Taras Grescoe has made a speciality  cultures for such publications as *The* ....*ational Geographic Traveler*, the *New York Times*, the *Independent* and *Condé Nest Traveller*. His acclaimed bestseller *Sacré Blues: An Unsentimental Journey Through Quebec* won the Edna Staebler Award for Creative Nonfiction and the Quebec Writers' Federation's Mavis Gallant Prize for Nonfiction and First Book Award. He lives in Montreal.

THE END OF ELSEWHERE

Travels Among the Tourists

TARAS GRESCOE

Library of Congress Catalog Card Number: 2004103020

The right of Taras Grescoe to be identified as the author
of this work has been asserted by him in accordance
with the Copyright, Designs and Patents Act 1988

First published in Canada by Macfarlane, Walter & Ross,
an affiliate of McCelland & Stewart Ltd

First published in the UK in 2004 by Serpent's Tail,
4 Blackstock Mews, London N4 2BT
website: www.serpentstail.com

ISBN 1-85242-867-8

Printed by Mackays of Chatham, plc

10 9 8 7 6 5 4 3 2 1

To Karen, for whom I'd go to the ends of the earth.

Contents

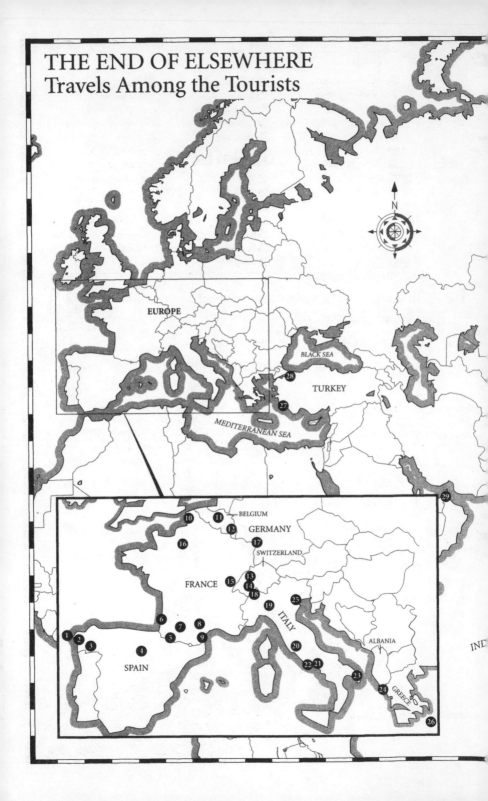

THE END OF ELSEWHERE
Travels Among the Tourists

EUROPE

BLACK SEA

TURKEY

MEDITERRANEAN SEA

BELGIUM

GERMANY

SWITZERLAND

FRANCE

ITALY

ALBANIA

SPAIN

GREECE

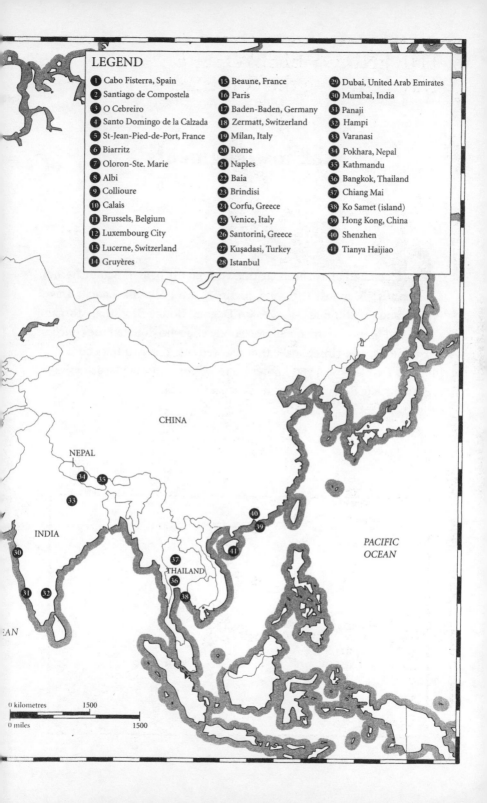

LEGEND

1. Cabo Fisterra, Spain
2. Santiago de Compostela
3. O Cebreiro
4. Santo Domingo de la Calzada
5. St-Jean-Pied-de-Port, France
6. Biarritz
7. Oloron-Ste. Marie
8. Albi
9. Collioure
10. Calais
11. Brussels, Belgium
12. Luxembourg City
13. Lucerne, Switzerland
14. Gruyères
15. Beaune, France
16. Paris
17. Baden-Baden, Germany
18. Zermatt, Switzerland
19. Milan, Italy
20. Rome
21. Naples
22. Baia
23. Brindisi
24. Corfu, Greece
25. Venice, Italy
26. Santorini, Greece
27. Kuşadasi, Turkey
28. Istanbul
29. Dubai, United Arab Emirates
30. Mumbai, India
31. Panaji
32. Hampi
33. Varanasi
34. Pokhara, Nepal
35. Kathmandu
36. Bangkok, Thailand
37. Chiang Mai
38. Ko Samet (island)
39. Hong Kong, China
40. Shenzhen
41. Tianya Haijiao

CHINA

NEPAL

INDIA

THAILAND

PACIFIC OCEAN

0 kilometres   1500

0 miles   1500

Acknowledgments

This book couldn't have been written without the help of Scott Chernoff and Jennifer Ménard, Lara and Justin Aydein, Shauna Lancit, David Freitag and Dominique Balas, Alain Dagher, Bouke Bergsma, Morgane Callec and Mano Bourdet, and everybody else who donated the couches, spare futons, and closet space that allowed me to get to the end of this journey. Thanks – and you know you're welcome at my place anytime. I also appreciate the support of the Canada Council.

Introduction

The Hotel at the End of the Earth

*A Sunset Walk – Shipwrecks on the Coast of Death – The Hotel in the
Signalling Station – Drawbacks of a Travel Addiction – The Long
Voyage Ahead – The Sole Cause of Man's Unhappiness – Toasting
Wanderlust with Spanish Cognac*

If any part of Europe is haunted, it must be Cabo Fisterra: Finisterrae in
Latin, Finisterre in Castilian – the end of the road in Europe, no matter
how you spell it. Medieval pilgrims died on this headland by the hundreds,
their ships deliberately wrecked by the *raqueiros*, or ground pirates, who
attached lanterns to cows' horns on stormy nights to lure seamen to the
rocky shore. The five-kilometre-long cape is surrounded by the submerged cadavers of 140 ships, whose names – *Tang Castle, Nouveau
Conselle, Skuld Stawanger, Good Lion, Ermoupolis* – sound an international
registry of wreckage. Just last month, the bodies of three women were
found on shore, carried hundreds of kilometres by the tides after a
highway bridge collapsed in Portugal. For the cartographers of the middle
ages, Fisterra was the beginning of the Mare Tenebrosum; beyond this
cape there was nothing save sea dragons and a vast world's-end waterfall,
where the ocean poured into the ether.

My poky bus has arrived at its last stop, on the bay of a fishing village
where blue and red skiffs float in a tiny harbour. I've come to Spain's Coast
of Death to see the sunset at the End of the Earth, but it's beginning to look
as though the sun will beat me to the horizon. Already, window panes on

1

the opposite shore are flaring into golden pixels as they catch the last lateral rays of dying light. The bus driver follows me out the door, stretches, and laconically points out the road to the Faro, a silver-domed lighthouse perched on the tip of the headland. Shouldering my backpack, I stride up a serpentine road that hugs the sides of a thistle-covered cliff plunging into the Atlantic.

Fisterra, of course, is not the only Land's End in the atlas. England has its own in Cornwall, and there are Finisterres in Brittany and off Baja in Mexico. But Spain's version, at the end of the Iberian peninsula, has an ineffable finality and remoteness to it. As does Galicia itself, that Celtic land never fully tamed by Romans – Imperial or Catholic – a place whose lichen-splotched hills are haunted by flying witches, seven-headed snakes, and kobolds. I fear I've spotted two of these mischievous sprites above me. A pair of men, a bag full of beer bottles beside them, are seated on a granite outcrop, yelling at each other in drunken Galician.

The road finally reaches the crest of the cape, just before the land runs out in a headland, and I'm rewarded with a panorama of ocean and sky. The sunken civilization of Atlantis may be out there somewhere, along with the vanished bombers of the Bermuda Triangle and the drowned centurions in the inundated Celtic city of Dugium. The dying of the light is mushy and anti-climactic, the sun veering yellowish-grey as it disappears into a bed of horizon-hugging cumulus, as if swallowed by some mid-Atlantic smog bank. As the cool dusk wind kicks up from the west, I sit down on an elephantine concrete step set into the hillside and contemplate the task before me.

From now on, my path leads east, towards the sunrise at the other end of the world. For the better part of a year, I'm going to travel away from home, friends, and family, from the tip of Spain to the extreme end of China, not stopping until I reach a place called Tianya Haijiao on the island of Hainan – the End of the Earth in the cosmology of the ancient Chinese. My route across the Eurasian landmass, from sunset to sunrise, will take me through landmarks in the history of travel, but there's also a more nebulous personal goal for the voyage.

Ever since I was a teenager, I've been leaving behind friends, lovers, and family in favour of a headlong rush into the unknown, to bruise my knees on the serried seat backs of beach-bound charter planes, rattle my spine over the rear axles of unsuspended Indian buses, and jettison my calamari over the taffrails of dented Greek ferries. I return to a petrified forest of house plants and a hallway sprayed with disconnection notices, feeling rootless, cut off from old friends, already nostalgic for abruptly severed foreign affairs – in a limbo of my own making. This travel sickness, which no amount of Dramamine can cure, is expensive and exhausting; I pay for the euphoric rush of movement with back pain and tropical infections, lost luggage and friends, and escalating feelings of disorientation and rootlessness. It's time that I discovered, once and for all, what I'm running to or from, and whether I should quit all this vagabonding and finally teach myself to just stand still.

"The sole cause of man's unhappiness," wrote the philosopher Blaise Pascal, "is that he does not know how to stay quietly in his own room." Shivering on hostel floors and ferry decks, stuck ticketless on tropical isles, I've often asked myself the question I am now travelling to answer: why in God's name can't I just stay put?

As night falls over Cabo Fisterra, the question seems more apposite than ever. The beer-guzzling kobolds have noticed my presence, and the dusk wind is wafting what sounds like mocking hoots in my direction. I'll have to walk the two kilometres of twisting road back to the village of Fisterra in the dark, and no doubt I'll have these louts nipping at my heels. In a last surge of hope, I walk towards the Faro, whose horizon-sweeping beams are now turning the world into a vast planetarium. I spot the backlit glass of a soft drink machine and, atop a concrete staircase, the cream-coloured walls and green shutters of a stone building. To my surprise, there are lights inside, and people sitting in upholstered chairs watching television, as a woman behind the counter works a row of beer taps. Pushing open the door, I enter a lobby filled with dried flowers and spot rows of keys behind a desk.

There's a hotel at the End of the Earth. It's a rather good hotel, too, and since this is the low season, rooms are going cheap. The bartender writes out the price on a bar napkin; I nod acceptance and walk up creaking stairs to a spacious room of varnished hardwood planks, complete with a colour television, a deep bathtub, and a telephone next to scallop shell ashtrays. The manager explains that until new technology made it obsolete 40 years ago, the building was a navy signalling station. Recently, it's been converted into a haven of *ecoturismo*, attracting weekend trippers from Santiago de Compostela and Madrid. I would have been happy with a dirty bunk in a youth hostel; this is enough to set me dancing a flamenco of gratitude.

Back downstairs, I decide to celebrate this unexpected godsend. Eight years ago, I gave up drinking, and more severe forms of self-indulgence, when it was becoming clear I had a penchant for taking inebriation to dangerous extremes. But these are extraordinary circumstances, and I vow that in the months to come I'll mark my progress across the continents by indulging in ceremonial samplings of local intoxicants – for literary purposes only, of course. After a dinner of coquilles St. Jacques and a fish called San Martiño served with peas and tomatoes, I return to the bar and order a dark Spanish cognac. It tastes not unlike Sloan's Liniment, I observe, with a slight afterburn of Sterno. In spite of its cankerous bouquet, the liquor makes me blithely optimistic. Suddenly, the prospect of months on the road seems less daunting than exhilarating.

It is here, in this little hotel bar at the End of the Earth, with a head corrugated by high-octane fumes, that I vow to complete my endeavour, come what may. In a world exhaustively explored, from pole to antipode, from mountain peak to ocean trench, in which an entire sub-genre of literature is devoted to *repeating* the voyages of Shackletons and Hemingways, it's time to look back on the history of travel and figure out how all this running around got started in the first place. The route I've inflicted on myself, a deliberately anachronistic trail through *belle époque* spa towns, Grand Tour hot spots, and Club Med islands, will throw me into situations I'd normally avoid like botulism. Travel writers tend to seek out the world's ever-diminishing pockets of authenticity, but I'll make a point of going exactly where the tourist ruts have been plowed the deepest. With self-consciousness about my own status – whether tourist, traveller, explorer, or anthropologist – set aside, I'll be better able to observe the impact a couple of millennia of tourism have had on the globe.

And, ultimately, I might even figure out why I find it so hard to stay quietly in my own room.

Chapter 1

A PILGRIM'S REGRESS

Confession of a Superstitious Traveller – The Pilgrim's Credential – Risks of Walking Backwards – Lunch with a Budget Travel Snob – How St. James Came to Spain – Waylaid by a Galician Peasant – Heatwave and Highway – Mistaken for a Medieval Pilgrim in the Cathedral of Santiago – The Camino of the Lovelorn – Insomnia and the Snoring of Germans – The Merits of Medieval Guidebooks – Dinner Chat with an Anarchist – Ill Omens and Nightmares – "Oriental Herbs" and the Templars – Sharing a Bunk with a Beautiful Blond Pilgrim – The Pyrenees in the Fog

I'm not a Christian. As a child, the only time I was lured into my local church was when the neighbourhood priest offered five-pin lessons in the basement bowling alley. Though I was born outside belief, I'm also morbidly, self-indulgently superstitious. Maybe it comes from too much German expressionism, too young, but the more I travel – and the more protracted any single journey becomes – the more my unconscious is seized by an involuntary horror of evil portents and ill augurs. I cancel room reservations when I see a black cat lolling on a hotel windowbox; I trade in my ticket when I learn the #13 Express is leaving from track 13 at 13:00; and a lone raven perched on a roadside gravestone is enough to make me change continents.

So it was with a mixture of profane skepticism and weak-minded, almost medieval dread that I set out to walk the Camino de Santiago, an 850-kilometre pilgrimage route that traverses the peaks and plains of northern Spain. Since the middle of the tenth century, Christians from every corner of Europe have been walking to the town of Santiago de Compostela to worship at the tomb of the Apostle James, whose remains, they believe, were revealed by a circle of stars that appeared over a Galician field in the year 813. For most of them, Cabo Fisterra is the unofficial finish line. I, in contrast, had resolved to walk in the opposite direction, from the Atlantic Ocean to the French border, rather than following the more conventional, east-to-west direction favoured by Charlemagne, St. Francis of Assisi, Isabella of Castile – and, come to think of it, every other pilgrim who, over the last millennium, has approached this path with a befitting sense of gravitas and reverence.

As I retraced my steps down the winding coastal road to the village of Fisterra, I wondered again what I was getting into. For seven years I'd cobbled together a living as a freelancer, doing articles for travel magazines that had me flying to far-flung corners of the globe at short notice. Several promising relationships had dissolved because of my sudden departures to Hanoi, Barcelona, or Havana. I was in my mid-30s, and I'd never owned a car or a condo. I had neither a stock portfolio nor a mortgage. Lately, I'd even given up the luxury of an apartment: in anticipation of this trip, I'd put my possessions in a warehouse and taken to subletting for a month or two at a time, or sleeping on the couches of friends.

Almost with my first steps, I went through the familiar bipolar shift. I loved travelling, I thought, as my gaze lingered on the coastline. A couple of hundred metres later, a pebble found its way into my shoe, and I recalled how much I hated travelling.

Fortunately, a more immediate issue demanded attention: I needed a plausible cover story to explain my contrarian odyssey. From a pilgrims' office in France, I'd been mailed a *credencial*, the gate-folded paper passport that allows pilgrims to sleep, free or for a small donation, in the network of hostels that dot the trail. To prevent people from simply hitchhiking over vast swaths of the Camino (Spanish for "path"), pilgrims are required by religious authorities or hostel-keepers to solicit dated stamps in the towns and villages where they sleep. The questionnaires that pilgrims fill out when asking for their *credencial* admit of only a few legitimate incentives for walking the Camino: spiritual, religious, cultural, or historical. My real motivation – to meet as many pilgrims as possible, to get an idea of the motives that have driven people to take this arduous road over the ages – just wouldn't fit on the form. Nor, I suspected, would my rationale for walking backwards: I wanted to maximize my encounters with other pilgrims and avoid getting tangled up with any single group of walkers. By any standard, I was approaching this endeavour in extremely bad faith: my plan was tantamount to skipping counter-clockwise around a Himalayan stupa, or pausing outside the Kaaba in Mecca to glue a false beard on my chin.

In the tiny school that was doing double-duty as Fisterra's pilgrim's hostel, a young woman in rubber boots was sweeping the floor.

"*¿Peregrino?*" she asked.

"*¡Sí!*" I replied, emphatically.

She sighed, dropped her broom, and beckoned me towards a paper-covered desk in an adjoining room.

"*Credencial, por favor.*"

I handed her my pilgrim's passport. Noticing that it was free of stamps, she looked at me with wide eyes.

"But, where are you coming from?"

"Cabo Fisterra," I replied – less than an hour's walk away.

"Then, where are you going?" she asked, incredulous. "Only to Santiago?"

This gave me pause. I couldn't really tell her that my goal was St.-Jean-Pied-de-Port, the border town where many French pilgrims begin the Camino, for that would reveal my wrong-walking ways and expose me to accusations of perverse impiety. Nor did I want to leave myself open to suspicions of dilettantism by saying I was walking only as far as Santiago.

"*¡Me voy a Roma!*" I blurted.

Which was true. I would be going to Rome – eventually, many weeks later – just not, as it happened, by foot.

"*¡Dios mío!*" she said, crossing herself.

On the front of my *credencial*, she wrote: "*FISTERRA A ROMA*," and the date. Then she solemnly branded the last page with a Galician-language stamp that read: "*Fin da Ruta Xacobea – Concello de Fisterra.*" Upside down, which seemed appropriate. Following me to the door, she said to a toothless man reading a tabloid on a bench outside: "See that guy? He's walking to Rome."

Though I wasn't particularly proud of my fib – or unpardonable heresy, depending on your outlook – it soon became clear I needn't have worried. The Camino has been walked by so many crackpots, full-time hoboes, criminals, and New Age flakes that one non-proselytizing secular humanist wouldn't do it much harm. Besides, there is a long, respectable tradition of backwards-walking on the Camino. Any Galician pilgrim from Fisterra would have been obliged to head east to get to Santiago, and in the days before the RENFE state railroad, coach tour pilgrims, and the Lavacola airport, most pilgrims who walked to Santiago had to turn around and walk right back home again. Far from being a heretical nonconformist, I would be the champion of an authentic medieval tradition: the Camino bush-telegraph, in which east-going pilgrims gave west-going pilgrims the heads-up about bad dogs and good tapas in the miles to come.

First, though, I needed lunch. I spotted a harbourfront restaurant, the Bar Miramar, where the specials were chalked on a blackboard. A good sign, I thought. A tiny woman with an apron around her waist bustled out of the kitchen – a still better sign – and asked me what I wanted to eat. Without quite remembering what they were, except that they came from the ocean, I opted for the *chipirones*.

"Good choice," I heard a voice behind me say in a south London accent. "I just had them. They were bloody exquisite."

I turned to see a red-headed man in his 40s, with several days' carroty stubble on his jowls and a red bandana tied around his neck, staring at me through thick glasses, his elbows planted in a ground zero of crumbs and oil-stained napkins. He motioned for me to sit at his table.

"Yes, *mar*vellous food in Galicia. I had a long conversation with an old fisherman last night – entirely in Spanish – and he told me the best seafood to order in Fisterra is *gambas*, the San Martiño, and octopus. You've definitely picked the right place by coming here. And it's inexpensive, too."

His name was Stephen, and he'd walked all the way from France. The pockets of his plaid wool shirt bulged with receipts and notes scribbled in a shaky hand.

"This is by far the best part of the Camino. Not so many bloody pilgrims. And then there's the sea – you can taste the salinity in the breeze." The tip of his tongue darted between his lips, as if he were snatching salt crystals from the air. "I slept out on the cliffs last night, next to the lighthouse. Such a relief not to be surrounded by snoring idiots."

Stephen, it seemed to me, was a bit anti-social. In fact, it quickly became apparent that being a miserable sod was a matter of principle with him. The cook brought my lunch, which turned out to be a plate of tiny cuttlefish, swimming in olive oil and onions, their guts as tender as warm ricotta cheese. I asked Stephen whether he was Catholic.

"Oh God no," he snorted. "My interests are cultural and historic. In fact," he said, picking his teeth, "I walked the Camino much more quickly than other people, so I'm just trying to decide what to do for the rest of the week. Perhaps Bilbao."

When I mentioned Frank Gehry's Guggenheim Museum, he rolled his eyes.

"Listen, I've just spent 25 days visiting some of the most exquisite 12th-century Romanesque churches in the world. I don't see myself going to the Basque country to see some bloody video installations."

Right. I was dealing with a type rampant on the road, the budget travel snob, connoisseur of the primitive, whose pleasure consists in informing you of all the authentic experiences he has enjoyed and you – poor uncultured yob that you are – have managed to miss. Paying my bill (it wasn't *that* cheap), I told Stephen that I really had to hit the road.

"Yes, you had better," he agreed, miserably, turning his attention to a photocopied map of northern Spain. "You'll never get anywhere if you start this late in the day."

At least, I thought, I'll get away from you.

And so, hefting my bag, I walked out into the humid, overcast Galician afternoon, set my sights down the long road to Santiago, and promptly got lost. As I picked my way over slippery boulders on a deserted beach, suppressing an image of the scuttling black crabs below gnawing on my broken-backed corpse, I reflected that it wasn't surprising the motives of the first pilgrim I'd met on the road were so patently non-religious. The 85-kilometre path to Cabo Fisterra is a kind of pagan coda to the Catholic pilgrimage route, and the 10 percent of Santiago pilgrims who continue on to land's end tend to be of either the esoteric or profane persuasion. From all I'd read, even the motives of historic believers on traditional pilgrim roads – from the Mecca-bound *hajji* to the Japanese *henro* paying his respects to the 88 holy places on the island of Shikoku – weren't always pellucidly pious. True, medieval pilgrims left home to visit faraway shrines, earn indulgences, or fulfill a vow made to a saint. But many were also escaping debt or bad marriages, fleeing stultifying routine, seeking sex with strangers, or simply taking the air. The same mix of motives, in fact, that drives people today to take a beach vacation in the Bahamas, ride on bus roofs across Kashmir, or pay half a year's salary to scale K2. (Or, in the case of Stephen, to have a dirt-cheap Spanish adventure holiday so he can feel even more superior to the poor sods back home.) The pilgrimage could be a sincere path of enlightenment, spiritual growth, and atonement. But, reading between the lines of Chaucerian verse and Buddhist haiku, it also looked like one of the earliest forms of leisure travel and a direct ancestor of modern mass tourism.

I'd never know, though, until I found the damn road to Santiago. I'd read that the route was marked with yellow arrows brushed onto barns, cemetery gates, and the silhouettes of giant bulls, but these seemed to be thin on the ground in Galicia. Rounding a point, I came upon a long, curved beach, where the sand blended with solid ground in a curtain of bending reeds and the tideline was strewn with scallop shells. An auspicious sight, my superstitious side told me: the scallop shell, or *concha de venera*, was the traditional badge of the Camino, and over the ages the shells had cost pilgrims many a peseta in souvenir shops on the road to Santiago. I stopped to safety-pin a particularly becoming blue-grey specimen onto my backpack and was heartened to see the first of many *mojones* – stone pillars, emblazoned with a yellow scallop shell, that indicated the distance from Cabo Fisterra. Gosh – I'd already walked 4,183 metres.

Only 845,817 to go.

❧

According to medieval legend, a knight fell into the sea off the Galician coast and was rescued by a saint, emerging from the waves draped in garlands of cockleshells. The saint was Santiago, a.k.a. the Apostle James, fourth of Jesus' recruits, who from a bit part in the gospels was recast as the featured star of the Camino. James, Catholic lore tells us, came to the Iberian peninsula to proselytize among the savages, converted a grand total of seven of them, and upon his return to the Holy Land in A.D. 44 was beheaded by Herod Agrippa. His friends put his decapitated body onto a stone boat, which journeyed without oars or sails past Gibraltar and on to Galicia in seven days, where his handful of Spanish disciples buried him on a hilltop. Almost eight centuries later, his remains were discovered by a hermit called Pelayo and moved to a shrine in Santiago de Compostela. Since then, they've become the chief draw at what is, after Jerusalem and Rome, Christendom's most venerated pilgrimage site. In recent holy years, especially after the end of General Francisco Franco's dictatorship, up to a hundred thousand foot pilgrims have come to Santiago to pay tribute to Saint James's bones.

With its awkward return trip to northern Spain and the clumsy gimmick of the self-steering stone boat, I found the Santiago story an inelegant legend, a clear attempt to dignify an obscure corner of Christendom with a decent Biblical connection. (I was more inclined to credit the profane historians' conjecture, which blamed it on the *lapsus calami* of a squint-eyed monastic scribe who confused *Hispaniam*, Latin for Spain, with *Hierosolyman*, Latin for Jerusalem.)

Things got even more convoluted as subsequent myth-makers had Saint James appearing in a cloud at the battle of Clavijo in 852, leading Christian horsemen to victory against the Moors. This apparition would signal the beginning of the Reconquest of the Iberian peninsula – and the end of a well-irrigated, scientifically advanced Muslim kingdom that had brought unwonted justice and tolerance to a land that has since suffered the Inquisition and Fascist dictatorship. On church porticoes and restaurant menus, Saint James is depicted as a humble pilgrim, dressed in a broad-brimmed hat and carrying a simple calabash gourd on a stick – as sanguine in his way as Ganesh, the elephant-headed overseer of Hindu pilgrimages. Later, in churches in Burgos and Logroño, I would see him as the sword-wielding *Santiago Matamoros* ("Moor-slayer"), a sanguinary Kali trampling swarthy, mustachioed heathens under the hoofs of a white charger.

Lured by the renown of this pilgrim-knight, travellers left their hometowns to join a network of routes that coalesced at Santiago as capillaries lead to veins, veins to the heart. The French followed four distinct roads;

Castilian pilgrims walked the Vía de la Plata, the Silver Way; and the English – 925 boatloads of them in 1428 alone – made most of the voyage by sea, to La Coruña on the north coast. Armenians and Greeks, Venetians and Viennese, Parisians and Frankfurters would share inns, wineskins, and prostitutes, learn to mock each other's customs, and return home with either renewed hatred or qualified respect for their very Christian neighbours. Europe, Goethe would famously aver, was formed journeying to Santiago. Not to mention, I thought, marching over the graves of slaughtered Muslims.

Though I had no desire to worship some truculent racist icon, I also resolved to be open to whatever the road had to offer me. On my first day of walking, it threw up magnificent coastal panoramas, clearing skies that soon branded my neck and forearms with a brutal farmer's sunburn, and an utter dearth of pilgrims. Late in the afternoon, after losing the Camino's *mojones* a half dozen times and covering a mere 14 kilometres, I finally walked into Cée, a small port town populated by frantic dogs and bored teenagers. That night I slept on a dirty hospital bunk, the only pilgrim in the basement of the local civil defence centre, a disused school where an amused volunteer fireman stamped my *credencial*.

Getting up before dawn, I resolved to put in a good day's walking. Heartened by the sight of my first *flecha amarilla* on the other side of a telephone pole – those yellow arrows would come to haunt my dreams – I left the paved road and walked between ruined stone walls into the Galician hills. In fields dotted with purple, blue, and yellow wildflowers, floccules of mist tangled in thistles, and a foghorn blurted and sighed in the bay behind me. I passed strange *hórreos*, rectangular granaries topped by crosses, poised atop toadstool-like stone platforms to protect the corn and wheat from pests. On a hillside switchback, a squat woman with cheeks that managed to be at once rosy and leathery urged a herd of cows to pasture with cries of "*Ho! Ho!*" Planting her rubber boots before me, she interrogated me with a stream of pure Galician – it sounded half Welsh, half Portuguese. When she extended what sounded like an invitation to wed and bed her stocky daughter, whom I glimpsed lurking behind a heifer, I shrugged and pointed at my shell, hoping (ill-advisedly, I would discover) that this would be interpreted as a symbol of chastity. As the fog lifted, I saw I was in a travel writer's paradise: a winding path through a savage landscape, peppered with peasants doing ancestral chores and architecture picturesquely succumbing to moss and moisture.

Galicia is supposed to be as damp as Ireland, but by noon it felt like the Mojave. I took a dip in a stream, eyed warily by tiny frogs, and walked for the rest of the day with a soaking T-shirt tied around my head and my sombrero pulled low over my eyes, the heat turning my delight with Celtic quaintness into irritation at everything Spanish. On a hilltop pasture where I sat to eat the first of many tuna *bocadillos*, a farmer backed his tractor into position, threw a switch, and sent jets of fermenting, liquid manure arcing into the air, to land with fetid splats next to my picnic spot. Forced to walk on a stretch of country motorway, I was sucked backwards by the slipstream of lumber trucks and sent scuttling down the embankment by a pair of polo-shirted yuppies in a speeding black Mercedes with Madrid plates. By the time I reached the hostel in a village called Vilaserio just before sunset, I'd covered 33 kilometres of the Camino. Taking into account my wrong turns and backtracking, I calculated the total was closer to 40.

That night, I slept among pilgrims for the first time. A German in his 50s was sitting on a lawn chair outside the hostel, reading a pocket-sized New Testament and writing with a thin pencil in a tiny travel journal.

"The place is filthy," he proclaimed. "There are no beds or showers. It is shameful."

Inside, a half-dozen French and Spanish pilgrims were arranging their sleeping bags on pieces of cardboard on an unswept floor. Upstairs, I found cobweb-draped closets and evidence of unchallenged squatting by local rodents. It was as though we were gypsies, and the villagers had banished us to a field on the edge of town to keep us away from the decent folk.

When I awoke, I was alone, the more experienced pilgrims having set off early to beat the heat. The day started as a rural idyll, a ramble through dewy fields glazed by slugs entwined in slimy orgies. Soon, though, the mounting temperature caught up with me. I would later learn that, thanks to a record-breaking late-spring heatwave, virtually every city dweller with a car had gone to the beach that weekend. Which meant I had to walk the last uphill kilometres approaching Santiago de Compostela on the narrow concrete shoulder of a highway filled with *cerveza*-and-sun crazed drivers who liked nothing better than to play "spook-the-*peregrino*" on their way back from the seashore.

Sweaty, unshaven, and unwashed, I finally walked into an expertly groomed park outside the old city, attracting stares from families in their Sunday best. I felt like a gypsy bum; I felt like a poseur and a fool; I felt like checking into a five-star hotel. But as I got my first glimpse of the intricate, wildflower-and-lichen covered spires of Santiago's cathedral – a fantastic, barnacle-covered reef looming over rows of stone houses – a funny thing happened: I also felt like a pilgrim. The towers went blurry, and I had to look at the ground to prevent tears and a tightening throat from crumpling my face. Exhausted by heat and lack of sleep, I felt an overwhelming connection with all those who, over the ages, had risked losing home, family, and life itself to follow wild rumours to some marvellous place at the edge of the earth.

By then, nothing could keep me from the cathedral. As I strode up stone stairs towards the Praza do Obradoiro, the churchfront square that is always packed with bus tourists, a man in knee-length shorts and pulled-up socks took my photo – I had become, I realized, a medieval icon, a picturesque element in a tourist snapshot. Inside, the cathedral was a cool cavern, and I wandered, pack on my back, hat in hand, staring up at the gilded baroque altar surmounted by Santiago on horseback, smiting, as was his custom, a posse of craven infidels. As I approached the Crypt of the Relics, where Saint James's bones are kept in a silver chest, a stout, bald man with a guidebook asked me where I'd come from.

"From the Ends of the Earth," I intoned, relishing my role.

He looked sincerely awed.

"*¡Qué fuerte, peregrino!*"

I'd arrived in time for the mass after Ascension, and as the tourists were shooed out of the cathedral, I leaned my backpack against a pew and sat through the ceremony, bare calves twitching as I rose and fell with the congregation. After shaking hands with the elderly woman in the black dress beside me – I blessed her for accepting my backpacker's stench with a graceful smile – I hit the back streets of Santiago. I needed a cheap hotel, a long shower, and 16 hours of sleep. I had a lot of walking ahead of me.

§

Naturally, my exhaustion coincided with a week-long civic holiday. Brass bands and drunken university students spent the night queuing beneath my shutters to deliver impromptu Galician renditions of "Guantanamera." I've often fantasized about living in ancient cities like Santiago, but the fact is, the acoustics of narrow roads, stone facades, and teeming street life would have made laudanum and ear plugs bedside necessities for medieval urbanites.

Crawling out of bed at noon, I found myself in Santiago's old town, a maze of crooked pedestrian streets. The red-headed bagpipers droning in the Praza da Quintana bespoke the Celtic heritage Galicia shared with Scotland; the beat cops checking identity cards bespoke a bourgeois provincial town's long tradition of hassling the itinerant. The Rua do Vilar, a colonnaded street full of *hostales* that led to the cathedral, was filled with people with peeling noses, formless hair-dos, drooping T-shirts, and multi-pocketed walking shorts – fellow pilgrims, I presumed. Many were seated at café terraces writing postcards, or window-shopping in souvenir shops that sold corkscrews topped by Saint James on horse-back, sets of shot glasses with silhouettes of the Santiago skyline, and shirts with insipid slogans like: "Somebody who loves me brought me this T-shirt from Santiago." A middle-aged woman caught me pricing a *concha de venera* ashtray.

"All the commercialism these days is terrible, yeah?" she said, with an Australian accent. "Strictly Made in Hong Kong, this trash."

I couldn't have disagreed more. Not only was the ashtray Made in Portugal, there was nothing particularly modern about Santiago's commercialism: since the ninth century, the city's raison d'être has been as a service centre for pilgrims, and I wasn't surprised that local restaurateurs and hoteliers had a hereditary knack for fleecing foreigners. I bought a *bordón* – a long, varnished walking stick with a pointed steel tip, good for spearing snakes and scaring off dogs. At the uncrowded Museo das Peregrinacións, devoted to the history of pilgrimages, I found a display case of souvenirs that had been sold in centuries past from stalls in the Praza do Obradoiro, including tiny medals in the shape of St. James and plates etched with images of the church steeples.

Souvenirs of arduous voyages have a long history in world religions. Muslims from Turkey and Sudan brought myrrh, frankincense, and jewellery home from Mecca. Hindus had long returned from Varanasi's Shiva temples with souvenirs of glass linga, or phalluses, to decorate their homes. Perhaps the most memorable of these mementoes was the bottle Boccacio's Father Cipolla brought back as a souvenir of the Holy Land in *The Decameron*. It was filled, he solemnly assured listeners, with the clanging of the bells of Solomon's temple.

Apart from a strange, bird-like pilgrim girl who flew through the rooms and perched beside me only long enough to chirp, "Is so boring, *no?*" I was the only visitor in the museum. A wall map put Santiago into cross-cultural perspective, showing it as one of many dots on a globe of sacred travel destinations, among them Kandy, home of the Buddha's tooth; Haridwar, where the Ganges descends from the Himalayas; and Medina, where Muhammad is buried in the Mosque of the Prophet. If a pilgrimage is a journey to a goal held sacred, surely Jim Morrison's grave in Paris – surrounded by Italian Lizard Kings offering joints to Swedish girls – qualifies for a dot on the map as well.

Most religions have a tradition of sacred travel, and many predate the earliest Christian pilgrimages. While European tribespeople were still dancing around pointy boulders, the third-century B.C. emperor Ashoka, an early convert to Buddhism, distributed relics associated with the Buddha's life in 84,000 stupas around India and built a network of roads, rest houses, and watering stations for fellow pilgrims. The origin of the modern Olympics lies in the eighth-century B.C. festival of Zeus, in which a truce between warring states was declared so that pilgrims from across the Hellenic world could come to Olympia, where the featured relics were the massive bones of the hero Pelops (now thought to be dinosaur bones).

Long before the first recorded Christian pilgrimage, Jews were coming to see the Ark of the Covenant at Solomon's temple, and vegetarian Jain ascetics wandered naked between mountain shrines.

In fact, it wasn't until A.D. 326, when the Emperor Constantine's mom, St. Helena, visited the Holy Land and claimed she'd found the True Cross, that a real tradition of Christian holy travel began. Even then, Christian pilgrimages have had a comparatively spotty attendance record. Every 12 years, during India's famous Kumbha Mela, up to 15 million Hindus come to Allahabad to bathe at the confluence of the Ganges and Jumna rivers. In Islam, last-born of the world's major religions, the pilgrimage to Mecca is a doctrinal necessity, and as many as two million Muslim pilgrims make it to the birthplace of Muhammad every year.

Relaxing over a *café con leche* after visiting the museum, I found an article in the local tabloid *La Voz de Santiago* that helped put the Santiago pilgrimage in context. The Camino across Spain consists of 31 steps of one day each, though most foot pilgrims manage only five, covering a mere 100 kilometres. In the last Holy Year – any year on which St. James's Day falls on a Sunday – 1.4 million bus tourists visited the Cathedral. In contrast, only 151,620 pilgrims walked or cycled to Santiago. A mere trickle compared with, say, the pilgrimage to the Shinto shrine of Ise in Japan, which draws 8.5 million pilgrims a year, a million on New Year's Day alone.

Back in the cathedral, I queued up with German bus tourists, who pressed their spread fingers into a hand print, greasy with a thousand years of sweat, on the central pillar of the Portico de la Gloria. I poked my head into the pilgrims' office, where a Dutch woman sobbed as she received her Compostela, the frameable certificate of completion the Church issues those who have walked at least the last 100 kilometres of the Camino. Reconciled to the fact that a rightfully earned Compostela would never hang on my wall, I watched a volunteer add the woman's *bordón* to a collection of cast-off walking staffs behind the desk. On the landing, pilgrims were pinning messages to a bulletin board. I read one, in ballpoint pen, that foreshadowed the hidden dramas of the Camino: "ALICE, I hope see you again. I'm Gona be here until tomorow the 28th. Try contact me at Hostal Barbantes. Missing you so mucht. Anyway, call me. Marcelo Doyle."

He'd left a number in Brazil at the bottom of the note. Presumably one where his wife wouldn't pick up the phone.

§

One of the Camino's sayings is "*Ir romero, y volver ramera*" – Go a pilgrim, come back a whore. It was on my mind as I set off through Santiago's fog-swaddled, pre-dawn streets in the general direction of France. The first personal account of the Camino I'd heard was from a friend of a friend, a West Coaster of mixed Hindu and Presbyterian parentage who proudly called herself a witch. When we'd briefly met in Paris before she set off for Spain, it was clear she was in search of romance, and for weeks after our meeting she sent mass e-mailings, detailing swollen ankles and an amorous encounter with a married Brazilian restaurateur. Pausing in a town called Cacabelos, she'd fallen in love with a young Englishman who was running the local *refugio*, and they'd moved to Canada after she'd fulfilled her pledge to walk to Cabo Fisterra. The last I'd heard, they'd married and were expecting a baby.

It wasn't surprising, I thought, that Christian pilgrimages encouraged love matches. While Muslims swore off loose talk and transgression for the duration of the *hajj* to Mecca, donning chaste white robes, Santiago pilgrims stripped down to shorts and T-shirts, had their libidos stoked by long walks in the country air and nightly bottles of cheap Rioja wine, and slept in co-ed dormitories. Many started the pilgrimage alone, walking through mid-life crises, but finished by pairing up, skipping the refugios, and checking into hotel rooms under assumed names. As early as the fourth century, Gregory of Nyssa had recognized the perils of being a pilgrim, emphasizing the risk of sexual misconduct between female pilgrims and their escorts. Chaucer's Pardoner made no bones about being an outright rake: "I wal nat do no labour with myne handes," he'd swaggered, leaving the Tabard Inn in Southwark to ride to Canterbury. "Nay, I wol drynke licour of the vyne / And have a joly wenche in every toune." Spanish inns, notorious for drunkenness, forced guests to sleep at least two abed, and many provided prostitutes. Before charter flights to Ibiza and Cancún made it all too easy, a pilgrimage could be life's one opportunity to leave the fpoufe at the fhoppe for a little finning.

The next morning, as I passed a road sign that cancelled Santiago with a diagonal red line, I encountered my first pilgrims. There were northern Europeans dressed in polypropylene windbreakers, polar fleece, and shorts, with retractable high-tech alpenstocks, as athletic looking as Alpine hikers. A knot of Spaniards walked by, the women talking volubly, the men carrying tiny backpacks; I took them for much-hated support-car pilgrims, those who have their bags chauffeured between *refugios*. I could immediately recognize the French pilgrims; they inevitably answered my "*Hola*" with a "*Bonjour*" – after a month's walking on Spanish roads, they somehow still didn't deem it necessary to say "*Buenos días.*" (I could also spot the lone New Yorker, because when I told him I was headed for Rome, he shot back: "Yeah, and I'm coming from the Sea of Galilee!") By the time I'd got to the Monte del Gozo, the windswept "Mount of Joy" where pilgrims catch their first glimpse of Santiago, I'd counted 67 pilgrims, and by the end of the day, my headcount had reached 168. After encountering only 14 fellow walkers in my first three days, it felt like a torrent of humanity.

That evening I walked into a tiny village, without stores or restaurants, called Ribadiso da Baixo. The pilgrims' hostel was an idyllic huddle of traditional stone houses, surrounded by a lawn that ran down to a meandering stream. In what must have once been a stable, a Brazilian girl had her blistered foot in her boyfriend's lap, and she let out a string of "*Ay ay ay*"s as he cut the dead skin from her toes with cuticle scissors. I sat next to a pale pair in their 20s who were silently sharing a bottle of red wine.

"Looks painful, doesn't it?" the young man said, nodding towards the amateur podiatrist. He was Kelvin, from Manchester; she Michelle, from Melbourne. They'd met on the Camino, shortly after the French border; it wasn't clear whether they were lovers. When I refused Kelvin's offer of wine, he nodded. "I should be living up to my cultural stereotype and getting dead drunk. But I'm too knackered to get paralytic. I'll save it for Santiago."

Kelvin explained that, after graduating from university, he'd quit his job at a telephone call centre and started casting around for something to do before his unemployment benefits kicked in. He'd briefly considered walking through Scotland. ("Oh, can you do long-distance hikes in Scotland?" interjected Michelle. "What are they known for up there?" "Glue sniffing," replied Kelvin, not missing a beat.) Researching the trip at the local library, he'd found a *Lonely Planet* guide to walking in Spain and decided to head south instead. "It's warmer here, isn't it? And the wine is much better."

I asked them if they were Catholic. Both shook their heads vigorously. Michelle explained she was a physiotherapist and a midwife. "I'd been planning a trip to Europe for a long time, but the bottom fell out of the Australian dollar about a year ago, so I couldn't really afford most countries in Europe. I'm not religious at all; this just seemed like a good cheap holiday, a different way to see the country."

Though the sun hadn't yet gone down, my ability to make coherent conversation was waning. Pleading fatigue, I hobbled towards my bunk on tightening legs. Inside, a Spanish couple talked quietly at the far end of the room. Suddenly, a red-faced woman reared up from beneath her sleeping bag like Nosferatu out of his coffin, and issued a sibilant: "*Shush!*" When that didn't have any effect, she barked out a lengthy, self-righteous harangue in stroppy German. Satisfied that her *Weltschmerz* had trumped any nascent *alegría*, she rolled over and vanished beneath her shroud. Within minutes she was producing a gimlet-tipped snore that pierced even my fresh earplugs.

Snoring proved to be the Camino's major curse. Packed as we were into dormitories of up to a hundred pilgrims, many middle-aged, most exhausted and chloroformed by half bottles of Spanish plonk, that there would be some degree of nocturnal emission was a foregone conclusion. I hadn't foreseen the stentorian symphonettes, however, with their 20-part cacophony and occasional crescendos into primal screams. I decided a mandatory physical examination by a throat-and-nose specialist should be conducted at the Spanish border, and all who fail should be branded with a special symbol – a pig's snout pinned to the pack would do nicely – allowing innocent victims to select their bunks accordingly. Or perhaps a separate Camino should be waymarked for snorers. Through Bulgaria.

I woke in a perverse mood. Once again, I was among the last to leave, though this meant I was able to wave goodbye to Kelvin and Michelle.

"Santiago's that way, mate!" Kelvin yelled, as I walked east over a stone bridge.

"Yeah, but Rome's this way!" I yelled back, pointing towards the sunrise, allowing them to conclude they'd been dealing with a lunatic. I walked ten kilometres before I found a place that would serve me breakfast, stopping for a potato tortilla in a town called Melide. As I negotiated a narrow path between fields bound by barbed wire, I heard an amused American voice.

"Hi! How was Santiago?"

I looked up: he was in his late 20s, wearing a baseball cap, with pale calves and a relaxed smile. Alongside him was a woman with long dark hair and a tight purple top.

"Totally cool," I drawled. "Good DJs, great ecstasy. Cops are brutal, though."

They stared at me in surprise, and then – fortunately – laughed. We sat in the shade of a chestnut tree and chatted. He'd quit his job at an investment banking firm in Boston to travel around Europe. She was Danish, but a recent stint working in the United States had left her with a perfect American accent. They'd met on the Camino, and had been walking together for two weeks. When I asked how they'd heard about the pilgrimage, they looked a little embarrassed.

"Uh . . . we both read *The Camino*," he admitted. "But, don't get the idea we're New Agers or anything." I assured them I'd read the book by the famous actress too. Some latent sense of gallantry makes me think I should bestow pseudonyms on other literary walkers of the Camino. Frankly, though, the authors of *The Camino: A Journey of the Spirit*, and *The Pilgrimage: A Contemporary Quest for Ancient Wisdom*, don't deserve such consideration. Shirley MacLaine and Paulo Coelho (whoops! it just slipped out) are responsible for putting tens of thousands of credulous North Americans and as many addle-pated Brazilians on the road every year. Their books can be skimmed in one sitting, as there's a remarkable amount of white space between the lines and very few big words or troublesome historical details. Between MacLaine's flashbacks to a civilization where crystal-horned unicorns frolic among androgynous Lemurians who subsist on mangoes, and Coelho's description of Masonic rituals and astral displacement in Ponferrada's castle, they provide a crash course in the ill-annealed amalgam of appropriated religious traditions that is the New Age. Tragically, they're also the main reason a great many pilgrims are on the Camino. I would run into countless Latin Americans who were performing the rituals described in Coelho's book, digging their fingernails into their thumbs when they had negative thoughts or pretending they were a seed so they could suck energy from the earth. *All* the Americans I met – even the smartest – had read Shirley MacLaine's book, though most seemed pained to admit it.

"I didn't think it was very good when I read it," said the woman. "Now that I'm doing the Camino myself, I realize it's total garbage. All that stuff about past lives and mango eating! I don't even think she walked all the way to Santiago. Or if she did, she did the last part by car. And other people carried her bag for her."

"I heard she only walked six days altogether," added her hiking partner, with the scorn of the freshly graduated long-distance hiker.

When we parted, trading tips on *refugios* in the towns to come, I considered the literature that was cluttering my bag. I was carrying an English vade mecum, whose prose – "at a minor road KSO ahead, forking L 100 m later; KSO for 2–3 km more and at a clear 'T' junction turn R; 300 m later turn L down goat path," and so forth, for 237 pages – made it an exemplary soporific. As a guide for the backwards walker, though, it was practically useless (I'd considered reading the sentences right to left, *Exorcist*-style, but decided I was already pushing my luck).

My favourite volume was a slender translation of Aymery Picaud's guidebook, the fifth book of the 12th-century *Codex Calixtinus*. Though not much use as a guide, it made for great reading – particularly if you were a paranoid xenophobe. Picaud, a cleric from Poitiers, excoriated the Basques, whom he called "misshapen, perverse, perfidious, empty of faith and corrupt, libidinous, drunken, experienced in all violence, ferocious and wild, dishonest and reprobate" and most of the other adjectives in the thesaurus entry for "rascally." In contrast, the people of his hometown were "swift runners, elegant in their attire, handsome of face, ready of tongue, generous and hospitable." I suspected contemporary French pilgrims of approving Picaud's prejudices, and taking the absence of *Vache qui rit* cheese and Beaujolais Nouveau in supermarkets as further evidence of Spanish barbarity.

❧

The *Codex Calixtinus* joined the latest New Age tomes in contributing to an age-old tradition: the plowing of the tourist rut. Travel, even in this era dominated by the various incarnations of the screen, is a bookish endeavour. The inspiration for journeys still comes largely from accounts of previous voyages in novels and travel literature. When they leave home, pilgrims, tourists, and explorers pack their bags with guidebooks and maps, and so with the perspectives of the travellers who have preceded them.

The problem is that, unversed in the local language, their vision framed by the boilerplate of literature, they often fail to see the new land with their own eyes. Gradually, a kind of self-creating travel circuit emerges, reinforced by travellers who have read the same books; the route becomes populated by people enthusiastically confirming one another's prejudices. The French, forewarned by Picaud that the Navarrese wait beside poisoned streams with sharpened knives to carve up the cadavers of their horses, ended up huddling together at the end of the day in foreigners' hospices, complaining about the perfidious Spanish. Modern-day Brazilians, on the lookout for auras and mystical swords, mumble together about the import of the Masonic eye painted on the dome of the Santiago cathedral. The Camino is one of Europe's most durable ruts, created and colonized by successive and sometimes coexisting ideologies: the Masonic mysticism of the Knights Templar; the anti-Muslim continent-building that fuelled the Reconquest of the Iberian peninsula; and the hieratic hucksterism of the New Age. Fortunately, the personal challenge of walking the Camino makes these accounts look like the limited literary products they are. For all but the most blinkered ideologues, the textured adventure of walking an ancient pilgrimage road transcends the narrow claims of doctrine.

I knocked off early that day and dropped my bag in a room filled with German girls in their 20s, writing in their journals. That night, I shared a *menu del peregrino* with a pilgrim who asked me to call him Jacobo. A Dutch-born professor of Andalusian literature, he quoted the opening lines of a poem by Antonio Machado:

"*Caminante, no hay camino / Se hace camino al andar,*" he recited, in an urgent whisper. "It means something like 'Walker, there is no Camino, the Camino is made in the walking,' but the Castilian is so much more beautiful."

If this were 1936, I asked, would he have been on the side of the Catholics and the Fascists, or the Republicans and the Anarchists?

"There's no question: I'd side with the Republicans. Franco and the Fascists were pretty brutal, and the Church supported them all the way. They tortured Federico García Lorca before he died – they knew ways of making a man die slowly. But the Anarchists did their fair share of butchering too. It was a brutal war, as civil wars are."

Much as I relished the medieval architecture of the Camino, it symbolized an all-pervasive social control that, had I lived in Lorca's time, I would have found intolerable. I knew that, if this were the 1930s, my heart would have been with George Orwell, the Mackenzie-Papineau Battalion, and the Republicans rather than the Catholic church.

In the days that followed, I had glancing encounters with other intriguing characters. Pausing at a vending machine in a village called Gonzar, I talked to Ariel, a handsome red-headed Israeli who was lying in a grassy picnic spot with his shirt unbuttoned. A pretty Dutch girl named Marsha was resting her head on his thighs. They'd met on the Camino and were sleeping in barns after one too many nights of creaking beds in the *refugios*. They mocked what they saw as Catholic commercialism, the calabash gourd souvenirs to be hung from rear-view mirrors, but they also seemed a little sketchy on the whole religious side of things. When I told Ariel the story of Santiago – it was the first time he'd heard it – he interrupted to ask: "What is *apostle*?"

There were also pilgrims who seemed to have walked straight out of the Middle Ages. In Portomarín, a town that had been drowned by a hydroelectric project in 1960 and rebuilt a few hundred metres above the new lake, I met a young German furniture maker dressed in the traditional big-buttoned black vest of his medieval guild. He explained that, according to tradition, he had to stay 100 kilometres away from his hometown for three years – his *Wanderjahre* – to break old ties and learn new carpentry skills. For him the Camino, with its retablos and ornately carved screens, was a vast linear museum of ancient woodworking techniques. Rounding a corner in a village called Ventas de Narón, I came upon a scene out of *The Canterbury Tales*: a sorrel nag was tethered to a tree next to a tiny stone chapel; her owner had removed her saddle and was brushing down her sweaty flanks. He was wearing a New York Yankees cap, with a grey beard bracketing his deeply lined jowls, and I saw that his right leg was encased in a steel-and-plastic framework.

He told me his story, in manly, no-nonsense Castilian cadences. He was Segundo Borlán, originally from León, now living in Barcelona. He'd lost the use of his leg to gangrene but his life was spared, and to give thanks he'd walked to Santiago with a burro. When his daughter survived leukemia, he repeated the feat, and wrote a book about it (he handed me a colour poster for a paperback titled, simply enough, *1000 km del Camino de Santiago en burro*). This time he'd traded the donkey for a horse, Lorena, and was making better time.

"I do 25 or 30 kilometres a day, exactly like a person walking," he explained. "One month to get to Santiago, instead of two with my burro."

Later, I met a Brazilian woman, one of the few Latin Americans who *hadn't* been inspired by Paulo Coelho's book. Tiny, in her late 40s, with a complexion like clay, she carried a *bordón* that looked like a bishop's crozier and was half again as tall as she was. She shuffled along in white socks and sandals, like a great-grandmother escaped from a nursing home. Though it was a sweltering afternoon, she wouldn't stop at a shaded pump in a village square, and seemed to be carrying no water of her own. A concerned-looking French pilgrim explained that, though the woman's feet were covered with atrocious blisters, she refused to stop. She had been cured of pneumonia in São Paulo, and her parish priest had urged her to walk to Santiago to give thanks. I suspected that her gratitude for deliverance would finish her, adding another roadside cross to the many that commemorated those who had fallen along the way.

These devout pilgrims were a reminder of the medieval pilgrimage's reputation as an exacting and perilous path of penitence. In A.D. 333, less than a decade after St. Helena went to the Holy Land, a walker known as the Bordeaux Pilgrim took more than a year to make the return trip to Jerusalem from France, averaging 32 kilometres a day on well-paved Roman roads. From 638, when the Caliph Omar entered Jerusalem on a white camel, right up until the 20th century, pilgrims' access to the Holy Land depended on the humour of the occupying Muslims. The first pilgrims went to Jerusalem overland, via the Balkans and Constantinople, but the advances of the Turks in Asia Minor forced later travellers to cross the Alps and rely on often extortionate Venetian ship captains to take them through the eastern Mediterranean. Jerusalem was only briefly in Christian hands: the first wave of Crusaders, the Papal holy warriors against the heathens, slaughtered Jerusalem's Jews and Muslims in 1095, but the Egyptian sultan Saladin took back the city less than a century later. Though pilgrimage to the Holy Land continued – the caliphs had no objection to making money off small groups of infidel tourists – the pilgrims' interest increasingly turned to the more accessible shrines of Rome and Santiago.

Even these European pilgrimages posed serious risks. Travel in the Middle Ages was no cakewalk: pilgrims were seen as pretty pickings when alive but even tastier when dead. Ferrymen tended to overload riverboats, counting on the fact that their passengers could rarely swim, and then pillage the pockets of the drowned. The right of wreckage, in which shore dwellers were allowed to claim booty from shipwrecks – as long as no crew members had survived – tempted the ground pirates of the Galician coast to set misleading signal fires and then murder the gasping survivors as they came ashore. And the custom of groundage, which allowed a ruler to collect merchandise if a wagon's axle touched the ground, provided strong disincentive for road maintenance, leaving the hapless foreigner open to cart-jackers. Before a causeway was built to Mont St. Michel in France, the Norman monastery could be reached only by treacherous mud flats, and in 1318 alone, 12 pilgrims were buried in the quicksands and 13 suffocated in crushing mobs in the sanctuary. Today's solo pilgrims, almost Protestant in their emphasis on the inner voyage, would have been seen as foolhardy aberrations in the Middle Ages, when banding together to ward off wolves and thieves was the only sensible policy.

Such early pilgrimages led to the innovations that would encourage leisure travel in centuries to come. The Benedictine and Cluniac systems of monasteries, with their policies of hospitality for wanderers from afar, would become lodging networks that foreshadowed Holiday Inns. The wealthy and international Knights Templar, a military order established to protect pilgrims on their way to Jerusalem, allowed people to deposit money in one place and withdraw it with a letter of credit from another, anticipating both traveller's cheques and ATMs.

§

In ridgetop O Cebreiro, where the Camino mounts to 1,200 metres and Galicia meets León, my superstition started to get the better of me. I'd gone to a *taverna* that night and sat with some Americans who suggested I try a shot of the local moonshine, *aguardiente*, served from an unlabelled bottle – which, for some reason, contained a tiny plastic ladder. Remembering my pledge to experiment with local specialties, I gave it a try. It tasted not unlike bathtub tequila. The proud bartender insisted I try another, stronger distillation, this time chased by a glass of *jerez*.

By the time I lurched outside, culturally enriched and intellectually impoverished, a fog had descended on the village, blowing wraith-like tufts of mist between the ancestral *pallozas*, stone huts with thatched, bell-shaped roofs that Galicians have been building since prehistoric times. A fog-shrouded hound, straight out of the Baskervilles, sat atop a stone platform, baying at the creaks and clangs of rusting signs. That night, I tossed on my bunk as I dreamt that a bearded man with a broad chest – Santiago himself, I feared – barred my path, and that I'd murdered him by puncturing his heart with my steel-tipped walking cane.

Next morning, as I pulled on muddy shoes, I saw the *hospitalero* turn away a powerfully built man with wild black hair, a frayed black sweater, a black guitar case, a huge black malamute on a leash, and a broad white scallop shell dangling from his neck.

"He is some kind of 'artist,' not a *peregrino*," the hostel-keeper warned me. "If I let him in, he will steal everybody's wallet. When you leave, keep your head down. Ignore him."

This, I thought, might be a *coquillard* (from the French for scallop, *coquille*), a false pilgrim, one of many who had taken advantage of the hospitality of the Camino's *refugios* since the Middle Ages. As I left the refuge, the guitarist caught my gaze with dark, Andalusian eyes and tapped a finger to his head.

"*Está loco*," he said, referring to the refuge keeper. "I only wanted to use the shower."

I shrugged and walked east. Had I been a medieval pilgrim, I might have described the morning's encounter as a meeting with a demon who had tried to lead me astray. As this thought occurred, I looked into a drainage ditch and saw the rotting corpse of a dead fawn, covered with flies. (Nothing unusual about that.) A few hundred paces later, I saw a dead green lizard with an arrow-shaped head in the middle of the path, lying upside down and pointing towards Santiago. (Steady on. Next you'll be believing in hobbits and hobgoblins.) A half hour later, I came across a scallop shell with a red cross painted on it that had been abandoned on roadside. (Stop this insanity, you fool. *Leave now.*)

By the time I reached Ponferrada, I'd let these portents convince me something wicked was definitely my way coming. I decided I would skip the next part of the Camino, the infamous Meseta, a 200-kilometre stretch of flat and featureless land where, I'd heard, you could spend an entire day walking towards a single tree. The sunburnt pilgrims I'd met in O Cebreiro talked of a record spring heat wave – 42 degrees Celsius on some afternoons – and of the many walkers who had quit and gone home. Boarding a train in Ponferrada, I was at first exhilarated to be covering so much ground so quickly. Even though the train smelled like *sangría*-scented piss and had a burgundy-and-umber colour scheme straight out of 1975 (which, in Spain, didn't come along until 1985), it was a wrenching leap into something like modernity. Abruptly, I was racing along at 20 times my walking pace, watching telephone poles flash by like the pickets of a fence. Occasionally, the train tracks would parallel the Camino, and groups of pilgrims would lift their *bordones* and wave; I sheepishly ignored them. In three and a half hours of train travel, I'd eliminated ten days of walking the Camino. Somehow, though, I didn't feel like I'd saved a couple of hundred kilometres; I felt like I'd been robbed of ten days of rich experiences.

After my train ride, it wasn't easy to reconcile myself with the Camino. In Burgos, I strolled through the aisles of the Gothic cathedral, muttering about the scaffolding that obscured the nave. In a town named after the 11th-century monk Santo Domingo de la Calzada – literally, St. Dominic of the Asphalt – who built bridges, hospices, and roads for pilgrims, I paused before an elaborately painted stone chicken coop in the transept of the cathedral. A group of pilgrims stood before it, gazing upwards expectantly: legend has it that if the cock crows, you will succeed in reaching Santiago. Growing impatient, they shuffled, mumbled, and then left. As soon as they'd walked out the side door, the rooster blessed me with an emphatic *cock-a-doodle-doo* (or rather, a Hispanic *quiquiriquí*), not once, but three times. In the circumstances, it seemed more observation than prediction.

In nightly encounters in the *refugios*, I noticed I was gravitating not towards the middle-aged Catholics that composed the great mass of pilgrims, but towards the exceptions and the eccentrics. In a town called Puente la Reina – where two branches of the route coalesce into the Camino Francés, the French road – I descended to the basement *refugio* of a hotel. One corner was filled with shirtless French men, sunburned purple, who were drunkenly teasing a pair of middle-aged honeymooners. On the other side, candles had been lit around the bunkbeds, and a Gallic Don Quixote and Sancho Panza were unpacking their camping equipment, next to a quiet blond girl with curly hair.

I turned left, choosing atmosphere over rambunctiousness. The Don was Hervé, tall and skinny, his snaggle-tooth smile bracketed by bushy sideburns. He'd recently left the French air force, where he'd repaired the ejector seats in fighter planes, and walked from his hometown of Tours. He'd met his Sancho, a solidly built sailor from Montpellier named Jean-Mary, while crossing the Pyrenees.

"I'm doing the Celtic Camino," explained Hervé, showing me a three-looped triskelion ring on his index finger. "The Knights Templar came along and built their churches on places the Celts had been using for centuries. Rivers, natural springs – these people were no fools. You can feel the energy. I'm conducting experiments as I go, meditating in churches, studying the geometry. You should come along with us. I'll show you things you've never seen."

"Him, he's making his own cocktail of different religions," snorted Jean-Mary, who considered himself a non-practising Catholic.

They were travelling with Iris, a 20-year-old with a Botticelli face who'd walked alone for the last three months from a small town near Amsterdam. I was intrigued enough by Hervé's tales of Templar crosses and Celtic influence, a side of the Camino I'd missed, to agree to retrace my steps for a day and walk back to Estella with them.

They proved to be great company. As we walked out of Puente la Reina the next morning, Hervé paused in front of the Romanesque Iglesia del Crucifijo in the town's long main street. He pointed to the ornate motifs on a 12th-century arch. "Have you seen this somewhere before?"

Perhaps, I answered. The long-tailed birds looked like Irish engravings.

"Yes – like in the Book of Kells, in Dublin."

After crossing the town's graceful six-arched bridge, built by a queen of Navarre to free pilgrims from the power of exploitive ferrymen, we walked into the hilltop town of Cirauqui, whose name means "nest of vipers" in Basque. Hervé pointed out a low stone cross at the foot of an archway, carved with intricate rosettes.

"I'll bet there's something on the other side. Take a look," he said.

I leaned over and saw, on the side closest to the arch, hidden from view, a prominent Templar's cross.

"This doesn't surprise me," he said. "They were all over the Camino. Their churches were built using precise geometry, which concentrated their force. *Tu imagines!* They spent so much time in the Orient, they knew all the secrets of the East."

We paused for lunch in a passageway that was the Camino's route through the old city walls. As we cut baguettes and cheese, a succession of pilgrims walked past us, including a man with the white beard and fixed gaze of an Ancient Mariner, whose right hand clutched a set of rosary beads wound around his *bordón*. Wide-eyed and focused as a Hindu sadhu, he declined our offer of coffee and strode onwards.

"I talked to him yesterday," Iris told us. "He's come all the way from Rome. He says he walks up to 65 kilometres a day. His socks were falling apart, so I gave him a pair of mine."

After we'd packed up our picnic, Jean-Mary announced it was time for some Oriental herbs. Pulling out a plastic bag of weed, he rolled a giant spliff, which he shared with Hervé. After that, our pace slowed. Jean-Mary and Hervé became fascinated by the irregular paving stones on a length of Roman road. They also started looking over their shoulders, convinced they were being shadowed by a group of undercover Guardia Civil who they claimed had followed them in the Pyrenees. I told them I thought they were getting paranoid.

"*Écoutes, mon vieux*," drawled Hervé. "I've been in the army. I know what military men look like. After all, we crossed the border. We could have been Bretons bringing explosives for Basque terrorists."

As the day wore on, the slow pace of the Celtic Don and his sardonic Sancho got to me. Besides, Hervé's appreciation of the Camino's mystical underbelly seemed less profound when I realized it was largely drug-induced. After they'd smoked another joint outside the church at Lorca, I peeked in to see what was keeping Hervé. He was conducting another of his "experiments," which meant sitting cross-legged in front of the altar with his eyes closed, ripped on his Oriental herbs. I told Jean-Mary I wanted to make it to Estella before sunset, and spent the rest of the afternoon walking with Iris.

I quickly decided that not only was Iris blue-eyed-blond-haired gorgeous, funny, and charming, she was also brave and entirely admirable. I listened mesmerized as she told the story of accepting a decrepit nobleman's invitation to his mansion in the French countryside.

"He was very strange. He was in his 50s and wore rouge and eyeliner. I think he had psychological problems – he washed his hands 30 times while I was there, and he told me he didn't talk to his family anymore. But I was freezing, and he offered me a warm meal and clean clothes. He made me take a shower before dinner, and then gave me a special kind of perfume, and eyedrops."

It was beginning to sound downright Hitchcockian – I expected to hear that a portrait of a woman who looked exactly like her hung over the fireplace.

"Then he offered me a huge bed with fresh linen. Of course, when the lights were out, he crawled into bed with me. I ended up yelling '*Non!*' and slept on the floor."

It finished well, she said: when she got up in the morning, unravished, her clothes had been washed and were drying on the line. I told her, sounding avuncular, that she should be wary of strange men.

"I knew what *he* wanted, but I wanted a warm bed, a shower, and clean clothes. And I got what I wanted!"

As we walked into the ancient town of Estella, I began to suspect my motivations for retracing my steps weren't as abstract and academic as I'd thought – a dangerous attraction was building between us. Dangerous because I'd started a serious relationship some months before I'd left, and I'd told myself, and my girlfriend, I'd be faithful for the length of my travels. Dangerous, too, because I'd been walking alone for too long, through invigorating Spanish landscapes. Dangerous, finally, because in the *refugio* Iris and I chose lower bunks that had been pushed together. When the Don and Sancho finally caught up with us, Hervé looked at our sleeping arrangements and commented with an insufferably insinuating, "*Ah, oui, je vois.*"

That night, after the snoring had started, Iris rolled over and whispered in my ear. "Oh, I should have brought a tent with me. That would be nicer for us."

True, I said.

"I wish they didn't lock the door of the hostels at night."

It is inconvenient, I mumbled.

"Because tonight would be such a nice night for a walk by the river."

I could only agree. And could easily imagine leaning over and meeting Iris's parted lips. But I could also call to mind the woman I loved, and quietly reached into my toiletry kit for a sleeping pill I'd packed for just such emergencies. As it dissolved under my tongue, I heard Iris sigh three times. And then, praise St. James and Stilnox, I lost consciousness.

§

The next morning was the only time I relished the *refugios'* cold showers. I found Iris sitting in the kitchen alone, sucking on a box of orange juice, looking not a day over her 20 years. I told her I wanted to start early, and she nodded as I bade her adieu with chaste kisses on the cheeks. Then I headed to the road and stuck out my thumb; within half an hour, a car had taken me the whole distance I'd walked from Puente la Reina the day before, and I was alone again on my backwards Camino, walking towards France.

"*Ir romero, y volver ramera,*" I muttered to myself. The Camino's age-old reputation as being the pimp of the pilgrimage trails had almost turned this *romero* into a full-on road whore.

Gradually, as the Camino came to an end for me, I began to grasp the advantages of walking, the oldest and simplest form of travel. The more I walked, the more materialism and concern about self-image seemed to slough away. Arriving in a new town, I'd pass the Zara and Benetton stores with no sense of avarice, gazing over the shop windows to read the ancient armorial crests above the signs for spring sales. I sought to divest myself of books and clothing, and gladly gave the heavy coins in my pockets to beggars, seeking only to fill my belly with nourishing food. I realized I had never truly seen the world go by at this human pace, four kilometres an hour, hour after hour, day in, day out. I learned about the warm westerly wind that sometimes crosses the land just before sunset, the cool *tramontana* from the north, and the afternoon breeze that sends iridescent ripples through the fields, as though columns of silver-backed lemmings were rushing through the wheat.

Watching the slow transition from ox-plowed fields to eucalyptus forests to rolling valleys and the vineyards of Rioja, I came to a new understanding. Only by seeing the seagulls on the Galician church spires, the storks on the Riojan chimney stacks, and the hard-working sheep dogs of the Basque country did I start to understand Spain and the subtle way its culture derives from still-flourishing rural traditions. Such things you can understand only when you're on foot, when, as Robert Louis Stevenson put it, you "get down off this feather bed of civilization, and . . . find the globe granite underfoot and strewn with cutting flints."

The Camino, in the end, had made another convert. I vowed to seek out new opportunities to use the oldest and most enriching means of travel: putting one foot in front of the other.

I finally crossed into France in a dense fog. The Pyrenees were an illusion: rams and cows occasionally surged out of the mist, along with shepherd's huts and stone crosses. Just before the French border, on a deserted forest path at an elevation of 1,300 metres, I came across an abandoned car, apparently dumped by Spanish joyriders, with a "Leicestershire Constabulary Vehicle Watch" sticker on its back window and a six-month-old copy of the *Observer* in the back seat. (Which reminds me: Will the owner of a green Ford Sierra, licence plate E601HJF, please remove it from the Ibañeta Pass?) I walked into St.-Jean-Pied-de-Port, the French village from which so many pilgrims start, and went to the pilgrims' office.

Staffed by French volunteers, mostly coiffed women in their 50s, the place announced that I was no longer in Spain. As a woman named Nicole pressed the last stamp into my *credencial*, she complained about the latest crop of pilgrims. "*Oh la la!* It's not like when I walked the Camino. These days, they have all read the book by that Brazilian. Now the Camino is full of South Americans; they piss against houses, they sleep on the ground." She finished with a melodramatic sigh: "*En effet, il est devenu un chemin de clochards.*"

A path of hoboes. True enough. But it was also a path of grateful survivors of pneumonia and gangrene, of *coquillards* and medieval furniture makers, of bored clerks looking for new love, of Quixotes and Sancho Panzas, of rogues and heroes.

Which meant, come to think of it, that not much had changed since the 12th century.

Chapter 2

MILLE BORNES

Fuck my feet, I muttered to myself. My stinking, calloused, bruise-toed,
pale-as-bacon-lard feet. After three weeks of walking, I needed a clean
shirt, a shave, and the addresses of some good restaurants. Most of all,
though, I needed wheels.

In the tiny train station at St.-Jean-Pied-de-Port, I left three days of
stubble in a sink and my *bordón* in a corner – which felt only slightly less
heartless than abandoning a baby bear in the coat check of Paddington
station. As I watched the low green peaks of the Pyrenees recede while my
graffiti-covered train criss-crossed the meanders of the Nive, I reviewed
the next step in my plan: to advance boldly from the 12th century to the
beginning of the 20th, exploring the south of France by rented car. This
was the country, after all, that invented automobile tourism. It's true that
the United States, home to the Motel 6 chain and Big Boy drive-ins, the
Model T Ford and the Winnebago, has a claim to pioneering the road.
Eventually, Americans paved their nation with a 68,000-kilometre
network of interstates, ensuring that anything of interest could be reached
by anybody who happened to be interested (somehow making everything
less interesting in the process).

But France had Michelin. Long before adventurers on America's first coast-to-coast road, the 1913 Lincoln Highway, were getting bogged down in their Wintons in the Iowa mud, moneyed *automobilistes* from Lyons and Paris were reading exquisitely detailed Michelin maps, rolling on demountable Michelin tires, and following Michelin-donated signposts to Michelin-recommended hotels. I'd used Michelin guides before – poking around the ramparts of St.-Malo, chasing down a one-star bistro in Montmartre – but never as they were intended: as vade mecums for the leisured motorist. *Bonheur,* for a certain class of European, was a late-model Citroën, a glovebox full of Michelin maps and guides, and a week to drive around Provence. I would become that gentleman motorist, moseying from village to village as I filled my backseat with local specialties, guided by Michelin's star-studded triage of the French countryside.

In the United States, such a rich cultural experience might have been possible in the *Grapes of Wrath* heyday of mom-and-pop diners, before superhighways were gouged into every county to further the inalienable North American right to patronize Wal-Mart and Krispy Kreme. The French countryside, similarly cross-hatched with asphalt, seems infinitely more varied, each hillcrest promising a different slice of terroir, a new monk-brewed beer, a more pungent goat cheese, or a fattier cassoulet. Blame it on the family-run multinational tire company from Clermont-Ferrand: through constant lobbying, they not only made sure there was a road for French drivers to hit, but also that there was something to get to when they did.

I rolled into Biarritz after a slow ride on a *train à grande vitesse.* The shops had closed, and I wandered the town centre with my backpack, scanning the sidestreets for hotel signs, gazing longingly at a rack of Michelin guides behind the locked glass doors of a *librairie.* Fortunately, French law requires hotels and restaurants – Le Crillon and the seediest Pigalle clip joint alike – to post their rates next to the entrance, an immensely civilized measure that spares tourists like me endless humiliation. A glance showed that a *chambre simple* at the Villa Etche Gorria, without *w/c,* but with *en suite* sink, might not be beyond my means. Entering through a small garden full of pink hydrangeas, I was directed up a wooden spiral staircase to a top-floor room that would have had a great view of the beach if it weren't for a much larger hotel, much closer to the beach, standing in the way. The bed was firm and the 19th-century mansion nostalgically decorated. Delighted, I told myself the guidebooks would surely approve my choice.

Alas, Michelin was having none of it. At the newsstand, I riffled through a metal rack full of maps and picked out *4064 Pyrénées-Atlantiques*, at a scale of 1:200,000. I then bought the latest edition of the *Guide Rouge* – the name had recently been changed from the *Guide Michelin* – with its 1,728 Rizla-thin pages of hotel and restaurant recommendations, as well as a French-language *Guide Vert* to the Aquitaine, the Atlantic coast area that includes Bordeaux, Bayonne, Biarritz, and Pau. Piling my literature on a tiled counter in the town's covered market, I sipped an *express* and discovered, to my surprise, that my hotel hadn't made the cut. My charming villa was apparently no more than a mediocre budget hostelry. Without Michelin, I was just another easily satisfied foreigner, laughably ignorant of the worthiest addresses.

My *Guide Rouge* came with a timely lagniappe: a facsimile of the first Michelin guide, dated 1900, shrink-wrapped to the cover. Compact as a hymn book, it devoted fully 178 of its 399 pages to *belle époque* motoring concerns – ads for Renault Voiturettes, instructions for changing the tires of Vélocipèdes, tables for noting one's daily consumption of such extinct gasoline rivals as Moto-Naphta and Automobiline. The core of the volume was an alphabetical listing of French cities, from Abbeville to Yvetot, including populations, distances from Paris, and, for the largest centres, maps of important streets. Flipping to the "B"s, I learned that turn-of-the-last-century Biarritz had 10,544 inhabitants, a train station, a telephone and telegraph office (where calls to Paris cost two francs and 25 centimes a minute), and three major hotels, of which two had darkrooms for developing holiday snaps. Michelin's mania for pictograms started early: a little three-roofed Monopoly-style hotel symbol next to three asterisks indicated that one should expect to pay more than 13 francs a day (wine included) at the Hôtel du Palais, the best address in town.

In the latest edition, the ads had disappeared, the tire-maintenance advice had been collected in 36 blue-bordered pages at the back, and the serried-roof symbol indicated a hotel's relative comfort. The Palais now got five Monopoly roofs, indicating a "luxury" hotel (as opposed to a hotel offering "top-class comfort," or, at the bottom of the list, "simple comfort"), where a double room would set you back 465 Euros/3,050 francs (wine, alas, no longer included). What's more, the Monopoly roofs were printed in red ink, indicating a particularly "pleasant hotel," and the little red pot-bellied silhouette in a rocking chair meant a "quiet and secluded situation." Passing a pop quiz in the semiotics of such Michelin entries, I suspected, was the secret to being granted full membership into the French haute bourgeoisie (extra points if you can do it while changing lanes on the Parisian *périphérique.*)

I wouldn't be staying at the Palais. Nor would I be eating at the Café de Paris – one of Biarritz's top three restaurants – whose four crossed spoons and forks indicated "top class comfort." I had suitable respect for Michelin's culinary rosettes, or "macaroons" as French hoteliers called them, introduced in 1926: their removal, after all, had been known to provoke suicide. (In 1966, when the inspectors downgraded Paris's Relais de Porquerolles after deciding its famous bouillabaisse wasn't what it used to be, chef Alain Zick shot himself in the heart.) It wasn't until 1982 that a British restaurant got three stars. Even then, the chef at London's Le Gavroche had been a Frenchman – the first English-born chef would have to wait till 1995 to receive his third star. (The British have had the last laugh. The chief editor of the *Guide Rouge* is now Derek Brown, an Englishman.) Of the 4,116 restaurants recommended in the Michelin guide to France, only 21 were three-star establishments, and my bankruptcy-prevention program involved avoiding all of them.

Since the 1980s, when superstar chefs spun their Michelin stars into culinary empires, dinner in most three-star restaurants in France has meant booking tables six months in advance and putting up with the corrections of supercilious career waiters. (So I've heard, anyway. I've yet to part with $500 for *foie gras* at Le Grand Véfour or lobster at Lucas Carton.) My strategy for using the Michelin guide would be simple: I'd scan the margins for the "Bib Gourmand" symbol, the bust of a smiling Michelin man that indicated "good meals at moderate prices," and hope I could wangle a seat.

But first, I wanted to use my new *Guide Vert* to explore Biarritz. In

1917, the patriotic Michelin brothers published the first of their *Guides to the Battlefields* – a rather optimistic editorial decision, given that the Kaiser's armies still occupied a good part of France. (Other collectible oddities would include the 1930 *Guide aérien* to France and North Africa, which recommended hotels and restaurants near landing strips, on the assumption that private planes would follow automobiles as the next wave in tourism.) The series would eventually entail more conventional guidebooks to the regions of France and foreign countries, becoming the familiar, long-spined green guides – which focused on churches, castles, and curiosities – with the first volume (Paris) appearing in 1946.

For most of the 20th century, the *Guide Vert* was a sober affair, with fine-lined drawings of church facades enlivened by the occasional engraving of a beret-sporting Michelin man saluting a flamingo with a baguette, or something equally whimsical. I was a little dismayed to notice that Michelin had recently succumbed to the lure of modern page-layout software, and that my guide to the Aquitaine featured colour photos, vast margins, and trendy hypertext sidebars. *Plus ça change*, something stodgy in my soul griped, *plus c'est de la merde*.

"At the beginning of the 19th century," I translated as I walked towards the beach, "Biarritz was a simple whaling port, where the people of Bayonne came on muleback to swim." The mules got the heave-ho when Emperor Napoleon III visited in 1854 and built the Villa Eugénie for his wife. At the turn of the 20th century, two casinos were built (I came upon one, a streamlined Art Deco affair), attracting such Jazz Age celebrities as Stravinsky, Cocteau, and the omnipresent Hemingway. While the movie version of *The Sun Also Rises* was being shot in the area in 1957, the American screenwriter Peter Viertel sent to California for a "curious board that mocked the waves," launching Biarritz's reputation as Europe's surfing capital.

Arriving at the curving Grande Plage, "a hotspot of Biarrote animation both day and night," I scanned the waves for surfers or, indeed, any sign of animation. Since it was overcast and windy, I found only a few etiolated Poles chasing the occasional patch of sunlight around the beach. Using the guide's small colour map, I followed a beachfront promenade to the Rocher de la Vierge, an offshore rock linked to the mainland by a metal walkway built in Gustave Eiffel's workshops, and nodded *bonjour* to the "immaculate statue of the Virgin, something of a symbol of Biarritz." Peckish, I poked my head into Chocolats Henriet, "a reference when it comes to the subject of chocolate," and bought a bag of *rochers de Biarritz*, a crunchy confection made of bitter chocolate, almonds, and orange peel. To this day, it is my reference when the subject of chocolate rocks comes up.

What I liked about Michelin was that it put stars not only next to fancy restaurants, swank hotels, and picturesque towns, but also alongside features – rood screens, grottoes, ossuaries – of buildings and landscapes. I walked along a beachfront promenade called La Perspective in search of the view** of the "three last summits of the Basque coast: la Rhune, Trois Couronnes and Jaizkibel." Soon, I started performing my own subjective triage; it was beyond my control. Stars appeared next to my first espresso** of the day, the copy of the *International Herald Tribune** someone had left on a table, and that unguarded men's room*** in the market. In fact, it took all my willpower to stifle my delight at this meta-textual contrivance* and resolve to use it with restraint.

§

Michelin, of course, wasn't the first guide to rate the world's attractions for the convenience of tourists. In the second century A.D., Pausanias, a Greek living under the Roman Empire, travelled the Mediterranean cataloguing the temples and monuments of Hellenic civilization, offering step-by-step directions and cranky dismissals of local treasures, commenting on Corinth, for example: "Behind the hero's shrine of Aratos are an altar to Isthmian Poseidon, and a Placable Zeus and Ancestral Artemis made without the slightest skill at all."

When recreational travel boomed in the Edo period, 18th-century Japanese tourists carried guidebooks printed on the back of fans, or folded like maps. The most famous, the *Ryoko Yojinshu*, advised pilgrims on their way to the Ise shrine that "applying ox dung to the soles of your straw sandals will keep away evil beasts, snakes, vipers, and poisonous insects at night." When movable type, first used in Europe in 1455, widened the availability of books, wealthy young gentlemen started carrying slim volumes like the 1642 *Instructions for Forreine Travell*, in which King Charles II's clerk James Howell advised the eastbound traveller to "go to Venice, where he may agree with a Janizary to conduct him in company of a Caravan all the way through the Continent of Greece as farre as Constantinople."

Guidebooks intended for a middle-class market, and with them the star-system, didn't really emerge until after the Napoleonic Wars. The first professional guidebook writer, an English traveller named Mariana Starke, published her *Guide for Travellers on the Continent* in 1820, rating pictures in major galleries with one to four exclamation marks. Her publisher, John Murray, brought out his *Hand-Book for Travellers on the Continent* in 1836, promising "matter-of-fact descriptions of what *ought to be seen* at each place, and is calculated to interest an intelligent English traveller." Karl Baedeker, a Koblenz-based bookseller and publisher, reprinted a guide to the Rhine a year before Murray's first handbook, though he would not truly launch his series of German guides until 1839. Quickly translated, Baedeker's was the first guidebook series to rate attractions with stars. Pretty soon, English, German – and, later, American – tourists could be seen following invisible constellations through the French and Italian firmaments, noses stuck in little red *Hand-Books*. Such guidebooks eventually influenced the reality they attempted to describe: Kaiser Wilhelm I made a point of standing in a particular window of his palace at noon because, he explained, "It is written in Baedeker that I watch the changing of the guard." In the 1942 "Baedeker raids," the Luftwaffe bombed York, Bath, Exeter, and Norwich – all of them starred attractions in pre-war German travel guides.

Inevitably, the reliance on guidebooks led to the tiresome and persistent Romantic anti-tourist discourse, in which lusty bluestockings – usually eccentric, often English – who had drunk too much Chianti made *carpe diem* speeches imploring travellers to cast aside their guides and live, yes *live!* The heroine of E. M. Forster's *A Room with a View*, for example, is scolded by an older countrywoman: "You are not, not, *not* to look at your Baedeker. Give it to me; I shan't let you carry it. We will simply drift." Predictably, Lucy Honeychurch, after dropping her trusty *Handbook to*

Northern Italy and drifting through Florence's Santa Croce, witnesses a knife fight in the Piazza Signoria, proving that real life is lurking just outside the margins of travel literature. Frankly, I've dropped my guide-book many times, and what usually happens is: 1) I walk the wrong way and spend an enriching afternoon exploring some industrial suburb; 2) I take the metro to the gallery and find it's closed on Tuesdays; or 3) I cave in to hunger and have a bad pizza in a fast-food joint and discover, when I pick up the guide again, that I could have lunched on splendid gnocchi with pesto in a bargain trattoria down a nearby sidestreet.

Michelin's originality lay not in its stars (Thomas Martyn's one-off guide to France, published in 1787, had beaten even Baedeker on that score), nor in its lapidary style, but in its targeting of a new breed of trav-eller: the auto-tourist. The first edition's press run of 35,000 may have been wildly optimistic – especially considering there were only 2,897 automobiles in France in 1900 – but it was a prescient publishing move. Baedeker's and Murray's had been tailored to travellers going by train. The very existence of the Michelin guides increased the popularity of touring by car, which permitted motorists to discover, for example, the excep-tional Grand-Marnier crêpes at Mère Brazier's bistro in the Col de Luère, which in turn led to calls for better roads out of Lyons. By 1920, the *Guide Rouge* was 815 pages long, and the company announced it would no longer give the book away (a decision hastened when one of the founders saw a stack of them being used to prop up a rickety table in a provincial garage).

I, for some reason, was still on foot. Without a car and the glove com-partment to put it in, my Michelin guide was beginning to feel like an otiose accessory, as though I'd become the owner of a high-speed modem for my Underwood. Biarritz was pretty – in a blue-rinse Disneyland kind of way – but I'd explored enough pretty towns on foot in Spain. Now I wanted the whole auto travel experience: the chocolate deliquescing around the Petit Écolier biscuits in the back seat, the restless punching of radio buttons, the calculation of distance to rest stop in kilometres versus bladder capacity in millilitres. So I took a city bus to the Biarritz airport and dropped my credit card on the counter of a car rental agency. The attendant directed me to the parking lot, where a chipper little Citroën Saxo – green, to match my guidebook, and rolling, I was satisfied to note, on Michelin radials – awaited. Ten minutes later, I was making a panicky entrance onto Autoroute 63, zooming north towards Bordeaux at 140 kilometres an hour. When I really wanted to be heading east towards Pau, at something like 50 kilometres an hour.

Actually, I didn't want to be on the highway at all. I'd meant to spend the early afternoon checking out nearby Bayonne**, particularly the Gothic cloister* of the Sainte-Marie Cathedral and the Goya canvases in the Musée Bonnat**. But one roundabout had led to another, an old Négresses Vertes*** song was playing on the radio, the sun was shining, I had a full tank of Moto-Naphta – er, diesel; and the exquisitely groomed French highway invited me to follow its gracile curves.

In the time it took to shift up to fifth, I'd again become the Hyde my mild-mannered pedestrian Jekyll so despises: the driver. Cars have always brought out a side of me I don't like – an impatience, an arrogance, a kind of inner Parisian – which perhaps explains why I've never owned one. (Oh, and there's the fact they're incredibly costly and the leading emitters of the greenhouse gases precipitating catastrophic climate change.) Such was my transformation that, if I'd encountered a grubby pilgrim sweating up the shoulder just then, I might have swerved his way a little, just to throw the fear of God into him.

In only five minutes I'd covered 12 kilometres – a morning's walk – albeit in the wrong direction. Pulling into a gas station–rest stop, I unfolded map 4064, which turned out to be the size of the Von Trapp family's picnic blanket, and determined that if I left the curvy red-and-yellow line I was now on, took vermicelli-tangle *échangeur* 7, and followed the N10 in the direction of St. Vincent-de-Tyrosse, I would in no time be on a squiggly red line with a green shadow, which meant – hold on – "itinéraire agréable-Reizvolle Strecke-scenic route." Sounded good. After stopping to dunk a coin into a toll-booth basket, I was released from intercity commuting hell and found myself driving over stone bridges and singing Louis Jourdan's "C'est Magnifique" at the top of my lungs.

French roads are nice, I thought, as hawks circled over fields dotted with hay ricks and the pavement mirrored the meanders of the Gave d'Oloron. One drives past leprous murals for Dubonnet, Suze, Byrrh, and other endangered aperitifs flaking off the walls of ancient bakeries. There's always some corbelled château lurking about, a farm that sells its own pear cider or shrivelled ancestral cheese, those cigar-shaped *Tabac* shop signs, and a guy in a black beret signalling a left by sticking his arm out the window of a rust-gnawed 2CV. Tombstone-shaped mileage markers, or bornes, still line the roadsides. They always remind me of the Parker Brothers version of the French card game Mille Bornes, whose excellent Puncture-Proof or Driving Ace cards allowed you to be the first to accumulate a thousand kilometres. It would have been perfect if not for the budding Terence Conran types I sensed lurking in the corners, unscrewing vintage Primagaz signs from gas stations to take back to their Notting Hill boutiques.

French drivers, unfortunately, aren't so nice, a fact I remembered when the first in a long series of cars passed me on a blind corner. This is such a cliché I'm inclined not to linger over it, but it is interesting to note exactly *how* French drivers are not nice. Whereas Italian and Spanish drivers drive fast for the sheer joy of it and it's all a kind of *fantastico* game, ¿no, Señor?, the French are actively mean: they want you to know you've been passed.

As I made my way along the D936, a Renault came storming up behind me, overtook me on a bridge, then slowed so abruptly that I had to pump my brake pedal to keep from ramming it. Only when I'd been forced to acknowledge his fabulous celerity and infinite dexterity – yeah, whatever, François – did he continue on his way. This is the infamous *queue de poisson* – in which the faster motorist administers a fishtail slap to the seaslug he's just passed – and it sums up, in a single act of automotive arrogance, what makes the Australians, Irish, Americans (and other nationalities that tend to pride themselves on their candour) hate the French. It also went a long way to explaining the Gallic popularity of Mille Bornes, which, I realized, was quintessentially French because it encouraged you to maliciously slap hazard cards on your opponents: Out of Gas, Flat Tire, and my favourite, Accident. *Chacun pour soi*, and I'll be sipping my *apéro* in St. Tropez before you, *mon vieux*.

There was enough of the pilgrim left in me to laugh off such peccadilloes with the detachment of a Benedictine beekeeper. Besides, a good portion of the drivers passing me would eventually end up wrapped around roadside plane trees, those exceedingly effective traps for existentialists. In Biarritz, I'd read in the daily *Libération* that a protester had recently damaged 96 such trees with a chainsaw after a friend had lost control of his motorcycle and crashed into one of the roadside colonnades. The editorialist, while admitting that 38 percent of France's 7,000 annual motoring deaths were caused by such "lateral obstacles," also made a sentimental appeal to save the rows of ancient trees that had provided shade for both Louis XIV's carriages and the cyclists of the Tour de France (not to mention – and of course he didn't – all those columns of invading German soldiers).

That's what distinguished the French from, say, the genetically cautious Swiss or the lawsuit-spavined Americans: they were willing to forgo trifles like public safety for the sake of aesthetics. Even French truck drivers had style, I noted, as a semi loomed in my rear-view mirror. A dropsical Michelin man was bolted to the roof, and the driver had wrapped a striped scarf around the mascot's neck, which flapped jauntily in the slipstream, even as the truck overtook and forced me to brake in the now-familiar way.

§

The Michelin man has a name, of course: it's Bibendum, from the phrase *Nunc est bibendum*, which means "Now is the time to drink!" (A motto whose aptness for the French road I would only later come to appreciate.) This was Horace's toast to the defeat of Antony and Cleopatra at the battle of Actium, but in turn-of-the-century Michelin publicity the slogan appeared above a man-shaped stack of whitewalls wearing a pince-nez. In one gloved hand this monster of rubber held a cigar; in the other he was lifting a goblet full of nails, broken glass, and horseshoes. It was an oblique way of illustrating the slogan: "The Michelin tire drinks up the obstacles!" Bibendum was the brainchild of André Michelin, who, with his brother Edouard, had moved from Paris to the provincial town of Clermont-Ferrand to save the family's failing rubber factory. In 1890, they founded Michelin & Cie., where, in addition to selling bouncy balls and brake pads, they did minor repairs to rubber goods.

When a local character named Grand Pierre came in with an early bicycle whose Dunlop brand tires were punctured (inflatable tires had been patented, though not perfected, by a Scotsman in 1845), the brothers spent almost a day wresting them from, and then reattaching them to, the wooden rims. Seduced by the air-cushioned ride, they vowed to create a *pneumatique* – an inflatable tire, as opposed to the bone-rattling solid rubber models then current – that would be easier to repair. The resulting prototype, the demountable tire, was tested in an 1891 bicycle race from Paris to Brest. When the rider they'd sponsored beat the competition by nine hours (in spite of the nails the brothers had sprinkled along the course to prove how quickly they could change their tire) the new invention took off, and within a year, 10,000 cyclists were rolling on Michelin tires. The first practical automobile with an internal combustion engine had been tested by Karl Benz in 1886, and soon Michelin tires were adorning the cars of Czar Nicholas II, King Edward VII, and Europe's burgeoning class of motorists.

My goal for the afternoon was a place called Oloron-Ste. Marie – 11,067 inhabitants, altitude 224 metres – "a somewhat austere town," the *Guide Vert* told me, "like those one often finds in the mountains, that seems to whisper its family secrets between the walls of tall houses coiffed with slate tiles." Formerly a stop on the road to Santiago de Compostela, it was known for its Basque berets, a sugary confection called the "russe," and the magnificent Romanesque portico** of its Sainte-Marie Church. Oloron would be my lunch stop. As I left the D936 and drove down Rue Casamayor-Dufaur, I pictured myself in a rakishly tilted black beret, sketching the church finials from the terrace of a good-food/moderate-price bistro, eavesdropping as the dark-eyed provincial beauties at the next table sibilantly exchanged family secrets.

It didn't quite work out that way. Leaving my car next to the local *pelote* court, I determined that, first, the portico** of the Sainte-Marie church was completely obscured by polyethylened scaffolding; second, the beret factory, though housed in the charming brick-and-smokestack Maison Beighan off a fountain-filled civic park, was not only locked tight, but showed no signs of ever having retailed its creations to passersby; and, finally, upon closer inspection, the only Michelin-recommended bistros in Oloron were actually at least 15 kilometres *outside* Oloron. To make matters worse, all the restaurants around the square were closed until dinner, and an all-pervasive odour of chocolate had me salivating like a hypoglycemic hound. When I asked a tiny woman in a cardigan where the bakery was, she had to give my question some thought.

"*Ah, oui,*" she finally said, creakily. "That is the Lindt factory up on the hill you smell. There is always an odour of chocolate around here."

Well, shit. A town whose very streets are perfumed with chocolate: how very Willy Wonka of them. I decided to return to the church square, where, my guide promised, the Maison Artigarrède would at least sell me a *russe*, "a house specialty for three generations, a cake prepared with almonds and praline cream whose recipe remains a family secret." I was vaguely hoping some sparkling-eyed Juliette Binoche*** would lure me into the back of the confectionery, but all I got was the usual dismissive singsong of "*Bonjour, monsieur*" – cake in the box – coins slapped in change tray – and, "*Au revoir, monsieur.*" Feeling rather morose, I walked back to my car, rummaged through my backpack, found a can of Catalan-style tuna* left over from the pilgrimage, and had a sad-sack picnic with my legs poking out the passenger door. The *russe* turned out to be a tiny rectangle covered with powdered sugar, an insubstantial, sickly-sweet *mille-feuille* that the family should consider keeping secret from the next generation.

As I started the Saxo, smearing powdered sugar all over the gear shift, a familiar feeling stole over me. By travelling in a car, I was missing the point. Had I walked into Oloron as a pilgrim, I would have spent a leisurely half hour exploring the church, eventually found an open bakery and a supermarket, and enjoyed a quiet lunch on the banks of a purling stream on the outskirts of town. Instead, I'd breezed into Oloron with a guidebook-inspired to-do list, and now I was rushing out of town, resenting this charming little place because it hadn't delivered value-for-money in the half hour I'd allotted it. That's the problem with auto-tourism: you never really feel like you're fully anywhere. Freedom of movement reduces your attachment to any one place, and if you're mildly dissatisfied with one piece of topography, you can be somewhere else in ten minutes.

As a pilgrim, I'd felt like an integral feature of the landscape; now, I was merely a consumer of the countryside, swallowing up kilometres and local specialties indiscriminately.

Scenes of a post–high school trip through Europe, courtesy of a friend whose father ran a car rental agency, came flooding back. The endless circling of medieval town cores in our Opel Kadett, "Take on Me" and "Summer Holiday" playing on Radio Luxembourg as we searched in vain for a parking space. The trio of gendarmes rapping on our window and demanding our *cartes d'identité* after we'd emptied two bottles of wine and passed out in our seats in the shadow of the Eiffel Tower. And, when we got back home, the tales of Swedish girls in wagons-lits from friends who had done Europe the *right* way, with a backpack and a railpass. I felt the same resentment and alienation stealing over me. There was clearly an art to mastering this French tradition of auto-touring.

What's more, I was getting lonely. After the easy camaraderie of the pilgrimage, I was finding it hard to adjust to a conversational repertoire that was being inexorably eroded to "*Faites le plein, s'il vous plaît*" and "just try to pass me, you *trou de cul.*" So, when I saw a couple standing on the side of the road with a hand-lettered sign saying "Pau," I pulled over and told them I was going to Pau.

"*Genial!* You're going to Pau!" they said simultaneously as they piled into the back seat, immediately making me feel like a taxi driver.

In the rear-view, I could see that he was unshaven, with a black singlet and a reddish Afro, and she was skinny, with dirty blond hair, and that both were deeply tanned. They were shepherds-in-training, had just completed their classroom studies, and were doing their two-month-long field work. This seemed at once wonderful and strange to me. Wasn't the shepherd's trade passed down from father to son, along with the familial crook and *pépé*'s recipe for wormwood *eau-de-vie*?

"*Non non non!*" they insisted. He was from Paris, she from Bordeaux, and as with all things in bureaucratic Europe, being a shepherd now required a couple of years of training, and a certificate with unpronounceable initials. Which kind of takes the rustic fun out of the trade, particularly if some inspector from Brussels can come along, demand your shepherd's licence, and upend your sheep for a quick udder-check. Still, from their tales of banquets in the Spanish Pyrenees, mead-soaked lute recitals, and the antics of faithful sheepdogs, it sounded like the pastoral life still had its moments.

"You can't leave without trying the ewe's cheese!" they shouted, merrily, as we parted company in a vast parking lot in the middle of Pau.

This sure wasn't Montana, I thought. There, the best culinary advice you could hope for from a hitch-hiker would be directions to the Denny's on the I-90. After he'd tied your wrists, taken your keys, and warned you not to move until you'd counted to a thousand.

Far from easing my loneliness, sharing a stretch of road with the happy-go-lucky hitchhikers had made me feel like a lonely freak with too much discretionary income, and I braced myself for a solitary meal. Consulting my *Guide Rouge*, I saw that most of Pau's nine recommended restaurants were closed for lunch, a few were closed for lunch on Tuesdays, and some were closed for lunch on Tuesdays during their annual holidays from April 30 to May 13. Besides, it was no longer exactly lunch time: it was that uncomfortable post–2 p.m. slot when waiters give you "*Ce n'est pas un fast-food ici, monsieur*" look. Which is exactly what I got when I sat down in a mediocre-looking bistro down the street from the parking lot and pointed grimly to the sidewalk sandwich board that promised a *gratinée* of seafood. "I think I have one left," said the waitress, and I thought I heard her checking in the fridge for an emergency stock of frozen supermarket meals. I was beyond caring, and I gratefully stifled my *russe*-provoked sugar shakes with an inconsistently microwaved crabmeat-and-grated Emmenthal casserole. Spreading my maps and guidebooks on the table (the waitress, who had abhorred me as a tourist, now openly despised me as a malingerer), I quickly realized I needed more maps and guidebooks.

In a bookstore I bought a 1:1,000,000 scale map of southern France and picked up a *Green Guide* called *Languedoc-Roussillon-Tarn Gorges*. To my delight, the English-language guides had the familiar margin-to-margin text, the almost imperceptibly unidiomatic translations ("in the midst of cork-oak groves, a group of former cork-cutters have set up a cork museum") and the obsessive attention to castle date (in century), mountain height (in metres/feet), and cathedral decor (in Romanesque/ Gothic). I also went to an Internet café across from the Musée des Beaux-Arts, checked my e-mail account (an urgent message regarding Herbal Viagra awaited me), and instantly fell in love with Michelin's Web site. After I typed in my location, it gave me precise driving directions from the parking lot in Pau to my next destination, Albi***, including highway tolls (Six British Pounds), weather conditions (currently 24 degrees in Albi, visibility 10,000 metres, winds from the NE), and a foolproof purple line over a zoomable map that showed me, down to the last on-ramp, the roads I had to take to get to Albi. The drive should take two hours and 28 minutes, of which all but 17 minutes would be spent on the autoroute. This was the contemporary equivalent of last century's Bureau de Tourisme in Paris – where motorists could consult maps and guides free of charge in a well-appointed reading room, and leave with a tailor-made driving guide – and it was great.

❦

Before Michelin undertook its taming of the European roads, touring by car must have been a daunting proposition. One hundred years ago, the best maps available were those of the geographical service of the French army, designed for digging trenches rather than finding hotels. Roads were waymarked as they had been since Roman times, with a bewildering array of signposts intended to be read by pedestrians and engineers, rather than motorists travelling at speed. Introduced in 1909, Michelin's series of four-colour, 1:200,000-scale accordion-folded road maps, which used special symbols to warn of unpaved roads and axle-snapping obstacles, opened scenic backroads to vacationers who until then had preferred to take trains to seaside resorts.

In 1912, Michelin started marking French roads with its distinctive distance panels made from volcanic rock quarried in the Auvergne. Michelin's cartography was so precise that in the 1930s the French army adopted them as their official road maps, and American officers invading Normandy were issued a reprint of the 1939 *Red Guide France*, stamped "For Official Use Only," to navigate their tanks through the streets of

medieval towns. Michelin's Web site was just the latest in a series of seem-
ingly altruistic services to the traveller, which briefly had me wondering
why they hadn't won some kind of Nobel Prize for Tourism – until I
remembered that it was all a nefarious plot to hawk rubber tires.

After printing out my itinerary, I hit the road. Only as I turned right
onto the North Pau access road for 0.4 miles, before merging onto the A64
in the direction of Toulouse, as per instructions, did I realize I'd neglected
to see the Notre-Dame Cathedral*, the 14C Château**, the panoramic
view*** of the Pyrenees, or indeed anything in Pau** besides a parking lot,
a bad restaurant, and an Internet café. In spite of the advice of the hitchhikers, I hadn't even picked up any fresh ewe's cheese. An irrational voice,
familiar from previous road trips, prevented me from turning back: I had
to make time, *haddamaketime*, or I'd never have a place to sleep that night.

Sliding counter-clockwise around the *périphérique* that encircled
Toulouse, catching tantalizing glimpses of rain-soaked red roofs and
church steeples, I seethed as a tangle of rush hour traffic played havoc with
Michelin's prediction that I could complete the trip in 148 minutes.
Slowed to an unconscionable 60 kilometres an hour, I drummed on the
steering wheel and felt a tantrum looming. Lured by the myth of the open
road, I'd become the auto-tourist who sets off to escape the grind of daily
commuting, only to find that, even in his leisure, he's competing with
thousands of other freedom-seeking commuters for parking spaces, hotel
rooms, and some kind of spurious precedence on the road. The people in
the metal-and-glass cocoons around me weren't fellow travellers, potential comrades on a shared adventure, as the walkers on the pilgrimage had
been. These drivers were obstacles to my enjoyment – and the ones in
rental cars were out to steal my hotel room for the night.

Albi looked pretty, I noticed as I rolled in (three hours and 22 minutes
after I'd left Pau), but I'd have to see about that later. Following a series of
parking lot switchbacks down to the Tarn River, I finally found a free spot
in an ill-lit, secluded lot occupied by a louche-looking motorhome whose
curtains rustled as I dumped my backpack into the trunk. *Guide Rouge* in
hand, I canvassed the medieval town centre and came up blank: the only
recommended hotel in the non-luxury category, the Hostellerie du Vigan,
was *complet*, the desk clerk informed me with a what-did-you-expect

grimace. The other drivers had beaten me, and I'd have to sleep next to the gypsies. Or I could forgo my Michelin and check into the charming-looking Hotel St. Clair, down a narrow pedestrian sidestreet, which, judging by the keys dangling next to the reception, was half empty, and certainly half as cheap as anything in Michelin. I was directed to a room with a good view of a red brick wall – not as bad as it sounds, really, being a vine-covered, sunlit brick wall in the south of France. I decided it was time to review my happy-go-lucky, no-reservations policy.

Miraculously, I was granted a corner table in Le Vieil Alby, a restaurant next to the house where Henri de Toulouse-Lautrec was born. Its two crossed knives and forks indicated it was a "comfortable" restaurant, and the guide told me it had a "traditional menu." "Comfort" here meant a peculiar French brand of stodginess, in which middle-aged couples sat in funereal silence at tables with pink cloths, rolling wine in their glasses and staring past each other's eyes. "Tradition" meant the Midi favourite cassoulet, "a thick, sumptuous stew of haricot beans, sausage, pork, mutton, and preserved goose." The first few bites were heaven: a succulent, rich feast in a pottery dish. The last many bites were purgatory: the cassoulet was on closer analysis a bunch of adipose white beans bursting out of their pallid skins, going down for the third time in a pool of melted fat. Walking home was hell: I wanted to hail a passing wheelbarrow and ask to be dumped in the alley next to my hotel.

The next day was, er, sluggish. Besides being a demi-abstainer, I'm also a semi-vegetarian, and my digestive system has gotten used to chugging along on fish and tofu for months, followed by a sudden assault of bison burger* or cobra steak. But cassoulet was something else again, and for the next 24 hours I struggled with the sensation that I'd swallowed a pound of Crisco. Visiting the Musée Toulouse-Lautrec**, I found myself comparing the pasty flesh of the portly Montmartre prostitutes on the canvases to goose fat. Staring morosely at the hollowed-out cane*** the artist had used for smuggling alcohol into a sanatorium, I wondered whether chugging a half bottle of Calvados would cut the grease in my gut. In Albi's vast brick cathedral, I knew I should have spent more time inspecting the rood screen***, a Flamboyant Gothic masterpiece of lacy stonework. But instead I was riveted by the star-free Boschian 15C mural beneath the

organ, with its scenes of leering demons inflicting appropriate punish-
ments for the Seven Deadly Sins. I understood the symbolism: the gluttonous, who had funnels stuffed in their mouths, were having a tureen of
cassoulet poured down their throats. And the gape-mouthed greedy – who
were being churned pale and naked in a pot by a devil that was clearly part-
goose, part-sow – were in fact howling haricot beans. The Last Judgment
was nothing more than a medieval allegory of indigestion, inspired by the
favourite dish of the Midi.

Deciding a little exercise might clear my head, I followed a one-hour
Michelin-guided walking tour of Old Albi**. A prosperous centre of the
textile industry in the 16th century, Albi boasted an agreeable promenade
along the turbid green waters of the Tarn, which contrasted nicely with the
red brick of the Renaissance mansions of dyer's woad merchants. This had
been the centre of the Albigensian heresy, a medieval sect of vegetarian
zealots who believed that while God ruled the spiritual world, Satan was
responsible for everything in the material realm (including cassoulet).
Also known as the Cathars, they were powerful lords and merchants
whose involvement with textile traders from the Levant probably brought
them into contact with an obscure eastern sect that preached patience,
humility, and chastity, ideals rather at odds with the day-to-day practice
of the 12th-century Roman Catholic clergy. Under orders from Pope
Innocent III, the Parisian knight Simon de Montfort drove the Cathars
into strongholds in the hills south of Albi, and after a series of spectacular
sieges, the last Parfait – or Perfect One – was roasted alive in 1321.

All this would have been chilling and evocative if it weren't for the
other guidebook-toting tourists I kept running into, reading exactly the
same eerie story in *Der Grüne Reiseführer*, *La Guía Verde*, and *De Groene
Gids*. Whatever *frisson* this heresy might have stirred in my superstitious
soul quickly turned into a shudder as I saw how thoroughly it had been
converted into a pre-packaged tourist circuit. The Michelin guide told me
that "Pays Cathare" was now a trademark of the Aude General Council. I
could catch a Catharama multimedia show in a nearby citadel, or partici-
pate in a forkless medieval spit-roast in the castle stables on the site of
Cathar immolations. Bracing myself for a kitschfest, I made a quick trip to
a supermarket to stock up on Yop Énergie*, Lu Hello Brownies***, Babybel

wax-coated cheese**, and other high-calorie road staples that I hoped would put me on a level playing field with French drivers.

The drive south to the walled city of Carcassonne***, which ended along a plane-tree-shaded stretch of the Canal du Midi that links the Mediterranean to the Atlantic, was leisurely. Not because the drivers were less patient – they weren't, and I wished Accident and Flat Tire cards on every one of them – but because I'd had the sense to reserve in advance. Arriving at the Hôtel du Pont Vieux just before sunset, I felt pretty slick. "Your recommendation is self-evident if you always walk into a hotel Guide in hand," the *Guide Rouge* hinted in red ink, and indeed, when I sauntered into the medieval-lodge–like lobby and slammed the guide down on the desk, the jovial, bearded owner seemed to guess I'd read about his establishment in Michelin. I asked him whether he used the series himself.

"Ah, Michelin," he sighed. "Now there's a value you can count on!" (Then again, he would say that. He's in the fucking thing.) He heaped scorn on other guidebooks, including a series popular with French baby boomers.

"If you don't pay a fee for their absurd signs, they take you out of the guide. Not with Michelin. You'll notice there's no Michelin plaque outside my hotel – they don't offer one. If you say that you're in their guide in any form of advertising, you're barred forever."

With that, he bumped me up to a larger room, with a private balcony and a stunning view of France's Masada. That was it: I was going to have fake Michelin inspector's ID made up, guaranteeing better hotel rooms and respect from maître d's for the rest of my life.

(Come to think of it, I might be able to do a pretty good job of impersonating an inspector. I'd met a Michelin man while working on an article on budget French hotels for an American travel magazine. Nondescript, vaguely amiable, wearing a yellow tie and a squint behind his thick glasses, he'd introduced himself as Bernard Renaud – which, it occurred to me later, was the French version of John Smith. "Renaud" looked like a travelling salesman, the kind you'd expect to have a range of samples of some obscure but pricey foodstuff in his briefcase. When he flashed his wallet card with the Michelin logo, the desk clerk at a Right Bank hotel across from the Opéra Comique froze like a Périgord pig caught scarfing a truffle. Renaud explained that he was one of about 20 hotel inspectors who combed the land, and allowed me a brief glance at what looked like a pre-flight checklist for the Space Shuttle, with highly specific boxes on hallway rug condition and mattress rotation. When he saw my hand-scrawled, photocopied rating sheet – sample entry: "hairdryer? yes/no" – he chuckled condescendingly.)

§

The next morning, I explored Carcassonne, which should really be called Catharland. In 1209, this apparently impregnable town – the largest fortress in Europe – fell to the pope's armies after only two weeks, apparently because the Perfect Ones forgot that even they needed to drink water. Eight centuries later, it was still under siege, by a far more redoubtable enemy: the tourists of the world.

"*S'il vous plaît*, come right in," a barker for the local Torture Museum cried to passersby. "It's the most beautiful museum in Carcassonne, all the Cathar torture instruments, you won't be disappointed . . ."

When I paused to glare at sidewalk bins full of plastic maces, pikes, and Templar-crossed tabards, an Englishman with a couple of pints of 1664 down his gullet snatched a rubber sword out of a scabbard and challenged me to a duel. As I leaned against a barbican, a Central European tourist a hundred metres away yelled at me because I was blocking her snapshot of the rooftops of the lower city. I wasn't surprised to learn that the resident population of the old city was only 139 – presumably only the deaf had chosen to remain. When I stumbled upon the Maison du Cassoulet, whose facade was spread with a backlit blow-up of a bowl of haricot beans glistening with fat, I decided it was time to leave. While I settled my bill at the Hôtel du Pont Vieux, the owner gave me the lowdown on the Cathar Country.

"I used to work as a tour guide around here. Most of this stuff isn't very interesting. All the English people go to Rennes-le-Château, for example."

I'd been thinking of going there myself: I'd read that in 1891, the local priest started living in fabulous luxury – some said because he'd discovered a trove of medieval treasure.

"You'll notice it doesn't get a single star in the Michelin guide. That's because there is strictly *nothing* there. Unless you want to see a bunch of New Age bookshops and some *rosbifs* with metal detectors looking for the treasure of the Cathars. You're better going off to Lagrasse – at least you can visit some nice wineries there."

Thanks to the innkeeper's advice, I had my first perfect day of autotouring. Lagrasse, I learned, had been voted one of the most beautiful villages in France, and after visiting its sprawling Benedictine abbey, partly in ruins, I sat on a tree-shaded boulevard and sipped my new favourite drink, the *diabolo-anise*, a fizzy lemon water and licorice-syrup that made me feel like a teenager in a Jean-Luc Godard film. Before leaving, I stopped in the high street shop of the Domaine du Cadran, a 40-hectare winery. The young owner, Edouard, shook my hand with an overly warm grip that suggested he'd been testing his product without spitting. He opened a bottle of old vines Carignane and poured it into a glass poised atop a barrel.

"*Nunc est bibendum!*" I shrugged; it's against my principles to refuse a drink offered in hospitality. It was delicious.

"We're already in the Gault et Millau guide," he told me, beaming, "and we've only been open four years." When I bought a ridiculously cheap bottle out of politeness, he offered me a complimentary glass of rosé. I protested that I was driving.

"*C'est pas grave,*" he said, insouciantly. "Most French people like to drive a little drunk." Ah ha! This explained why they used their cars like a four-year-old uses a crayon.

"It is true. You've got to be a little careful here when you're going around the corners."

A timely reminder, I thought: driving through French vineyard country after lunch, even on a brilliantly sunny spring day with 10,000-metre visibility, is a feat of devil-may-care bravado. (Driving through Calvados country in the fog, it is universally acknowledged, is a desperate cry for help.) The French, per kilometre driven, are the most accident-prone drivers in Europe, and I learned to favour the shoulder on most turns, even if it meant grazing the sculpted calves of Tour de France wannabes from time to time.

The next couple of days were everything the Michelin guides promised the auto-touring experience would be. I opted for tiny roads that led past ancient aqueducts and roadside crosses, and set a German shepherd barking as I took a long detour to stock up on a nicely pungent goat cheese called *pelardon*, which I purchased straight from the farmhouse. The hills were daubed with yellow swaths of broom and perfumed like a *bouquet garni*, and I spent the afternoons following winding roads to the Cathar castles of Quéribus* and Peyrepertuse***, those "citadels of vertigo" that commanded magisterial views of the Corbières plateau.

One evening I drove into Cucugnan, a village poised on a rock in the middle of a sea of grape vines. Though it had a year-round population of only 128, it supported two Michelin-recommended establishments. After visiting a church that contained one of the world's few pregnant Virgin statues, I checked in at the Auberge de Cucugnan and could only agree with Michelin's attribution of the little black-ink rocking chair man that betokened a "quiet situation." As I strolled through the maze of streets and emerged on the grassy hilltop above the last roofs of the village, the sun disappeared at the end of the valley, and the only sounds were the barking of a distant dog and the cooing of nearby doves. This was Bibendum in paradise, the apotheosis of auto-touring: excellent cuisine, high-standard lodgings, picturesque panoramas, charming curiosities. And, best of all: Free parking***.

§

The next day, succumbing to the lure of the seaside, I drove to a promising-sounding fishing town called Collioure**, where Matisse, Braque, and Picasso summered long, long ago. As I approached, I was churned in the centrifuges of three-lane roundabouts on coastal highways that called to mind the congestion of South Florida. I arrived in Collioure to face constant parking anxiety. In the two minutes it took to tote my bags to the desk of my beachfront hotel, a cop on a moped had pulled up and told me to beat it, directing me to a vast parking lot next to the Château Royal that dominated the harbour.

The lot operated on an escalating scale, each hour more expensive than the last; stabling my Saxo for 24 hours would cost far more than my own lodging. To cut my losses, I came back at midnight, after the streets had cleared of day-tripping diners, and cruised the labyrinthine back-streets for 45 minutes in search of a spot, then undertook one of those 12-point continental parking manoeuvres best attempted with Vaseline and a shoe horn. The rest of my stay in Collioure was spent paying neurotic visits to the Saxo, checking whether the vehicles I'd wedged myself between had conspired to compress it into scrap.

Collioure was a pretty town. Its tiny harbour featured pebbly beaches and Catalan fishing boats painted in gay and glossy colours, and culminated in Notre-Dame-des-Anges, whose cylindrical stone clock tower and wave-lapped Mediterranean setting made it seem more lighthouse than church. Painters had set up their easels on the beachwalk, and galleries in the old Mouré quarter sold neo-Impressionist canvases. Tourists walked around with multi-scooped ice cream cones or queued for excursions to Spain in small sailing ships. When I asked the clerk in an overpriced grocery store where I could get some good seafood, she smirked.

"Not in Collioure. Try Port-Vendres – that's a real fishing town."

Then Collioure wasn't? What about the fishing boats in the harbour? Wasn't this a centre of the anchovy fleet?

"Anchovy fleet!" she scoffed. "Those boats are for tourists. They pack the anchovies here, they sell them here, but they haven't caught them here for ages."

Come to think of it, the vanes of the windmills on the low dry hills that cupped the harbour never seemed to move, and all the artists in the galleries were American or British. Collioure was another pseudo-place – like Carcassonne, reconstructed German town centres, and much of Paris's Latin Quarter – carefully maintained for its tourist appeal.

In his famous deconstruction of *Le Guide Bleu*, one of Michelin's competitors, Roland Barthes looked at the travel guide as a chapbook of the bourgeois mythology of humanity. For him, it masked the real spectacle of classes and social struggles, turning the people of an entire country into a kind of vast classical ballet, a backdrop to what the middle-class tourist found really attractive in a nation – its monuments. It was true: when I envisioned roaming France with a Michelin guide, my mind focused on starred restaurants and Romanesque churches, rather than the French themselves – who were in fact a potentially annoying footnote to my idealized auto-touring experience. The perfect Michelin tour, permitting both optimal driving times and no six-month waits for three-rosette restaurants, would be in a France that had been selectively neutron bombed, sparing only castles and toqued chefs. Collioure, from this perspective, was an enormous stage set, a town frozen in late Modernist amber. Charming, picturesque, it merited its stars. But, when it came down to it, I didn't want anchovies with good taste. I wanted anchovies that tasted *good*.

There was only one Michelin-recommended restaurant in town, the harbourside Neptune, which ominously featured three crossed spoons and forks, but no rosettes, promising high pretentiousness and higher bills. An appearance in Michelin seemed to set many restaurants in aspic, locking them into a menu of specialties and bland, frilly decor designed to soothe the sensibilities of anonymous Messrs. Renauds. I was sick of following the guide, then enduring a lonely meal next to *les waters*. Leaving Bibendum in my hotel room, I asked a hip-looking young woman in a sandwich shop where *she* went to eat. She gave me a rave review of a bar down the road. "It doesn't look like much, but the tapas are great."

I sat at the bar while the latest Manu Chao album blared and people smoked and laughed. The waiter wrote my orders on the bartop with a grease pencil, and I was presented with a series of dishes – grilled octopus, garlic-dosed *anchoïade****, spicy olives**, and deep-fried calamaries** – by a grinning chef whose long white hair was pulled back in a ponytail. A Michelin inspector would have decamped the second he saw the cook's dirty T-shirt, but who wants to hang out with Michelin inspectors? I took part in an argument about the difference between Romantic and Romanesque with a group of DJs at a nearby table who talked me into trying the local specialty, the sweet dessert wine Banyuls. (It tasted not unlike fermented Robitussin.) For an hour, at least, I'd broken out of my cocoon, the signposted and symbol-studded world of Michelin, which has so diligently rated, measured, and alphabetized every feature of the touristic world. It is indeed a good thing to know how to use a guidebook. It's better, though, to know when to put it down.

§

Next morning, I ran to the car with a laser-printed itinerary in hand. The goat cheese was stinking in the back seat, the Yop had gone off, and it looked like I'd have to repeat my adolescent automotive marathon. I'd forgotten I had an appointment with a bus in Calais in less than 24 hours, and an Internet café had shown me that Collioure, on the Mediterranean, was about as far as you could get in France from the English Channel. Michelin's Web site told me I had 1,179 kilometres to drive, practically the length of the nation. For a North American, I blustered – not really convincing myself – it was a Sunday outing. With a good supply of Moto-Naphta, a complete set of Michelin maps, and a Driving Ace card*** on my dashboard, I'd be there before sunset.

Chapter 3

SEVEN BORDERS IN SEVEN DAYS

My Coach Awaits Me – Thomas Cook Started It All – My Roommate Thinks I'm Gay – The Tour Guide Is a Lush – The Bus Has No Bathroom – How to Visit Brussels Without Seeing the Manneken Pis – If This Is 10:45 a.m., It Must Be Luxembourg – The Ground Has Gone Sour, Pt. 1 – Eating at Rest Stops – A Brief History of American Music – The Ground Has Gone Sour, Pt. 2 – The Perfect Snapshot – Frank Plays the Alpenhorn – Cook & Son Rule Egypt – Gruyères Without the Cheese – Beaune Without the Wine – A Single Bed in Paris – Dangers of Local Specialties – The Outrageous Cancan – Frank Organizes His Own Tour of Fontainebleau

The history of travel is the history of vague yearnings, spurious promises, and frustrated expectations. Spawned deep in the loam of the psyche, the yearnings tend to evanesce when real overland motion begins. The sight of a freckle-faced hiker with a rucksack in Thomas Mann's drear Munich led Gustav von Aschenbach to a daydream of a crouching tiger in a tropical marshland beneath a reeking sky; to the vague pursuit of a Polish youth on the Lido; to a pathetic death in Venice. In his *Journey Without Maps*, Graham Greene tried to account for his penchant to travel to West Africa rather than Switzerland, only to be frustrated as "words and images, witches and death, unhappiness and the Gare St Lazare, the huge smoky viaduct over a Paris slum, crowd together and block the way to full consciousness." Travel books, cruise ship brochures, and palm-treed posters are the parasites on our subconscious cravings, offering to appease lacks we can rarely fully define. But generations of travellers succumb, lured abroad by Sir John Mandeville's accounts of dog-faced men and twin-headed geese, or the latest island resort Web site promising Sex on the Beach and other erotic cocktails. Spuriouser and spuriouser.

Awaking clotted and shaky after a six-hour sleep in a rest stop a hundred kilometres from Calais, I'd cursed the nebulous desire for freedom that had made a French road trip sound attractive. Here I was, stiff and road-glazed, feeling like a teenager who'd blown his bus pass money on video games. Tossing aside my *Guide Rouge* after paying the car rental bill in the agency next to the Calais ferry terminal, I pulled another fraudulent appeal to unspoken desires out of my backpack: the plastic-bound travel wallet of a tour bus company called Global, containing the brochure for its week-long "Taste of Europe" excursion. I'd booked the trip a week before I'd left home.

"'Host service on the Continent,'" my Basque-born travel agent Maria had read aloud, gazing low through her bifocals. "'Eight continental break-fasts; three dinners; private first-class air-conditioned motorcoach; Lake Lucerne cruise; Sightseeing with local guides: Chillon Castle and Paris' – doesn't sound too bad." The itinerary had also looked promising: "Visits to Luxembourg, Lucerne, Interlaken, Cheese factory and Gruyère village, Lausanne, Beaune; Scenic highlights: Swiss Alps and Lakelands."

After a call to the head office, Maria had said they were willing to accommodate my strange request to start the tour in Calais, rather than London. "They must be desperate for clients," she'd speculated.

The price had seemed right – Global's slogan was "Quality Cut-Rate Touring" – they'd set up room-sharing so I wouldn't have to pay a single supplement, and they shaved off two nights of English hotel fees and the Channel ferry fare. "You'll probably have room to spread out on the bus," Maria had said, handing me my tickets. "I just hope for your sake you get a good roommate."

Walking across the vast ferry terminal parking lot towards the foot pas-sengers disembarking from the P & O Stena Line's *Provence*, my relief at abandoning my car was neutralized by the feeling I was about to relinquish the hard-won autonomy of adulthood and undergo a horrible regression to adolescence. The sight of dozens of fishermen on a long pier ending in a green lighthouse had provoked a bout of déjà vu: I'd been to Calais, at age 14, on my first trip to Europe. It was meant to be a Mediterranean cruise, but two weeks before sailing our ship was commandeered to serve as a troop transport in the Falklands War. The HMV *Uganda* was traded for a tour bus, and I spent a fortnight with 40 other barely post-pubescent North Americans gaining a connoisseur's knowledge of Heineken-filled vending machines at rest stops on *Autobahns*, *autostrades*, and *autoroutes*.

Highlights of that trip had included a morning announcement not to imitate Kurt, who'd "whiddled in the bidet," and the night some girls discovered the unlocked minibar in their room and vomited their fondue over the balcony of a four-star Zurich hotel. I barely noticed the ceiling of the Sistine Chapel, too involved in a conspiracy to torment greasy-haired Greg, a cop's son who was the designated loser in our group dynamic. My friend Bill and I decided the summum of cool was the punks we'd seen in London, and infuriated everybody with clumsy impersonations of Johnny Rotten and Sid Vicious. We tried to smuggle a broken gargoyle head out of the bell tower in Notre-Dame Cathedral, and spent most of a free afternoon in Venice shopping for switchblades. It was an inauspicious start to a life of travelling, but it was also my first brush with Dijon mustard, flirtatious Italian girls (for months after my return I received cheaply perfumed letters sealed with smudges of pink lipstick), and the Uffizi Gallery.

It was also remarkably similar to the itinerary of the circular tours of the Continent organized by the pioneer of the package tour, Thomas Cook. The Baptist cabinetmaker was struck by a thought as he walked along 14 miles of track to a Leicester temperance meeting one morning in 1841. Why not use the recently generalized train system to organize a rail excursion of like-minded teetotallers? After negotiating with the Midland Counties Railway, he marshalled a crowd of about 570 and charged them a shilling each for a holiday excursion to Loughborough, where they spent an afternoon of anemic fun enjoying ginger beer, biscuits, and games of "Lost My Slipper" (rather than the usual Industrial Revolution gin-house amusements of bull-baiting, prize-fighting, and "Lost My Lunch").

Spurred by his success, Cook printed up a handbook for a Special Pleasure Train to Liverpool that would have 350 "trippers" visiting Caernarvon and scaling Mount Snowdon without the aid of Fiend Alcohol.

Excursions to the Isle of Man, Wales, and Scotland followed. He conducted groups to the Hebrides, where in 1861 the local poverty inspired his tourists to donate enough for the building of a fleet of 24 fishing boats, including one christened the *Thomas Cook*. (That same year, he provoked outrage on Iona by shooting a rare golden eagle – the first in living memory to alight on the island – neatly presaging mass tourism's mixed economic and ecological impact.)

By 1855, Cook was a confident enough tour guide to make his first expedition across the English Channel, taking 25 excursionists to the diamond shops of Antwerp, to the Cologne Cathedral, on a boat trip down the Rhine, and on a promenade along the Champs-Elysées. The major difference between my teenage odyssey and a 19th-century Cook's Tour – apart from the volume of alcohol consumed – was the means of locomotion. Just after the First World War, Cook & Son had started running six-day tours of the battlefields by motor coach, and by the 1920s buses were coming to supplant trains as the tour vehicles of choice. The dignity of rod-and-rail gave way to the banality of rubber-and-road, as Nelson's Monument and Notre-Dame Cathedral were remorselessly encircled by cordons of diesel-spewing Contiki and Wallace Arnold buses.

🛡

Near the ferry, I walked along a row of white-and-orange Setra coaches that were filling with passengers. Beside the bus marked Tour 4520, a driver was loading luggage under the watchful eyes of a covey of tourists. "Hand it over, love," she said, grabbing my backpack, "unless you want to be wearing that jumper for the next week."

We filed onto the bus, and a red-capped Global representative told us we'd be met by our tour guide and a new driver in Brussels. We should also feel free to take advantage of the toilets outside. A small man, whose extravagantly wrinkled face called to mind the early phases in the desiccation of an apple head doll, leapt up as if electrocuted and exclaimed: "Jeez, I've got to pee-pee!" Outside the bus he'd been telling everybody and nobody he was Frank, from Kalamazoo, Michigan. I'd glanced at a passenger manifest open beside the driver's seat, and noticed, with a premonition of doom, that I was slated to share rooms with a certain *Mathers, F.*, nationality: American.

"Let's see if Ol' Gertie wants to start," said the driver, Ruth, in pure Cockney. As we hit the flat coastal roads of northern France, she engaged in badinage with Frank (who'd snagged the shotgun seat) about governance, cloning, the merits of fresh fruit, and the vicissitudes of the American auto industry. She was particularly opinionated on the subject of royalty.

"The queen's going to hang on to the crown as long as she can. They'll have an IV drip running up the side of the palace before she leaves." After almost sideswiping a Mercedes (and muttering "Stupid cow!" when the driver had the temerity to honk), Ruth continued: "Charles, he's a big mother's blouse, he is. Imagine him as king – he'd be wandering around the castle talking to his plants! A thousand years on the island, and we get a mucker like 'im."

"That Prince Charles was born with a silver spoon in his mouth," said Frank, displaying a fine republican disdain for monarchy.

"Your George W. Bush was born with one, too!" snapped Ruth. "And I hope they both choke on it." She glanced at Frank appraisingly. "Where's your wife, then?"

"I left her at home. I have my bank account, she has hers. It's my third marriage. She's seven years younger than I am, but I still want to swap her in for another model – Ha! I'm only kidding! Twenty-five years of struggle, and now we can enjoy ourselves." Just not, apparently, at the same time.

I idly watched two dignified Indian men in suits ahead of me eating savoury balls and unwrapping mango chocolate treats, even as Ruth complained about passengers soiling her bus.

"Stuffing apple cores into the ashtrays – dis-*gus*-ting," she spat. "Things they wouldn't do at home. Putting diapers into the toilet – dis-*gus*-ting."

A small blue sign marked "België" announced we'd crossed into a Flemish-speaking part of Belgium. The scenery consisted of off-ramps for towns that sounded like the eructations of a tippler with a gastric ulcer – Gistel, Jabbeke, Brugge, Oostkamp, Beernem, Burst, Erpe. I turned to a copy of Evelyn Waugh's *When the Going Was Good* for distraction.

"What are you reading there?" said Frank, leaning over the aisle. "*How to Get Fat?*" He whacked me jovially on the thigh. "Ha! Just kidding, there, buddy! I'm Frank!"

I shook his extended hand. When I told him I thought we'd be sharing a room that night, he started in genuine alarm, but quickly recovered.

"Don't worry!" he stage-whispered. "I'm not like that –!" He let his left wrist go limp.

I widened my eyes in perplexity, hoping he'd elaborate.

"You know what I mean!"

He took a good look at me. I'm slender and tall, and my hair is permanently unkempt. Artsy type, not a good ol' boy. Frank's jovial look disappeared, and he inched away from me on his seat.

Hmm, I thought. He'd pegged me for a skinny gay bookworm. The next week could be interesting.

Ruth wheeled us into the suburbs of Brussels two hours after we'd left Calais, and deposited us at a Holiday Inn across from the rusting Atomium, a scaled-up model of an iron crystal molecule and *chef d'oeuvre* of futurist kitsch from the 1958 World's Fair. In the lobby, a wan, dark-haired English woman in her 20s, eyes marked by the kohl-like circles of professional sleep deficit, introduced herself as Emma, our tour director for the duration of the trip.

"After you've checked into your rooms, you'll perhaps want to have dinner. Which isn't included in your package tonight, actually. However, you'll find you can enjoy some lovely mussels and french fries across the street at the Bruparck, next to the stadium. Here in Belgium, they're famous not only for their lace, tapestry, and chocolate, but also, you'll be happy to hear, for their *beer*. There are approximately 464 different kinds of beer in Belgium, actually, and they're all served in different glasses." Emma's love of the word "beer" – exacerbated, no doubt, by Global's rules that tour directors couldn't drink on duty – was matched only by her predilection for the word "actually." Liberally swizzled with figures culled from fraying copies of Michelin green guides, Emma's utterances could be distilled to their essence in the phrase: "Alcohol, actually." Which I took as the poignant response to the unspoken question, "What do you miss most when you're working?"

Looking at her manifest, Emma confirmed my worst fears: Frank and I were indeed bunking together. After we'd gone up to inspect our room – a quaint scale model of a North American hotel room, with narrow beds just distant enough to quell Frank's incipient homophobia – I asked what he was doing for dinner.

"I'm going to check out that there Atomium across the street."

I said I thought I'd try to find a restaurant in downtown Brussels. We'd be leaving in the morning, so this would be our only chance to see the city.

"You go ahead, there, buddy. You can tell me what it looked like tomorrow." He probably had visions of me playing footsie with him under the table.

I crossed the street to a metro station, and saw on a wall map that Global had us lodged at the end of the line – practically at the airport, with the downtown a good dozen stops away. After riding the boxy metro, I wandered past the gilded bourgeois buildings and woody bars of the Grand-Place, then ate in a Vietnamese restaurant where I was serenaded by an itinerant accordionist and ignored by the rose peddlers (one of the few advantages of solo dining in European capitals). Catching the last metro back to the hotel, I sat across from a victim of Trappist beer who burped uncontrollably every 20 seconds: "Gistel!" I thought I heard him belch. Then: "Jabbeke! . . . Brugge!" As the car emptied stop by stop, I consoled myself that three hours in Brussels' twee centre was better than nothing. ("Oostttttkamp!") Even if once again I'd failed to find the much-loved emblem of Belgium's diuretic beverages, the Manneken Pis. ("Burst! Erpe!")

§

"Rise and shine!"

Frank was an early bird, I realized with dismay, and he invariably burst into consciousness with some non sequitur hauled from the depths of an unexamined psyche.

"Yeah, we had two springer spaniels, and we named them Duke and Duchess after Wallace and Edward VII."

I looked at the clock radio: 5:59 a.m.

"What did you say?"

"'Course, we don't have royalty in America, but I did up my family tree, back 20 generations, and I'm descended from Henry VIII. You know – the bastard-maker!"

I soon understood that Frank didn't so much expect me to converse with him as encourage his blurts with the occasional nod or grunt. I'd eventually learn that I could take a shower, go buy a soda from the machine in the hall, and return to find Frank enjoying his solipsistic universe unaided.

Down in the dining room, after navigating through a breakfast buffet of slate-coloured cold cuts and piles of prunes, I sat at a table with ten other Global excursionists. Ina, a jovial, roly-poly, born-again Christian from Goa who now ran an office-cleaning company in Mumbai, expressed shock at local prices.

"Everything is so expensive in Europe!" she told me, with a disbelieving wobble of the head. "I have already spent lakhs of rupees on this vacation. I wouldn't mind so much if the food wasn't so bland. Potatoes and mayonnaise – all the food is white! And don't they use spices here?" Mentally comparing the toast and soft-boiled egg on my plate to a nice masala dosa, I wasn't inclined to contradict her.

With the exception of an Australian couple, John and Mary, no one else seemed to have spent their time in Brussels by actually going to Brussels, opting instead to eat in the food court Emma had recommended. Perhaps it wasn't surprising, given that our hotel was probably closer to Ghent than to downtown Brussels.

On the bus, Emma picked up the microphone and – though no one showed evidence of being hung over – began the day with a jocular announcement.

"Well, I hope too many of you aren't recovering from your experiments with Chimay, Leffe, and other Belgian beers – paracetamols will be forthcoming!" Despite the puzzled silence, she soldiered on: "You'll notice that we have a new driver today, Manu – say hello, Manu – who is from Belgium, actually. And indeed you'll notice that we have a new bus. Now, we don't actually have a toilet" – a chorus of groans – "but, as those with nicotine habits will also be happy to hear, we do allow regular breaks.

There is no eating on the bus, except for sweets and water. Hopefully, we'll have a safety-free – whoops! – a safety-*conscious*, week."

Emma called for a show of hands. Frank and a woman with a thinning black bouffant from New Jersey represented the United States; the couple from Australia and a blond Kiwi who spent her time teletexting messages into a cellphone made up the Antipodean cohort; East Asia made a good showing with several Vietnamese, Koreans, Malaysians, and a Thai couple; and, though Emma had to be reminded of our geopolitical existence, there were four Canadians. Thirty-three passengers in all, with the largest show of hands coming from India. We were a hearteningly post-colonial crew, returned from the outposts of empire for a cut-rate inspection of history's humbled colonizers.

It was a singular contrast to Thomas Cook's 19th-century clientele, who were almost overwhelmingly English, using their new-found wealth to explore a world cowed and unified by the Pax Britannica. It was the growth of railways – the first steam-powered passenger service started running between Liverpool and Manchester in 1830 – that began the democratization of travel. Until then, only the aristocratic English could afford a Grand Tour of the Continent in costly diligences, and they moved no faster than Roman senators on horseback had, 2,000 years before them. As rail systems spread through the Continent, travel got not only speedier but cheaper, and Cook, arriving on the scene in the propitious period of peace that followed the Napoleonic Wars – an era whose coinages would include the terms tourism (1811), guidebook (1814), and sight-seeing (1824) – showed a talent for negotiating all-inclusive fares with the new railways. His chief innovation was the through ticket, in which a traveller paid a single fare (£1, say, for a third-class return ticket to Paris in 1861, or £18 for a first-class return to Alexandria in the 1870s), saving much haggling at the wickets of ferry companies and foreign train stations.

As history's seminal vulgarizers of travel, Thomas and his son John Mason Cook got a bad rap for packing the cathedrals and beauty-spots of Europe with gaggles of Cockneys and governesses. To be fair, neither the package tour nor the all-inclusive ticket was their invention. In the 15th century, Jerusalem-bound pilgrims could pay Agostino Contarini or his rival Pietro Lando, who flew their banners in Venice's St. Mark's Square,

60 gold ducats for an all-in Holy Land cruise package, including guides, bribes, and two hot meals with wine daily. (Apparently, clients experienced a kind of "If this is Shrove Tuesday, it must be Bethlehem" sensation, complaining of being rushed through on-shore sites in less than a week.) The first reduced-rate group railway excursion had taken place five years before Cook's 1841 outing, and Henry Gaze, Cook's chief competitor, had sent tourists on package tours to Paris as early as 1844. It was Gaze who probably inspired Cook's system of hotel coupons, prepaid eight-shilling tickets that in 1872 entitled the bearer to a room, including two meals and tips, in one of more than 150 Continental hotels.

After the first altruistic Cook outings of clerks and working men, most Cook clients travelled independently, without guides, carrying their tickets in a green leather or cloth case with COOK'S TOURIST TICKETS emblazoned on the cover – not unlike modern European railpass bearers. (Their "circular notes," which inspired American Express's traveller's cheques in the 1890s, were redeemable at Cook-approved hotels, a system that would only disappear in the 1920s, when fluctuating currency rates made it impractical.) What Cook & Son, eventually the world's largest travel agency, was really responsible for was simplifying and cheapening foreign excursions, transforming travel-for-the-few into tourism-for-the-masses. By 1872, Thomas Cook himself could boast of conquering the world, personally guiding a tour group to the Rocky Mountains, Singapore, and the Taj Mahal in a 222-day round-the-globe rail-and-cruise odyssey. It was nice to see that, in the 21st century, the middle classes of India and East Asia – exchange rates permitting – could now come to England and the Continent to return the compliment.

I had Thomas Cook to blame for Global's whirlwind style of touring, as well as the fact that the first and last act of our day in Belgium consisted of *leaving* Belgium.

"Imagine!" said Emma over the loudspeaker. "You'll be able to tell your friends back home that you had breakfast in Belgium, a coffee – or a *beer*, actually – in Luxembourg, lunch in France, and dinner in Switzerland. By the way, I was very impressed with how on time you've all been so far. If you keep on doing this, you'll see me wearing a smile, not a frown."

A *New York Times* writer had early on remarked on this tendency to infantilize tourists. "So strongly," he had written, in 1872, "is the average Cook's tourist impressed with the feeling that he has been thrust back into his school-boy days, that it is rumoured that tourists have abstained from smoking, except by stealth, and have even run away by night from the hotels to which they have been committed, with vague ideas of working their way back to London and appealing to the charity of prosperous uncles." In the gloom of a rainy Sunday morning on a highway in the Ardennes, as I heard Frank repeating to all and sundry that he was the great-great-great-great-etc. of Anne Boleyn, I realized that my transformation into halfwitted toddler, capable of great naughtiness but not independent thought, was well underway. Once a foot-proud pilgrim, so recently a discerning Michelin motorist, I was being turned into a sheepish package tourist. The wound, as usual, was self-inflicted.

◆

Luxembourg, the rest stop of nations, is tailor-made for bus tours. It has ample parking, free lavatories, and plenty of souvenir shops, and it is too small for even the directionally clueless to get lost in. A quick dose of quaint, you're in, you're out – half an hour, tops. It was only as we left that I read in a tourist office brochure that I'd missed a cliffside elevator that led to the Bock Casemates, a 23-kilometre network of underground passages beneath the town castle. But Emma didn't want her charges wandering too far, so when we parked in a ravine-side lot overlooking the meanders of the underachieving Pétrusse River, she neglected to mention the attraction.

"Luxembourg City is the capital of the Grand Duchy of Luxembourg. There are many banks here, and many government headquarters. We'll be walking you to the tourist office, where you can get your passports stamped. And today, we'll be saving you some money. Because it's Sunday, actually, and most of the shops are closed."

She might also have mentioned that it was raining, the streets were dotted with impossibly wack multicoloured life-sized papier mâché cows, and you couldn't even hope for a watery espresso in the Place d'Armes because the cafés were still closed.

After following Emma's raised umbrella to the tourist office (where Frank videotaped me having my passport defaced with an entirely unconvincing "Luxembourg City Tourist Office" stamp), our group split up. Some couples headed straight for the Pizza Hut in the square, but most went window-shopping in the deserted streets. It took me about 12 minutes to confirm that, except for comparing bank machine graphic interfaces and pushing over cows, there was nothing to do in Luxembourg at ten o'clock on a Sunday morning.

As we drove past the Lexus dealerships and Ikea stores that lined the road to the French border, Emma passed around sheets outlining the tour's many optional excursions. Global apparently low-balled the competition on their initial quote by making virtually all tour activities paid extras. If you wanted to go up a Swiss mountain, see Versailles, or even say goodbye to everyone at the farewell dinner in Paris, you had to sign up in advance and fork over $60 or risk sitting alone in your hotel room all night. There was much discussion of the cabaret night; the pamphlet warned of adult scenes and semi-nudity, and advised parental discretion. A young Malaysian couple, Allison and Andrew, got into a lengthy debate about signing up for the Mt. Titlis Ice Flyer.

"We have never seen the snow," they finally explained to me. "Do you think we will need gloves?" I told them they could probably get away with keeping their hands in their pockets for an hour.

"You'll notice that we have now crossed into France," announced Emma, "where we'll soon be pausing for lunch. Some people say that the French are quite abrupt, but if you do try a few words of French with these French people, they'll be quite nice to you, actually. And don't worry, if you say the word 'beer' they'll understand you in any language, and you'll get a nice, cold glass of beer." For a second, I thought I could hear a faint but insistent clicking coming from across the English Channel: the sound of teetotalling Thomas Cook's teeth gnashing in Leicester Cemetery.

We pulled into a highway rest stop next to a giant electrical plant, whose high-voltage lines ran over green fields on rolling hills dotted with yellow flowers.

"Yeah, that's wild mustard," announced Frank, for the second time. "They plant that when the ground's gone sour." (I would have had more faith in his country savvy if he hadn't told me he'd worked in a General Motors factory all his life.) In the rest stop, which had the usual collection of overpriced toothbrushes and 1970s-vintage coin-op espresso machines, we queued for undercooked french fries and ratatouille swimming in yellow oil. I found Allison and Andrew at a linoleum table, pushing pieces of cold ham around a plate of rice, commiserating with Ina about the food.

"This is the first rice we have had since we came to Europe," said Allison. "The food is so cold and greasy here. We are missing our chilis." Frank joined us, digging into his oil-limp fries with gusto. He stared at Ina blankly for a second, until her ethnicity seemed to trip some deeply buried neuron.

"I was a kid when that Mahatma Gandhi died," he said. "That made a big splash over our way at the time. What was he trying to overthrow? The government? He was trying to overthrow something." Though Ina's eyes widened in disbelief, she suavely ignored his question. I was starting to like her.

Our introduction to French cuisine had left many people grumbling. John from Australia, on the overweight side of solid, seemed particularly disappointed.

"Of all the places we could have eaten in France," he said, "we stop at a crap petrol station restaurant."

"I hope you all appreciated our stop," Emma said over the intercom. "Now, please, try to enjoy this French scenery, while we whisk you off to enjoy some Swiss scenery."

As Frank indiscriminately took snapshots, oblivious to the glare on the window, I reflected that the scenery, with its fat cows, cute peaked-roof houses, and rolling pastures, would have been perfectly quaint – if it weren't for the great ugly tour bus full of prying eyes right in the middle of it.

As we approached Basel, Emma announced: "We've just crossed another border. You're now in Switzerland. Do you feel any different?"

"Our bottoms are sore!" cried Ina, and then, charmingly, covered her mouth and blushed. Frank, putting his chin on a seat-back antimacassar, asked Emma whether she was married.

"No. I'm still trying to find my rich, successful boyfriend, actually."

"What about Prince Charles?"

"He's a little too old for me, don't you think?"

"Age is just a number!" Frank bellowed. "I'm 68, but you know what they say: there may be snow on the roof, but the fire hasn't gone out in the furnace!" He turned to the Indian gentleman across from him: "Ha! That's what I tell the young girls. Makes 'em think they've got a chance with me."

Another country, another rest stop. This one bore the evocatively Italian name of Passagio, and called to mind the Ponte Vecchio, in that it had shops that could be reached by staircases at either end. (The resemblance would have been complete if the Florentine bridge were made of Lego-toned plastic rather than stone, crossed a multi-lane Swiss motorway instead of the Arno River, and sold microwaved rösti instead of Etruscan goldwork.)

In the cafeteria I spied Manu, our driver, staring vacantly out the window at the six lanes of traffic below us. An epicene francophone with the voice of a castrato, he wore a droopy white cardigan and a slick cowlick, and seemed to get pastier and paunchier as the week went on, as though sucking up all those kilometres of European highway in his carapace of metal and glass was transforming him into a giant Belgian mussel. He told me that he had been a professional bus driver for 15 years, four of them for Global. I asked him how he travelled when he went on vacation.

"Never by bus." He flattened a palm, imitating a plane taking off. "I'm going to the Cook Islands, north of Australia, in two years. There, I'm going to lie in a hammock between palm trees. No highways, no rest stops, no parking lots."

I detected disenchantment with the glamour of a travel industry career in his tone, and hoped the fact that we could communicate in French might lead us to connect. The next day, however, he caught me with the edge of my shoe on an armrest of his bus, and his glare contained such reproach I knew I'd destroyed any budding sense of trust.

Meanwhile, Frank was bonding with a young Indian boy, whom I'd pegged as an 11-year-old but who turned out to be 16. His father told Frank the boy was depressed because his wallet, filled with American dollars, had been stolen on the cross-channel ferry.

"Well, that's too bad. Why don't you come over here and sit down," said Frank, patting the seat next to him. "What's your name?"

"Vikram," replied the boy, smiling shyly.

Frank was nonplussed. "Victor? No? Vincent? No? Well, your name's too hard for me. I'll just call you 'little buddy.' See those yellow flowers over there, little buddy? That means the ground's gone sour."

As we pulled over at a gas station to allow the two Indian gentlemen to urinate – they'd smuggled tall cans of Beck's beer on the bus – I listened to Frank explaining American music to Vikram.

"First there was country. Gene Autry, Roy Rogers, Hank Williams."

"I kind of like Guns 'n' Roses," said Vikram, softly.

"That's good, little buddy. Then you had your vocalists like Frank Sinatra and Tony Bennett . . ." The monologue stopped only when we emerged from a ten-kilometre-long tunnel drilled through a mountain near Lucerne. We were now surrounded by lofty Swiss snow-peaks. The sight made Allison and Andrew squirm in alarm.

That night, we stayed in a wooden lodge in a village called Sisikon on the eastern shore of the Urner See, a mountain lake that is a crooked coda to the larger Vierwaldstätter See. There was a highway on one side of us, and red electric trains slipped by on the other, but otherwise the setting was idyllic. I strolled through the village, where a precipitous mountain torrent was directed through a concrete channel next to the church. It was clean and very quaint, and with its cool mountain air and towering mountains rising out of the lake, Sisikon would have made a nice night's stop in a typical Swiss village – if it weren't for the fact that we bus tourists outnumbered the locals on the streets two to one. Realizing there was nothing else to do but follow my fellow tourists' example and go to bed, I returned to my room.

I found Frank lying in bed, with one eye open. "I sure am missing my wife tonight," he said. "Night, buddy."

I noticed he'd erected a barrier of chairs and luggage between our beds.

§

"Up and at 'em!" roared Frank. My alarm clock read 6:01 a.m. "Yeah, they're going to be setting up a new plant in Salvador pretty soon. Man, they're getting big."

Another day, another non sequitur. "What are you talking about, Frank?" I muttered, yawning.

"My company. They're expanding all over the place."

I was in a foul mood; I'd slept poorly in spite of all the Swiss silence, and I wasn't amused by Frank's impersonation of *Good Morning America*. On the bus, we were welcomed to our Swiss morning by the lowing of a cow: Emma had up-ended one of those barn-animal-in-a-can noisemakers next to the intercom. The day's itinerary had us going back through the ten-kilometre-long tunnel to Lucerne, with Manu's execrable soft rock hits, including "I Write the Songs," "Seasons in the Sun," and "I Just Called to Say I Love You" providing a soundtrack to the sheep clinging tritely to mountainside meadows. When John from Australia saw me malingering as we disembarked in Lucerne in the riverfront Pfistergasse, he grumbled, "C'mon, tourist." I growled back: "Who you calling tourist, tourist?"

Indeed, my status as a single male, in his 30s – lone package-tour clients tend to be female, and in their 50s – who appeared fluent in French was exciting comment among the other passengers. As was the fact I was constantly scribbling in little notepads. The night before, one of the older Indian men had cornered me in the Hotel Eden's dining room.

"I was wondering whether you could render me a service," he said, officiously.

Depends, I replied, suspiciously.

"Could you please provide me with your jottings at the end of the trip, so I can note all of the timings and distances?"

I hemmed: "Frankly, I don't think you'd understand my handwriting." Anticipating an objection, I hawed: "Besides, these are more notes of my personal thoughts and impressions. For my travel journal. And they're personal."

He accepted this, but I could tell that my cover identity – as an entertainment listings editor for a Montreal weekly – wasn't satisfying everybody. Paranoid Frank wasn't a problem: I could just play the overgrown catamite, whose raging hormones might soon force him to barricade himself into a bathroom. But John, who had worked as a military cop and emigrated from England to Australia when he was 15, didn't seem convinced. After all, I was still young enough to be thumbing rides, chasing

French girls, and getting into adventures, not riding on a cushy bus. I pleaded a sheltered life and a desire for a quick overview of Europe before coming back to get to know it better.

Our morning in Lucerne turned out to be a shopping excursion. We were encouraged to enter the shop of H. Rüttimann, watchmaker. I took one look at the Swatches and cow bells, picked up a complimentary map, and wandered up to the town's fortifications, deciding that Switzerland was the kind of country where they painted the lines on the road afresh every morning. When I got back to the bus, everybody was showing off their new purchases. Cindy, a fellow Canadian, had had a Swiss Army Knife engraved with her name. Ina offered me a sweet from a capacious bag of Swiss chocolates. The frog-faced North Vietnamese bureaucrat in a three-piece suit, travelling with two comrades who also seemed to speak no English, came back with a Longines watch. For my part, I proudly showed John the earplugs I'd picked up at the pharmacy.

"You're bunking with Frank?" he asked. "Poor bastard. Aren't you ever tempted to search under his coat and see if you can't turn down his volume knob?"

We were driven 300 metres to a dock by the train station and herded onto the upper deck of a small tour boat. As we looped the lake, everybody swept dismissive hands at one another, making sure there would be no tourists' heads wrecking their snapshots. For me, it was the essence of tourism: a bald-faced denial that one's experience was anything but unique. For generations, the ease of access and familiarity of a place like Switzerland had ensured it would be chiefly populated by tourists rather than travellers. But even tourists long for authenticity, the evidence of some real encounter with the foreign. So when they finally reach the longed-for Leaning Tower, Mount Rushmore, or Jungfrau, they can barely control their resentment of the devil's equation that has made ease of access directly proportional to the number of other tourists blocking their sight-lines. *You* are the traveller, the old quip had it; the tourist is the other guy. Now that I was in the company of people who were undeniably, manifestly, tourists, it was interesting to note that even *they* seemed to hate tourists.

That night, I got a high-grade dose of unapologetic tourist kitsch. I'd
signed up for the optional Swiss Folklore Evening, and after a quick dinner
at the Hotel Eden I joined Frank, dressed in a sports jacket and bowtie, and
a dozen of our number in the lobby. Consternation was general as we were
taken to a bigger, better Global shuttle bus that not only had its own toilet
but also an Italian driver with a hint of a sense of humour.

Back in Lucerne, we parked alongside five other tour buses outside the
Stadtkeller Restaurant, a cavernous beer hall with a capacity of several
hundred. As we filed past tourists from all nations seated at wooden
benches covered with beer steins, the night's master of ceremonies, a
woman in a white lace collar and black top and pants, joined her hands
beneath her chin and greeted Ina, who was wearing an attractive golden
salwar kameez, with a bow and a "Namaste." When three meagre casseroles
of fondue were deposited on our table with a shout of "Good Appetite!' the
glum Indian couple from Chennai seated next to me looked at the caldera
of bubbling cheese with alarm. John promptly ordered a huge stein of beer.

On stage, which was flanked by the crosses of billowing Swiss flags and
bunches of roses, Trudi, the MC, proved to be something of a martinet.
When her introduction of a spoon-player was not greeted by immediate
silence, she addressed a withering "Thank you for your kind attention!" to
a table of riotous Japanese salarymen well into their kirsch. This was followed by a spoon-and-tap dance number, a musician in loafers who
played the "Love Theme from *Dr. Zhivago*" on a saw, and then Trudi
herself, who directed if looks-could-kill glances at noisemakers until there
was silence. As I desperately sought an exit from this folk prison, the audience participation segment began. Frank didn't have to be asked twice:
when they hauled out a banister-sized alpenhorn, he leapt on stage.

"Careful," Trudi cautioned the line of volunteers, "you need a lot of
breeth!"

An abdominous cheese-eater from Wisconsin could elicit only the
mildest bleat, but I felt an odd sense of pride when Frank's able lungs provoked a resounding blurt, a reminder of his stirring wake-up announcements. After a beer-drinking contest, a dancing cow burst out of the men's
room and led the group – a whooping Frank bringing up the rear with a
red-faced Japanese businessman – in a reeling conga line.

Social anthropologists refer to this kind of reheated heritage as staged authenticity, though this Swiss version was so flagrant it qualified as self-parody. It's hard to imagine anybody believing that the cutting-edge, quartz-timed Swiss are still yodelling in sod chalets; but the same impulse that draws people to Hawaiian folk villages to watch hula-wearing Filipinos apparently permits them to swallow a restaurateur's lucrative re-enactment of folk dances along with their tureens of lukewarm fondue. It's all good fun, as John – whose bibulous smile suggested he'd finished a second stein of ale – said to me, with an "oh-well, what-do-you-want" shrug. Yeah, until the Emmenthal congeals in your stomach, I thought, and it starts to rankle that you've maxed out your credit card to be fooled, patronized, and ushered around like a refractory child for a week. Better, in such circumstances, to keep your head full of beer. I noticed that it was at this point that John started to up his alcohol intake.

🛡

"Yup! That was a Mercedes bus we were in last night."

It was half past six in the morning.

"I could use another hour's sleep," I groaned.

"Better believe it," Frank replied, "Your big buses like that – that's why Chrysler's going out of business."

Frank's subconscious dreamscape, I realized, was a Meccano romper room filled with monster trucks and round-the-clock assembly lines.

On the bus, Rajput's wife was rocking back and forth, mumbling her morning puja.

"Interlaken is a man-made town," announced Emma when we parked next to a dozen other tour buses a couple of hours later.

Better than those gopher-made towns. As I tried to fill an hour pricing ribboned cow bells at Heidi's Shop and reading the menu at the Schwyzer Country and Western Pub ("You will feel like entering a good old saloon in the West of the States. Beautiful wall painting, solid wooden tables, classic saloon doors, and real jail"), I changed my mind: if gophers were city planners, the town they'd build would look a lot like Interlaken. With its cog railways, flower clocks, and the *belle époque* Grand Hotel

Beau-Rivage, the place would have appealed to the sensibility of a Disney rodent. It didn't surprise me that Interlaken, with its lacustrian setting within day-tripping distance of Jungfrau, was one of the favourite resorts of early Cook's Tourists. Virginia Woolf's father, Leslie Stephen, consoled himself by reflecting that such Alpine resorts were like fly-paper. By attracting Americans and Cockneys, they did "not indeed diminish the swarm of intrusive insects, but profess at least to confine them to one spot."

Stephen was commenting on the gradual establishment of a Victorian travel rut, principally encouraged by Cook's system of hotel and rail coupons. While previous cohorts of Grand Tourists had at least made a pretense of learning foreign customs, Cook's tourists – called Cookies by snobs, *i Cucchi* by Italians, and *i Cookii* by Egyptians – spread bourgeois English tastes, and the rumbustious reputation of John Bull, throughout the world. They ate potted salmon, Yorkshire pudding, and English ham in tents in Palestine, had snowball fights on St. Gotthard and bathing parties on the Italian coast. Loved for their money and loathed for their vulgarity, Cookies were soon ubiquitous.

By the late 19th century, a Cook's tourist could also travel a world that the firm of Cook & Son itself seemed to have built. She – women made up most of the clientele – could ride to the top of Vesuvius on Cook's funic-ular, saving painful scrambling over scree and ashes. She could exchange currency coupons, purchased at Cook's main office in Ludgate Circus, in branch offices in Yokohama, Hong Kong, or New York. Arriving in Egypt, the observant tourist might notice that the entire nation seemed to be the domain of Cook & Son. In Alexandria, she would be greeted by a turbaned dragoman with "Cook's Porter" emblazoned on his blue gown. She could take a Cook's train from Cairo to Aswan, air-conditioned to 25 degrees Centigrade by air blowing over 135 kilograms of ice, or opt for one of the 24 Cook's steamers, their decks dusted with ostrich feather brooms, that plied the Nile. And she would probably stay in Cook's luxurious chain of hotels, perhaps the Semiramis in Cairo, or the Winter Palace in Luxor. Many Egyptians were under the impression that John Mason Cook was the king of England.

Like the pilgrimage roads to Santiago de Compostela and Jerusalem, and the starred sights of Michelin guidebooks, the Cook & Son infrastructure encouraged the plowing of a durable travel rut. Even if they weren't part of a guided tour, Victorian travellers in Europe, by carrying coupons redeemable only at the few hundred Cook-approved hotels and travelling on pre-arranged rail itineraries, could be certain of spending much of their time abroad in the company of their countrymen. Such burgeoning middle-class tourism was an expression of an economic imbalance, with the financially empowered English free to roam in the lands of the less powerful – in Switzerland, Italy, Egypt, and India – just as post–Second World War Americans would later frolic in the $5-a-day Europe of ration books and Marshall Plan recovery. Armed with guidebooks confirming national prejudices, shuttled around in buses, and congregating in enclaves like Interlaken, Cook's tourists and their successors were ensured that their experience of the foreign would be primarily visual, a three-dimensional slide show of landscapes and church facades.

"That was of course Interlaken," said Emma, as the bus door whooshed shut. "And perhaps some of you visited the Casino, where many people come to make more Swiss francs, because of course things are more expensive in Switzerland."

Not likely, I thought, given we'd been allotted an hour, and she hadn't mentioned the existence of any casino. Staring out at the peaks of the Bernese Oberland, I compared the tour bus window to a television screen, transforming a real landscape into unspooling images on glass, and the tourist into a viewer, incapable of real interaction, only passive voyeurism. Except, of course, with other spectator-travellers – like Vikram, who asked if he could sit down next to me. He passed the time telling me jokes.

"What do you do when a Sikh throws a pin at you?" he asked, breathless. "Run! He has got a grenade in his mouth! – Lovely, isn't it?"

I learned that his father, seated ahead of us, worked for the Indian Institute of Technology, and sent Vikram to an expensive private school in Mumbai. This wouldn't have bothered me, except that I'd heard the man boasting he made sure to spend more than six months out of the year living outside India so that he didn't have to pay income tax. In other words, in a nation where 60 percent of children were severely malnourished, Vikram's father didn't spend a rupee of his earnings improving the lives of his fellow citizens. Instead, he used the money to take his family on European vacations, where his son could tell strangers racist jokes.

"I have another," said Vikram, giggling. "How did the Sikh student get to be the top of his class? – Somebody gave his turban a good hard pull!"

I shouldn't have been so hard on Vikram, who was a nice kid, but we'd already covered 1,100 kilometres, and I was bored out of my skull. I was vaguely looking forward to our stop in Gruyères, source of the fondue cheese. When we pulled off the highway into a parking lot outside a demonstration cheese dairy and were invited to eat in a sterile-looking cafeteria, I got antsy. I overheard Vikram's father asking Emma about the village of Gruyères.

"It's about an hour's walk from here," she told him. "And unfortunately, because some people were late this morning, we only have time for a 45-minute stop."

In the parking lot, I asked an old Swiss man about the white-walled castle I could see, perched on a low hill like a camembert on a cheese tray, less than half a kilometre away.

"*Ça? C'est le village de Gruyères*," he replied.

I speed-walked up the hill, and in five minutes found myself in a charming medieval town. Surrounded by 12th-century ramparts, Gruyères's main street was lined with bakeries and restaurants and led to a turreted castle with a courtyard filled with flowers. After buying a freshly cut slab of Gruyère in a family-run grocery, I had a quick baguette-and-cheese picnic on the ramparts and then strolled back to the bus, arriving while the group was still paying their lunch bills.

"Where did you get to?" John asked, as I climbed onto the bus. I told him about Gruyères. "It was that close?" he muttered. "I visited the village last time we were in Europe. It was beautiful. That was one of the main reasons we chose this tour."

Brussels without the Manneken Pis; Luxembourg without the castle; Gruyères without the cheese. The package tour's relentless schedule, meant to give tourists scenic value-for-money, had been devised by a man who, early in his career, was famous for commanding groups with orders like: "Shoulder shawls – pick up carpet bags – quick march!" Emma and Global continued the Cook tradition. When we'd groaned about another 6 a.m. wake-up one evening, our director had pedantically scolded: "I'm afraid this is a tour, not a vacation!" Misinformation was evidently part of Global's arsenal of crowd control techniques, sparing the overtired driver and tour director the inconvenience of chasing down errant clients.

That night, we slept in Vevey, the stodgy lakeside resort where Charlie Chaplin had gone to lick his wounds after his Hollywood peccadilloes. For once, our hotel was a dignified two-star, and I watched three sofa-ensconced businessmen roll their eyes and leave the lobby as our group mobbed the front desk for keys. Half of me – the tourist who just wanted a shower and a nap – thought: "Go to hell, you snobs, I've got a right to be here too." The other half – the traveller who had too often groaned as a tour bus pulled into a quiet piazza – fully sympathized. In my reading, I'd encountered enough choice morsels of the hackneyed and venerable Victorian anti-tourist discourse to vow not to waste too much time enriching the canon. *Charles Lever* was contemptuous on the subject of Cookies: "Anything so uncouth I never saw before, the men mostly dreary, sad looking; the women somewhat younger, travel-tossed but intensely lively, wide-awake and facetious." *The Rev. Francis Kilvert* was hyperbolic: "Vulgar, ill-bred, offensive and loathsome . . . No wonder dogs fly at them and consider them vermin to be exterminated." *W. H. Mallock* was more subtle: "As for the excursionist . . . it can hardly be said that he has ever left home at all. He has virtually sat still and looked at a moving peep-show." The metaphors were endless, never flattering: tourists were intrusive insects, sheep, vandals, circus animals.

Strangely, by the time Thomas Cook died in 1892, his son, reputedly a first-class snob, was concentrating on attracting a better sort of tourist. John Mason Cook could eventually boast of organizing tours for the Archbishop of Canterbury and France's Empress Eugénie, as well as conducting the Prince of Wales's sons through the Holy Land and Kaiser Wilhelm II up Vesuvius. Briefly, Cook & Son became a prestigious brand name, like Louis Vuitton and Chanel. But the damage had been done: thanks to the package tour, the masses had forever been set in motion.

Trying to nap in my narrow bed in Vevey, I realized the early critics might have had a point: without Cook & Son's innovations, Frank's braying New World voice, which I heard echoing down the street, would never have disturbed the tranquillity of a Swiss evening. On the other hand, without mass tourism's economies of scale, a 16-year-old Indian boy like Vikram, with whom I chatted about life in Mumbai as we strolled on the lakefront that night, might never been exposed to another continent. And I wouldn't have had an hour-long talk about the tenets of Theravada Buddhism with an Asian couple over salmon and boiled potatoes. (They told me they'd find a wife for me if I ever visited them in Thailand. "Thai women really know how to straighten your finances out!" the woman boasted.) A bus tour wasn't the best way to travel – it wasn't *any* way to travel, really – but it could at least whet the neophyte's appetite for new horizons, as it had whetted mine when I was a teenager. And show the traveller how *not* to voyage in the future.

Sadly, some people never found the courage to try anything else. The Thai couple told me that this was the *fifth* time they had taken the same Global tour. The next day, my last full day in the bus, we stopped in Beaune, a winemaking village among the vineyards of Burgundy, and I sat down with a quiet Canadian couple, Bruce and Peggy, who were eating sandwiches in the town square. In their 70s, they told me they'd toured Europe several times before, sometimes on their own, sometimes with groups. I asked if they were happy with the experience.

"Well, we aren't told or warned about things," said Bruce.

Why not travel independently, then?

"We're getting older," Peggy replied, "and when I see some of the distances we've covered on the highway, I don't think I could handle it any more. And some countries we've been to on other trips, like Hungary, you almost need to be on a tour. The language is so different, and the border crossings – they'd take up to two hours. And if you've noticed, they also pack a lot into a day."

Bruce looked wistful. "Maybe I could have made it on my own, though."

◥

"Well, I hope you enjoyed Beaune," Emma announced, "where we had a chance to have a typical glass of French wine. And perhaps you'll have a chance to come back and spend some more time here, and hopefully not get too inebriated."

The rest of the afternoon was strangely subdued. John was sprawled out on the back seat, his head in Mary's lap, after finishing a bottle of Burgundy at lunch. Even Frank was silent, staring dreamily at the fields of wild mustard. The tour was coming to an end, and people seemed to be realizing how badly they'd been short-changed. When Emma handed out some customer evaluation forms, there was much vehement scribbling.

There was still hope, though: Paris, City of Light! As we merged with rush hour traffic on the *périphérique*, the immense ring road that girdles Paris, Emma worked through a checklist of clichés. "Paris is a magical city, a very cosmopolitan city. The Parisians aren't all rude, actually, but they are very self-absorbed. They don't care where they park, and traffic lights are purely decorative, so be careful when you cross the street. There are lots of pickpockets around, so men, if you want to lose your wallets, keep them in your back pocket."

I squirmed at these inanities. I'd lived in Paris for four years, and I'd never had my pocket picked. (True, my wallet had never been fat with francs, either.) I'd come to France at the age of 22, after a bad year in my hometown. A late adolescent predilection for acid, pot, and whatever booze I could get my hands on, had, after I graduated from university, become a slow-motion slide into downers and heroin, complete with blackened spoons, blunt needles, and bruised forearms. I shook myself out of the deepening addiction long enough to earn the money to buy a one-way ticket to Europe. It was a simple case of what the French call *fuite en avant*, running away from one's problems by plunging ahead. I didn't know who or where I wanted to be; I just knew I needed to get myself away, be elsewhere. I settled on Paris as my new centre, a likely spot for reinventing myself. After all, it had worked for Henry Miller.

Within a year, I was living with a dance student from Brittany, speaking passable French, and giving English lessons to accountants and doctors. Unfortunately, I'd also discovered that French pharmacists were willing to dispense over-the-counter paregoric, opium-laced cough syrup, and barbiturates. I swallowed them all, chasing the mix down with cheap red wine. My new self, then, was not a nobly toiling bohemian but a slurrer of subjunctives, a stumbler over cobblestones, a chronic misser of the last metro. Travel was a form of escape, but so were alcohol and drugs; and I'd discovered an exile within my exile. It took three more years of hangovers and declining health, culminating in a drug-induced epileptic fit, to end my expatriation. I went home, swore off drink and drugs, married my French girlfriend, and started to write. The marriage ended, amicably, after a couple of years, but I stayed clean, and did on my own turf what I couldn't do abroad: I began to make a living as a writer.

I'd never completely untangled the idea of travel – of geographical escape – from the more complex issue of escape from self. If the promise of travel was also the promise of release from sexual and social restraint, for me it was also bound up with the self-evasion of intoxication. On recent trips, I'd allowed myself indulgences – pub crawls through Barcelona, binges on absinthe – explaining them away as transgressions deliberately undertaken for journalistic purposes. It was also something to look forward to: every few months, I'd go abroad to write a travel article or two and get mildly sozzled on some local specialty. This time, however, I had months of uninterrupted travel before me. The potential for sampling local specialties seemed endless. After a week on the bus, Frank's braying and the low-grade boredom had me eyeing the complimentary bottles of plonk on the dinner table with real intent.

The flashing green cross of a Parisian pharmacy caught my eye. A quick trip to the drugstore, and I'd have everything I needed to smooth out the dull hours and sleepless nights. With an effort of will, I stowed the impulse somewhere deep inside me.

"Hundreds of people are employed in Paris every year just to sweep up dog poop," Emma maundered on.

Global had us bunked in a no-man's-land outside the city limits, across the *périphérique* from the Porte de Montreuil, in a towering, 325-room chain hotel. After getting our keys from two overworked desk clerks, Frank and I rode the elevator to the 18th floor. The room was tiny, the sleeping quarters of a plastic submarine. The curtains stank of dark tobacco, the windows wouldn't open, and, to Frank's horror, there was only one bed.

"I'm going down to give 'em hell!" he yelled.

He came back a few minutes later, fuming. The desk clerks had told him to look under the covers: there were two contiguous single beds that could be pushed apart. He set to work violently rearranging the room, making sure there was no possibility of accidental contact.

I decided to dispel any doubts about my heterosexuality. "I'm going to see the cancan show," I told Frank. "I love watching French girls dance. You coming?"

"Naw," said Frank. "You go knock yourself out, buddy."

Hmm. It occurred to me that maybe I was the one who should have been careful.

In the hall, I ran into the officious Indian gentleman who had requested my notes. "The cabaret show is now?" he asked. He'd dressed up for the outing in a three-button suit, with a Rotary pin on the lapel.

We drove along the *périphérique* to Pigalle, and as we parked next to a Contiki bus full of hollering, beer-soaked Australians, I noticed that the upper floors of the Haussmann-era apartment buildings had signs on their balconies that read *"Non aux Autocars!"* (No to the Tour Buses). Our group walked *en masse* to the Nouvelle Eve, a poor man's Moulin Rouge where a half bottle of champagne nonetheless cost 73 euros. As we stood in line on the Rue Fontaine, waiting for the early show to clear out, I chatted with John and Mary. Dapper in a blue suit, John told me he'd stopped drinking to excess after one memorable hangover when his esophagus went into peristalsis, drawing bile from his stomach to his mouth. The tour was clearly shaking his resolve, however, and when we'd been seated by an Asian waiter in a tux, he partook of his free glass of champagne. (As did I. It tasted not unlike warm Baby Duck.)

The show was a Gallic version of the Swiss Folklore Night, tits-and-ass taking the place of taps-and-alpenhorns. Leggy, small-breasted dancers crab-walked in front of cut-outs of painted backdrops of the Eiffel Tower and the Arc de Triomphe, endlessly chanting *"C'est la Nouvelle Eve . . . C'est Formidable!"* I was seated so close I could see the acne beneath the pancake makeup and the runs in the fishnets. While Mary was in the bathroom, I admitted to John I was surprised he'd taken a bus tour – it didn't seem his style.

"It's true, but Mary wanted to try it. If we were living in the U.K., we probably wouldn't do it this way. We'd rent a car, do it on our own. But when you live Down Under, it's not easy to get to Europe. And they do pack a lot into every day." That's what Bruce and Peggy had told me, too. And, like John, they'd groaned about how little they'd actually seen.

A Venetian blond with a Central European accent picked four victims out of the audience, among them Rajput from Chennai. She challenged them to a dance contest, and Rajput, in cardigan and loafers, did a creditable version of the funky chicken as 70s-era disco blared. John turned to me after a Canadian with his fly halfway down, his stage-fright progressing to panic, returned to the audience without attempting a single step.

"You Canadians really are the most timid bunch," he proclaimed. "Comes from letting the Mounties tame the frontier for you."

"*Touché*," I replied, bilingually. Since I also possessed the national trait of diplomacy, I politely refrained from making any cracks about the gene pool of alcoholic felons in his adopted home.

Back at the hotel, Frank was lying awake, watching a dubbed Steve McQueen sweating it out on L'Île du Diable. "There were girls, Frank," I enthused. "Beautiful ones. With no tops on. You should have come."

He looked unimpressed, as though this was just a ploy to get him to drop his guard. "Good night, buddy. Don't let the boogerman get you."

I skipped out on the next day's tour of the Eiffel Tower and Notre-Dame – the thought of being herded around this stylish city, my former home, was too much humiliation for me. When I got back around dinnertime, Frank burst into the room like a whirlwind, a new red beret in place of the Tyrolean cap he'd bought in Switzerland.

"I just got back from Fountain-blow!" he said. He had the video to prove it, and showed me a shaky recording of the château at Fontainebleau that Napoleon had built for Josephine. "You're real lucky you didn't go on the tour this morning. They ought to be ashamed. We didn't even stop at those Tool-eries gardens like they said they was gonna. We was in and out of Noter-Dame like that!" he yelled, running one flat palm over the other. "The Eiffel Tower, we had only five minutes. I went down to Fountain-blow on my own, could walk around all I wanted to. That tour this morning was a farce. A farce!"

I had to hand it to Frank. He roared, he complained, and, because he expected service for his money he usually got his way. Most of the people on the tour – my fellow Canadians in particular – had passively grumbled about conditions, but Frank showed rare resourcefulness. While Ina and a group of women gave up on exploring the *quartier* and came back to the hotel with McDonald's bags, Frank had arranged his own expedition to a castle outside Paris.

I asked if he'd take a Global tour again.

"Hell, I could do this better myself!" he shouted, livid. "I saved my customer evaluation form for today – oh, you bet I'm gonna let 'em have it!"

Next morning, I went down to the breakfast room to say goodbye. My bus mates were on their way back to London. Vikram gave me his e-mail address, Ina invited me to visit her in Mumbai, and Frank wrote down his phone number in case I ever made it down Kalamazoo way ("And bring your girlfriend!" he added, still dubious). Emma was smiling – she had just learned that she had three days off before her next tour. I asked how she'd fill the time.

"Well, believe it or not, I'm going to sleep, actually." (I rather suspected she was going to pass out, actually.)

Manu, pale as a bivalve, no doubt dreaming of Polynesian coconut cocktails in Rarotonga, mustered a limp wave before closing the door.

I watched the Global village pull onto the *périphérique*, merging into lanes jammed with similar communities of tourists, until it was just another silhouette among all the other buses from Italy, Croatia, England, Poland, Holland. Back in my room, I stared out the filthy window, which couldn't be opened, of a soulless hotel on the outskirts of Paris. The Global brochure sat on the bedside table, filled with colour photos of French girls flouncing their furbelows beneath the Eiffel Tower – the eternal, undefined promise of exotic foreign travel. Strange how industrial-strength tourism could reduce Europe to a tedious road movie viewed through a seatside screen, a nagging sense of having been cheated, and a sore bottom.

I shook myself, tipped the brochure into the garbage can, and hit the streets of Paris for a long walk.

Chapter 4

CLASS, DISMISSED

Declining Standards in the Gare de l'Est – My Illustrious Ancestors – The Luxuries of the Golden Age of Travel – Finding Suitable Lodgings in Baden-Baden – The Allures of Hypochondria – I Drink Radioactive Water – The Promise of Nude Mixed Bathing – Most Satisfactorily Scrubbed with a Horse Brush – The Birth of the Spa – Shopping for Tinctures – German Fashion Tips – In the Old Days, the Rich had Class – Nicht Gehts Mehr – Chastised in a Sauna – Caesar Ritz Started It All – Among the VIPs – In Which I Lose My Rented Shirt at Roulette

Ah, for the grand old days. If I'd been standing in Paris's Gare de l'Est in, say, 1908, I wouldn't have had to fumble beneath my shirt to get my *billet* out of my money belt so I could stamp it in the machine, all the while keeping an eye on the muttering, scab-faced junkie circling my backpack like a vulture. I'd surely have sailed from New York on the *Amerika*, the first luxury liner with an elevator, where I would have chosen from a menu planned by Auguste Escoffier, been served on fine china by a staff trained by César Ritz, and slept on a feather bed in a cabin decorated by Charles Mewès. When I'd disembarked in London, porters would have transferred my Louis Vuitton trunks to Pullman cars waiting in Victoria Station, and a white-jacketed steward would have served me coffee and smoked salmon sandwiches on the way to Dover. A quick hop over the Channel, and I'd have boarded the luxurious *Calais-Mediterranean*, where I'd have played solitaire all the way to Paris. My baggage would have been transferred to an eastbound train, and I could have whiled away the few minutes before departure by looking at the royal blue wagons-lits of the Constantinople-bound *Orient Express*, departing from the next track.

Patience, I would have consoled myself: the Sultan's harem will have to wait for another trip. This time, I have come to Europe to take the Cure.

Travelling these days wasn't quite so elegant. Beneath the arched glass ceiling of the Gare de l'Est, there were no porters to be seen, so I'd had to lug my own bag to a clapped-out second-class wagon at the far end of the SNCF train. Just before we'd left, a deaf-mute had dropped a pair of folding scissors on the ripped vinyl of my seat, and a beggar had recited a lengthy resumé of misfortunes before being chased off the train by a conductor. The five-hour trip to Strasbourg had been a sonata of cellphone tones, and when, after another change in Offenburg, we arrived at the utilitarian Baden-Oos station, I'd waited for a city bus to take me to the town centre. Had I arrived in Baden-Baden in the heroic epoch of luxury travel, I would have disembarked at the neo-Renaissance train station and spent my time beating off the ruddy-featured drivers of horse-drawn fiacres and droshkies competing for my custom. It's come to this, I thought ruefully, as I struggled onto the bus: public transit.

Actually, if this were the *belle époque* I almost certainly would have been one of the red-faced droshky drivers, not a privileged passenger. My ancestors are from County Down and Kiev, and if there's anything rarer in the pages of the *Who's Who* than Irish aristocrats, it's globetrotting Ukrainian noblemen. (Unless I'm missing someone: The Duke of Donnybrook? The Marquis de Mogilev?) In the 19th century, the aspirations of people of my genetic stock were limited to finding ways to make liquor out of turnips. We didn't tour: we emigrated.

It was a testimony to the democratization of travel, I thought, that a classless New World mongrel could breach the citadels of a venerable watering hole for European royalty without so much as a passport check. Baden-Baden, after all, was created to exclude people like me. The upper classes had long been the most enthusiastic of travellers – indeed, they were among the very few who could afford to go on Holy Land pilgrimages or lengthy Grand Tours. But as the spread of railroads set the hoi polloi in motion, the happy few began to seek refuge in exclusive resorts, creating a golden age of unsurpassed elegance in travel. About the time Thomas Cook was conducting his first tourists around the globe in 1872, a network of luxury transatlantic steamers, first-class sleeping cars, and palatial grand hotels was coming into its own, making world travel a pleasant matter of gliding through foreign climes in Pullman cars and Cunard liners. Encouraged by a period of European peace – brought on by the unification of Italy in 1861 and Germany's rise to statehood after the Franco-Prussian war – the crème could travel between the world's *salons privés*, hotel lobbies, and first-class waiting rooms as though they were merely far-flung wings of their sprawling mansions.

While train travel had brought Cook's hordes to the Riviera, the Alps, and Niagara Falls, rail barons soon found a way of making the railways an instrument for the demarcation of class. Since Cook's first excursion in 1841, an ever more labyrinthine rail network had spread its rhizomes into Europe and North America. The invention of dynamite in 1867 hastened the piercing of Mount Cenis, permitting direct service from Geneva to Turin without having to resort to muleback. Soon Rome could be reached from London in three days, rather than the three weeks it had taken in 18th-century post-chaises. By the end of the 1870s, a grid of steel rails, intersecting in grand railway station nodes, linked the great cities of Europe from Paris to Warsaw.

During its first decades, rail travel was uncomfortable and undignified. Most European trains were unheated, and few had toilets or dining cars; passengers had to rush to bathrooms and buffets during brief station stops, and were likely to finish their trips with eyes streaming, backs aching from wooden benches, and dickies bedizened with soot. It was in the United States, where great distances were traversed in great discomfort, that a Chicago entrepreneur named George Pullman built the first luxury rail car. His Pioneer, a confection of brass, walnut, and deep pile, got its big break when it was used to convey Abraham Lincoln's body in state between Chicago and Springfield. The resultant tabloid publicity made Pullman's fortune, and 48 of his sleepers were circulating on the American rails by 1867.

The first such cars were simple affairs of curtained bunks ranged down a long corridor – Jack Lemmon entertained Marilyn Monroe in a mock-up of a Pullman bed in *Some Like It Hot* – and they shocked European sensibilities by placing men and women in the same wagons. A Belgian named Georges Nagelmackers convinced an imprudent Pullman to give him a tour of his workshops, and the young banker promptly returned home to convince King Leopold II to invest in a firm that would come to be called the Compagnie Internationale des Wagons-Lits. His separately managed sleeping cars, attached to regular trains and open to passengers who paid a supplement, converted European-style individual compartments into bedrooms with fold-down berths that could sleep four with a more seemly degree of privacy. Pullman and Wagons-Lits (as well as the short-lived but excellently named Mann Boudoir Sleeping Car Company) would come to compete in Europe, but together they introduced an unprecedented era of opulence in train travel. Pullman service started to Brighton in 1879, and Nagelmackers's triumph, the Orient Express, first left Paris for Constantinople four years later (return fare cost about the same as the annual rent for an elegant London townhouse). The wealthiest travellers, of course, had their own cars. In America, industrialists boasted about their "varnish," well-polished private rolling stock with wall safes and butlers; financier Jay Gould travelled with a favourite cow, whose butterfat levels soothed his dyspepsia.

Coupled with the launch of the White Star Line's *Oceanic*, the first real luxury transatlantic steamer, improvements in rail service meant that by the 1880s a network for nabobs was firmly in place, ensuring that the upper crust could voyage without risk of having to hobnob with the humbler classes. Baden-Baden, with its killer triumvirate of Grand Hotel, Casino, and Spa, was one of the most prestigious stops on what became a latter-day grand tour for grandees. Along with Monte Carlo, Aix-les-Bains, Nice, and all the other Germanic Baden, it offered refuge for the social elite: Napoleon III lived at the Stéphanie les Bains Hotel, and Queen Victoria, Kaiser Wilhelm I, and Czar Alexander II sojourned in their own villas. Today, Baden-Baden is an anachronism, a Black Forest enclave that somehow escaped bombing in the Second World War and is even now guaranteed immunity from the indignities of bus tourism by its high prices and the 3.5-kilometre tunnel that keeps Autobahn flotsam out of the town centre.

The watering hole's filtration system clearly wasn't perfect, though: after all, it let *me* seep through. Wandering the chestnut-shaded promenade next to the River Oos with my ratty grey backpack, I was an obvious contaminant in a well-regulated ecosystem. I felt like I was breaking a half-dozen civic ordinances just by breathing (*ein*: having the intention to jaywalk; *zwei*: attempting to make eye contact with passersby; *drei*: being under 60 in a public place – 500 Euros, *schnell!*).

At the Trinkhalle – the Pump Room where the *souffrant* once took their waters, now Baden-Baden's tourist office – a helpful, French-speaking clerk ran her long fingernail to the bottom of a list and wrote down the address of what she said was a reasonably priced hotel.

Walking up a staircase next to a Gargantuan statue of Bismarck, I was braced for the worst. It was Friday the 13th, after all, I was in the Black Forest, I didn't speak German, and I was surrounded by rich people. But the Hotel Am Markt, on a church square beneath a terraced hillside atop which a castle squatted, seemed to be fine. The precise, bespectacled manager gave me a room which, though toilet- and shower-free, had a desk and a sink. Had I been paying attention, its major disadvantage would have been immediately evident. When booking a room, it is wise to ask the following questions: Is your establishment next to a row of civic bottle recycling containers? Is there a rooster in the vicinity? Finally, and most crucially: Is there a great hulking church with a huge bell right across the street?

In the case of the Hotel Am Markt, the answer to the last question was, of course, *Bong!* In the week to come, I would get to know the bell-ringing habits of my punctilious neighbours at the Stiftskirche, whose rear the local skateboarders had – aptly, I thought – spray-painted with a flaming "666." In the mornings, the church's quarterly tintinnabulations acted like a kind of mandatory public snooze alarm, defeating sloth in all but the Pilsner-comatose. (I wasn't surprised to learn that it was the good people of the German Schwarzwald, rather than the Swiss – *pace* Harry Lime and his "five hundred years of peace and democracy and what do you get" jibe – who had invented that work-ethic gimcrack, the cuckoo clock.) If I dared to lie down for an afternoon nap, it was always just before a clan-gorous carillon recital that had me trying to thread my pillow-bolster through my earholes. I wondered what the reaction in our supposedly egalitarian and multi-confessional western cities would be if, one Sabbath morn, mosque muezzins, synagogue chanters, and stupa gong-ringers dared to match the decibels of their swaggering Christian brethren.

This would never be an issue in Caucasian-toned Baden-Baden. A fresh rain had just rinsed the pavement spotless, and the water washed in an orderly fashion over rectilinear curbs. The place was so white it made Lucerne look funky. The cabbies drove cream-coloured Mercedes, and on the main pedestrian shopping drag, the cobblestoned Langestrasse, even the buskers were high class: a long-haired string quartet had opened a violin case, now full of banknotes, and was doing a soporific rendition of "Yesterday." Women with deeply encrusted foundation and padded shoulders walked out of hat shops, and a handful of skateboarders milled outside the town McDonald's, eating esoteric snack food like "Schwip Schwap" Cola Mix and "America Cream" Flavored X-cut Crunchies. Thank God for what little immigration Germany has, I thought as I assuaged my hunger with a Vegetarische Kebap in one of Baden-Baden's few Turkish restaurants.

That said, Baden-Baden was a comely place, in a town-of-a-certain-age kind of way. The chastened River Oos (which should have been called the Trickle), carried families of mallards beneath wrought-iron bridges that led to dignified stone villas. The centenary beeches and plane trees of the central promenade, the Lichtentaler Allee, blended into the hillocks of the Black Forest, among which were hidden the mansarded roofs of stolid houses. Walking back to my hotel, I stifled a yawn that threatened to turn into an existential shudder. Given my past proclivity for pills and my growing interest in local specialties, Baden-Baden was going to be a place where I'd have to watch myself. I wasn't exactly sure how I was going to make it through the next week – maybe I could hang with the skateboarders or launch a career as a gigolo with the Chanel set – but one thing was certain: I was finally going to get in touch with my inner hypochondriac.

§

I'd long been intrigued by the stodgy allure of a spa vacation. Images of bygone elegance queued in my head: in Louis Malle's *Murmur of the Heart*, the asthmatic adolescent hero is hosed down naked by white-jacketed nurses, and wiles away a grand hotel summer reading Proust's recollections of the Norman coastal resort of Cabourg, which he fictionalized as

Balbec. I pictured myself with a rarefied condition like gout, sciatica, or lumbago (anything, in fact, that required walking with an eagle-headed cane) that could be alleviated only by recondite treatments like Lymph-drainage and Elektro-Therapie. Like Dumas, Stendhal, and Balzac before me, I would be a gentleman scribe seeking inspiration and solitude in the moss-carpeted paths of the Black Forest.

In the breakfast room of my hotel, frail old men in suits with elbow patches lined up beside me for bowls of pre-milked muesli, brown-shelled eggs kept warm in a tureen of sand, and dark buns covered with sunflower seeds, and then hobbled alone to their tables to read copies of *Die Welt*. Outside, it had started to rain again. I walked around the Stiftskirche, skirted the base of the wooded Florentine hill that led to the castle, and descended a staircase beside the bath house.

The hillside, thick with dark foliage and shot through with gated-and-locked utility tunnels, was the source of Baden-Baden's reputation: in the first century A.D., Roman legionnaires found hot water burbling up through the stone and built a bath house on the site. The ruins of the sol-diers' baths were preserved behind a glass wall in an underground parking lot, and I squeezed past a Mercedes station wagon to get a better look. Using a booklet I'd bought in the Trinkhalle, I made out the tepidarium and the arched-roof furnace in the gloom.

In the third century the Emperor Caracalla was cured of a wound by taking the local waters, and in his gratitude expanded the baths to include facilities for officers and noblemen. The Alemanic tribes – like most barbarians, they were none too keen on keeping clean – had reduced the soldiers' baths to a three-metre-high pile of brick pillars and crumbling mortar. The ruins of far more elaborate Imperial baths, still unexcavated, lay beneath the Stiftskirche – an additional argument, if one was needed, for tearing the noisy eyesore down.

Outside, a niche had been gouged into the rockface. A stream of water poured from a spigot into a carved stone basin, which was covered with unhealthy-looking green and brown mineral buds. A stained stone plaque said this was the Fettquelle, one of the 23 springs that produce 800,000 litres of fresh mineral water every day. The water percolates through Black Forest granite from a depth of 2,000 metres, and the Höllquelle, or Hell

Spring – the hottest in Europe – pours forth at 68.8 degrees Celsius. All the springs are radioactive, and a shot of Baden-Baden water is brimming not only with salt, potassium, and iron, but also arsenic and strontium. Filling my plastic water bottle, I drank deep, barely repressing a spit as the salty, metallic liquid washed over my taste buds. Not unlike getting a mouthful of tepid Caribbean water, I thought, with a barium swallow as a chaser.

People used to drink that *every day* – though, apart from a few stray tourists choking down a glass in the pump room, I didn't see a single modern-day *curiste* imbibing during my entire stay. Feeling queasy, I walked a hundred metres to the pompous entrance of the Friedrichsbad. Also known as the Roman-Irish baths – which conjured up better-repressed images of naked leprechauns cavorting with legionnaires – the name referred to a supposed Celtic penchant for using fire-heated stones to create backwoods saunas. Like most bathhouses, they had a mild erotic charge. A whole fatuous sub-genre of French academic painting is devoted to hammams full of nubiles being scrubbed by Nubians, and spa propaganda through the ages has focused on the titillation of mixed bathing. The Friedrichsbad's colour pamphlet was no exception: it featured pert-nippled vixens in their 20s, with towels slipping off their pinkening buttocks as they bent to drink from swan-necked fountains. The promise was clear. As in the decadent days of the early Roman baths, when men and women bathed together and the *bagnio* became synonymous with the brothel, a trip to the Friedrichsbad would be an affair of sly sideways glances and steamy encounters in Rococo wading pools. The coy caryatids on the facade, ditzily failing to hold their togas over their breasts, seemed to offer a foretaste of the delights within.

"Go up the stairs," said the woman at the desk, dismissing my sly inquiries about Fango Treatments and *Krankengymnastik* with a shrug that indicated her job description didn't include detailed replies in English. "Woman to left, man to right."

On the second floor, in the changing room, I stripped naked and left my clothes in a cubicle, grabbing a thin white towel, lengthy enough to be worn like a toga, from a pile on a chair. As I wrapped it around my waist, a middle-aged beer keg of an attendant grunted at me to take it right back off, pointing to a row of wall hooks in the shower room. Two further grunts seemed to mean I should put on a pair of white rubber sandals. Now in that most humiliating of conditions – shod but otherwise naked – I flip-flopped over to an enormous stainless steel showering device, which looked as if it had been commissioned from Hector Guimard's workshops by Buck Rogers. The monosyllabic attendant demonstrated its use: by turning a comically prodigious lever through a vast arc, I could produce a flow of water through thousands of holes set in a streetlamp-sized shower head.

"*Kalt*," he said, pulling it to the left. "*Warm*," he elaborated, pushing it to the right. After a quick but thorough soak, I retrieved my towel, and the attendant led me to the adjoining *Warmluftbad*.

"*Fünfzehn*," he said, venturing into disyllables as he pointed towards a row of slatted wooden recliners. "*Zehn*," he continued, nodding towards a thick curtain and holding up ten spread fingers. *Ah, so*: this was the number of minutes to spend in each room – the whole bath experience, I was to learn, was run on schedule, and if I malingered beyond my allotted three and a half hours, I'd have to pay a supplement. There were clocks in all the rooms, *natürlich*, with big minute hands that jerked forward to help you regulate your "relaxing." I spread my towel and sat down, passing the time by inspecting chinoiserie wall tiles of herons and plovers wading among reeds and lily pads. This was the warm dry air bath, and when it failed to raise even the slightest of sweats, I went through the curtain to the smaller *Heißluftbad* – the *hot* dry air bath – whose dome was pierced by a glass oculus. This was marginally warmer, and after a few minutes eyeing the centenary mould in the grouting, I swallowed hard and headed to the lair of the infamous *Seifen-Bürstenmassage*.

The complete body soap-and-brush massage, an experience either excoriating or invigorating, depending on one's squeamishness, was the therapeutic core of the spa visit. Two men in their 30s, in damp yellow polo shirts and with fingertips puckered into pale prunes, awaited me. One, with red hair and a goatee, took my towel, lay it on the bed, and motioned for me to lie down. Setting to work with a stiff-bristled round brush, my invigilator began the flay-you-alive treatment, removing layers of what were surely still living cells. Once he'd determined I didn't speak

German, he started a paranoia-inducing conversation with his colleague, which I loosely interpreted:

Masseur: "Ha! This *Ausländer* is so scrawny and girly-like! With just a little more pressure from my knotty forearms, I could rub him into a stain on the fabric."

Co-worker (snickering): "*Ja*, why don't you use the 'horse-brush.' That made even Helmut Kohl's cheeks stream with baby's tears."

Just as I was beginning to feel like the "Human Nervous System" plate from *Gray's Anatomy*, my masseur soaped me up and ran his linked fingers up and down limbs as though they were well-greased sausages. Stepping back, he then shouted: "Over!" Assuming he meant over – as in finished – I got up, but he shook his head.

"*Nein!* Over – turn!" He flipped his palm. After scraping my back and hastily massaging my shoulders, he chuckled: "Now – *Ende!*" and pointed me to the shower.

Exfoliated as never before, pink and sanded to the grain, I felt ready to enter the mixed bathing section. Thus far, my fellow bathers had been older men. In the *Thermal-Dampfbad*, a steam bath where sulphurous spring water poured through a series of seven saucer-shaped basins set into the wall, I sat among sweating BMW board members whose genitals flopped over the clammy tiles like beached jellyfish. Moving on to the *Thermal-Vollbad*, I shared a pool of warm mineral water in a high-ceilinged room with two patrician types with Roman profiles who whispered conspiratorially, mouths just above water level. A Venus Pudica statue, her hand held modestly over her crotch, announced that we were about to enter the centrepiece of the Friedrichsbad, the unisex thermal exercise bath. Through an archway on the other side of the circular pool I could see the corresponding *Thermal-Vollbad* on the distaff side, which promised similar titillation for the women with a reproduction of Michelangelo's buff David.

Mustering my dignity, I walked into the vast domed room and, as indolently as I could, descended the steps into the tepid exercise bath. Placing my cheeks on the steps, I languidly glanced upwards, towards the circle of cherubim that underpinned a coffered dome whose skylight cast a sensual half-light on the pool. Slowly lowering my gaze, I prepared to take in a scene of decadence straight out of Petronius's *Satyricon*.

It was the Fellini version. A bespectacled man with wild tufts of black hair protruding from his back was giving me the eye as he paddled clockwise around the pool. At the swan-necked tap where the blond maiden in the brochure had been, a one-armed man bent to rinse off a prosthesis. The only woman in the pool was rake thin, with the alligator hide that bespoke decades of pre-sunscreen tanning on the Riviera.

Well, I thought, shifting to the burbling waters of the jet spray thermal bath, it made sense: people who have come to take a cure aren't likely to be the picture of health. Still, as I found a spot in the shallow, room-sized Jacuzzi and gazed at the flaking skin and bypass scars, I began to wonder what I was doing sitting in a solution filled with radioactive isotopes, heated to a temperature ideal for the multiplication of bacteria colonies, soaking in the same water as people with arcane medical conditions. Samuel Pepys, observing the filthy men in waistcoats and the powdered ladies in gowns cavorting in the waters at Bath in 1668, sensibly noted: "Methinks it cannot be clean to get so many bodies together in the same water." Good point, Sam. I got up and gave myself a good long shower.

On the way out, I was intercepted by the grunting beer keg. Thinking I'd overstayed the allotted time, I started to make my excuses, but he wordlessly tossed a warm towel over my shoulder and led me to a circular salon filled with plush beds on platforms. I saw a dozen man-shaped forms on the beds, face up, wrapped in sheets. This must be the morgue, I thought, where they'd put the clients who had succumbed to the soap-and-brush treatment. The attendant threw my towel onto a free bed and, gesturing for me to climb up, wrapped me in flannel with firm hands. "*Ruhe! Dreißig Minute*," he ordered, and clumped out of the room. That much German I knew: Relaxation – half an hour. Arms bound to my sides like a mummy, with only my nose poking out towards the creamy grey ceiling, I began to relax. Thus swaddled and warmed, I felt as womb-wrapped as Proust's narrator when his Maman gave him his bedtime kiss in his room. Soon, lulled by a chorus of Euro-snoring, I dozed off.

◆

I awoke in a pleasant daze. Wriggling out of the sheets, I covered myself with cream from a wall-mounted dispenser and dressed in a fog of endorphins. Outside, the mossy odour of the Black Forest perfumed the air. The Friedrichsbad, I decided, wasn't a sensual experience, but it was a sensuous one, inducing a low-key aesthetic hum rather than an erotic jolt. I found it touching, not to say bizarre, that for centuries upper-class Eloi had favoured a ritualistic form of enforced leisure that had them moving in somnambulistic fashion through clouds of vapour in various states of undress, to have their unspectacular frames manhandled by gruff Morlocks.

It was certainly a venerable tradition. Bathhouses built around hot springs were inaugurated at Delphi by the Greeks, who retired for a public dip after a wrestling match or a philosophical chat. Baths were refined to sumptuous heights in Rome, which, by the fourth century A.D., had 11 imperial *thermae* (bathhouses with recreational facilities) and 926 smaller public baths supplied by ridiculously labour-intensive aqueducts. The Baths of Diocletian, which could accommodate as many as 3,000 bathers at a time, were so immense that the renovated *frigidarium*, or cold bath, was able to house the entirety of Michelangelo's Santa Maria degli Angeli church. As the Roman Empire spread, springs were commandeered for soldiers' baths – Aquae Sulis on the site of present-day Bath, Vicus Calidus in what would become Vichy – until the savage tribes of Europe won the day and turned the *caldarium* pools into troughs for their sheep.

The notion of drinking spring water to cure ailments probably comes from the town of Spa, a resort founded in the Ardennes, in what is now Belgium, in 1326. The effervescent water of the Sauvenière spring was said to cure infertility, rheumatism, and respiratory inflammations. Gradually, the internal as well as external use of water became a popular treatment. In England, Richard "Beau" Nash encouraged the gentry to drink their three daily glasses of water in Bath's pump room.

The real salad days of the spa came in the 19th century. As the perfection of luxury trains encouraged the mobility of the wealthy, the spas started to specialize. One went to Vichy for a shot liver, to Karlsbad for gastrointestinal disorders, to Bad Gastein to have one's flagging hormones revivified by radium mudpacks. A typical sojourn in one of the Germanic Baden began with a visit to the *Kurarzt*, or spa doctor, who laid out a regimen for a visit of several weeks, often with the warning that hotel and sanatorium informants would be monitoring how closely the patient observed his diet. Baden-Baden's waters, richer in minerals than most, were said to be especially good for arthritis, respiratory diseases, and neuralgia.

Judging by the telephone book, Baden-Baden was still a paradise for the *malade imaginaire*. The yellow pages listed 35 general practitioners, three plastic surgeons, and 19 specialists in something called "Innere Medizin." Pharmacies were as thick on the ground as espresso joints in Seattle; every couple of hundred metres, a neon letter "A" in Gothic script announced the presence of another Apotheke, competing with its neighbour in opulence. On the tree-shaded Sophienstraße, Dr. Rössler's Hofapotheke, founded in 1831, with its sliding wooden and glass doors topped by the coat of arms of Baden-Baden, made me long to be a full-blown neurasthenic. Stepping inside, I gazed in awe at the wooden shelves lined with porcelain pharmacy pots, the hundreds of pill drawers, the sculpted snakes entwined around the stems of golden flowers. It was like a fantasy from my days of pharmaceutical abuse, a baroque temple to the pill. As I approached the polished counter, the pharmacist looked at me with the usual suspicion reserved for healthy young men in drugstores.

"Do you have anything for the nerves?" I asked. Part of me, the aficionado of local specialties, was hoping he'd propose a German equivalent of Mrs. Winslow's Soothing Syrup or a vial of Bayer Brand Heroin.

"Maybe some Baldrian tincture," he suggested, skeptically. He wrapped up a bottle of Valerian extract, and I picked up some ginseng pills in case I felt a bout of melancholia coming on. Perfect: with enough syrups and tablets, I'd have my incipient hypochondria licked in no time.

The problem was, once the day's bath and pill shopping were over, there wasn't much to do in Baden-Baden. I paused outside the office of the *Badisches Tagblatt*, the local weekly newspaper, and used my pocket dictionary to translate a bronze plaque on a stone. "Here stood the Baden-Baden Synagogue," it read, "destroyed by arson on 10 November 1938." Right: between spins of the roulette wheel, even the citizens of Germany's most elegant resort participated in the harassment and murder of Jews on Kristallnacht.

I spent the balance of the afternoon – I could easily have spent the summer – idly cataloguing German fashion mistakes. In a land where socks and sandals (so *hygienisch!* so *praktisch!*) were *de rigueur*, and checkered bell bottoms could still be worn without irony, I'd soon filled half a notebook. Sitting on the Langestrasse, eating bad gelato, I noted it was entirely possible for a German man to wear a blue polo shirt tucked into black-and-white striped referee-style shorts, set off by white sneakers and black socks pulled up to his knees. It was good, even encouraged, for an adult male to put on white trousers and a long-sleeved rayon shirt covered with parrots, carnations, or palm trees. The lumpen Baden-Baden look, whose palette ran from beige to taupe, tended to polyester-and-visible-panty-line and mullet-and-single-ear-ring. Just as I was going to draw a grand conclusion about dowdiness and the Teutonic character, one of the rare groups of bus tourists I'd seen in town rounded a corner. Elderly, dressed in Gore-Tex and iridescent pants with elastic waistbands, they carried McDonald's milkshakes. Most wore straw hats, the bands covered with jaunty maple leaves. After noticing the word "Canada" written across their formless red nylon jackets, I stuffed my notebook into my mouth.

The very rich, at least the few who showed themselves in public, avoided the worst fashion crimes. I spotted a rare cluster at the terrace of the Capri Eis Café, sucking back overmilked cappuccinos. Clothed in Chanel, Ralph Lauren, and Burberry, the women wearing "don't you know who I am?" black sunglasses, they shared tables but stared off in different directions, as if perpetually awaiting somebody more interesting. I imagined the bright-eyed terriers that frolicked at their heels would make better company.

It was too bad, because in their heyday, the upper classes could be brilliantly individualistic – real *Kurschrecks*, or spa terrors – particularly when relaxing together in their Continental enclaves. In Monte Carlo, for example, the exiled Grand Duke Michael of Russia won a bet by putting a napkin over a chocolate soufflé and sitting on it for an entire banquet. James Gordon Bennett, founder of the *New York Herald*, was so miffed at being kept waiting for dinner one evening that he bought the Café Riche in Monte Carlo, fired the manager, and gave the restaurant deed to his favourite waiter as a tip. In Baden-Baden, the Duke of Hamilton – a

Scottish landowner who died a most excellent death by taking a drunken header down the steps of a Paris brothel – won a bet by leading a calf down the Lichtentaler Allee on a blue-ribbon leash.

None of the conformist stiffs at the Eis Café looked like they had the wit or arrogance to pull off such eccentric coups. Being chic in Baden-Baden seemed to involve slavish deference to anything French, and the epitome of this francophilia was the casino. In 1837, after the gambling houses in Paris's Palais Royal provoked one suicide too many, the French decided to ban games of chance. The Parisian casino owners moved to Germany, where gambling was still legal, and transformed the dowdy spas into stylish palaces for the international elite.

§

One morning, I got up early and walked to the *Kurhaus* for a guided tour of Baden-Baden's casino. The colonnaded building was fronted by a row of six-armed gas lampposts, and looked, as the poet Alfred de Musset so neatly put it, like the bastard son of a hay barn and the Parthenon. I joined a German tour group, composed of 20 large men with feathered hair and pot-bellies sporting T-shirts with an image of a short man with a huge Afro, a bushy moustache, and smoked glasses. The man himself – Germany's Weird Al, I assumed – was there in the flesh, wearing a tight-fitting leather jacket. As we wandered through the gaming rooms, the tour guide occasionally offered me some explanation.

"This is the Winter Garden," she said, emitting one English word for every paragraph of German. "It is wery beautiful."

In the Florentine room, whose roulette tables were spread beneath five chandeliers and a ceiling painting of an orchestra of angels, the tour group sat down for a private lesson – prep work, perhaps, for an upcoming "Weird Hans Does Vegas" video. The tour guide led me to a roulette table in an adjoining room, called over a croupier, and offered a perfunctory translation. The casino had been founded by Jacques Bénazet and lavishly decorated by his son, Edouard – the renowned "Duc de Zéro" – who called in a set designer from the Paris Opera to bring the establishment to its current levels of opulence. Germany itself banned games of chance in

1872, and during that time, when the *Kurhaus* became a dancing hall and Baden-Baden was primarily a spa (the Friedrichsbad wouldn't open until 1877), the fashionable set moved down to Monaco, on the French Riviera.

"But they gambled here again during the Second Great War," my guide explained. In fact, Hitler, in need of foreign exchange, reopened the games rooms in 1933. Noticing the green baize covered with French gambling terms – *Marque-Passe-Impair-Pair* – I asked the croupier whether he still said "*Les jeux sont faits*" before every spin.

"No. In the time of Hitler and the Nazis, they wanted not to have anything French, so they said only in German '*Nicht gehts mehr*,' which we have kept to this day."

The tour guide put a chip on the red, and the croupier gave the wheel a counter-clockwise spin. "The little ball arrives in one of the 37 slots," she said, her eyes following the ball until it settled in 11 black. "There! I have just lost 5,000 Euros!" she joked. When she handed me a blue chip as a parting gift, I asked whether I could come back and use it to place my first bet.

"No!" she scolded. "Sentimental walue only!"

The early diaspora of French gambling magnates helped set the tone in the upper-class resorts of the 19th century. François Blanc, driven from Paris by the gaming ban, opened a casino in the principality of Monaco. This state between Nice and Menton, no bigger than London's Hyde Park, was transformed when Blanc cut a deal with the Grimaldi princes, giving them 10 percent of casino profits. Monte Carlo became Europe's foremost haven of elegant vice, the place where Sarah Bernhardt tried to kill herself with the barbiturate Veronal after losing a fortune, where Nijinsky danced in his bollock-cuddling white tights, and where a secret cemetery was said to be filled with the corpses of gambling suicides.

"Monte" was a key stop on the aristocratic grand tour that saw people repairing to the Riviera in winter, the Norman resorts of Deauville and Cabourg in summer, and St. Moritz and Davos year-round for rest cures (with excursions to Constantinople or Cairo for the adventurous). Chefs such as Antonin Carême and Auguste Escoffier were hired to create architecturally ambitious dishes, and wherever the upper-class traveller went he would encounter a menu drawn from a limited repertoire of French haute cuisine. Whether at Shepheard's in Cairo, the Savoy in London, or the Taj in Bombay, the gluttonous Baron Renshaw (pseudonym of the Prince of Wales) could be confident of finding his favoured crepes Suzette, Poulard Derby, and pâté de foie gras with asparagus.

The well-to-do may have mocked Cook's tourists for travelling the world in conducted groups, but they were caught in their own upper-crust rut, slavishly conforming to French manners and separated from day-to-day foreign life by an impenetrable gauntlet of doormen and porters. In a sense, the very rich weren't travelling at all: they were merely changing decor. The wealthiest packed their prejudices along with their Asprey's luggage, and went abroad to impose their standards on other shores. There was the example of the Russian count who, when in Monte Carlo, had a servant crush a half-dozen baskets of strawberries to a pulp every morning – and later remove them uneaten – so that he could inhale their perfume. Except for the magnificence of the gesture, was this any different from the Cookie's loud insistence on kippers and steak sauce in a *pensione* in Sorrento? No matter what the class, by expatriating one's vision of the world while travelling – and by favouring consumption over exchange – one was committing tourism rather than practising travel.

§

I spent another morning taking the waters, this time at the Caracalla Thermae, the Friedrichsbad's newer and brasher neighbour. Completed in the postmodern mode of the mid-1980s, it was a mishmash of stylized columns, ribbed domes, and outdoor thermal pools. In an area called Saunaland, I was confronted by the naked hordes. I watched a pair of pot-bellied men remove their swim trunks and put them in cubbyholes. Shrugging, I followed suit. Finding a place on one of four tiers of cedar seats in a 90-degree-Celsius sauna, I joined the other naked bathers staring blankly at a radiant purple amethyst. Just as I was achieving melt-down, a young woman pointed at a sign on the wall and read it aloud, word by word, in German. I protested that I didn't understand.

"Carrying – a – towel – is – mandatory," she translated, loudly. I could purchase one, she added, at the reception.

Well, that was humiliating, I thought, as I stormed out of the sauna, stamped down the hall, and clambered back into my trunks. If this had been Italy, or some other country populated by *real* human beings, no fellow bather would have taken it upon herself to turn sauna cop. Then again, I realized as I paid far too much for a tiny black towel, if this were Italy I wouldn't have been sitting around naked in public at all.

Thomas Coryate, an early Grand Tourist, had remarked on this phenomenon on a visit to Baden-Baden in 1611. "I have noted another strange thing amongst them, that I have not a little wondred at. Men and women bathing themselves together naked from the middle upward in one bathe . . . [The husbands] were beholding their wives not onely talking and familiarly discoursing with other men, but also sporting after a very pleasant and merry manner." Verily, even 400 years ago, the Germans were consorting stark naked in a jocular and salubrious manner.

Returning to the sauna with my towel – Fräulein Spa-Polizei had unfortunately left – I gazed at the Bratwurst bellies and unselfconsciously sagging breasts and wondered at how this healthy attitude could make nakedness so damn unsexy. Give me a little Mediterranean shame any day. The flash of olive skin beneath a black dress and the gift of an active imagination were worth a Jacuzzi full of chortling Teutons.

The next day, at noon precisely, I lugged my backpack up Lichtentaler Straße, past the parked Jaguars and Saabs, and entered the lobby of one of the grandest of the world's grand hotels. Before leaving home, I'd glanced through a guidebook, obnoxiously titled *The Best Spas*, at the local library. It advised that at the Brenner's Park-Hotel, "the look in general is posh, well-heeled, conservative, elegant, classic, and correctly *sportif*... For men, Prince Philip, Prince Charles and Ralph Lauren advertisements are good fashion images to bear in mind." Right: bear in mind, you snot, that I'd been sleeping fully clothed among vermin on the floor of an abandoned Spanish schoolhouse just a few weeks before. The closest thing to respectable garments my "packing list" included was a worn pair of cords and a threadbare black sweater. Yes, I looked like a vagrant, but I was a vagrant with a credit card. Which is really all that counts these days, darling.

"How long will you be staying with us?" the woman at the desk asked, with commendable professionalism.

"About 23 hours," I replied, glancing at my watch.

A bellhop grabbed my bag and hurried me out of the lobby and into an elevator. I'd picked the cheapest room, stuck in the mansard roof on the fifth floor, but – as I dismissed the bellhop with a bill folded between my fingers, Dino-in-Vegas style – it looked like paradise to me. After two months of bashing knees and elbows on bunks and bedside sinks, I could lounge in a bathrobe monogrammed with my room number and spit grape seeds from the complimentary fruit basket towards the ashtray. For a whole *day*. I whistled as I stuffed the pillow-top truffle, the face cloth, and an array of Bulgari green-tea-scented *eau de toilette* and shampoo containers into my backpack. The rich, by the way, really are very different from you and me. They get much better *en suite* toiletries.

The Brenner's Park-Hotel got its start in 1872 when a tailor named Anton Brenner bought a small but well-placed hotel on the Lichtentaler Allee. A decade later, his more cosmopolitan son took over, bought some neighbouring villas and a fair swath of the park that led to the River Oos, and decorated the hotel with rare carpets and antiques. The hotel started attracting maharajas and kings, statesmen and industrialists. Walking down the long corridor, I understood the appeal. Layers of green and auburn leaves, shading to blue in the distance, were the only things visible through the French windows, and the silence was troubled only by bird-song and the carillon from the nearby Russian Orthodox church. It was as if, through some miracle of perspective, we were no longer in a town of 53,000 but on the secluded estate of a Schwarzwald margrave.

The development of such grand hotels was the final link in the upper-class travel circuit. Since the Middle Ages, the best a weary traveller – even a wealthy one – could hope for at day's end was a glorified inn with no real public spaces. Travel historians credit Boston's Tremont House (1829) – with its French chefs, dining room that seated 200, domed lobby, and bar offering mint juleps – with being the first true luxury hotel. New York's Hotel Astor, with its roof garden, would soon follow, and it was in America that such innovations as private bathrooms, door locks, and hot-water plumbing were introduced. The first European grand hotel was the Great Western (1852), near Paddington Station in London, soon to be followed by the Grand Louvre in Paris.

But the real pioneer of Euro-lux was an ambitious Swiss citizen born into a family of peasants. César Ritz, whose early career waitering in Parisian restaurants brought him into contact with J. P. Morgan and the Prince of Wales, took over the Grand Hotel in Monte Carlo in 1877. There he hired the great Auguste Escoffier, inventor of Melba toast, cementing his reputation as a hotelier to the elite. Striking out on his own, he founded the Ritz Hotel in Paris in 1898, whose innovations included bathrooms in every room, indirect lighting, and hygienic muslin and paint in place of dusty damasks. Ritz's chain opened hotels in London and New York, and his imitators created a worldwide network of pseudo-châteaux for the tycoons and parvenus of the Industrial Age.

Brenner's, which bore a distinct resemblance to Buckingham Palace, was a fine example of the genre, numbering two staff members for every room. I walked the length of the corridor past other guests – Arab men, two blond youths chatting plummily about Wimbledon, well-tended women in their 50s – many of them wearing white bathrobes en route to the spa, a diminutive version of the Caracalla Thermae, where a push of the button in the intimate steam baths would perfume the air with the odour of birch, peppermint, or orchids. In a darkened lounge, I sat on a white leather recliner, and the man next to me showed me how to work the remote control. As vibrating seatback knobs traced curving paths on either side of my spine, I asked him if he was vacationing alone.

"No," he replied, warily. "I am here with my wife and two children. We come once a year, for two or three days."

He was German, blond and blue-eyed, in his late 30s, working for a hydroelectricity company Switzerland. Had he been doing much gambling?

"No. I never leave the hotel. I come here to get away from it all, and do nothing but relax. This is a hotel where Bill Clinton has come. Frank Sinatra has written in the guest book – he says this is the best hotel he's ever stayed in. There is even a Princess of Arabia staying here right now, in the Presidential Suite. It is not a business hotel – it is a Wee Eye Pee hotel."

"There is only 100 rooms," he added. "It is very expensive."

Well – I had noticed that.

Michael soon roused himself. "You will have to excuse me," he said. "Now, I am going to find my wife." He'd seemed unnerved by my inquiries;

Brenner's apparently wasn't the kind of place where one unduly importuned one's fellow guests.

Back in my room, I noticed a rather disturbing sign by the door, a cartoon image of an unshaven man in an open-collared shirt, whose comically ruffled hair looked a lot like my permanently dishevelled locks. It read: "Most of our lady guests appreciate the gentlemen wearing, if possible, a dinner jacket or a dark suit at night." Great: the sun was going down, and, bereft as I was of Ralph Lauren and Burberry, I'd soon be *persona non grata* in the corridors of Brenner's.

That was the problem, it seemed. While it had proven easy to step into the skin of the pilgrim and the bus tourist, impersonating the luxury traveller required the one thing I didn't have: wads of ready cash. Even if I did have the resources to become a *Stammgast* – a regular – at Brenner's, there was little hope I'd be able to strike up an acquaintance with fellow travellers in this income bracket. Not only were the rich able to smell a pretender from across a hotel lobby, they could outdistance me merely by buying a ticket for the Concorde or a first-class seat on a bullet train. Private jets had long since replaced "varnish," and the prestige of owning a country estate had yielded to the cachet of owning one's own island, but the essential mechanism for discouraging the mixing of the classes remained in place: money. I didn't have it – at least not enough to tread long in the watering holes of the rich without gasping for credit. I would have to content myself with being the most fleeting of visitors in the land of the Wee Eye Pees.

§

One haunt of the wealthy was open to everyone. The casino was the most democratic of institutions, after all – anybody could lose money there. Beneath the *lampadaires* of the Lichtentaler Allee, I imagined Dostoevsky roaming in a dazed funk. He had come to Baden-Baden in 1863, launching a career as a spectacularly bad gambler and an equally trying correspondent. He wrote to his mother-in-law: "Here in Baden I have lost everything at roulette, absolutely and completely everything. I have lost more than 3,000 francs. I have now only 250 francs in my pocket . . . I shall be in Turin without a farthing, and will pawn or sell my watch." To his brother: "When I arrived in Baden I went to the tables and in a quarter of an hour won 600 francs. This goaded me on. Suddenly I began to lose, could no longer keep my head, and lost every farthing . . . after paying the landlady we were left with six *napoléons d'or* for the journey. In Geneva I pawned my watch." It must have been hard to be such an excitable visionary. Even harder, though, to be his watch.

I decided that Aleksey Ivanovich, the touchy hero of Dostoevsky's novella *The Gambler*, would serve as my model at the Baden-Baden roulette tables. Entering the casino one night with 20 friedrichs d'or, he leaves with 100,000 florins. I'd forborne from wearing a carnation – terribly bad luck for gamblers – and carried a lucky stone, plucked from a pass in the Pyrenees, in my pocket. Approaching the desk in the *Kurhaus*, I paid my admission and was asked for my passport. Which, of course, I'd left at the hotel.

Half an hour later, I was back from Brenner's, documents in hand. This time I didn't have enough money for the jacket rental, and the bank machine in the lobby was out of service. After locating a Deutsches Bank beyond the Kolonnaden, I returned, picked out an electric-blue blazer and a clip-on tie, and strode into the Florentine room, ready to bust the bank.

As I bought a handful of chips from the cashier, I considered tactics. I could try the Martingale system, which involved doubling-up on bets after losing, or the d'Alembert method, which consisted of increasing by a chip after a loss and decreasing after a win. Finally, I decided to use Dostoevsky's mystical method, which he explained to his wife thus: "I have proved by experience that if, on approaching the table, one plays coolly, calmly and calculatingly, it is *utterly impossible* to lose!" (He would never lose faith in this system, explaining his immense losses as temporary lapses into passion.)

As coolly as I could, I leant between two seated players and tossed a chip on the red. With a little flick of the wrist, the croupier sent the wheel spinning. The ball landed on black. That's cool, I said. I waited a couple of spins, during which a pair of Asian men raked in a pile of chips.

"This roulette wheel was obviously made in China," said a British man, which got a chuckle out of the croupier.

I calmly tossed a chip on Manque, the numbers from 1 to 18, but it landed in the Passe zone, on 21. I went to another table, where a Russian man with a shaved head and an eggplant-coloured suit over a Hawaiian shirt was feeding the tall black woman in a white cocktail dress next to him chip after chip. I bet on the first Colonne: if the ball landed in one of the twelve numbers, I'd win back twice my bet. It landed on 2, in the second column. Very cool, I muttered, calmly. A tuxedoed croupier came up behind his seated colleague, gave him an affectionate flick on the shoulder as if dusting off dandruff, and replaced him, flipping over the cushion before he sat down. Just before the new croupier announced "*Nicht gehts mehr*," I tossed a chip on Impair, the odd numbers. It landed – *c'est la vie!* – on 24. The Russian, who had lost again, rolled his eyes. Down to my last chip, I adopted the Count von Zernsdorff technique and bet it all on 17 – if I won, the bank would pay 35-to-1 odds. The ball spun, jiggled, and dropped into the aluminum slot: 19. The Russian raked in a stack of chips and his girlfriend yelped with pleasure. Dostoesvksy was a stupid loser, I muttered, and stalked towards the bar in a sulk.

I spent the rest of the night wandering among the tables, watching the gamblers. Most people were smoking, but few were drinking. There was an Omar Sharif type, lit cigarette always held between manicured fingers, with a fierce brow, black beard, black eyebrows, and black ponytail. He always pushed through the crowd to scatter his chips at the last second – but never seemed to win, though he bet on a half-dozen squares at a time. He would have been commanding and impressive if he weren't wandering around muttering ironic comments to the croupiers, which they ignored. There was an epicene Asian, wearing a tuxedo, whom I'd decided was male until I saw her emerging from the toilets for *Frauen*. A hunchback was at the high-bet table, scribbling notes on past falls of the ball, looking for patterns in the numbers like a kabbalist.

Nobody seemed happy or triumphant. Again and again I watched the croupiers clear the tables of chips with their plastic rakes. Though this was one of the world's most elegant casinos, there were no James Bonds breaking the bank with a smirk. There were, on the other hand, many dowdy, big-shouldered German women with bouffants and nicotine skin, and men dressed in the checkered suits of Trabant salesmen. People looked blank-eyed, hypnotized by the rotating wheel. As I left, I glanced over my shoulder. In spite of the magnificent frescoes of fountains in classical courtyards, I had the feeling I was looking back into the gloom of a seedy bar from a sunny street, at people as locked in an addiction as skid-row alcoholics.

Must be interesting, I said, as the doorman removed my suit, to work in a place that had attracted the likes of Ivan Turgenev and Marlene Dietrich.

"Yes," he said, "a lot of people have gambled here." Any famous ones? "Most of the famous ones are in prison now. There was the manager of a bank, from a nearby town. Every night he was at the tables, for months. He lost millions. Now he's in jail. You are better, maybe, to leave early."

Well, I hadn't lost enough to feel really depressed about my bad luck. As I walked back down the Lichtentaler Allee, I reflected that while travel sometimes makes you realize who you could be, it is as often a reminder of who you weren't. Many travellers had sought to shed their class abroad, from the Cockneys who became feudal lords in India to the lords who became slumming remittance men in the Pacific islands. Though they might have fooled others, they could rarely fool themselves. Much as I enjoyed being the Pauper on the Prince's estate, even for a week, I would never be at home in this world.

Nor was moving through the upper-class bubble of luxury liners, grand hotels, spas, and casinos my idea of travelling. As a separate sphere, a gated community for superconsumers, it had a certain anachronistic charm. But the world of wealth – particularly inherited wealth – has always struck me as being suffused with sadness, divorced as it is from the stakes of everyday life. In its own way, it too is a tourist rut, insulating people from the conditions of the places they're travelling through. I suspected that the elite travellers who journeyed to affirm their position in a global realm of shared values and prejudices were no more broadening their horizons than was the business traveller who shuttles through interchangeable airports, steak houses, and Hiltons. For the super-rich – the original tourists – a brush with the authentic would always be a matter of slumming.

Outside the casino, the night was fresh and cool. I sauntered down a Lichtentaler Allee shiny with another drenching of Black Forest rain and recalled, happily, that the following day I'd resume travelling in the class to which I'd long been accustomed.

Namely, second.

Chapter 5

AT PLAY IN THE BEAR GARDENS

Euphoria on a Swiss Train – On Certain Mad Travellers – Dysphoria in a Cheap Hotel – Severely Dissed on the Glacier Express – The Daily Goat Herding Pseudo-Event – The Alps as 18th-Century Eyesores – A Foot Race with Middle-Aged Tourists – Not With a Bang, But a Whymper – Drowning in the British Fluid – A Modest Proposal for Saving the Alps – The Japanese Guide to Switzerland – Cellphones on the Matterhorn – The 102-Year-Old Guide – The Climbers' Cemetery – In Which I Scale a 4,000-Metre Summit – Joggers on the Breithorn

I was in the spotless toilet of a Swiss ICE train, between Bern and Brig, when I remembered what kept drawing me back to the road. Jostled as I brushed my teeth, I stared blankly at the sealed plastic cups of drinking water the porters had set beside the sink. In that odd, windowless, vibrating room of plastic and metal, I settled into a familiar euphoria. Plunging into a land where I had no history, I was free. There were no attachments tethering me: only novelty, horizons beyond horizons, and endless possibility. I had no cell phone, no landlord, no idea where I was going to sleep that night. It didn't matter that centuries of tourists had beaten the Swiss travel track as deep as an ocean-floor trench. At that moment nobody knew exactly where I was and I knew nobody on the train, nor even the name of the canton we were travelling through. I could ditch my plans, disembark at the next station, and use the tracery of European rail lines and roads to lose myself in any one of a thousand different directions – or

I could stay put, though paradoxically in motion, in this shaking, locked rail car bathroom. Suspended between running *away* and rushing *towards*, I was perched on the knife's edge of travel, shearing forth in an endlessly renewed present. This felicitous sense of being entirely in my body – of feeling the accretions and compromises and sedimentations of life swept away in the breeze-blast of simple, perfect movement – was where I found my purest motive for travelling.

Somebody tried the door handle. I rinsed, spat, and regained my seat, catching sight of my first red-cheeked garden gnome and the first vein of snow on an Alpine peak. Strange how the memory of such euphoria could infiltrate a hometown winter afternoon and lure me, again and again, into dropping everything and hopping a plane. It matters little, after all, what first impels one to move. An eccentric uncle's invitation abroad, teenage ennui and an empty seat in a southbound Oldsmobile, a vague suspicion that things are ordered differently in the next valley. It's like the first whisky or pill that awakens a lifelong aptitude for debauchery: the important thing is not why you crossed the line (curiosity, boredom, hazard – the motives for the first flirtations are banal), but what you discovered there, and why you kept returning for more.

A couple of decades of travelling had already left me with a bag full of mnemonic madeleines to relish at my leisure. There was the memory, for example, of renting a chair for a few pesetas at the head of the Ramblas and watching, unwatched, the parade of elegant Catalans strolling down Barcelona's promenade on a warm fall evening. Deskbound in the routine of writing, I could tease forth the image of a troupe of robe-wrapped Sikhs advancing towards me with pikes and swords as I approached a ruined hilltop fort in Gwalior. Inspired by a few lines from an out-of-print guide-book, or an evocative name in the crease of a map – the traveller's pornography – I could project my imaginative will onto a distant, never-visited spot. Quite often, a few weeks or months later, I would find myself approaching this vapour-wrapped Solfatara, colonial Martinique, or other Persian-tinged Balbec, and see my anachronistic mental image replaced by a picture that included (I should have known!) touts, admission fees, all the scaffolding of modernity. Yet somehow, months or years later, even the memory of this reality-adjusted image could set me back on the road.

I stopped in Brig, a railway hub and convergence point of several Valais mountain passes and the traditional gateway to the Simplon Route to Italy, and found a room at the Hotel du Pont. Dropping my bag on a sagging bed, I gazed for a minute at a Technicolor-tinted print on the wall. Beneath the cracked glass was a panorama of a departing cruise ship, pulling away from a crescent of golden sand, with a caption that read: "La Promenade des Anglais, Nice." Outside my hotel, at the end of the southbound highway, picturesque mountains loomed. I wondered if, even now, some backpacker was sweltering on a stained mattress in a cut-rate hotel on the French Riviera, gazing longingly at a photo of a cool Alpine summit.

After a silent dinner of train-station sandwiches on a bench in the town square, I felt myself succumbing to the dysphoria that is the valley after the manic peak of travel intoxication.

I knew what was happening to me. Before leaving, I'd read a book that had named my condition. In *Mad Travelers*, the Canadian philosopher Ian Hacking focused on the phenomenon of the fugue, first observed by a French clinician in 1878. The earliest sufferer was Albert Dadas, who lived an uneventful life as a gas fitter in provincial Bordeaux. At regular intervals he was overcome by headaches, anxiety, and insomnia, prey to a compulsion to drop everything, abandon his family and job, and just up and leave. Pausing for a ritualistic drink of orgéat in a local bar, he would set out – sometimes on foot, walking up to 70 kilometres a day, more often using the new network of railways that made this kind of "pathological tourism" possible – and eventually find himself in Moscow, Constantinople, or Algiers, without identity papers or a single sou, sobbing alone in a hotel room, confused and homesick. "Albert's obsessive and uncontrollable journeys," Hacking had written, "were systematically pointless, less a voyage of self-discovery than an attempt to eliminate self."

Though my voyages were never exactly pointless – I always managed to find a goal to justify my journeys – there was a little of Albert in me. Back home, I could lead a circumscribed existence for months on end, patronizing the same cafés, laundromats, and grocery stores. Gradually, though, a kind of toxin seemed to accumulate in my tissues, like lactic acid in tired muscles. Objects carefully chosen, cherished at the moment of purchase, would begin to weigh on me, every souvenir and book a reminder of what I'd become and what I'd always be. The only way to shake off the mounting lethargy and depression lay in imagining myself *away* – moving towards elsewhere. And inevitably, one morning I'd find myself stuffing a bag with quickly chosen travel clothes, taking a ritualistic final drink, and hitting the road. As I slammed the door, I'd feel what Albert must have felt: the euphoric hope of forever shedding one's old sense of self.

Lying sleepless in the cheap travellers' hotel in Brig, I feared I was becoming an inveterate *fugueur*, and that my continent-spanning endeavour was subtracting me from what little life I'd established for myself at home; that, in the end, the only freedom I'd won was the freedom to dine alone in a strange town. I knew that in the clinical sense, I was not one of the clan of mad travellers – they were, after all, unable to master their impulses. I suffered from a constitutional impatience, some addiction to stimulation that made the promise of an overheard place-name, and the journey towards it, seem the path to happiness. As a teenager, I'd discovered that the infrastructure of modern tourism – airport waiting rooms, intercity trains, no-questions-asked traveller's hostels – offered me repeated access to a state of statelessness, where all becomes hope, promise, and new horizons. The fugue was a *petite morte* of the identity, as addictive in its way as orgasm or opiates.

My girlfriend had quoted me a proverb before I'd left: the body may travel by train, but the soul travels by donkey. I'd tried to call her that night, but she wasn't home. I knew what she'd tell me, though. Stay where you are, Taras. Wait for your soul to catch up to you.

❧

Brig, I saw next morning, was no place to await a metaphysical reunion. I boarded the Glacier Express, famous for passing through 91 tunnels in the 290 kilometres between St. Moritz and Zermatt. After passing the town of Visp and heading into the mountains along a turbid, jade-coloured river, I examined a landscape that seemed to approach the Platonic ideal of picturesqueness (if Plato had been a rather conventional eight-year-old with a pencil case full of primary colours) – a village church, with its wooden steeple; a gabled house, with gaily painted shutters, flowerboxes, and a white-crossed Swiss flag; a brown and white cow, with its big bell, standing in a vividly green Alpine meadow.

At the centre of the landscape was our train, attaining a degree of train-ness that verged on self-parody: glossy red, charmingly boxy, and so unscuffed it seemed to have been removed from its box that morning. Given the scenery, I understood the impulse of the adolescents of Bern and Lucerne to deface any available underpass or factory wall with elaborate tags. Sadly, even the Swiss graffiti was technically excellent; I suspected the vandals of being subsidized by government grants.

Overhearing two men speaking English, I asked if I could sit down with them. Al, the taller of the two, was an engineer at Boeing whose greying sideburns, piercing blue eyes, and full head of swept-back silver hair made him resemble Clint Eastwood. Steve was a banker, already retired though only in his 50s, wearing a thick wool shirt open over a white T-shirt. Both were from Seattle, both were tanned, and both had crushing, dry-palmed handshakes. The kinds of guys, I decided, who had built their own homes. Not to save money, but for the sheer, manly satisfaction of it. They told me they were mountain climbers.

"We're not professionals, though," said Steve. "I climbed the Matterhorn back in 1995. I've also crossed Ellesmere Island and climbed in the Andes. The conditions are far from ideal on the Matterhorn right now. Two people were killed this week. There have been a lot of storms, and a lot of snow. We're going to do some hikes on the smaller mountains instead."

Al looked me up and down, appraisingly. "You going to Zermatt?" he asked. I admitted I was. "It's a mountain-climbing town. You'll see lots of ice picks and backpacks on the main street. It's totally dominated by the Matterhorn."

We were silent a moment, gazing through the vertical slats of a tunnel at a snow-peak that flashed by as though in a zoetrope. Must be an incredible setting to grow up in, I ventured.

"The Swiss used to think there were dragons living on top of the mountains," said Steve. "It's amazing – they lived alongside the Alps for centuries and never thought to go to the top. It took the English mountaineers to do it."

Wasn't it more amazing, I said, that anybody would want to climb them at all?

Steve and Al stared at me, as if judging how long I could hold onto the end of a rope. Not very long at all, their looks seemed to say. After a minute, Steve pointed out the window. "There's another slot canyon," he said to Al.

I'd been appraised and dismissed.

Steve and Al got off the train in the town of Tasch, and we exchanged curt goodbyes. Clearly, we were different kinds of travellers. I thought I'd glimpsed in their steely gazes an *Übermensch*-like contempt for the trappings of civilization. While my attention was easily distracted by the Swiss conductor with the adding-machine-style ticket dispenser around his neck, theirs had been fixed on geological strata, glaciers, and overhangs.

I asked myself why I had never travelled abroad to scale mountains, cliff-dive into tropical atolls, or bungee-jump off suspension bridges. On a globe already fully mapped, where the flags of all nations have long since been planted on the major peaks, adventure travel had always looked to me like an involuted manifestation of the impulse to conquer, its practitioners forced to set themselves ever more masochistic challenges. First to unicycle across Bhutan; largest whitewater rafting expedition among the headhunters of Borneo; second blind man to scale Everest – if it was remote, frozen, and strewn with land mines, there was some overpaid dilettante ready to reconquer it. When the locals couldn't be avoided altogether, they were recruited as porters and background colour for photo essays. For today's connoisseurs of risk, a foreign country was just an excuse for an exotic dateline.

Perhaps I was missing the point. Apart from some abortive forays into rock climbing and caving, I had never really tested my mettle in extreme environments or tasted the rarefied thrill of treading where few had dared go. I had chosen Zermatt, the place where people had first started climbing mountains for the sheer thrill of it, in hopes of slipping into the skin of the adventure traveller. Little matter that these mountains had been conquered centuries ago – any climbing would be challenge enough for a beginner like myself.

The Glacier Express pulled into the train station – the end of the line –

and I walked out onto the main drag of Zermatt, the Bahnhofstrasse. The shark-finned, canine-toothed, white-walled Matterhorn loomed at the end of the street, a child's drawing of a scary mountain. Against a background of blue sky, a horizontal stream of cloud intersected the summit, as though the protruding peak was provoking a disturbance in the empyrean, an earth-claw raking the stratosphere. I thought of the Paramount Pictures logo, muesli boxes, and Toblerone, trying to undermine the mountain's impact with everyday trademarks. Rising white and alone from a pedestal of meadows and evergreens, it foiled all attempts at trivialization: the Matterhorn was a genuinely fear-inducing sight.

The main drag, on the other hand, was as familiar as a high street on a bank holiday, filled shop-to-shop with elderly Japanese tourists, American college students, and Germans in hiking gear. A man with a hiking stick in hand yelled "*Attention!*" and pointed at the electric cart coming up fast behind me, ferrying luggage from the train station to one of the hotels.

Zermatt's spine was the milky-green Mattervispa. Bracketed in the town limits between grey stone walls, the river roiled unconstrained down the same valley I had followed in the Glacier Express, flowed into the Rhone at Visp, and eventually carried the Matterhorn's meltwater all the way to the Mediterranean. The buildings of Zermatt were strewn along both sides of the river, climbing the valley walls in rows until the wild-flower-dotted slopes got too steep to build on. In the square by the railway station, where the horse-carriage drivers were lined up to welcome the latest trainloads of visitors, I picked up brochures in the tourist office. There were 106 hotels and guesthouses in Zermatt, I read, and 17,000 beds. All told, there were 35 mountains of more than 4,000 metres in the area, their slopes linked by a spider's web of 36 cable cars and gondolas.

Outside McDonald's, the tourists around me fumbled for their cameras. A troupe of long-haired goats was being driven up the street, bells a-jangle, by a teenager in shorts carrying a shepherd's crook. A French boy yelped as a billy goat pushed its beard into his palm and swiped a jujube. The animals left a trail of glossy crottes in their wake, promptly swept up by men in overalls. For a moment, I entertained the idea that I'd happened upon the transhumance, a genuine pastoral ritual.

Of course, at 4:30 p.m. the following day – and on every afternoon I spent
in Zermatt – precisely the same pseudo-event was staged, accompanied by
the click of a thousand camera shutters.

§

Once upon a time, Zermatt was a real village, not a chamber of commerce
concoction. In the lanes between the tennis courts and five-star hotels, I
saw rundown mountain huts overgrown with grass, and quartz-topped
granaries poised on stone disks on wooden posts – Swiss versions of the
vermin-foiling *hórreos* I'd seen in Galicia. When the pioneering Alpine
explorer and scientist John Ball came in 1845 to explore the local glaciers,
he'd found only "a crowded assemblage of dank, dirty-looking wooden
houses" and been forced to lodge with the local priest.

Only relatively recently, in fact, had the Alps attracted visitors in
sizable numbers. Until the 18th century, mountain scenery was considered
the grimmest of tableaux, and tourists rushed through Switzerland as
though they had wolves on their tails – as often they did – many of them
blindfolded against the vertiginous horror as porters carried them in
sedan chairs. In the 1780s, Goethe considered the Alps "zigzags and irritating silhouettes and shapeless piles of granite, making the fairest portion
of the earth a polar region." The poverty-stricken mountain Swiss were
often afflicted by cretinism and dangling neck goitres, the result of iodine
deficiency. Cowed by stories of demons, they ventured into the high
mountains only to hunt marmots, crystals, and chamois (a kind of goat
crossed with an antelope). As late as 1723, a Zurich physics professor
devoted an illustrated chapter of a learned volume to the natural history
of cave-dwelling alpine dragons.

For Grand Tourists before the Industrial Revolution, for whom fertile
fields and goodly croppes were the ultimate scenery, the Alpine peaks
could only represent sterility, famine, and sudden death. As urbanization
and industry crowded Europeans into dirty cities, however, a landscape
formerly barren and fearsome came to be equated with purity and spiritual challenge. During his 1790 "Pedestrian Tour" of the Alps, Wordsworth
hiked 25 kilometres each day before breakfast, praising the therapeutic

pleasures of hiking, the virtues of peasant life, and the "sky-roofed temple of eternal hills." By the mid-19th century, when England became the first nation where more people lived in cities than in the country, urban over-crowding, pollution, and tuberculosis had combined with such romantic notions as the cult of the noble savage to revolutionize attitudes towards mountain scenery. The Alpinist Professor Tyndall could aver in the 1860s: "There is assuredly morality in the oxygen of the mountains, as there is immorality in the miasma of a marsh . . . the Alps improve us totally, and we return from their precipices wiser as well as stronger men." In the course of a century, the miserable and irritating Alps had become the healthful playgrounds of Europe.

These days, Zermatt's English Quarter, set back from the fondue and pizza joints on the Bahnhofstrasse, amounts to a Protestant chapel, one of the town's oldest hotels, and the little Alpine Museum, a two-storey build-ing that looks like a ski chalet. I paid my admission and crossed worn wooden floors covered with dusty stuffed ibexes and mountain goats, examining botany textbook prints of wildflowers and butterflies pinned to particle board. In a room full of primitive rucksacks, long wooden skis, and flimsy-looking leather boots, a portrait of Horace-Bénédict de Saussure, who had climbed the nearby Klein Matterhorn, reminded me of the mixed motives – both scientific and adventurous – of the earliest mountaineers. The Geneva-based scientist had offered a reward to the first person to scale Mont Blanc, at 4,807 metres the highest peak in western Europe. Two men from Chamonix summited in 1786, and de Saussure himself made the ascent the following year.

It was the English of the Victorian era – the leisured, moneyed citizens of an increasingly powerful empire – who came to dominate mountain exploration. The Alpine Club was formed in 1857, enlisting mountaineers, scientists, and literary men such as John Ruskin, Matthew Arnold, and the guidebook publisher John Murray. After the glaciers had been explored, the empirical justification for risking one's neck got harder to swallow. Adventurers began to leave behind their boiling thermometers and barometers, favouring instead pitons, national flags, and bottles of cham-pagne for the peak parties. A dash of derring-do and aristocratic style came to be *de rigueur*: Sir Alfred Wills ascended the Wetterhorn in cricket flannels, and Charles Fellows and his porters went up Mont Blanc with eight joints of meat, a dozen fowl, and 42 bottles of red wine, brandy, *capillaire*, and syrup of raspberries. In a back room of the Alpine Museum, I found a photograph and handwritten letter dated 1894 from a 20-year-old Winston Churchill, recommending a local guide. The future prime minister, bearded and slender, overcame sunburn and mountain sickness to ascend nearby Monte Rosa, the highest mountain wholly in the Swiss Alps. It was a hint of the degree to which a session of Alpine climbing was an important rite of passage for the young English gentleman.

Dispirited by this evidence of Victorian fortitude, I crossed the river to a pizzeria called the North Wall and had a cup of coffee at the bar. A meeting point for climbers and skiers, the restaurant was empty that afternoon. I idly flipped through a guest book at the bar. Among the usual backpacker doggerel ("This week I have mostly been eating yogurt – Jessio"), there were precise ballpoint-pen sketches of the Matterhorn, and square-jawed connoisseur's comments such as: "Great bolted route to the left of thermometer C on the Riffelhorn. Superb Exposed Crux." A bartender named Chris, with a gentle manner and a Prince Valiant haircut, caught me poring over a tourist office map of the local mountains.

"Looking to go for a hike?" he asked, with a South African accent. I told him I'd like to, but didn't have equipment or mountaineering experience.

"Why don't you go to the Rothorn-Hütte?" he suggested. "It's only about six hours there and back. This time of year, you probably won't be walking through much snow."

That was all the encouragement I needed: I stocked up on Birchermuesli, orange juice, and trail mix in a supermarket and headed for the hills. Taking a path from behind the Alpine Museum, I found myself among sloping meadows, waymarked with little brown wooden signs indicating the estimated time between villages such as Edelweiss and Zmutt in increments of a quarter of an hour. (These signs, I decided, had been posted by a 19-year-old extreme athlete with an amphetamine habit.) Unseen crickets were stridulating all around; white-tailed hares bounded up the hills and wildflowers made the fields look like an endless embroidered bath mat. It was like walking into an Alpen cereal box, and as I inspected a Heath Robinson–style pulley system, which apparently allowed groceries to be delivered from a lower meadow to a mountain hut perched on a rocky outcropping high above, I had to squelch a repetitive subconscious chorus of "The Sound of Music."

After crossing a bridge below a waterfall, I followed the Triftbach River, climbing a snaking path up an ever-ascending gorge. On level ground in a stretch of forest, I passed a fit couple from Leeds, who looked to be in their late 40s.

"From Canada, are you?" the man asked me. "Our son is working in Banff – we went to visit him last year. We've just now arrived in Switzerland. Not really in training, yet."

I wasn't exactly sure what his point was, but I bade them good luck as I walked on. Passing me as I paused to rub in some sunscreen, they barely acknowledged my second hello. I'm a strong uphill walker, so within a few minutes I overtook them again.

"We hate you, you know," the man said, a grimace almost trumping his smile. It was meant to be jocular, of course, but it seemed mean, a revelation of petty competitiveness.

I soon forgot about the encounter. After passing families sitting at picnic tables at a mountain guest house, I skipped from stone to stone over a vast tract of scree, dampening my shoes in shallow meanders fed by snow melting from the sides of the Zinalrothorn. The path followed the ridge of a dramatically rising zigzag slope. As I walked alongside a sharply pitched snow slope to my left, a barechested hiker let out a whoop and leapt, bootheels first, onto its surface, churning and sliding a couple of hundred metres downhill, miraculously maintaining his balance until he disappeared from view.

I soon arrived at the Rothorn-Hütte, a two-storey building, one of many built by national mountaineering societies to shelter climbers. On the terrace, hearty Germans in fluorescent ski pants were drinking beer, and I joined them in inspecting a panorama of snow peaks – at 3,200 metres, we were 1.6 kilometres above Zermatt. Within half an hour, the English couple appeared below, climbed the stairs, and walked onto the terrace. I greeted them cheerily, but they were tight-lipped. Shouldering my bag, I started down again. Soon I heard the scuffling of rocks behind me. Sure enough, there they were; the husband, leaping over the rocks at a half-run, his wife struggling to keep up. I suspected that the fellow was subjecting his wife to a foot race with a younger man to salve his pride.

Having passed me, however, they couldn't keep up the pace. I followed on their heels for half an hour, watching the man stumble as he picked his way through the scree, imagining her increasing frustration with his behaviour. I hated myself for not sitting down for five minutes and forgetting about the absurd contest; but I confess to a little perverse satisfaction in driving them on with harassing footfalls. Finally, the path widened near the mountain guest house at Trift. The man stopped, put his hands on his hips, and looked about in exaggerated satisfaction.

"Well, we'll be stopping here for lunch," he said. "Perhaps we'll see you back in Zermatt, then."

For the remainder of the walk, the Englishman's wry admission of hatred, as naked a glimpse into his state of mind as a Shakespearean aside, stayed with me. This view of the world as a playing field, of people on the trail as competitors rather than fellow travellers, disturbed me. I knew it lived within me, too, and that it sometimes poisoned my interaction with the world. I suspected it was this flinty core of pettiness, married with tenacity and glorified as sportsmanship and national pride, that had driven many mountaineers and adventure travellers.

Back in Zermatt, I emerged next to the shuttered facade of the Hotel Monte Rosa. A plaque next to the door bore the name of Edward Whymper, explaining that he had left from the hotel on the morning of July 13, 1865, to complete the first successful ascent of the Matterhorn. There was no room, evidently, for the epilogue: Whymper's expedition not only cost the lives of four of his comrades, it also launched a mode of adventuring for the sake of adventure that would make the fortunes of Zermatt's hoteliers, lead to the conquest of Everest, and send generations to the coldest, deepest, highest, and bleakest corners of the globe for reasons even the most lucid of them could scarcely explain.

❧

Whymper, son of a wood engraver, had been introduced to the Alps when a publisher asked him to go to France to make some engravings for the

Alpine Club. More attracted to scaling the peaks than drawing them, the young man conquered several virgin summits and made seven attempts on the Matterhorn. In the summer of 1865, he learned that a guide from the Italian side, Jean-Antoine Carrel, was mounting an expedition to climb the mountain. Whymper, then 25, hastily assembled a team that included three local guides, Lord Francis Douglas (18-year-old brother of Oscar Wilde's lover), Reverend Charles Hudson, and an inexperienced climber named Roger Hadow.

The weather was clear, and though Hadow had to be helped much of the way, the team made good time up the northeast ridge. Worried about the Italian group's progress, Whymper and the Chamonix guide Michel Croz unroped themselves and made a dash for the summit. Arriving at 1:40 p.m., Whymper saw the Italian team on a ridge far below. "We must make them hear us; they shall hear us!" Whymper yelled at Croz. He would later write: "I seized a block of rock and hurled it down and called upon my companion, in the name of friendship, to do the same . . : The Italians turned and fled." On the way down the mountain, Hadow slipped and dragged Croz over the side. Though Whymper and the two Swiss guides braced themselves, the rope below them broke. Four of the seven climbers – including the young Lord Douglas – plunged 1,200 metres to their deaths on the glacier below.

I'd seen the frayed ends of the rope – it was no thicker than a clothes-line – in a glass case in the Alpine Museum, as well as a signed copy of the report Whymper had given to authorities. If there had been little contro-versy about the accidental nature of the disaster at the time, there had been outrage about the senselessness of it all. Charles Dickens thundered that the Alpine Club "contributed about as much to the advancement of science as would a club of young gentlemen who should undertake to bestride all the weathercocks of all the cathedral spires in the United Kingdom."

A pall briefly dropped over the largely English climbing community, but before long they were at it again. Only three years after the Matterhorn tragedy, the great Alpinist A. F. Mummery climbed the mountain from the more difficult northwest side, ushering in a new era in climbing. From then on, it was the technical challenge of the climb that set the standard. By the beginning of the 20th century, when all the great Alpine peaks had been conquered, attention turned to the peaks of the Himalayas. As even those peaks fell – and Everest is almost twice as high as the 4,478-metre Matterhorn – new challenges had to be invented: climbing without oxygen, going solo, or scaling the more difficult north faces. Two centuries after modern mountaineering began with the scaling of Mont Blanc, a blind man made it to the top of Everest.

I thought I could hear the echo of Whymper's "We must make them hear us!" in the "We hate you, you know" the Englishman had tossed at me. It was the men of England, the first nation to be industrialized, who had the leisure to turn conquest, exploration, and adventure into a sport, and the economic power to impose their whims. In Switzerland, they insisted on separate tables and dinner jackets at meals, and frowned upon conversation with strangers. (The Swiss called them "Yes and No" tourists, because of their haughty refusal to engage the locals in anything but monosyllabic conversations.) Chastised for low standards in John Murray's *Hand-Book*, the owners of local inns – the Bear in Grindelwald, the Monte Rosa in Zermatt, the Engadine Kulm in St. Moritz – began to offer four o'clock tea, footbaths, and *table d'hôte* dinners with English mustard. By the 1850s, an Alpine travel rut was well established. French author George Sand, observing a group of English, wrote: "Albion's islanders [have] with them a peculiar fluid which I shall call the British fluid, enveloped in which they travel, as inaccessible to the atmosphere as is a mouse in the centre of a pneumatic machine."

Gradually, the Alpine preserve fell to middle-class tourism. Beginning in 1852, English contractors and financiers helped build the rack-and-pinion railways that would take tourists high into the Bernese Oberland, and engineered the tunnels that would link Switzerland to Italy. By the 1880s, Switzerland was attracting a million visitors a year, and English tourists brought the Norwegian pastime of skiing to Davos, descended the Cresta Run in St. Moritz on toboggans at 110 kilometres an hour, and skated in boisterous packs at the rinks in Grindelwald. The critic and essayist John Ruskin, whose "Of Mountain Beauty" was one of the earliest aesthetic appreciations of the mountains, waxed eloquent on his compatriots' desecration of the mountains in 1864: "You have made race-courses of the cathedrals of the earth. The Alps themselves, which your own poets used to love so reverently, you look upon as soaped poles in a bear garden, which you set yourself to climb and slide down again with 'shrieks of delight.'"

After my hike, I walked into a bar called the Pipe Surfers' Cantina, which advertised non-stop surfing videos and wet T-shirt contests. It was mid-afternoon, but pints of ale already lined the bar in front of two bleach-blond, shiny-eyed women and a man in a singlet.

"What do you want, mate?" he asked, with a beer-blurred South London accent.

I gestured towards the plexiglass-shielded Internet terminal, behind his stool.

"Computer nerd! Computer nerd!" he shouted. I eased past him and took a seat; just then, the shaven-headed bartender, bristles sprouting from his thick neck, emerged from a back room and planted his feet solidly before me.

"Who said you could use my computer, then?" he bellowed. The crowd at the bar laughed appreciatively.

"I didn't know you knew how to use a computer," one of the blonds said to the barman.

"He doesn't," said the man in the singlet. "He's still trying to figure out what ISDN means."

Drawing himself a pint, he retorted, "I do – it means Inside Some Dumb Nigger. Which is where I'd like to be, come to think of it."

"In your dreams, mate," the man in the singlet shot back. The women groaned.

I checked my e-mail and left, relieved to be released from the British fluid.

§

The English, though they still had their enclaves, were a minority in Zermatt these days. Shortly after the creation of the British Alpine Club, the Swiss, Italians, and French founded their own national climbing organizations. European industrialization meant that prosperous Germans and Austrians invaded the skating rinks and toboggan runs. On the mountains, English climbers found they were being raced to the top by the Swiss who had once been their guides. A Norwegian, Roald Amundsen, beat Englishman Robert Scott to the South Pole in 1911. The Austrian Heinrich Harrer was part of a team that solved the last great Alpine problem, the treacherous north face of Eiger, in the name of Hitler's Third Reich.

The Swiss, derided as cretinous peasants by the first English visitors, established a capital-raising and banking system to finance a tourist infrastructure of lake steamers and railways and came to have one of the highest living standards in Europe. By 1950, the English, saddled by postwar rationing and currency restrictions, found themselves poorer than their former innkeepers. These days, an estimated 50 million people are drawn to the Alps' 600 resorts and 41,000 ski runs every year. Only one in 20 of the visitors is English.

On the Bahnhofstrasse, the shops sold sugar-topped Matterhorn pralines, key chains, souvenir mugs, and even yo-yos. I'd read that one ton of postcards was mailed from Zermatt's post office every year, most of them bearing an image of the famous mountain. In only a couple of days, the Matterhorn had lost its impact on me, a natural wonder turned to cliché by a hyperactive tourist industry.

In a similar process, a couple of centuries of human influence have made the Alps the world's most threatened mountain system. The million trucks that cross the chain every year bring acid rain and poor air quality. As the world climate changes, the snowline creeps higher. In the next century, half the Alpine glaciers are expected to disappear. It was time, I thought, to advance a modest proposal. We should take the familiar attractions – the glass-fronted *Mona Lisa*, pollution-pitted Notre-Dame, climbing-rope-cluttered Matterhorn – bundle them in burlap, stick them in a time capsule, and banish them from view. Only after a century should they be unveiled, renewing our ability to regard the western world's leading attractions without irony.

The largest contingent in Zermatt was surely the Japanese, who walked the streets in conspicuously tight-knit groups. They seemed ravished by Switzerland, enthusiastically buying alpenstocks and floppy sun hats. The country's reputation for pure air, safe streets, and orderly public life must have corresponded to some Japanese ideal of the good life. I studied the menu outside Myoko, one of several Japanese restaurants in town, noting that a single piece of tuna sushi cost four Swiss francs. A bespectacled Japanese man in his 40s, in shorts and white T-shirt, poked his head around the sign.

"Food is very good!" he said. "Sushi not so good, but the yakitori and tofu salad – you know tofu? – very good."

I asked whether he'd tried Swiss food.

"I had . . . ooh . . . fondue? But I don't like." He rubbed his stomach, frowning. "Too heavy." He'd made another reservation at Myoko that night. "It was recommended!" he said, showing me a guidebook.

I sat down on a bench to eat a sandwich, and five minutes later he was back, presenting me with his card.

"Please, take my guidebook," he said, explaining he was moving on to Milan the next day. "As a souvenir!"

Thanking him, I flipped through the "Gio Globe Trotter" guide, whose cover featured a line drawing of a man with a telephoto-lens camera staring through a hotel window at the Matterhorn. Picking out the English among the Japanese characters, I could see that Asian tourists were advised to dine at Fuji's of Zermatt, stay at the four-star Schweizerhof Hotel, and seek information at the Japanese Tourist & Information Centre. Aided by guidebooks with excellent maps and hundreds of colour pictures, the Japanese evidently followed their own distinct rut, convening throughout Europe in such Asian-friendly tourist bubbles as Zermatt.

◆

In the 1850s, rough Swiss guides had congregated against a stone wall outside the Monte Rosa hotel, waiting for an English "milord" to hire them for an expedition. Now there was a two-storey Alpin Centre, where helicopter skiing trips were booked via e-mail. I waited in line on the upper floor, and asked a harassed-looking woman at the desk, who fielded phone inquiries between clients, what I needed to climb the Matterhorn.

"You need to have climbed a high mountain before," she said, pushing a photocopied sheet at me.

"To attempt climbing the Matterhorn you need to be in *top physical condition*," it read, "to have *some rock climbing experience*, and to have done *some practice with crampons.* Inexperienced climbers are advised not to attempt such a difficult mountain as the Matterhorn for their first climb." Another issue was price: the cost of the trip, including the guide's fee and a night in the hut, was 937.50 Swiss francs.

"Could you recommend a smaller . . . and . . . uh, cheaper mountain?" I asked.

She brightened. "Why don't you start with the Matterhorn-Hütte? Then, for people with not so much experience, we suggest Breithorn." She gave me a sheet that outlined the ascent of Breithorn, "one of the easiest 4,000-metre mountains in the region." Noting the 125-franc fee with relief, I booked a meeting with a guide for the next day.

The ascent called for an intimidating array of climbing paraphernalia. In the basement of a rental outlet across the street, a gruff man, who dealt with Italian, German, and French clients in their respective languages, saddled me like a dray horse. After fitting me with a scrotum-hugging harness, he showed me how to attach crampons – bear-claw-like metal strap-ons that give you purchase on ice – to a weathered-looking pair of size 44 boots. It was just noon, so I decided I'd take advantage of my gear and do a day-hike to the hut at the base of the Matterhorn.

Linked gondolas took me to 2,582 metres, and I emerged at the Schwarzsee, the small Black Lake where the meadows end and the approach to the great mountain begins. In a half hour of cable-car riding, the Matterhorn had turned from disempowered postcard image to awesome towering threat, its pristine white flanks revealed as rocky corrugations cross-hatched with snow. I hiked over a chaos of broken quartz that looked like a fossil seabed from which an antediluvian tide had retreated, and up metal staircases bolted into rock face, twisted by ominous dents that suggested recent boulder impacts. Walking over a slope of mushy snow, I paused to chat with a cheery Nepalese man in wraparound mirrored shades who explained that he was hired to come to Switzerland every summer to clear the mountain paths. After a challenging two-hour hike in which I gained 700 metres, I reached the Matterhorn-Hütte – the base camp for all the assaults on the peak.

"Can I have another cappuccino?" a man with an American accent asked as I crested the last slushy incline. On a wooden platform before the shuttered building, a waiter took the orders of a couple of dozen people sitting at picnic tables. Many had video cameras trained on the peak, whose incline started in earnest just behind the hut. A cellphone rang.

"You'll never guess where I am!" a man in a denim shirt said, ruining my day.

I sat down and glanced at the menu for the Berghaus Matterhorn. Here, at 3,260 metres, I could enjoy spaghetti bolognaise or Matterhorn rösti with ham and cheese, followed by a Nescafé latte. The platform gradually got more crowded. Soon, I counted 45 people, many carrying state-of-the-art photographic equipment. When a dozen of the elder Japanese I'd seen on the cable car appeared, panting, dressed in identical sun hats, I decided it was time to leave.

When I was a boy, my father gave me a copy of a book by Richard Halliburton, the great American horizon chaser. In *The Royal Road to Romance*, published in 1925, Halliburton writes with a swashbuckler's insouciance of swimming in the pools before the Taj Mahal at moonlight, posing as a pilgrim to get into Mecca, and fighting nausea and frostbite as he clawed his way to the top of the Matterhorn. He always seemed to be the only traveller amidst a backdrop of desert Bedouin or bearded Greek monks. It was a world of wonders, Halliburton told his readers, whose pleasures the adventurous few could taste if only they had the courage to leave their armchairs.

By now, I'd visited many of the places Halliburton had described in his books. I'd be hard-pressed, however, to spin a romantic legend out of my visit to the Taj Mahal, where I'd had to queue with hundreds of bus tourists before I could stand on the marble plinth. Since Halliburton's time, mass tourism has gained ground, and those with the urge to explore are forced to issue themselves increasingly arcane challenges. In 1946, Wilfred Thesiger made a deliberately anachronistic camel-back crossing of Arabia's Empty Quarter, when he could easily have gone by Land Rover. Tourist-cum-explorer Redmond O'Hanlon, a combination of Bill Bryson and David Livingstone, had to go to the very heart of the shrinking Amazonian rainforest to meet a tribe, the Yanomami, with its traditions intact.

The vogue for travelogues in which narrators follow in the footsteps of Richard Burton, Ernest Shackleton, and George Mallory is a recognition that all the great voyages of discovery have been made. Adventure has long been a repudiation of the self-indulgence and indolence of tourism – the icy aridity of the Poles a reproach to the white sands of tropical beaches – but lately the two have come to overlap. These days, adventure travel has veered into its decadent phase, with travel agencies offering package tours to war zones, and writers like Robert Young Pelton promoting guidebooks to *The World's Most Dangerous Places*. A century ago, my visit to the Matterhorn-Hütte might have made a good episode in a European travelogue. Now, in a world where diet and gyms have made good health commonplace, it was a banal day-hike for fit grandparents.

§

Back in Zermatt, I stopped for a pizza at the North Wall. It was a slow afternoon, and Chris, the bartender, was chatting with a client about the Austrian Stefan Gatt, who had just snowboarded down Everest, without oxygen, in minus-28-degree conditions. It reminded me that I would be climbing to the top of a snowy peak the following morning, and I took Chris up on his offer to loan me some clothing. He brought out two thin sweaters.

"Just layer yourself," he advised. "You should be all right."

I'd noticed that Zermatt's oldest living guide would be signing autographs that afternoon. I feared a human zoo – a withered fellow trotted out to the local shopping mall in a wheelchair – but in fact the signing was a dignified affair in a small gallery. Ulrich Inderbinen, born in 1900, had made his final ascent of the Matterhorn at the age of 90. He sat behind a table covered with postcards, a small man with abundant wrinkles and a bushy white moustache curled at the tips. I asked whether the Matterhorn was really as tough as it looked.

"Matterhorn is not the most dangerous, says Ulrich." The mustachioed gallery owner was interpreting. "Others are more difficult. But it becomes the most dangerous because there are so many people. Some days there are 100 climbers. They drag their ropes around, and this loosens rock. If there are not so many people, it is not so dangerous."

Paying for the postcard he'd inscribed for me, I told him it sounded like climbing a highway.

"*Ja – Matterhorn Autobahn*," chuckled Ulrich.

That evening, I visited Zermatt's little cemetery, down by the Mattervispa River, where flames in orange votive candles danced on the gravestones. It was true, the Alps had long since lost their mystique. In the summer climbing season, dozens of people might summit the Matterhorn in a single day. Grandmothers have made it to the top, and musicians have played concerts on the peak. Still, the Matterhorn is a deadly mountain, provoking 20 deaths in a bad year. In the last couple of weeks alone, two Japanese men had been killed 180 metres from the summit, and a 58-year-old British woman had fallen to her death on an icefield. The cemetery was filled with mountaineering monuments: a Cambridge man "killed by a fall on the Riffelhorn"; a pair of Spaniards "*desaparecidos en el Monte Cervino*"; two Germans "*Gefallen Am Matterhorn*" on the eve of the Second World War. A monument commemorated Hadow and Hudson, Whymper's ill-fated companions.

I paused, surprised, before the memorial to Donald Stephen Williams, from New York City. An orange ice axe was affixed to the grave below the lapidary declaration: "I chose to Climb." I was more impressed by his place of death, however: "23 July 1975," the inscription read, "on Breithorn."

Wait a minute: people die on Breithorn? Wasn't it supposed to be the easiest of the 4,000-metre summits? That's why I'd declined to pay the 30 Swiss francs for an insurance policy at the Alpin Centre, deeming the need for a helicopter rescue unlikely.

That night I slept poorly in my attic room, kept awake by a sore on my foot where my rented boot had peeled a patch of skin off my ankle, and dreamed about becoming another *Bergtod*, a mountain corpse. When I awoke before sunrise, I saw that the face of the Matterhorn was already illuminated, a buccaneer's sail billowing over the dark streets of the sleeping town. I shivered in my thin summer pants as I approached the gondola station and introduced myself to Ricki, a tall, taciturn man in his late 20s, with sunscreen spread unevenly over his nose. (I would learn he was the son of Richard Lehner, a famous mountain guide who had climbed the Matterhorn 600 times). His sister, Maya, and his girlfriend, Yvette, a good-natured French-speaking woman from a nearby valley, were coming along "for the fun of it." We rode two gondolas, picking up a pair of Germans, with white beards and brand-new polar fleece jackets and ski poles, at the second station. On the third and last gondola – the highest in Europe – I struggled silently with vertigo, as the car seemed to rake the sheer bare rock of the Klein Matterhorn.

We passed down a long tunnel and emerged squinting onto a snowy plain in dazzling sunlight. Yvette looked surprised by all the skiers and snowboarders. I asked if this was unusual.

"No," she said. "It's just that, I say to myself, we've got enough winter here, why go skiing in the summer?"

"You're a little underdressed," muttered Ricki, cinching the harness around my pants. "It is going to be maybe minus 5 degrees on the mountain. But we won't stay long." Bound together, we began a slow, single-file march across a vast field of névé, granular snow that hadn't yet hardened into glacier ice. Ahead of us, the rounded summit of the Breithorn rose from the plain, and I could see lines of climbers strung out in zigzags along its face, calling to mind the photos of would-be miners scaling peaks in the Klondike gold rush. Just before the slope started in earnest, we strapped crampons onto our boots, and I heard Ricki offering advice to the group of Asians next to him.

"You speak Japanese?" I asked, surprised.

"You have to in Zermatt!"

The ascent began in earnest. I had to concentrate to keep my crampons from catching the rope dangling from the waist of the German man before me. Everybody was silent, planting one foot in the firm, crusty snow, lifting the other, moving up in increments. After a switchback, we took a more intense angle upwards, finally coming to a ledge beneath the ridge that led to the summit.

"Kodak-Stop!" said one of the German men, who paused to document the ascent. We followed a narrow, wind-blasted ridge, and I looked with dismay to my right, where the mountain slipped away in a vertiginous incline, plunging towards a glacier hundreds of metres below.

"Put your feet wide!" Ricki yelled back at us. "Don't let your crampons get caught in the ropes!" I stared at the ground ahead of me, banishing the drop from my peripheral vision. Finally, we stepped down from the narrow ridge and approached the slightly flattened peak. We had made it to the top. We exchanged handshakes, and Yvette planted three kisses on my cheeks. One of the Germans pulled out a video camera and filmed his friend, providing a dramatic, reality-show-style voice-over for the benefit of the microphone, in which I could make out the words *"Breithorn"* and *"4,160 Metre."*

The wind was fierce, and two more groups of tethered climbers were approaching, so Ricki motioned for us to move to a lower, broader ridge on the lee side. The view was a panorama of Alpine peaks, dominated by Monte Rosa to the east, soaring above the snow, and the Matterhorn and its smaller parody, the Klein Matterhorn, in the foreground. Yvette pulled out her cellphone and showed me its digital display: it read "Telecom Italia." Breithorn straddles the Swiss-Italian border, and I could see the green valleys and the smaller peaks of the Ligurian Alps on the other side of the ridge. The Germans gestured at me to lean backwards, as I was interfering with their panning shot of the twin peaks of Castor and Pollux.

The great Alpinist Frank S. Smyth took in the same view in 1946, gazing over the peaks he'd spent his career climbing. "Treading that snow slope," he wrote in *Again Switzerland*, "was like treading the snow-covered roof of the highest building in the city, and seeing beneath thousands of other roofs extending as far as the eye could travel . . . views such as this are meant not for men but gods." He couldn't resist a little Anglo-Saxon chauvinism, admitting to relief that a group of Italians he'd met on the névé field hadn't followed them. "We were thus enabled to enjoy a prospect unalloyed by the presence of our fellow men. This may sound an ungenerous statement, but not where Italians are concerned, since this race is incapable of any form of restful meditation either on or off a mountain, and must needs jabber at all hours of the day and night."

Smyth would have been appalled at the scene before me: a dozen or so groups of day trippers were roped together – including a boy not older than ten and a woman in her 60s – jabbering in a whole range of Asian and European tongues. There were at least 60 other climbers on the peak. A couple of hundred metres below us, a helicopter hovered over the snowfield.

Then I saw an apparition. A man wearing sports shoes and leotards, and carrying two ski poles, seemed to *run* up to the summit. He hurried

past us, then disappeared over the edge of the mountain, back towards
the névé. I got up and looked over the edge: he was descending – straight
down – the face we'd just spent a laborious hour climbing up in a zigzag
approach.

"I think he's part of the Skyrunning Championships," Yvette said.
"They are extreme athletes – they have to run up mountains as part of
their marathon."

As we started back down, Yvette and Maya leading the way, we saw
that the helicopter was filming a race. Runners with fluorescent Fila and
Vibram jerseys cut across our serpentine path, climbing vertically at an
absurd pace. As we paused to take off our crampons, a pack of runners
rushed past.

"These people," muttered Yvette. "I think they will have problems with
their health in ten years." The athletes looked muscular but cadaverous,
sleek and sexless, as though shedding their body fat had somehow
shrunken their gonads, giving them an unattractive androgynous intensity. I mentioned to Yvette that they looked like wealthy executives.

"Yes, yuppies!" she said. "The extremes, all the extremes, there is
something *malsain* – how do you say it, unhealthy – about them. I think
there is a hole, something missing in the lives of these people."

We started off across the snowfield. Ricki, silent, seemed pissed off
about these foreign athletes on his turf. We followed the path we'd taken
up, and every few minutes a runner passed us, red-faced and unsmiling.
One came by shirtless, and Maya's head swivelled to follow him.

"*Domani – rosso!*" she said to Yvette. Given the intensity of the sun's
rays at this altitude, tomorrow he'd be beet red.

We heard a man's voice behind us: "*Pista!*" – Italian for "Give way."
Ricki kept on course, and a fellow made mostly of bundled muscles rushed
past us, cursing. As he passed our roped team he pushed first me, then
Maya, almost knocking us to the ground.

"*Va funculo!*" I shouted at him, using up 5 percent of my Italian
vocabulary.

"*Ils sont fous!*" said Yvette, twirling a finger by her temple.

After walking back to the gondola station, we unharnessed, said goodbye to the German men (who were already reviewing their documentary),

and sat down for coffee at a place called the Terminus Café. Yvette's work at an emergency response centre, where she fielded up to 500 calls a day, had her deciding whether to send helicopters or rescue teams to save tourists who had gone astray. They'd recently had to rescue four snowboarders who had gone off-track and fallen into a crevasse. I asked her about the men who had died on the Matterhorn last week.

"A German and a Spanish. But you know, there is more than the Matterhorn around here. There are dozens of mountains. And people go without guides. Then they get into trouble, and we have to send a helicopter. And when a helicopter can't go in, people like Ricki risk their lives to go and save them – or find their corpses."

Ricki introduced me to Rudi, a colleague at the next table.

"You a guide?" I asked.

"Yes," he replied.

"Hi," I said. "I'm a tourist."

Rudi laughed. "But you aren't a *bad* tourist. We have some . . ." he said, shaking his head. "I had a group of five Japanese the other day, for example. It took us five hours to go up Breithorn! You could go up faster crawling." When they started swapping horror stories about clients in Swiss German, I took the hint, said goodbye, and hopped the relay of gondolas back to Zermatt.

I couldn't shake the memory of the extreme athlete's shove, which lingered in my body for the rest of the day. On the Internet, I looked up the race we'd seen that afternoon: the Sky Marathon had competitors from 22 nations running 42 kilometres across moraine and glaciers with an elevation gain of 2,600 metres, for prizes of $50,000.

Yvette had been right: too many people had holes in their lives, and they travelled absurd distances to undertake ludicrous challenges rather than mustering the courage to stare into their personal abyss. Whatever sense of sportsmanship and high ideals had existed in the time of the explorers and early Alpinists, they have perished in our age of steroids, mass tourism, and mindless competitiveness. For me, the most disturbing thing was the adventurers' sense of entitlement and arrogance. The first English mountaineers had dismissed beliefs about Alpine dragons and bribed locals into guiding them up forbidden peaks. The French are notorious travel imperialists, letting their beards grow as they grip the wheels of cigarette-company-sponsored all-terrain vehicles, knocking over stray children and village wells in their heroic "raids" of West Africa. A famous American expedition to Mexico's Huautla ignored Mazatec beliefs about the sanctity of underground burial sites in order to be the first to explore the world's deepest cave system.

The core of my own travel addiction, I was beginning to understand, was a constant sloughing of a calcified identity – a refusal of routine that produced an illusory sense of eternal youth – intensified by the kinetic rush of motion and the novelty of new experiences. Compressed in foreign streetcars and subways, where every gesture was a new code to be broken and even figuring out how to buy a ticket was an adventure in semiotics, I felt as alive and wide-eyed as when I was a kid taking my first solo bus ride downtown. It was the side effects that justified the addiction: jostled and upturned by exposure to new turns of phrase and thought, I could imagine the world through the eyes of the Vietnamese rice farmer, the Colombian documentary filmmaker, the Muslim teenager in the Parisian suburbs.

Though I certainly had my own holes to fill, my reasons for hitting the road seemed mostly positive. My most successful trips involved exchange and discovery, not self-glorification, patriotic swaggering, and consumption.

The exponents of extreme travel, I'd been convinced, weren't travelling at all. For them, foreign lands were just far-flung theatres for staging dimly perceived psychodramas. Hence the continuing attraction of mountain summits, war zones, Arctic islands, desert sands, and Alpine peaks-turned-jogging tracks – all the blasted and barren places from which the troubling complexity of human affairs are banished.

Chapter 6

THE GRAND RUT

*Sir Fopling Flutter Does Europe – All You Need Is Let's Go and a Railpass –
The Flying Pig, the Love Parade, and Cheap Beer in Prague – The Original
Grand Tourists – Travel Panic in the Milan Train Station – Too Much
Garlick – Discussing the McPink at Fawlty Towers – The First Travel
Ghetto – Goethe Gets Laid – Cruising for Backpackers on the Spanish Steps
– A Disgraceful Pub Crawl to the Campo dei Fiori – Bubbled and Poxed by
the Neapolitans – Il Gabinetto degli oggetti osceni – How to Cook Canned
Spaghetti – Byron Got It Right*

Travel is an orgy. The sideways glance in the terminal lounge, the
memory of an airplane bathroom sex scene in a French soft porn film, the
woman in fishnet stockings in the row ahead. The suspense, as the express
pulls into the station, over whether some svelte Anna Karenina or suave
Dr. Zhivago will burst into the compartment. The bronzed Lotharios in
bulging Speedos swaggering past pale northern Shirley Valentines. The
Swiss chambermaid with the charming blush, the Venetian gondolier with
the bold stare, the worldly Turkish tour guide who can set you up with a
belly dancer for a little baksheesh. Suzie Wong is looking for a new
boyfriend this week, and the almond-eyed Algerian houseboy wants to take
the man with the green carnation in his lapel to a special bathhouse in the
souk. Friends, family, the one you left behind can't possibly know how free
and easy things are here. Besides – *You'll never see these people again.*

The subtext of sex was permanently inscribed into the tradition of
travel with the Grand Tour, an 18th-century ritual in which packs of British
fops and dandies, most of them still in their teens, went whoring and
gambling through the Continent under the guise of completing their

educations. Accompanied by their tutors, or "bear-leaders," barely post-pubescent dukes and baronets would run riot through Paris, Venice, and Naples, bringing home counterfeit Canalettos, a half-dozen phrases of unidiomatic Italian, and doses of clap as souvenirs. Sir Fopling Flutter and Lord Macaroni, wearing the tight waistcoats and powdered wigs some *perruquier* had overcharged them for in Paris, were roundly mocked for cluttering English coffee houses abroad and affecting effeminate Continental manners at home. Yet, by jingling the silver in their satin breeches loudly and often enough, they forged the template of European travel, creating a network of foreigner-friendly inns and restaurants that has served as the prototypical tourist rut ever since.

The Grand Tour of Europe still takes place. It is now dominated by middle-class Americans, Australians, New Zealanders, and Canadians, typically with a year or two of college behind them. The 21st-century version wends its way from Amsterdam to Prague by way of Venice and Corfu, its boundaries determined only by the restrictions of Inter-rail and Eurail passes. It is a rite of passage approved, and usually bankrolled, by parents who wish their offspring to have some exposure to European culture. Its ostensible objects are the same: rounding out one's education, seeking enlightenment in the galleries and theatres of foreign capitals. Its actual goals, now as then, are binge-drinking, unsupervised sex, and boisterous partying – usually in the company of one's fellow travellers, rather than actual Europeans.

It was easy enough to join this circuit. All I had to do was find the local hostel, which in Zermatt was a wooden building hung with American, Japanese, and Australian flags, its porch cluttered with fluorescent backpacks. Walking down the narrow staircase, I inspected the accommodations: metal-framed twin bunkbeds were spread with grey wool blankets and wedged four to a room next to changing-room lockers.

By a pay phone, I picked up pamphlets for other hostels on the circuit – the Amphora in Istanbul, the Best in Budapest, the Funny Farm in Interlaken – just as a tall guy who'd been calling his parents was hanging up. I noticed his paperback edition of James Joyce.

"Molly Bloom keeping you company?" I asked.

"Oh – have you read *Ulysses*?" he asked. "I haven't got to her monologue yet, actually." He introduced himself as Thomas, from Arizona. The wispy blond hair on his high forehead, already thinning, made him look older than his 21 years.

"I'm carrying about ten books in my backpack," he said. "If you're looking for something to read, you should take a look. They're breaking my back." I told him I could definitely use a good book. "My brother and I are going out for dinner in a couple of hours. Want to come?" We agreed to meet at a restaurant near the Catholic church.

I had a hunch about the Café du Pont. Before leaving home, I'd armed myself with the two items essential for a modern-day Grand Tour: a European railpass – mine offered five separate days of travel, though most backpackers I'd met had the more expensive month-long version, good for unlimited trips – and the latest edition of *Let's Go: Europe*. Created in 1960 as a mimeographed pamphlet handed to Harvard students on student charter flights to Europe, it was now the world's best-selling travel guide, a 955-page backpacker's bible, listing countries from Andorra to Yugoslavia.

The original Grand Tourists had packed Thomas Nugent's *Grand Tour*, published in 1749, a four-tome guidebook that served as an earnest catalogue of the major buildings and sights of Europe. (Many undoubtedly preferred the rival *Gentleman's Pocket Companion for Travelling into Foreign Parts*, whose phrasebook gave a model dialogue on luring German, French, or Italian chambermaids into one's bedroom.) Short of reading material, I'd flipped through *Let's Go* and couldn't help noticing a certain bibulous editorial slant. On the Greek island of Ios: "It's your mother's worst nightmare – people swilling from wine bottles at 3 p.m., condoms scattered on dirt roads, people dancing naked in bars." On a Dublin distillery tour: "If you're lucky, you'll be selected to be an 'Irish Whiskey Taster' . . . Sure, the certificate is nice, but the haze is even better." Before a list of Czech bars: "The most authentic way to enjoy Prague at night is through an alcoholic fog." The restaurant Thomas had picked was one of the two recommended in the half page that *Let's Go* devoted to Zermatt.

The Café du Pont looked like a Swiss mountain eatery should, all rough wood panelling and long benches, but the people hunkered around the tables were college-aged, and they were all speaking American-accented

English. I was introduced to Alan, bespectacled and acne-corrugated, and Thomas's brother, Philip, brown-haired, a year younger, who seemed the most adventurous member of the trio. Philip went to Northwestern, in Chicago, and Thomas had graduated from Harvard, with a degree in computer science. Alan, a member of a mountaineering club at Harvard, had talked the brothers into coming to Zermatt, but they were already thinking of moving on. Thomas made the case for Interlaken and Paris, while Philip argued for the upcoming Love Parade in Berlin. A yearly DJ-and-dance party, the Love Parade sees blaring tractor-trailers snaking towards the Brandenburg Gate on a Saturday afternoon, and was described, in a half-page screened box in *Let's Go*, as an "annual techno Woodstock, the world's only million-man rave." It was clearly a highlight of the modern Grand Tour.

"If we had somewhere to sleep, then maybe you could convince me," said Thomas. "There's going to be like 1.5 million people walking through town. I don't want to sleep in the park."

"It's summer," I chided, "and the Tiergarten is pretty big. Couldn't you guys just find a secluded place there?"

"We should just buy hammocks!" Philip said. He tempered his enthusiasm with entrepreneurship: "We should *buy* used hammocks here and *sell* them in Berlin at a mark-up!"

"Why don't you guys just take ecstasy and stay up for the whole weekend?" I asked, playing the devil's advocate. That would have been my solution when I was 20.

"Yeah, right," said Thomas, dismissing my suggestion. "Maybe we could book rooms at the Ritz," he mumbled. "I'm sure it isn't going to be full."

"You're right, Thomas," conceded Philip, "we shouldn't sleep in a park. I remember in Vienna there was some talk about the effect that millions of gallons of piss would have on the plants in the parks there. Can you imagine? With all the beer the Germans drink? We'd be swimming in it."

We moved on to the Post Hotel, a giant après-ski complex with a basement disco full of teens in glitter makeup, where signs offered "Mad Cow Vodka Jellys" for five francs a pop. As we sat on stools made of wooden beer barrels, I asked them where else they'd gone in Europe.

"We just came up from Venice, Cinque Terre, Florence, and Rome," said Philip. "I hated Rome! Hot, crowded, and smelly. We were in the subway, and I felt someone brush up against my leg. Dude had his hand in my cargo pants! I thought he had my wallet, so I chased him through the station, but it turned out I'd scared him off before he could grab it."

They were sarcastic about Holland. "I think going to Amsterdam has made me even less of a libertarian," said Thomas. "All those hippies sitting around smoking in coffee shops. What a waste of a life." Predictable attitude, I thought, from a guy whose father was paying his $30,000-a-year tuition. Their favourite stop, bar none, had been Prague.

"You could get a meal there for four dollars, a beer for 50 cents," said Philip. "It's ruined us for everywhere else." Thomas would be heading back home soon, to start a job with a Web-based bookshop in Seattle. Back at the hostel, he offered me a Milan Kundera novel he'd picked up in Prague. And then, violating the most basic backpacking ethos of barter and exchange, he charged me ten Swiss francs for it.

I told him to stay out of trouble. Though, judging from his attitude, trouble wouldn't be an issue.

§

The earliest Grand Tourists were also spies. In a Europe divided into Popish and Protestant zones, akin to the Communist Bloc and Free World of the Cold War, Elizabethan travellers were expected to note the dimensions of battlements and make discreet enquiries about armories, arsenals, and the size of armies. On his 1591 tour, Fynes Moryson, granted £20 a year by the queen to study the laws of the Continent, narrowly missed capture by pirates from Dunkirk, disguised himself as a poor Bohemian to foil freebooters in Holland, travelled from Rome to Naples with 60 musketeers to ward off *banditti*, and was finally robbed by disbanded soldiers in France.

Thomas Coryate, a parson's son and buffoonish courtier, financed a 1608 trip to Venice by making a bet at seven-to-two odds on his safe return, and roamed through France, Switzerland, and Germany documenting executions and corpses rotting on gallows before triumphantly returning to introduce the English to the fork and the umbrella.

The "Grand Tour" – a term coined in 1670 in Richard Lassels's *Voyage of Italy* – became an institution in the 1700s, when fear of the Inquisition and religious conflicts had abated enough for a Continental sojourn to be seen as an ideal finishing school for aristocrats. Europe, formerly the proving ground for the venturesome and ambitious, became the stomping ground for impudent lordlings stoked with their daddies' letters of credit.

The real heyday of the tour was from 1763, the end of the Seven Years War, to the beginning of the Napoleonic Wars. In the decade preceding the French Revolution, an estimated 40,000 Englishmen came to the Continent each year, with 3,760 pouring into Paris in one six-week period alone. They were young – the average age of the Grand Tourists was 18, and few were older than 21. They were rich – they typically spent £300 a year on their travels, at a time when the average wage in England was a pound a month. And, from all evidence, they were elitist, chauvinistic little sots.

Lady Mary Wortley Montagu, a worldly diplomat's widow who had explored the bathhouses of Constantinople, watched in consternation as the Grand Tourists overran her adopted Italy. "Their whole business abroad," she wrote a friend from Venice, "being to buy new cloaths, in which they shine in some obscure coffee-house; and after the important conquest of some waiting gentlewoman of an opera Queen, who perhaps they remember as long as they live, return to England excellent judges of men and manners . . . I look on them as the greatest blockheads in nature."

Save for a few celebrities such as Thomas Hobbes, Joseph Addison, and Adam Smith, their tutors were typically ineffectual clergymen, known for losing control of their charges as soon as they trundled them within eyeshot of a tavern or brothel. One disgusted bear-leader, John Moore, recounts how a Grand Tourist, realizing it was time to go home after lollygagging around Rome for months, hired a post-chaise and in only two days whipped through a checklist of sights it had taken Moore six weeks to show his own young charge.

"The grand object of travelling is to see the shores of the Mediterranean," Samuel Johnson once proclaimed, and most English fops, hearing tales of loose ladies and free manners, didn't have to be told twice. Typically, their tour began with a carriage ride from London to Dover, where, on a good day, the trip across the Channel could take as little as three hours. In bad weather, they might have to wait a week in a local inn before they could cross; if the tide was out at Calais, they'd have to be carried ashore by "watermen" in rowboats. Once customs officials had searched their pockets for contraband, they'd be written a passport for travel through France. (Modern passports, issued by the traveller's country of origin, didn't come into widespread use until the First World War.) The wealthiest Grand Tourists brought their own carriages from London, and hired horses at post houses, strung along the road at intervals of about six miles, which often offered lodgings as well as stables.

Most Tourists travelled in shared carriages: the six-passenger *carrose*, the 16-passenger *coche*, or the faster 30-passenger *diligence* – bone-rattlers whatever their size. In Paris, they bought powdered wigs and velvet suits and shopped and gambled in the arcades of the Palais Royal; often, they were lured into the company of a painted lady by some crooked chevalier and fleeced at cards. After side trips to Fontainebleau and Versailles, they headed for Lyons, where innkeepers justified their high prices by obsequiously dubbing them *grands seigneurs* and "milords," no matter what their rank.

From there it was on to Switzerland, where many importuned poor Voltaire – an early victim of the human zoo phenomenon – who once complained to a crowd of gaping Tourists: "Well, gentleman, you now see me. Did you take me for a wild beast or monster that was fit only to be stared at as a show?" Those with carriages had them stored or dismantled and carried across the Alps, but most hired sedan chairs mounted on long poles and were carried across the Mount Cenis pass by porters in nailed boots.

Once in Turin, their first major Italian town, they would bargain with a *vetturino*, a kind of package-tour guide, for transport. Arranging all transport and lodgings for a fixed sum, he often skimped on hotels and meals to pocket more profit for himself. Milan, Bologna, and Florence might be stops on the way, but Rome and Naples were the climaxes of the tour. From there, the traveller turned around and headed home through Germany and the Low Countries.

That, in outline, was the Grand Tour. Individual Tourists, of course, took different routes. The 22-year-old James Boswell, dogged by scolding letters from his strict Presbyterian father, in 1763 set out for ten months of study in Holland, before spectacularly busting loose from discipline, having his wallet lifted by streetwalkers in Dresden, picking up a dose of venereal disease in Florence, and seducing Jean-Jacques Rousseau's mistress in Paris.

Some travellers, like Tobias Smollett – at 43, a decidedly over-the-hill Grand Tourist – made for the south of France, sojourning in Montpellier and Nice before following the coastal route to Italy. Few went north of Hamburg, east of Prague, or south of the Pyrenees. Individual tours could last six months to four years, with Boswell's two-and-a-half year circuit falling close to the average. Packing for such a trip was no light undertaking: contemporary guidebooks recommended waterproof buckskin breeches, a dozen strong shirts, an inflatable bath with bellows, and such sundries as a pocket inkstand, a tinder-box, and a tea caddy. Optional was the Claude glass, a smoked, convex mirror with which the artistically inclined Tourist, his back turned to the countryside, could regard the scene in a sombre, wide-angle reflection that called to mind the idealized landscapes of French painter Claude Lorraine.

§

In Zermatt, I hopped a train for Italy. Changing in Milan, I strolled around the cavernous station late in the morning, noting the scowling eagles, SPQR symbols, and medallions commemorating Work and Commerce on the facade – Mussolini's enduring stone testament to that decade the Italian trains ran on time. In the bathrooms, I wondered why there were office-cubicle-length partitions between the urinals until I saw a bald man leering at me from an open toilet stall as he flayed something ornery in his sagging trousers. Retreating to the waiting room, I killed an hour cataloguing the possessions of latter-day Grand Tourists. Since I'd first travelled by rail in the mid-1980s, there were fewer guitars to be seen, but more technology. A guy in a white T-shirt and shorts was eviscerating his backpack on some plastic chairs, in the grips of that all-too-familiar syndrome: travel panic.

"Shit, man," he said to his girlfriend, pulling out three pairs of dirty jockey shorts. "I knew we shouldn't have left our bags at the hostel. That guy with the dreads was totally scoping them out."

He wrenched a John Grisham paperback out of a side flap, followed by a hacky sack and a Ziploc bag full of coins. The main compartment of the bag yielded Tommy Hilfiger shirts, a digital camera, a Discman, a Frisbee, and a Leatherman tool. Reaching arm deep into the bag, he emerged with a *Let's Go* guide and flipped through the pages.

"Shit shit shit!" he yelled, red-faced. "Now I'm going to have to wait like three weeks until the embassy gives me a new one!"

His girlfriend, unfazed, patted the side of his shorts. "Did you look in there?"

He unsnapped the pocket, and pulled forth an American passport. "That's like, *so* weird! I *never* keep it there!"

I had to sympathize: I've often started the morning in a dither, turning a hotel room upside down in search of a key that I find, half an hour later, stuck in the door.

My compartment was occupied by three Asian men in their early 20s, all wearing glasses, all in white chinos. One of them, in a yellow sweatshirt that read "California," spoke some English, and told me they'd been travelling for two weeks in Switzerland and were making a brief side trip to Rome before going back to Korea. This seemed typical of young Asians in Europe: hampered by exchange rates, short vacations, and the demands of jobs or school, they tended to roam for only a few weeks. American Tourists travelled for up to two months, but, for a nation of 285 million, they were surprisingly underrepresented in Europe (bolstering reports that only 17 percent of Americans actually have a passport). For the English, Europe had been a near-suburb since the mid-19th century, and they now went to Paris or Amsterdam for the weekend, by fast ferry, cut-rate airline, or Channel Tunnel, saving their Grand Tours for Asia. Canadians, maple leaf flags stitched to their backpacks, tended to travel a few weeks longer than the Americans. These days, only the Australians, South Africans, and New Zealanders consistently made a European Grand Tour worthy of the name – presumably to get the most, after their long and expensive flights, out of what might be a once-in-a-lifetime experience.

The same *carpe diem* rationale had made the young lords of the 1760s into privileged Goths, desperate to sow their oats. At once arrogant and insecure, they approached the Continental experience with the same mix of paranoia, hyperbole, and self-consciousness that is the hallmark of much British travel writing. William James once described a man who, convinced he'd written down the secret of the universe while ripped on nitrous oxide, awoke from his debauch to find he'd scrawled, "A smell of petroleum prevails throughout." For early British travellers, the smell that permeated Europe was not gas, but garlic. "I hate the French cookery," bitched Smollett, "and the abominable garlick, with which all the ragouts, in this part of the country, are highly seasoned." William Hazlitt called Rome "an almost uninterrupted succession of narrow, vulgar-looking streets, where the smell of garlick prevails over the odour of antiquity." Even Shelley, in open revolt against English society, betrayed a parochial streak: "What do you think?" he reported from Italy. "Young women of rank actually eat – you will never guess what – garlick!" The mock-aristocratic attitude was so ingrained in English culture that, even in the 1990s, the Britpacking authors of *Don't Lean out the Window*, a teenage travelogue about the Inter-rail experience, would describe a "Froggy" seat-mate as being "clearly of garlic descent," and dismiss a woman on the *croisette* in Cannes as a "cheeky bloody peasant."

Approaching Rome, our train slowly rolled into thickening clusters of satellite-dish-encrusted housing projects. A Grand Tourist in the 18th century would have arrived by coach, probably in the company of a half dozen other giggling fops, to be deposited in the Piazza del Popolo – the northernmost point in Rome at the time – where he would have found goats grazing at the base of the phallic Egyptian obelisk erected by Pope Sixtus V. Giddy with the Eternal City's erotic promise, he would have hired a cab and slipped between the bulging breasts of the twin-domed Santa Maria churches, penetrating the spread legs of the Via di Ripetta and the Via del Babuino by the tight labial opening of the Corso. Casting nervous glances down the side-alleys where the prostitutes worked, he would have checked into an *albergo* and later – what a coincidence! – run into one of his fellow travellers, freshly powdered and ready for revelry, on the streets of the world's first English tourist ghetto.

My train arrived in Termini, a vast station near one of the old city gates. By the metro entrance, middle-aged men with a feral look and sloppily photocopied badges that said "Rome Travel Assistance" tried to inveigle me into following them to their hotels, but I already knew exactly where I was going. On the train, I'd opened *Let's Go* and picked their first listing.

"Pensione Fawlty Towers. Fabulous! Co-ed dorm style quads. No curfew; night keys available." Perfect.

A block away, I entered the foyer of what looked like a residential apartment building. A plaque on the elevator cage read: "1° Casa Cicconi; 3° Marco Polo; 4° Sileo; 5° Fawlty Towors" – a homage, perhaps, to its namesake's chronically misspelled sign. Swivelling out of a tiny elevator on the top floor, I was admitted with a buzz.

"I think you have some luck," said the black-haired Finnish girl at the desk, looking through her registry sheet. "Somebody just left." As she wrote down my passport details, a backpacker with a pony tail and shorts bustled in, red-faced and panting, and dropped his *Let's Go* on the counter.

"Tell me you have a bed for tonight!" he implored.

"No, we are now full," the girl said, nodding at me. She recommended their sister hotel on the other side of the station.

"Is it good?" the backpacker asked. "I mean, is it a party place? I want to have fun tonight." The Finnish girl shrugged, and he shouldered his backpack and disappeared.

The hostel called to mind a Greek society house inhabited by foreign-exchange students. Bulletin boards were covered with tips on mailing packages home from the Vatican post office and catching ferries to Greece. I sat on the collapsed springs of a sofa in a rec room, where an amateurish mural showed a liberal adaptation of Klimt's *The Kiss* against a backdrop of the Colosseum and the Pantheon. The guestbook was open on a table. "Thanks for being the best bloody hostel in Italy!" one client had written, "and introducing me to not one, not two, but *three* hot Australian travelers!" Andie of San Francisco had gushed: "Thanks for a great Christmas, with microwave lasagna, chair-dancing cobra, and lots o' cheap wine. I had a blast."

While the original Grand Tourists stayed at the Prince of Orange in Calais, the Queen's Head in Amsterdam, and Charles Hadfield's popular inn in Florence, today's backpackers congregated at the Generator in London, the Flying Pig in Amsterdam, the Boathouse in Prague, and Wombats in Vienna. (Hard-core railpass travellers opted to forgo hostels altogether, saving room fees by sleeping in the trains.) I sat down at one of the three plastic tables on the rooftop terrace, next to a young man with long hair and braces on his teeth, acne half-hidden by a goatee, who was sucking up some microwaved noodles.

"*Buon appetito*," I said.

"They're just Ramen noodles, dude," he said. Another guy offered me a piece of cheese pizza he'd cut with a Swiss Army knife splayed on the table like a spider crab. He introduced himself as Trevor, from Nebraska. Pudgy and soft-spoken, he'd saved enough working two jobs after high school for a one-month tour of Europe. The noodle-eater, wearing knee-length orange shorts and runners without socks, was Mike, from Louisiana, who'd just come to Rome from Germany (which he insisted on calling "Deutschland"). Neither could have been older than 20. As we talked, Stephanie, who was going to university in Virginia, sat down and lit a cigarette. She'd been studying art in Florence for the summer and was showing her mother – a primary school teacher who lived in Bolivia – around Rome. She was bright and unconventional, and had done a fair amount of travelling in her 20 years.

Looking at the food spread on the table – pre-packaged luncheon meat bought from a supermarket, a bottle of porcelain-capped Fisher beer ("I only drink Deutsch beer now, dude," Mike explained), and a jar of Nutella next to some white bread – I asked if they'd discovered any good Italian food.

"This salami's good," said Mike, laconically.

"I went to McDonald's the other day," said Trevor, "and they have this thing called McPink. I think it's pork."

"I can't believe you come to Italy and go to McDonald's!" said Stephanie.

Trevor looked sheepish. "Well, it's cheap. And I really like their hamburgers."

Stephanie conceded that, in Florence, McDonald's had espresso machines and salad. A discussion of American fast food chains ensued, with Trevor favouring Denny's.

"In the South, white people don't go into Denny's, dude," drawled Mike. "I don't know if y'all have them up north, but we go to Waffle House in Louisiana. If we're on the highway at four in the morning, we see a Waffle House on the other side of the road – oh yeah! – you just *know* we're going to turn around. Bottomless cup of coffee, some golden-brown hash-browns, a couple of pecan waffles . . . that's serious good eating." He then did a spirited exegesis on the uncensored Deutsch-language lyrics of a death metal band.

I commented on the *Frommer's* guide Trevor had hidden beneath a pile of postcards.

"My parents gave it to me," he said. "I can't really afford any of the hotels they write about."

"Dude," said Mike, picking a salami rind from his braces, "you totally have to get *Let's Go*." He pulled a copy from his bag. "This is like my *bible*. Without it, I'd totally be lost."

What about competing series, like the *Rough Guide* or *Lonely Planet*? "No way," he said. "For me, *Lonely Planet* is the dark side of Europe. All those coffee shops in Amsterdam and raves they're talking about. I just stick with my good ol' *Let's Go* – they always tell you where to find the best brew."

Where was he headed next? "Back to Deutschland. But I'm going to stop in Interlaken. I'm going to do some serious paragliding. I hear they've got this 800-metre bungee cord there. I've never bungeed before – but when I start, I want it to be the best."

Christ, I thought, hitting the streets in search of a plate of agnolotti, had I ever been that age? My predicament – stuck with people 15 years younger than myself – was self-inflicted, but I found it exasperating to be in the Italian capital discussing the merits of the McPink. When I'd done my own European tour, I'd made a point of avoiding fast food joints and fellow travellers. I came to Europe for the third time when I was 22, after graduating from university. I flew to London one-way, using a ticket I'd bought, through a classified ad, from an emigrating Frenchwoman. I took a boat-train to Berlin, where I crashed with an artist friend, and got tear-gassed the next morning in the annual May Day riot in Kreuzberg. The Berlin Wall had just fallen – in fact, it was still pretty much intact, though being eroded by chisel blows every day – and I crossed the border into a zone free of billboards, where the department store shelves were empty and I could afford to eat in the grandest hotel restaurants. I made a drunken side trip to Prague, quaffing vodka and Pilsner in the train with my artist friend, and saw Václav Havel addressing a crowd of thousands in Wenceslas Square.

I eventually took a bus to Paris, where I stayed for four years. My personal Grand Tour of the Continent went completely off the rails of traditional travel and ended with a debauched expatriation. For all its negatives – the poverty, drugs, and aimlessness – it also left me with a raft of positive experiences. I gained a command of gutter French, roamed Paris so obsessively that I came to know every street in the city, and returned with a lifelong, ever-deepening appreciation of another culture. In comparison, all my previous travel experiences had been mere sightseeing.

Of course, expatriation wasn't supposed to be the fate of the good Tourist. The classical Grand Tour was a circular experience: the traveller left wet-behind-the-ears and returned competent in several European tongues, capable of discoursing on Italian landscape painting, stylishly clad but with a reinforced appreciation for the values of his homeland. Nugent's guidebook summed up the Tour's goals: "To enrich the mind with knowledge, to rectify the judgement, to remove the prejudices of education, to compose the outward manners, and in a word to form the complete gentleman."

Tourists were expected to carry notebooks and sketchpads, and a good tutor encouraged fencing and French lessons. Some European travellers really did make a point of broadening their minds: Boswell charmed his way into interviews with Jean-Jacques Rousseau and Voltaire and signed up for a six-day course in Antiquities and Arts in Rome. Goethe, arriving in Italy, reminded himself: "I am not here to enjoy myself after my own fashion, but to busy myself with the great objects around, to learn, and to improve myself, ere I am forty years old."

Italy usually proved too much for their resolutions. Goethe took up with Faustina, the daughter of a Roman innkeeper – his first documented sexual experience – and Boswell resolved to have a woman every day he was in Rome. In Switzerland, he had promised a servant girl he would take her and her children back with him to Scotland, and in Siena he had an affair with a noblewoman stuck in a loveless marriage. As he left her, she poignantly complained to him, "You go to greater and greater happiness, but you leave me here to go continually from bad to worse." Love 'em and leave 'em – from Cuba to Thailand, it's the classic refrain of the rakish traveller, pockets heavy with hard currency, for whom the next town and the next local girl always beckon. Boswell pardoned himself by concluding that, in Italy, "women are so debauched that they are hardly to be considered as moral agents, but as inferior beings." Many English travellers preferred the company of men. The *bardassi*, or "buggered boys," were notorious at the Italian universities of Padua and Bologna, and Venice's gondoliers had a penchant for sleeping with all comers – as Truman Capote and Cole Porter would discover three centuries later.

I spent the sultry evening walking through the centre of Rome. As the sun went down, drivers started honking, and girls with their faces painted orange and red rode past on the backs of Vespas, carrying football club flags. Parma had been trounced by AS Roma in an Italian league match a few days before, and the city was still jubilant. On the piazza around the chalk-white Vittoriale monument, where seagulls underlit by searchlights wheeled like insects around a porch lamp, somebody had spray-painted "*Roma Campione – Lazio Merda*" on the pavement. In spite of this boisterous upswelling of Roman pride, tourists seemed to dominate the centre of Rome. On the Via Veneto, next to the Hard Rock Café, an American boy had his ass crammed into a shopping cart and was drinking from a tall can of beer as his friend pushed him down the curving avenue. Next to the Pantheon, a long-haired busker crooned "Losing My Religion" to a crowd on a restaurant terrace, their nationalities revealed by the lettering on their guidebook covers. In the Campo dei Fiori I saw a guy in a black T-shirt marked "Staff" loudly assemble a crowd of American college students, hand out cans of beer, and then soak them – along with several Italian passersby – with the water from an ice bucket.

I finished the evening in the backpackers' ghetto. North of Termini there were a half-dozen nondescript streets, made up of five- and six-storey buildings, with cheap *pensiones* and hostels packed several to a building. There were laundromats (one boasted that it was "Soap Free") with Internet access, a Mailboxes Etc. for sending packages home, and cheap pizzerias and Chinese restaurants. Backpackers with shorts and Teva sandals were heading to the Eurail ticket centre in the station, many with their copy of *Let's Go* in hand. The closer I got to Termini, the seedier the streets got. *Carabinieri* with pistols in white holsters strutted past gypsy women with babies sucking on their exposed breasts. Strange that travellers would congregate in this dicey section of Rome, which was a long bus ride – on a route notorious for pickpockets – from the attractions of the Centro Storico. That night, as I wrote postcards in the rec room, an Asian-American man burst into the hostel.

"Do you know if anybody had anything stolen from here?" he asked, panting. I replied that I hadn't heard any complaints.

"Shit," he said. "I'm in the hostel downstairs, and we all had our things robbed. They got by the guy at the desk – he was like, passed out – and then they went through all the rooms while we were sleeping. They took tons of backpacks, went through them, and dumped them in the hall."

§

The next day, I rode a graffiti-covered metro train with nervous-looking Japanese teenagers wearing their backpacks on their chests. At the Spagna stop I passed through a long tunnel that emerged on the narrow Vicolo del Bottino. The original Grand Tourists' ghetto still bore traces of its heyday as an English enclave. This was Tridente, one of Rome's most pricey neighbourhoods, where artisans' workshops had long ago been supplanted by Gucci and Armani outlets. By Babington's English Tea Rooms, a tuft of mohawked punks with "Discharge" spelled in studs on the back of their leather jackets drank from tall cans of beer. I made a pilgrim's stop at the Keats-Shelley Memorial house beside the Spanish Steps, where charred bones, locks of hair, and other Romantic relics were enshrined in the tiny rooms where Keats died at the age of 25.

On Via Condotti, next to the Cartier shop, I found the Antico Caffè Greco, a genuine holdover from the Grand Tour – founded, according to a sign on the facade, in 1760. With its oval marble tables, the statues of dandies niched in the walls, and the murky landscape paintings browned with the nicotine of the ages, the Greco was a cabinet of curiosities preserved for posterity. I took a seat on a red velvet banquette between a group of Japanese girls with Prada bags at their feet and a middle-aged Italian man necking with an overdressed companion half his age. A bowtied waiter in tails that dangled to the back of his knees bestowed upon me a cappuccino that cost as much as lunch.

For the British, the Caffè Greco – patronized by shady Europeans like Casanova, Goethe, and Baudelaire – would do in a pinch. But, all in all, the Grand Tourists preferred to eat English-cooked meals at English-run inns like the Albergo Londra near the Spanish Steps, and to read the London papers in the now-defunct English Coffee House. The centre of the action was the Spanish Steps, the Rococo cascade of 130 marble stairs that purl down from the Trinità dei Monti church. In the Grand Tourists' day, the staircase was draped with languorous artists' models, and the Piazza di Spagna was filled with *cognoscenti* selling counterfeit paintings to the Tourists. Things hadn't changed much over the centuries. Tourists continued to seek out their national cuisine – the Americans now ate American food at the nearby McDonald's – the Steps were still covered with young Italian men, and persistent hawkers still tried to interest people in artwork. The market had degenerated a little, true. These days, the masterpieces for sale tended to Manneken Pis–shaped lighters that spurted fire from their phalluses.

I took a seat on the mottled stairs among bright-eyed Italian boys, who were teletexting messages into their cellphones or directing laser pointers at the exposed shoulder blades of passing women. Four blond German teenage girls sat down in front of me, exciting general interest. The men kept their profiles to the girls, always watching from the corner of their eyes, making little bird-like whistles to attract their attention and gradually closing in around the group. The girls huddled ever tighter, like sheep surrounded by wolves, until a man in a sleeveless T-shirt managed to bum a cigarette from a girl in Capri pants by using sign language and undulating eyebrows. Hemmed in, the girls stood up, wiped the Roman dirt off their asses, and walked towards the Trinità dei Monti. A flight lower, a pair of English girls sat down, and the process of predatory preening and demure flight repeated itself.

A tall girl with pink dreadlocks made her way among the groups of tourists on the Steps, pointedly avoiding the Italian men. She handed me a flyer covered with photos of shirtless hunks and tube-topped babes dancing on bar counters.

"You fancy going on a pub crawl?" she asked, with an Irish accent. "We're meeting down by the fountain in ten minutes. There's all-you-can-drink between eight and nine, free pizza and shots – we visit five or six pubs. It's good fun." A few minutes later, I introduced myself to Simon, a shaven-headed young Englishman with a twisted snake tattooed above his right ear. He handed me a brochure that outlined the pub crawl rules.

"It is legal to drink on the street, but make sure you get a plastic cup when leaving the bar. Please finish the drink before entering the next bar. – A 5 minute warning will be given at each Pub before leaving. – Remember that loudness, fighting or harassing behaviour will not be tolerated."

The pub crawl was a grim affair. Deciding there was ample journalistic justification for partaking, I swallowed Aqua Velva–toned liqueurs and overpriced Guinness in a series of mock-Irish pubs. Soon, we were walking en masse down the Via di Propaganda. I felt tempted to detach myself from this horde of screaming college kids with plastic cups in hand, a parade that forced Italian families off the sidewalks and into the gutter.

A Torontonian in glasses and a stained white T-shirt walked alongside me. "I've been in Italy for a month and a half," he slurred. "We're supposed to be taking a course in Classical stuff – Greece and Rome. Bunch of garbage! It's more like: how to be drunk every night for six weeks and still keep on functioning. We've been drinking sambuca on the Spanish Steps since four in the afternoon." His red-headed friend, who strode beside me, was carrying a nearly empty bottle of the liqueur.

"Man, this chick came up and showed me how to light it on fire while it's in my mouth," he told me. "Problem is, it spilled over my face when it was still on fire – I don't know how I'm going to explain the burns." Tiny blisters were already blossoming around his lips.

After the fifth bar, the crawl, which had never been particularly coherent, was falling apart. The Torontonian started vomiting between parked cars. Snake-eared Simon barely prevented a plastered frat boy from being hit by a Vespa as we crossed the busy Corso Vittorio Emanuele II. By the time we reached the Campo dei Fiori, a normally pleasant square of *enotecas* and caffè terraces, a third of our number had gone astray. Outside a dance club called Heartbreak, a shaven-headed staff member greeted the crawlers by shooting a fluorescent aperitif into drooling mouths with a giant plastic squirt gun.

By this time, the mixture of Italian Guinness and anti-freeze cordials was having its effect, and I worked my way to the back of the club in a daze. A chubby girl in a Day-Glo tank top, so tight it looked like her shoulders had been squeezed from a tube, was necking with the frat boy. A hipster from Nashville was grinding his pelvis against a chubby Pennsylvanian sorority girl. I looked around me: it was Delta House does Europe, with bad techno rather than decent rhythm 'n' blues on the soundtrack. Detaching myself from the ruckus, I walked to the middle of the square and sat down on the pedestal of Giordano Bruno's statue, which some soccer fan had draped with a red and orange "Totti" jersey. Elegant Italians around me were watching the familiar Anglo-American riot with jaded amusement. From a distance, confined to one corner of the square, it didn't look so bad. Since the first Grand Tours, Rome had learned to ghettoize its increasingly witless visitors who, these days, were too unversed in Italian to attempt making trophies of the locals. They seemed resigned to the crowds that overran their piazzas every summer. After all, when it came to barbarian invasions, Rome had seen it all before.

❦

I spent a couple of more nights at Fawlty Towers, until the drunken teenagers stumbling over my cot at two in the morning got tiresome, then hopped a Eurostar at Termini. We followed gap-toothed aqueducts as Rome's suburbs gave way to fields filled with yellowing rolls of hay. An hour later I was in Naples, the southernmost limit of most classic Grand Tours. In the 18th century, when it had been the most populous city in Italy, fully 10,000 of its 300,000 residents were estimated to be active courtesans. Neapolitans had a reputation for being free and easy: bronzed youths bathed naked on the seashore, and boisterous crowds spat orange peels into the pit at the San Carlo opera house, the world's largest. The notorious Emma Hart, a blacksmith's daughter, had married the ambassador Sir William Hamilton, and delighted Tourists by posing nearly naked in a series of "Attitudes" inspired by Roman antiquity. After the obligatory ascent of the still-smoking Vesuvius and a visit to the newly excavated Pompeii, the Grand Tourists could blow their cash at the famous casino. "Naples is a paradise, in it everyone lives in a sort of intoxicated self-forgetfulness," wrote Goethe. A paradise, as an Italian apophthegm had it, inhabited by devils – one where the German writer forgot himself so thoroughly he later deemed it prudent to destroy all of the notes from the Neapolitan stretch of his tour.

As I shouldered my bag, I remembered a travel writer's observation that in Naples's train station, one is always in the immediate vicinity of at least half a dozen master criminals. One of them was certainly my cab driver, who took me on a 20-minute detour through the hills before depositing me at a hostel that turned out to be a ten-minute walk away from the station. On the top floor of a decaying apartment building, it was run by an energetic Australian woman who had married a Neapolitan. It was one of the best hostels I'd seen, with spacious dorm rooms and a pleasantly chaotic kitchen. What's more, for the price of a McPink and a Coke, the Italian grandmother in the suite downstairs would prepare guests a fabulous vegetarian pasta meal.

Naples, a little too scary and real for North American college kids, wasn't a popular stop. I'd overheard the backpackers at Fawlty Towers regaling one another with stories of pickpockets and muggings. It was true: in Naples, you had to be on your toes, if only to avoid the helmetless 12-year-olds riding three-to-a-Vespa. Shelley witnessed a murder within minutes of his arrival, and one Grand Tourist reported seeing a street urchin steal a handkerchief from an English dandy at one end of the Largo di Castello and peddle it back to him at the other. Even today, Naples, with its genially shambolic street life, had something of Bombay to it. Patrick, a hostel guest from Limerick, told me about being offered a cut-rate carton of Marlboros in the market.

"Jesus," he marvelled, "the fellow was completely mesmerizing. I couldn't take me eyes off him."

The salesman took Patrick's money, handed him a well-wrapped Marlboro carton, and melted into the crowd. When Patrick tried to check his purchase, an accomplice appeared, ripped open the packaging, and showed him the cigarette packs were filled with nails.

"Then he panicked, as if the *carabinieri* were coming, and ran off with me bloody nails!" he said. "It was worth it, though, just to see the sheer artistry of those fellows."

At the desk, Diane, from Seattle, also cautioned me about scam artists.

"If you get offered a digital camera for like a hundred bucks in the market, *don't buy it*. You'll just open the box and find a block of wood or a bag of sand inside. It happens a couple of times a month to guests here. This is a good place to pick up counterfeit Gucci, though." (Later, one of my banknotes was pushed back to me at the rail station window. It was a colour-photocopied counterfeit. Naples – a town so crooked that even the bank machines rip you off.)

Over the next few days I got to like Diane, a pretty woman in her mid-20s, with big dark eyes that betrayed her Cuban-American roots and tight dreadlocks that spoke of her involvement with Seattle's anti-globalization scene. She'd been travelling for four months, mostly in Spain, and was looking for a change in her life. Over a glass of wine in the kitchen one night, she told me about her courtship of the Italian boys.

"When I arrived, I saw all those hotties on their scooters, with their sleeveless shirts, and I was like – *mmmm*, I gotta get me one of those." She gave her phone number to the guy who delivered the laundry, but he stood her up. "So, forget it, buster, I said. You know, these Italians are all spoiled by their mamas. They live at home, they've got a regular girlfriend they know they're going to marry. Until then, it's like: 'What can I get today?'"

Lately, she'd been hanging around the Piazza Gesù Nuovo, trying to score hash from the anarchist squatters, and she had high hopes for a guy from the local communist centre. She reminded me of myself when I'd been rattling around Germany and France in my 20s: a little lost, looking for something new – preferably a genuine relationship with a European, not a drunken one-night stand with another backpacker.

I'd come to Naples with a particular goal: the Secret Cabinet, a collection of erotic art in the National Archeological Museum that had been a required stop on the classic Grand Tour. For much of its existence the *Gabinetto degli oggetti osceni* could be visited only with a permit, and had actually been walled up by the Bourbons in 1851. Recently reopened after a complete reorganization, the collection was still kept behind a metal gate, and while our group waited to enter, I studied the petitions of English dignitaries asking the Bourbon kings for admittance. "The foreigners visiting Naples on the Grand Tour tended to indulge in ribaldry whenever the collection was mentioned," a sheet in a display case noted dryly, "and their comments could be decidedly defamatory with respect to life and morals, both ancient and modern, in the Kingdom of Naples."

A pretty young woman in a red top led us into the first of the Cabinet's five small rooms.

"Welcome to the Gabinetto Segreto, a collection of objects that were considered unmoral in their day. As you can see," she said, pointing to a cabinet of objects from the Borgia collection, "they are all in the shapes of virile members, uteruses, and breasts."

"Careful where you sit down, luv," an Englishman whispered to his girlfriend.

How the Tourist toffs must have tittered when they'd finally gained admittance. Many of the objects had been recovered from Pompeii and Herculaneum. Bakeries were advertised with images of erect stone phalluses – an allusion to rising bread – and bronze bells made up of clusters of penises had hung outside middle-class houses.

"These are pygmies, in a Nile scene," said the guide, gesturing towards a narrow fresco of naked, childlike figures from the House of the Doctor in Pompeii. "They were considered a very lascivious people, very close to nature, and were usually depicted with very large phalluses. Here you can see them involved in some very strange performances."

"Gives me some good ideas for my next trip to Egypt, that does," said the Englishman, *sotto voce*.

There were Kama Sutra–like frescoes from brothels, a marble of Pan sodomizing a goat, and a Venus in a bikini leaning on a tiny figure with a huge erection. (Or it would have been huge, if some Vatican censor hadn't snapped it off.) I was particularly taken by the Freudian symbolism of a bronze gladiator duelling with his own penis, which was turning on him like a wild beast. The Gabinetto Segreto must have been the 800-metre bungee jump of the 18th-century Grand Tour, providing Tourists with a new perspective on their long and dull Latin studies and fodder for dinner conversation for the rest of their lives.

§

Over dinner at the hostel that night, a 20-year-old from Minneapolis with a mass of curly hair made fun of me for buying capers and fresh basil. When I started on my rotini with *puttanesca* sauce, he came up to me with a can opener.

"Like, when you buy spaghetti sauce in a can, and you've got no microwave, do you take it out of the can *before* you heat it?"

Some of these kids had come to Europe straight out of the nest.

I showed him how to use a pot, and was joined at the table by a shirtless fellow with dreadlocks and a red face, displaying a sunburnt belly. The kid from Minnesota asked him where he'd been travelling.

"Portugal, the ex-Yugoslavia, Slovenia. Anywhere there isn't a hostel," he spat, adding: "Because they're these stupid pools of English people separated from the local culture." He told us he'd been travelling for two and a half years. "I was in Seattle for the riots, man. And now I can honestly say that I no longer think the United States is a democracy. I think it's a fascist state. A few people breaking windows doesn't justify what happened there. I've completely lost faith in my country."

Over the next couple of days, though, he never seemed to stray beyond the stupid pool of English-speaking people in the hostel. He walked around with his belly hanging over his black shorts, scowling, and stayed up all night in the television room watching *Independence Day* and videotaped American sitcoms.

Diane made a brief appearance. A friend had trimmed her dreadlocks, she'd put on a low-cut shirt, and she was about to head out to meet her Italian communist beau in the square. I wished her luck, admiring her courage. The original Grand Tourists, self-entitled as they'd been, had at least made fleeting attempts to learn foreign customs and pay court to the people they met on their travels. Some, such as Boswell, succeeded abundantly, using his British affluence with a connoisseur's flair, having experiences – interviews with philosophers and flings with countesses – that let him come home with a new world-view. Ultimately, however, the Grand Tour was the glorification of travel as consumption, with souvenir paintings, willing opera singers, and new waistcoats as prize items in the Continental catalogue. Tobias Smollett, always the Skeptical Traveller, summed up the fates of the Tourists nicely.

"One engages in play with an infamous gamester, and is stripped perhaps in the very first partie: another is poxed and pillaged by an antiquated cantatrice: a third is bubbled by a knavish antiquarian . . . all of them talk familiarly of the arts, and return finished connoisseurs and coxcombs, to their own country."

From what I'd seen of the kids in hostels and sleeper compartments, few got as far as being bubbled or poxed, and the only thing most of them would be able to talk familiarly of was variations in fast food menus. The contemporary Grand Tour was all about meeting other travellers, following *Let's Go*–approved itineraries from Amsterdam to Prague, and returning home unscathed and unchanged. It was a travel groove that allowed college kids to voyage far from home without leaving their frat and sorority houses.

The man who broke the Grand Tourist mould, and became a Romantic legend in the process, was of course Byron. His early tours of the Continent were as devoted to conquest as Boswell's, and soon he could recite a Leporello-esque catalogue that included 15-year-old Greek boys, king's mistresses, daughters, and mothers. But, somewhere along the way, something happened: Byron stopped being a Tourist and started living abroad. He avoided his countrymen, complaining Rome was "infected" with Englishmen, and that "Florence and Naples are their Lazarettoes where they carry the infection of their society . . . I never see any of them when I can avoid it." He preferred Venice, where in 1816 he lived with a baker's wife and finished *Childe Harold's Pilgrimage*. Rather than returning home, he plunged deeper into exile, fell in love with a 19-year-old Venetian girl, and became involved in the revolutionary politics of her family. He died at 36 in Greece, promoting rebellion against the Ottoman Empire, having made the great leap from travel to expatriation. This was the journey not only as rejection of home, but as acceptance and embrace of the foreign, and it made his fellow-travellers look like the Tourists they were.

I never discovered how Diane made out that night. I hope she started seeing her communist beau, enrolled in night classes in Italian, and got involved with the local leftists as they marched in protest against Silvio Berlusconi. She probably didn't need my advice, though. Unlike the Grand Tourist pub crawlers, slaves to their railpasses – for whom the next bar and town always beckoned when things threatened to get real – she'd already discovered one of travel's fundamental truths, something I'd realized in Paris years ago.

To stop being a tourist, sometimes all you have to do is start standing still.

Chapter 7

VENI, VIDI, VISA

Naples Goes to the Beach – Julius Caesar's Summer Place – Orgies of the Fishpond Set – Egyptian Tourists Deface the Pyramids – The First Travel Writer – Roman Roads, From Iraq to Scotland – Tourist Traps of Antiquity – Villas Claimed by the Waves – Sic Transit Gloria Mundi

The weekend had come to Naples. In the streets around the Piazza Dante, plump girls with big pink-tinted sunglasses hopped on scooters and buzzed out of town towards the litter-strewn beaches of the Tyrrhenian Sea. On the metro to Pozzuoli, a car full of thin-limbed boys cranked the bouncy Europop on their ghetto blaster ever louder as the palm trees thickened. Near the dormant volcanic crater of Solfatara, a suburban bus took me along a curving, car-packed coastal road that looked like the endless traffic jam in Jean-Luc Godard's *Weekend*. A barefoot mother threatened to smack her bawling children while, just ahead, a sub-compact pulled to the shoulder, disgorging six teenagers whose gesticulations vanished in a cloud of radiator steam. When an old man with a cane overtook the bus for the second time, I took the hint and hopped out the back door – left open to encourage the breeze – and carried on by foot. Sometimes, the oldest way of travelling is also the fastest.

The farther I got from the Bay of Naples, the easier it became to conjure up the past. Inland from the port town called Baia, I headed up a twisting, disused road, bordered by trees drooping with pink flowers as membranous as backlit baby's ears. A stocky farmer directed me up the hill and, at a ridge topped by ruined walls, I contemplated a panorama fit for an emperor. To the right, the severe planes of the Castle of Baia, an Aragonese fortress perched on a promontory before the cape of Miseno, western extremity of the Bay of Naples. To the left, looking toward the city, a hydrofoil picked up speed as it left Pozzuoli and skimmed across the azure gulf towards the island of Ischia. Below me, curving terraces covered with ruins descended towards the pleasure boats and coast guard vessels moored in Baia's harbour.

A pile of bricks, mortar, and marble chips stood before me. It took an effort of the imagination to reconstruct what I was seeing: the 140-metre-long ridgetop wall, overrun with weeds and spotted lizards, was once a porticoed series of rooms that opened onto this panoramic view of the bay – all that remained of the vacation home of Julius Caesar. Before I could erase the buzz of scooters and the sight of discarded water bottles from the scene, a hornet settled on my bicep, took a firm stance, and squeezed a jet of poison into my blood. Sleepy and halfwitted in the midday heat, I was recalled to the moment with a rush of adrenaline. It doesn't do to lose oneself too deeply in classical reveries on the Campanian coast. Modern Italy, that jealous paramour, never fails to pinch its daydreaming suitors back to the here and now.

Returning to Baia, I mentally draped the scooterback lovers in togas, and turned the satellite dishes on grilled balconies into amphoras full of Falernian wine. A man in an unbuttoned white shirt stirred from beneath the shade of a tree and wandered over to sell me a ticket to the *Parco Archeologico di Baia*. These were the terraces I'd seen from the ruins on the ridgetop, a series of broadening tiers that descended like crescents of theatre seats towards the proscenium stage of the bay.

On the upper level, I wandered past the walls of lozenged brickwork of the Villa dell'Ambulatio, whose long, sea-facing portico was strewn with broken columns. Peeking into an intact room, I could see the waxed-paper skin shed by a snake blowing across a polychrome floor tiled with a mosaic of theatrical masks. In another room, a phalanx of ants marched across the cherubs, sea panthers, and swans in flight carved into white stucco walls.

Following a staircase down towards the laundry-draped backs of the modern homes on the shorefront Via Lucullo, I came upon the remains of a semi-circular *exedra*, two bands of crenellated stone set around a circular cement depression. Beneath a bit of wall stucco, I could make out the date 1776 scratched next to an elaborate signature that read something like "Bouffon Cochon" – the graffito of some long-dead Grand Tourist. The place was evocatively derelict and entirely free of visitors, which is how 18th-century travellers described the Roman Coliseum before mass tourism, when weeds grew from Doric columns, goats grazed in the gladiators' pits, and hermits lived beneath its arches.

I walked into what looked like a Brobdingnagian brick pizza oven known as the Temple of Mercury. The building's dome, 21 metres in diameter, dates from the first century B.C., making it the oldest on such a scale in the world. A concrete platform led to the middle of an opaque pool, and concentric rings of wedge-shaped tufa blocks rose to the ceiling. It was like being in a post-apocalyptic Pantheon, stripped of Christian paraphernalia, in which the floor level had risen to the base of the dome. I let out an exploratory yelp, and the high note came careening back from the ceiling with a metallic, pinging echo.

Thanks to a phenomenon called bradyseism – the word means "a slow earthquake" – the volcanic land of the Phlegraean Fields rises and subsides, sometimes a metre in a single month, and the lowering of the ground level at Baia has hidden a natural spring that once flowed from a niche in the wall. The floor of the "temple," now invisible, was covered by a pool of green water so murky it appeared bottomless. I glimpsed a white cloud drifting against a deep blue background through the oculus, sensed the afternoon breeze carrying the odour of wild thyme and dill through four rectangular openings that spewed forth tresses of ivy. As water dripped lugubriously from the ceiling, I shuddered, feeling like a soul in Hades contemplating mocking images of a vanished life.

Eighteenth-century Tourists were convinced that a structure of this scale had to be an important place of Roman devotion, where priests and worshippers gathered for pagan mystery cults. But 2,000 years ago there was nothing sacred about the scene. The "Temple of Mercury" was simply the *frigidarium*, or cold room, of a much larger bath complex.

The Younger Seneca itemized the boisterous cast of such baths: "Toughs looking for a fight, the thieves caught in the act, and the people who enjoy hearing themselves sing in the bathtub. Don't forget the hair-removal expert forever forcing out that thin screech of his to advertise his services and only shutting up when he's plucking a customer's armpits and can make someone else do the yelping for him. Then there's the drinkseller with his various cries, the sausage-seller, the cake-seller, and all the managers of the restaurants, each hawking his wares with his own special intonation."

In their heyday, these public baths were surrounded by the villas of affluent senators, noblemen, and nouveau riche freedmen. This notorious vacation spot was, according to Varro, "a vortex of luxury and a harbour of vice," where "maidens were common property, old men turned into young bucks, youths experimented with homosexuality, no man escaped without a broken heart, and few women left with their virtue intact."

In other words, I was in the ruins of the Riviera of the Roman Empire, a classical St. Tropez, the first vacation spot where affluent urbanites travelled en masse to get away from it all. In Baia's 500 years as a fashionable resort, starting in the first century B.C. (when it was known as Baiae), its lakes resounded with choral song, its streets with the drunken serenades of aristocrats' sons, its shores with the riot of boating parties. During the reign of Emperor Augustus (27 B.C. to A.D. 14), an unbroken succession of villas came to stretch from Miseno to Sorrento; beachfront property was extended by erecting stone-pillared piers into the sea. Owning at least one *villa maritima* became a status symbol, and the "villa habit," as moralistic commentators called it, implied vast outlays on imported marbles, Greek statues, and exotic fish.

In their *peregrinatio*, their seasonal pilgrimage to their vacation villas, the Romans were the first people in history to undertake regular holiday travel. As the heat rose and the senate recessed, they left the stinking, noisy streets of the great capital and headed for the seaside in spring, the Alban and Sabine hills in summer. The annual exodus to the beach led to the first holiday traffic jams as wealthy Romans fought slow-moving carriage and mule traffic on the Via Domitiana. It was a four-day journey of 160 kilometres, and the richest rode in litters – curtained couches, borne on the shoulders of up to eight slaves – and stopped in their own rest lodges. Entire households, including slaves, maids, valets, and chefs, travelled in carriages with wooden wheels and iron tires, camping along the way in silken tents.

The trip was worth its jolts: the Campanian coast boasted Neapolis –
modern Naples, founded by Greeks – where young noblemen preferred
Hellenic *chlamys*, or shawls, to togas, and music, literature, and elegant
living to commerce and politics. Bustling Puteoli (now sleepy Pozzuoli)
was a cosmopolitan port, with restaurants and brothels, where hundreds
of thousands of tonnes of wheat arrived from Alexandria every year.
Cumae had sulphurous hot springs, famed for their therapeutic value, as
well as the Sibyl's grotto, where the mystified could address questions to a
minuscule, immortal Greek prophetess.

Best of all was Baiae, which had the oyster beds of Lake Lucrinus, and
whose artificial bay, created with stone breakwaters, allowed for nude
bathing at all hours. It was good to know somebody, of course – Baiae
hardly catered to the casual tourist – and better still to have one's own villa.
The Younger Pliny boasted six villas, and senators, sojourners, affluent
natives of the region, and resident intellectuals, often of foreign extraction,
competed for the most opulent lodgings. Consumption was lavish and
conspicuous. Formal gardens were watered with wine, and one of the chief
occupations of purposeful Roman leisure was the tending of elaborate
tidewater-fed pools. The *piscinarii*, or fishpond set, trained bearded mullets
to eat from their hands; the lampreys in the imperial fishponds wore golden
earrings. The headland now called Posillipo (where the exiled Oscar Wilde
later composed the "The Ballad of Reading Gaol"), owes its name to a villa
owned by a certain Vedius Pollio. When a clumsy servant broke a costly
goblet, only the intercession of Augustus himself prevented the villa-owner
from tossing the slave's body to his flesh-eating eels.

At the height of its magnificence, from 31 B.C. to A.D. 69, Baiae, the
leisure centre of the fabulously wealthy and spectacularly jaded, witnessed some of the most depraved extravagances of the Roman Empire.
Nero ordered floating brothels filled with noblewomen to be set adrift on
his arrival, and visited them in leisurely sailboat cruises. It was in Baiae
too that Nero's mother Agrippina – who had killed her ex-husband with
a poison mushroom – was put asea by her son in a ship with a leaded
canopy designed to collapse and crush its passengers. (When the
emperor's trap failed, he simply had three naval officers break down her
door and beat her to death.)

The most vivid picture of the Phlegraean Fields comes from Petronius's *Satyricon*. In this episodic picaresque novel, two slumming bisexual aristocratic bucks arrive in a town that was probably Puteoli. After getting into a screaming match over a pre-pubescent boy-toy sidekick and witnessing forbidden Priapic rites, they're kidnapped and one is jumped by a eunuch. "Before I knew it," says the well-endowed narrator Encolpius (the name means "Crotch"), "he had straddled me on the couch and, despite my resistance, pulled off my clothes. Then, for what seemed hours, he worked on me but without the slightest success. Meanwhile a river of sweat was streaming down his face, leaving his wrinkled cheeks so creviced with powder that he looked like some cracked wall standing desolate under a pelting rain."

The centrepiece of the novel is the dinner with Trimalchio, a freed slave who has made a fortune in the wine business and bought a villa so lavish and extensive that even he doesn't know how many slaves work the property. Reclining on sofas, our heroes are fed dormice dipped in honey and rolled in poppy seeds, served sauce from gravy boats with phalluses for spouts, and treated to a sow whose belly is stuffed with live thrushes. Their later adventures take them as far as modern-day Marseilles; en route they encounter anal dildoes covered with oil and crushed nettle seeds, incestuous voyeurism, and lots of homosexual rape. It is Trimalchio's feast, however – at which guests are encouraged to belch and fart at table, hands are rinsed in wine, and Ethiopian slaves are threatened with death for the slightest slip-up – that suggests just how debauched things got in the villas of Baiae.

§

Even before the Roman Empire, people travelled to satisfy their curiosity and indulge their leisure. The going wasn't particularly good, but they went anyway. The first cities, between the Tigris and the Euphrates in what is now Iraq, produced the first vehicles, little solid-wheeled Sumerian wagons drawn by oxen and wild donkeys that appeared about 3000 B.C. There is evidence, a millennium later, of Babylonian carriage roads capable of taking wheeled vehicles. The Egyptians travelled in chariots, and though it was mostly government officials who rode between cities, by 1500 B.C. tourism seems to have come to the Nile.

Wealthy Egyptians began to travel to see the monuments of their own civilization, especially the Sphinx and the pyramids of Giza – by then a thousand years old – visits attested to by graffiti on temple walls. One of the earliest of these "scratchings," dated to 1244 B.C., reads: "Hadnakhte, scribe of the treasury, came to make an excursion and amuse himself on the west of the Memphis, together with his brother, Panakhti." As there was no travel infrastructure, the brothers probably slept in a field or on the deck of a Nile boat. The first inns, originally hostels for travelling government officials, appeared in Mesopotamia and Crete. The innkeepers tended to be women, and from about 1500 B.C., they provided drinks, beds, hip baths, and prostitutes to their almost exclusively male clients.

The Athenians, after winning the last of their decisive battles against the Persian empire of Darius the Great in 479 B.C., were probably the first to travel for travel's sake. Their best highways had bridges, ferries, road signs, way stations, and stretches of pavement. (They also introduced "rut roads," in which carefully squared grooves, about 1.4 metres apart, were carved into rock or dirt surfaces to speed the passage of standard-gauge carts.)

The citizens of Greek city-states, scattered around the Mediterranean (as Plato put it) like frogs on a pond, would come from afar to such pan-hellenic festivals as the Olympic games, where they squeezed in some sightseeing at the temple of Zeus. Solon, the Athenian lawmaker, became history's first recorded tourist when he travelled to Egypt for pleasure after ending an arduous term of office. Herodotus, born in Asia Minor in 484 B.C., was the first to make a career of travel writing, roaming the Hellenic world and going as far north as Russia and as far east as Persia, finishing his days in Italy. He recorded the wonders of Babylon, including the natives' penchant for perfuming their bodies, wearing turbans, and carrying walking sticks, and picked up a smattering of Persian and Egyptian. A wealthy man, he was primarily motivated by curiosity about religious practices. (Art left him cold. Of the great temple at Karnak, he wrote only: "It is large.") Not above repeating legends, such as tales of floating islands in Egypt, hippopotami with horses' tails and cloven hooves on the Nile, and ants the size of foxes that mined for gold in India, he was quick to admit – unlike many subsequent travel writers – that he hadn't actually seen such marvels with his own eyes.

Travel in Hellenic times was not pleasant or easy, and people took to the pirate-ridden seas or the dusty highways only out of dire necessity – for trade, or in hopes of some miracle cure. It took the unified empire of the Romans, with its common currency, its lingua francas of Latin and Greek, and the absence of hostile borders, to make the concept of "leisure travel" more than an oxymoron. The Romans liked to build roads and were very good at it, engineering highways that might deviate from the true only a few hundred metres in the course of 30 kilometres. Starting with the surveying of the Via Appia, the "Queen of Roads," between Rome and Brindisi in 312 B.C., they bound the Italian boot from toe to calf with an exquisite cross-lacing of highways. Built on a bed of rounded stones in a matrix of clay, often bolstered underneath with tight-packed sand, the best of these roads were topped with polygonal stones of granite and basalt, 20 centimetres deep – all-weather paving that has lasted to this day. (Around the same time, the Han Chinese covered the Middle Kingdom with superb roads, wider even than the Roman *vias* – but since they paved them with gravel, not one has survived.)

Along the highways, a network of hostels offered food, beds, and a change of vehicles. If the traveller could wangle a cooperative official into granting him a *diploma*, a document allowing accommodations in the government post, he could stay in the more elaborate *stationes* intended for imperial parties. Maps such as the seven-metre-long Peutinger Table used Michelin guide-like symbols – a twin-peaked roof for a modest country inn, a square within a square for more luxurious lodgings. There were restaurants where one could eat reclining in couches, or the less pretentious *tabernae*, snack bars where one hoped the bartender didn't add too much water in the wine. By the first century A.D., the Mediterranean was ringed by roads, and by the time of the Emperor Trajan, who ruled from A.D. 98 to A.D. 117, a Roman citizen could travel from the banks of the Euphrates to Scotland, under a single legal system, on roads that wouldn't be surpassed for comfort until the 19th century.

Given these conditions, something like a Grand Tour of the Ancient World emerged, complete with fashionable resorts and must-see sites. For the Romans – only the very wealthy could afford leisure travel – Greece was what Italy would become for English Grand Tourists: a source of art and spirituality that a culturally insecure world power plundered for inspiration and consolation. A typical tour started at Delphi, with its sanctuary of Apollo and temple loot like Helen of Troy's necklace and the gold throne of King Midas. In Athens, tourists climbed the hill of the Acropolis and were shown around the Parthenon, marvelling at the sculptor Myron's bronze cow, so realistic that it was said to lure passing calves. At Olympia, where the games carried on through Roman times, an ivory statue of a throned Zeus covered with golden drapery, one of the Seven Wonders of the Ancient World, was a three-star attraction. In Sparta, if their timing was right, they caught the Feast of Naked Boys, in which aristocratic youths gouged out each other's eyes. Asia Minor – modern Turkey – was Homer country, and Romans felt a special attachment to Ilium, site of Troy, since Rome was said to have been founded by survivors of the Trojan War. Better still was the renowned statue of Aphrodite at Knidos, the first large-scale, free-standing nude of a woman. Local guides explained that the stain on its crotch was made by a smitten youth who had hid himself in the temple after closing time and made love to the gorgeous likeness.

From Asia Minor, travellers could sail across the Mediterranean to Alexandria. Filled with exotic monuments, easily accessible thanks to the boats of the Nile, Egypt was the *ur*–tourist destination. From the first sight of the 120-metre-high lighthouse at Alexandria, the Roman tourist found himself in a land geared to his needs. Renting a cabin cruiser with papyrus sails and an awninged reed shelter, he could head down the canal leading to Canopus, which was lined with resort hotels and nightclubs. At the pyramids, then covered with a smooth revetment carved with hieroglyphics, local boys offered to shinny to the top for a little baksheesh. At Crocodilopolis, the priests had trained the sacred crocodiles to open their jaws on command so that they could have their teeth brushed – a spectacle arranged for the benefit of tourists.

The key features of modern tourism could be found *in ovo* in the ancient world. There were marvellous attractions that performed on schedule. At Thebes, not far from the Valley of the Kings, stood the famous statue of Amenhotep III, originally 18 metres tall but broken across the torso by an earthquake. Each morning, as the air in the damaged statue heated, a loud pop, like the sound of a plucked lute string, could be heard: it was billed as Memnon, greeting his mother the dawn. The "talking" statue drew huge crowds – as attested by the 106 Roman and Greek graffiti on its base – until it was silenced in the third century A.D. by an ill-advised restoration. (When the skeptical geographer Strabo visited, he was pretty sure one of the bystanders at the base of the statue had imitated the sound to satisfy the expectant crowd.) There were guides, incompetent and chattering – they liked to claim the pyramids plunged as far into the sand as they rose into the air – and guidebooks that offered to free tourists from their tyranny.

Starting in A.D. 160, Pausanias, probably born in Lydia in Asia Minor, began his multi-volumed *Guidebook of Greece*, covering Hellenic civilization from Syria to Italy, with an emphasis on foreign religious practices. Quick-drawing miniaturists waited outside the Parthenon, ready to do a portrait sketch with evocative columns in the background, the ancestor of the Kodak moment. And there were souvenirs, as ubiquitous as snow domes and ashtrays today: cheap terra cotta models of temples were sold in tourist traps, people bought containers of Mount Hymettus honey in Athens, and upon return to Rome paid a 25 percent customs duty on such luxury goods as silks, spices, and perfumes.

Then as now, the tourist must have been troubled by the feeling that he was travelling through a spectacle created entirely for his consumption. The priests in Memphis would trot out the sacred Apis bull for exercise in the courtyard only when there were enough visitors around. The temple in Sparta had preserved the giant egg (now thought to be an ostrich's) from which Helen of Troy had hatched. The more perspicacious ancient tourist might have noted that the same image of Athena stolen by Odysseus was on display in Rome, Argos, and three Italian towns. A tame dolphin appeared on the beach at Hippo Diarrhytus, in North Africa, and allowed a boy to ride on its back. The resultant influx of government officials and curious visitors, with all their demands of food and lodging, quickly became a burden to the modest community. "In the last analysis," wrote Pliny the Younger, "the place itself was losing its peace and privacy. So the decision was taken to kill off surreptitiously what was causing the influx."

Of all the travel hot spots in the ancient world, the "golden shore of Venus," luxurious Baiae, provided the most intense concentration of both the blessings and the blights of tourism. It was, in the strictest sense, a non-place. Like the Mexican beach resort of Cancún, whose location was selected by a computer, Baiae didn't exist as a geographical entity before the arrival of tourists. Unlike Neapolis, Puteoli, or Cumae, it hadn't been founded by the Greeks, and there is no record of its having had its own magistrates, industry, or independent territory before the first villas appeared in the second century B.C. Contrived for hedonistic escape, exploited by speculators who recognized its ideal location, it was a resort pure and simple. John D'Arms, in his *Romans on the Bay of Naples*, concluded that it's "doubtful in the extreme whether these estates contributed anything of substance to Campania's economic health." Driven from Rome by boredom and stress, vacationers brought city slaves and imported luxury foods from Roman markets rather than buying produce from the local towns. At its best, Baiae was a Greek-tinted centre of the arts. More often, it was a haven for bored urbanites.

The one economic innovation the Romans brought to the Campanian coast was surely the brothel. Prostitution was rife in Baiae, and the materialistic grandees of Rome expected their pleasures to be promptly delivered. In the *Satyricon*, Encolpius, lost in a seaside town, is led by a little old lady to a house filled with languorous women and wall posters outlining the rates for various services. It might have been as seedy as the backstreet brothel that tourists still line up to visit at Pompeii, with its gloomy, cramped cells covered with amateurish erotic frescoes. "Slowly, much too slowly," complains the narrator, "it dawned on me that the treacherous old hag had led me to a whorehouse."

Almost as far back as we have records of people travelling, there are references to innkeepers selling women along with beds. From the start, wanderlust – the erotic undercurrent in travel – has been conflated with curiosity and restlessness and has been transformed into lust, pure and simple. In their age-old symbiosis, the world's biggest legal industry – travel – colludes with the world's oldest profession to turn exoticism, leisure, and freedom into a commodity purchasable with foreign exchange. For a fistful of *sesterces*, pounds, or dollars, travellers would come to grasp at the chimera of travel's essence with exotic shows of staged intimacy.

§

Bradyseism, lately in its downwards phase, has gradually lowered the land on which the vacation homes of Baiae stood. Most of the piers, restaurants, and *villae maritimae* are now hidden under the waters of the Mediterranean. When the tide is very low, you can see shell-encrusted pillars poking above the breakers, and (when the port workers aren't on strike) a glass-bottom boat takes tourists out to glimpse another epoch's vacation utopia. Beneath the waves, where seaweed grows from the roofs of the brothels, the eels once kept as pets now dart among the submerged villas of long-dead vacationers.

Sic transit gloria mundi. So passes away the glory of the world.

Chapter 8

PROSPERO'S STY

Boogie Night on a Greek Ferry – Put in a Headlock by Canadian Wrestlers – Debauchery at the Pink Palace – Growth of the Tourist Bubble – The Masses in Motion – The Durrell Brothers Turn in Their Graves – The Road Takes Its Toll – I Need a Club Med Vacation – The Birth of Sea, Sex, and Sun – Too Many Italian Men, Not Enough French Girls – A Cheap Holiday in Other People's Misery – The Holy Water of Forgetfulness – Chip Butty and Lager Louts in Kavos – Nazi Holidays – St. Spiridion versus the Barbarians

There's no missing your first Greek sunrise, I'd been told, so I arose to watch the rosy-fingered dawn pinkening the shores of Corfu. We had docked at our first stop, Igoumenitsa, and I gazed at the dry low hills of the Greek mainland, whose tufts of evergreens thinned near their tops like the fur of a mongrel with the mange. Alongside us, a ship dropped anchor and a rusty chain slid out of its port hawse hole with a calamitous rippling chug. As the sun's disk rose up over the hills, it illuminated the blue Ionian Sea, the sandy beaches of Corfu to the west – and the catastrophe all around me.

Upturned chairs, sticky with lager, were scattered over the deck. Backpackers were spread-eagled on air mattresses within makeshift windbreaks assembled from toppled deckchairs. A young man with a T-shirt that read "US Navy Police – Against the Wall and Spread 'Em!" was passed out with his head on a table, surrounded by cans of Fanta and Amstel beer. A stinking garbage can overflowed with half-eaten sandwiches and *cornetti*. Next to me, an elaborately bored, deeply tanned Italian, a Stars-and-Stripes bandana clipped to his scalp by mirrored shades, was meditatively gobbing into the wine-dark, oil-slick sea.

I could feel a serious case of travel spleen coming on. It was four months since I'd taken my first steps on the Santiago pilgrimage, and *everything* was beginning to annoy me. I'd left Naples 32 hours earlier on a midnight train, and my delight with Italian brio seamlessly bled into exasperation with Latin vacuousness as the chain-smoking woman in the seat behind me chain-phoned numbers from a faux leopard-skin address book. (What sort of woman has half a dozen friends she can chat with at 2:30 in the morning? A *Neapolitan* woman.) Later, I was kept awake by a bad case of logorrhea, as a pair of female wrestlers from Regina, fresh out of high school, lugged their maple-leaf-covered backpacks onto the train. They pinned a dazed-looking Mexican-American with an uptalk catalogue of wrestling injuries.

"She like totally had pus draining out of her ear? When we lanced it, it exploded in our faces! Her coach's ear has been ripped so many times it's like, swollen shut?"

Awakening in my seat, I'd felt like I'd spent the night locked in a Greco-Roman full nelson.

Brindisi, a port town halfway down the boot heel, is Italy's main gateway to the eastern Mediterranean, and as I'd walked down the pedestrianized Corso Garibaldi from the train station, clots of backpackers were milling outside the offices of the Blue Star and Hellenic Mediterranean ferry companies, clutching their railpasses. I'd bought a ticket for the evening sailing on a Fragline ferry and spent the day with my head on my backpack in the palm-tree-filled Piazza Vittorio Emanuele, watching white-shirted Polizia Municipale blow their whistles at anybody who dared to play hacky sack on the grass.

When my capacious white ferry finally pulled out of port, it was nearly 10 p.m. and I was exhausted. I'd purchased deck passage and watched in dismay as the aft deck swimming pool, tarpaulined and roped off like a boxing ring, was turned into an all-night disco. A band of cheering Americans stormed the floor and took photos of one another ripping off their shirts and voguing to "Shiny Happy People" and "Dancing Queen." In a stupor, I'd nested down on a dim stretch of foredeck on the lee side. I'd spent the damp August night shivering in layers of T-shirts as a group of indefatigable Italians on the deck below chattered and smoked until just before sunrise.

Which is why, as we crossed the short stretch of sheltered water between the Greek mainland and the east coast of Corfu, I hated the ferry, its passengers, and the bloody blue Ionian. The first sight of Byron's "shores of glory," with their vast Venetian forts and spiky cypresses, left me cold. Corfu wasn't on my itinerary for its mythological associations (this was the isle where the naked Odysseus, drifting on a raft after leaving Calypso's island, was said to have spied on the teenage Nausicaa as she bathed) nor its literary pedigree (as the early playground of the Durrell brothers and Henry Miller). I'd chosen it for its reputation as a paradise overrun by German package tourists and yobs in Union Jack shorts who emerged already legless from their charters to turn the Mediterranean into their personal vomitorium. Like the Spanish islands of Ibiza and Majorca, and like Ios and Mykonos in the Aegean, Corfu – Kerkyra to the natives, "Cor, Phew" to the lads – had the reputation of being an accessible, downmarket party centre, a kind of Blackpool-on-the-Med that offered moussaka-and-chips and 24-hour full English breakfasts. Now that I was here, in the 40-degree-Celsius sticky heat, I realized I couldn't have chosen a more perfect hell for myself than an over-touristed island full of boozed-up louts.

One isn't supposed to arrive in Corfu carrying a backpack. I'd snuck in through the back door, rather than arriving on one of the chartered jumbo jets that seemed to roar in from Düsseldorf or Manchester every 15 minutes. Milling with the other deck passengers near an exit staircase, I talked to a tall, red-headed man in his early 20s.

"You going to the Pink Palace too?" he asked. I nodded. "I hear they meet you outside the ferry and drive you right there. Sounds like a cool place."

Walking down the ramp, we were picked out of the crowd by a deeply tanned girl whose pink tube top made her look like a cocktail wiener wrapped in cotton candy. "Pink Palace?" she yelled as passengers left the ferry, and within ten minutes she'd assembled a crowd of two dozen backpackers, directing us to a parking lot outside a customs building devoid of inspectors. By the time I got to the shuttle bus, it was already full of hollering Italians, and an efficient-looking woman with a clipboard and a Greek accent clattered up to the girl in the pink tube top.

"Get rid of the Italians, *right now*. They are insufferable, they won't stop complaining about the heat."

She stuck us in a cab, along with a pair of garrulous young Irishmen from Cork, and the silent driver took us along curving roads overhung with tresses of purple bougainvillea.

Lawrence Durrell described Corfu as a sickle-shaped isle hard by the Greek mainland, the landward side forming "a great bay, noble and serene, and almost completely landlocked." To me, it looked more like a butcher's diagram of a swine's leg. Our ferry had docked at Corfu Town, on the hock of the hog's leg – it was on this mainland-facing hindshank that the most popular beaches lay – and we were now being driven to Agios Gordios, a beach on the Italy-facing foreshank. In total, this gruntling's leg measured 85 kilometres from ham to trotter, making for a lot of tourist bacon to carve up. Nabobs like Lord Jacob Rothschild and Princess Margaret had long ago claimed the northern haunch, living in isolated villas on pebbly coves on the shore that faced Albania, while the hoi polloi congregated by the tens of thousands on bucket-and-spade beaches nearer the pig's knuckles. When the tourists started arriving in May, full-time residents abandoned the coasts and high streets altogether, leaving the punters to wallow in their all-inclusive sty.

The Pink Palace, a legendary hostel, was an anomaly on Corfu, at once a magnet and a holding tank for backpackers who had arrived by rail and ferry. On the cab ride over, I'd been entertained by the boys from Ireland – the nation's software-and-higher-education boom has recently sent a new contingent of loquacious and very pale travellers on the road.

"Girls in Italy and France, they're all *tens*, like," said Cormac. A bird-like young fellow, he looked northern and virginal in the black singlet that drooped over his freckled skin.

"In Ireland," agreed David, "they're all fat, with great awful teeth, and when they smile all you see is their gums. All we've got back home is twos – and maybe a six, like, if you're really lucky."

We piled out of the cab next to a pink, porticoed building, and an Irish girl at the desk – a very pretty Irish girl, I thought, but *chacun à son gout* – told us to join a crowd of backpackers sitting at a dozen round tables in a room adjoining the reception. The manager, wearing a Hawaiian shirt and a strap-jawed grin that had something of the ventriloquist's dummy to it, explained the breakdown of rooms into A-Class, B-Class, and dormitory. All, I was saddened to learn, had to be shared.

Checking in took an hour. Our table was last to be called to the reception, and to stifle the grumbles, an employee did the rounds with a 1.5-litre bottle of pink ouzo. I took a shot and immediately regretted it: with no breakfast in my belly, two days of bad travel hit me like a mallet, and I could feel myself turning as pale as Cormac's chest.

"Jesus!" he yelped, after downing his shot. "That's worse than poteen! It tastes like toilet cleaner!"

Which didn't prevent him, I noted, from gulping two more shots. By the time we got to the desk, the Irish boys had attained new levels of loquacity, excitedly shouting in my ear about knackers and dust-ups. I begged the desk clerk for an A-class room, and, after being issued a pink identification card, was taken by the lethargic and hungover Irish girl to a nearby building. As we walked, I vaguely registered the "10 biggest lies at the Pink Palace" on the back of her T-shirt.

"1. I'm only staying one night," it began, below the nape of her neck. "2. I know how to ride a moped. 3. I'm never drinking ouzo again." The list concluded just above the henna tattoo on her lower back: "8. I just want to kiss you . . . you can keep your clothes on. 9. Of course I remember your name!" I'd found a place where drunk driving and date rape were sources of merriment.

"I think the other fellow in this room is an American, too," she said.

Before I could object, she'd opened the door. It was like walking into a frat house after a frosh-night keg explosion. Every surface was covered with beer and vodka bottles. As I stepped over a slimy condom, I saw the source of the mayhem: a broad-shouldered blond in stained boxer shorts, his arm dangling off the side of the bed, a smog bank of half-metabolized liquor emanating from his prone body. For some reason he'd torn the mattress from the other bed and piled it on his own. I turned to the Irish girl and earnestly implored: "Do you have any B-class rooms left?"

The Pink Palace, I would learn, can house 850 people in its 13 buildings, and when one too many boatloads of backpackers arrives, they simply requisition the neighbours' properties or let people sleep in beach chairs. (I had a nightmare vision of the contagion spreading, like pastel measles, until every structure on the island was stained pink.) I was conducted down a long staircase, along an olive-tree-lined lane, past a basketball court, to a wooden-sided row of rooms within sight of the waves at Agios Gordios. My roommate, mercifully, had left for the day, and I noted with approval that he'd arranged his toiletries neatly on the scratched table. Lying down, I heard the couple next door stirring to life. It was well past noon.

"Are you hung over?" he asked, with an English accent.

"Yeah," she groaned. "After you left, we went down to the hotel disco on the beach. I wasn't that pissed, but I started to vomit. It was the taste of the drink that made me sick, I couldn't stop myself. The lady from the bar was saying: 'Are you from the Pink Palace? Tell those people from the Pink Palace to stay away from here! Go puke on your own beach!' As if it was my fault!"

I had to hand it to myself: I had a knack for finding the best addresses.

◈

The Pink Palace was *The Lost Weekend* meets *How to Stuff a Wild Bikini* on a Hellenic Daytona Beach. Dinner, included in the room price, involved queuing for at least an hour with 500 sun-baked college kids in an open-walled, mosquito-plagued structure called the Palladium. As I waited for lukewarm moussaka, soggy noodles, and overcooked baby carrots served by a sneering cook (who never failed to ask: "You *sure* you vegetarian?") I wondered whether a prison canteen could be worse. The place was dominated by Americans and Italians, a volatile mix. In the dinner queue one night, a group of Italian men tried to jump the line.

"*O-kai!*" the ringleader said to an American who had objected. "We going to back of the line, but nobody tell me to fuck off!"

Shoving began, women screamed, and a group of security guards converged on the troublemakers and threw them down the stairs. One of the aggressively flirting Italians later punched an unresponsive American girl in the eye, and the next morning they trashed their room and pummelled the desk clerk who served their eviction notice.

The employees, mostly backpackers who'd run out of cash on the road, were paid three dollars an hour and packed into dormitories. I didn't envy them. They had to control a population of shirtless frat boys, Joe Boxer underwear riding high, who were often stumble-drunk by 11 in the morning. Most employees coped by drinking heavily, though some obviously relished their position. Working on a Nescafé frappé at the bar late one afternoon, I was joined by a squat fellow with a flowered shirt and a red porkpie hat.

"Top o' the morning to you, Madam," he said to the bartender facetiously.

"How's it going, Simon?" she asked, hoarsely.

"I've had a *won*derful day," he replied. "Yeah, I was sitting on the beach with a *lovely* girl named Lucy on one arm, and a *gorgeous* redhead called Amy on the other. Nothing happened, but still – this is *paradise*. Sounds like you've got Pink Palace voice, luv. We call it the 'Cor-flu.' Must be the climate."

More likely the cumulative effect of cheap liquor, sunburn, and bad food on the immune system. I saw Simon later in the evening, walking up the path from the beach, flanked by girls in bikinis. "Easy life, mate," he drawled as he passed, "easy life."

My roommate turned out to be Dave, a software designer from Seattle. He was, like me, a decade past the average age of the guests. After island-hopping in the Aegean, he'd flown to Corfu and was doing his best to forget that he had a girlfriend back home.

"The last thing she said to me before I left was, 'Be good.' So far I have been – but you know how it is. I mean, did you see those Swedish girls at lunch today? They were *hot*." He chuckled nervously. "I wouldn't want to have to lie to my girlfriend – but c'mon, we're guys! Sometimes the little head does the thinking for you."

He'd worked for an organization called Bust Loose in college, setting up spring break excursions to Cancún, Puerto Vallarta, and Mazatlán, and was nostalgic for the days of sex without commitment.

"I went down five years running, and became resort director. I had a fantastic time! Man, it was all about the chicks. I don't know what it is with girls on vacation – they want to have a fling. There's something about the beach, the sand, the sun – they'd do things they'd never do at home. You weren't supposed to drink on the job, but everybody did. You know: one tequila, two tequila, three tequila, floor!"

He had a trunk full of such Margaritaville slogans, which he'd regularly trot out with a mirthless chuckle. "You know what they say," he said when I caught him napping one afternoon. "If you wanna fiesta, you gotta siesta!"

At the Pink Palace pub that night, the manager explained they'd reduced the number of fights by banning Corfiots. "It's policy that local Greeks aren't allowed into the disco," he told me. "Too much friction. But there's still the Italians," he added, nodding to a group closing in on two blonds.

Near midnight, an announcement was made: Dr. George, the owner of the Pink Palace, was about to put on his famous show. We were instructed to sit in concentric circles around the dance floor, and a game of spin the bottle began. A solid, tired-looking man with a goatee took the microphone and delivered a message of love.

"People here from many nationalities, please! Any time the girl is having problem, let us know! We deal with problem, we want peace here only."

Then, as the slow-dancing theme from *Zorba the Greek* started up, Dr. George picked a plate from a stack and smashed it over the head of a seated girl. Walking around the circle, he brought down plate after plate, trailed by the manager, who kept him supplied from the stack of crockery in his arms. Sometimes Dr. George faked out a victim, pausing before he smashed; sometimes he flipped the plate like a pizza; always he brought it down with a thwack, so the shards tangled in people's hair or tumbled into their drinks. This display went on for ten minutes: a Greek hotelier shattering unglazed white plates on the heads of 400 drunken college kids with sadistic gusto. The Irish boy, David, picking a shard out of his eye, leaned over and said with delight: "He smashed *two* on me head! That was great!"

❧

Next morning, waking to the sound of my neighbour dry-heaving, I decided it was time to check out of the Pink Palace. At the breakfast hall by the beach I sat down with the Irish lads.

"I'm completely knackered," said Cormac, hand trembling as he tried to lift his eggs to his mouth.

"There was this fucking Canadian girl – no offence – following us around last night," moaned David. "She was *locked*. She peeled off her beer label and handed it to me, and told me that in Canada that means you want to sleep with somebody." I was about to tell him I'd never heard of the custom when he whispered: "Jesus! That's her!"

A girl flip-flopped over to our table, fresh from the beach, water pearling on her fleshy, broad shoulders.

"I'm like, still drunk!" she gushed. "What did I do last night? Omigod, don't tell me, I hope it wasn't like, too embarrassing?"

"Don't worry, I was pretty tipsy meself," Cormac reassured her chivalrously.

As she staggered off to pick up her breakfast, I told them I'd seen her before. She was one of the wrestlers on the train from Naples.

"That's why she came up and gave me a bear hug last night!" said Cormac, who couldn't have weighed more than 60 kilograms. "I thought she was going to break me bloody ribs. We walked her back from the bar and she was puking all over the bushes. I was trying to pretend I wasn't with her."

Dave, my roommate, joined us as two tall girls staggered in. One was alternately laughing and crying, and had an angry patch of raw, oozing flesh running down her arm from her shoulder.

"She pushed me off!" she yelled, shoving her friend. It wasn't clear whether she was drunk or in shock.

"You see that all over Greece," said Dave. "People getting off the ferries covered with welts and bruises and open running sores. It's brutal. You get two girls on a scooter, that's just asking for trouble."

Projectile vomiting, international brawls, road rash. I'd seen about enough of the Pink Palace. An all-inclusive backpacker's camp with its own small stretch of rocky beach, it was a cut-rate version of the self-contained holiday resorts the college kids' parents visited in the Caribbean or on the Costa del Sol. I'd put up with it because I'd been given a relatively quiet room, and I was so road-addled I'd been willing to bear the sounds of the late-night volleyball games. But too long in this Pleasure Island amusement park, I figured, and I'd sprout ears and turn into a braying, alcoholic donkey. I wished Dave luck with his next roommate and said goodbye to the Irish boys.

"Actually, we're thinking of moving on ourselves," said David. "We've been here three days, and we haven't seen one Greek person yet."

"Well, there was the cab driver, like," Cormac objected. He thought back for a second. "But then, we didn't talk to him."

§

Midway through the 20th century, a pernicious tendency in leisure travel – already embryonic in the pleasure enclave of Baiae – culminated in the perfection of the tourist bubble. Institutionalized in the inns and travel ghettoes of pilgrimages and the Grand Tour, it reached its apotheosis in the all-inclusive beach resort, which allowed people to travel halfway around the globe, to nations with distinct languages, traditions, and cultures, without encountering anything foreign. The fully formed tourist bubble relied on two developments: the generalization of paid vacations, and the invention of the jet airplane. Before that, a working-class beach trip was a local affair, a weekend excursion limited to Coney Island or Blackpool by the speed of omnibuses, charabancs, and trains. In England, the Bank Holiday Act, introduced in 1871, set aside a fixed number of vacation days at Christmas, Easter, Whitsun, and the beginning of August, flooding the beaches of Brighton and Scarborough with day trippers. The French upped the ante in 1936, when the socialist prime minister Léon Blum established a European standard by setting aside a generous fortnight to a month's worth of paid vacations, though stipulating they had to be taken in the summer (provoking the famous ghost-town effect familiar to anybody who's visited Paris in August).

Though the masses were increasingly free to travel, they couldn't afford to go very far. Before the Second World War, the choicest shores were colonized by those with the leisure and money to enjoy extended sojourns. In 1834, Henry Brougham, former lord chancellor of England, built a villa at Cannes, pioneering the foreign colony that would transform a derelict stretch of French coast into the Côte d'Azur. By the end of the

19th century, Nice had become the first modern western city with a tourist-based economy; wealthy British expatriates gathered beneath the palms on a Promenade des Anglais built for their strolling pleasure. It was strictly a winter destination: in the hot summer months, the best people still made for the Norman resorts on the English Channel.

It took a group of democratic American upstarts – upstarts with incomes, naturally – to popularize the out-of-season French Riviera. In 1922, the year the elegant Train Bleu started its Calais–Mediterranean run, Gerald Murphy and his wife decided to aestivate in a château that Cole Porter was renting. They convinced a local hotelier to remain open till September, and a free-floating community of bohemians, depicted in F. Scott Fitzgerald's *Tender Is the Night*, slummed in fishermen's caps, espadrilles, and striped shirts on the deserted beaches. The next year, Coco Chanel returned from the Côte d'Azur with a deep suntan – before the Industrial Revolution, such swarthiness had been an emblem of peasant labour – giving the vogue of heliotherapy the imprimatur of high fashion. Hoteliers started confecting Riviera resorts like Juan-les-Pins to attract the new breed of sun worshippers in streamlined bathing suits, importing sand and sweeping the beaches of flyspecked seaweed.

Those who could afford it went to the new resorts in Jamaica, Cuba, Martinique, and the Bahamas, sometimes by boat, but increasingly on that new plaything of the rich, the passenger plane. The world's first scheduled airline service had operated briefly between Tampa and St. Petersburg, Florida, in 1914, and after the First World War the Airco DH16, a converted bomber glassed-in by a sliding roof, began regular flights from London to Paris. As other European nations started scheduled services – the Dutch airline KLM was founded in 1920, Germany's Lufthansa six years later – airplanes became a costly novelty for adventurous businesspeople, diplomats, and showbiz types (until 1935, however, Hollywood stars were contractually forbidden from risking their valuable necks in planes). Though unheated, and so noisy that passengers had to communicate by handwritten notes, early planes could also be as elegant as first-class railway cars, featuring alligator-skin-upholstered wicker chairs and walnut panelling.

Such winged Pullmans were also expensive. In the 1920s, a 48-hour trip from New York to Los Angeles, which involved two transfers by train, cost

$351.94 – far more than a discount ticket on the same route today. When Pan Am launched the first transatlantic commercial air service in 1939, the Boeing 314 flying boat achieved a zenith in aeronautic opulence. With ship-style staterooms, an elegant dining salon that served lobster and *pâté de foie gras*, and a promenade deck, the airborne luxury liner known as the *Yankee Clipper* took 19 hours to fly from Newfoundland to Southampton.

Before the masses could afford to fly, something had to change. The innovations were both socio-economic and technological. In 1932, the first chartered airplane excursion had taken two dozen members of England's Polytechnic Touring Association from London to Switzerland. The Douglas DC-3 revolutionized the airline industry two years later; its soundproof cabin, reclining seats, and autopilot soon made it the world's most successful passenger plane. After the Second World War, the Boeing 707 was the harbinger of a new era, a pure jet (its predecessors had combined jet and propeller technology) that could carry 189 coach passengers at 960 kilometres an hour.

By 1958, with the introduction of the first transatlantic passenger jet service – a Pan Am Boeing 707 flight between New York and Paris – more people were crossing the Atlantic by plane than by ship. Tourist-class fares gradually put distant beaches within reach of lower middle- and working-class vacationers. The wide-bodied Boeing 747, tall as a six-storey building, capable of flying non-stop between New York and Tokyo and spilling 320 passengers at a time onto the runways of tiny island nations, was introduced in 1970. Cheap charter flights soon came to account for half of all plane travel in Europe. In 1950, 25 million people made some form of international trip. A half century later, thanks largely to the jet airplane, the figure had risen to 700 million.

For places like Corfu, the combination of capacious jet planes and cheap air fare was a disaster. When the Durrell family lived here in the 1930s, flying boats touched down once a week in Gouvia Bay; most foreign tourists arrived by ferry. They tended to be wealthy, educated, and – if not utter prats – passably acquainted with Mediterranean culture. Corfu was one of the most verdant Greek Islands, successively an outpost of the Byzantine Empire, a Venetian colony, and a British protectorate. It boasted impregnable fortresses emblazoned with the winged lion of Venice,

elegant colonnades modelled on Paris's Rue de Rivoli, and Sunday afternoon cricket games on the Esplanade, where locally brewed ginger beer
was served beneath café umbrellas. Prince Philip was born in the royal
villa of Mon Repos, and the Kaiser Wilhelm II left an eccentric legacy in
the Akhillion, an absurdly incongruous neo-Pompeiian villa near the
village of Gastouri. Shot through with a bewitching array of cosmopolitan influences, Corfu was an anachronistic retreat from the cares of the
world. "I cannot conceive why rich people live on the French Riviera
when there are places like Corfu left in the world," marvelled Evelyn
Waugh in 1930.

Then, after the Second World War, an airport was built a couple of
kilometres from Corfu Town. By the late 1960s, a new kind of invader was
beginning to take over, more insidious than the previous waves of Vandals,
Goths, and Normans. Package tourists could now fly to a distant land in
the time it had once taken to go overland to Brighton or Miami Beach. By
the 1990s, a million tourists were arriving every year – half from England
– overwhelming the full-time population of 105,000. Corfu appeared on a
tourist map that included Torremolinos, Majorca, Benidorm, and the
Algarve, becoming just another sun destination in the British brochures.
One where, the charter passengers were interested to learn, the people
spoke *Greek*.

It wasn't until I'd been on Corfu for three days, riding the bus from the
Pink Palace to Corfu Town, that I really started seeing signs in the Greek
alphabet. I'd waited on the road beside a shop called Gee Bees Super
Market, which sold day-old copies of the *Daily Mail* and *The Express*, and
crowded into a 1950s-vintage bus that juddered uphill past the cacti and
olive trees as though it were cranking its way up the tracks of a rusty cog-
railway. The bus stopped to pick up elderly Greek passengers, many of
whom were forced to stand because the seats were filled with tourists. A
Scandinavian man finally gave up his seat to a grey-bearded Orthodox
priest, who warded off the blond toddler staring at him by making the sign
of the cross before his face.

After checking into a suicide-inducing hotel on the shorefront road
on a diesel-fume-choked strip of the new port – the only place with a
room – I wandered through the old town. Cicadas stridulated in the trees

like the rattlers of an anarchic mariachi band, and cats slinked between the umber and ochre facades of the shuttered Venetian-style townhouses of the old Jewish Quarter. The backstreets were gorgeous, but the moment I stepped onto a main avenue like Nikiforou Theotoki, I was caught in a slow-moving *défilé* of glossy Italian women and British men in T-shirts that read "They tell me I was on Ios, but I don't remember." The pavements were crowded with gigantic bottles of moonshine Chanel No. 5 and counterfeit Ray Bans, their cheap finish already flaking onto the paving stones.

Determined to try something local, I bought an Eiffel Tower–shaped bottle of Koum Quat liqueur and used it to chase down a gyro stuffed with greasy chips. Suggestive of Grand Marnier distilled in a New Jersey chemical plant, it tasted not unlike a melted orange popsicle.

In a high street newsstand, I picked up a celebrated paean to Corfu, Lawrence Durrell's *Prospero's Cell*, a superior example of the literary current in which privileged expatriates reminisce about balmy paradises. Lately the genre has degenerated into the boomer Arcadian form, where culture is reduced to cuisine, the natives to soulfully eccentric rustics, and yuppies gloat about their years in Provence, their villas beneath the Tuscan sun, and – coming full circle – their houses in Corfu. In his heartfelt 1945 homage to the island, Durrell and his wife, Nancy, rent a fisherman's house on the north end of the island. Between nights of Greek jazz, letters from Henry Miller, and nocturnal fishing for octopi by the light of carbide lanterns, he spins an erudite and poetic – if sporadically pompous – history of an island that he argues could have been Shakespeare's model for *The Tempest*. To read it in modern-day, concrete-encrusted Corfu was to plunge into the cruellest bathos.

"A white house set like a dice on a rock already venerable with the scars of wind and water. The hill runs clear up into the sky behind it, so that the cypresses and olives overhang this room in which I sit and write . . . This is become our unregretted home. A world. Corcyra."

I glanced up from my Greek coffee. Pinkening British tourists were walking around with open cans of Heineken. Foul T-shirts hung in the arcade across the street, buffeted on their hangers by the sirocco. "Certified Muff Diving Instructor," read one. "Dry skin? Free lotion, Pump here," said its neighbour, above an arrow pointing crotchwards.

Lawrence's younger brother Gerald, the down-to-earth, animal-obsessed Durrell, wrote *My Family and Other Animals* (in which his poet sibling comes across as an uptight sot), enchanting generations of readers with a vision of a childhood Eden populated by rapacious house geckos and tortoises lurking beneath phosphorescent tides. After using the royalties from his books to fund his zoo on the Channel island of Jersey, he returned to Corfu in 1968, a year after the first Holiday Inn opened. His biographers speculate that Gerald's guilt over popularizing Corfu, and the touristic carpet bombing that ensued, hastened his breakdown and slide into alcoholism.

I sensed a similar depression gaining on me as I returned to my hotel. I found the Greeks in Corfu Town cynical and mercenary, jaded by contact with the tourists. An ad for a British cellphone company near the New Fortress read: "Current UK temperature 5° C. Go on, ruin their day. Phone home and tell them what they're missing." It seemed to encapsulate Corfu's new raison d'être, as well as the essence of the beach vacation: as an escape hatch for stressed northerners, an experience that only had value if it could be gloated over.

Maybe, too, the wear and tear of travel was blackening my mood. Sweating on the damp mattress in my hotel, I enumerated my ills. My bicep was still sore from the wasp's sting. An unknown insect at the Pink Palace had injected its acidic venom – or perhaps, I mused bleakly, its larvae – into my thumb, which throbbed priapically. The nail of my big toe, blackened by my assault on the Matterhorn-Hütte in those too-tight rented boots, was threatening to fall off completely. Plagued by pink eye, my right cornea was no longer responding to the antibiotics I'd picked up in Rome, and I had to bumble through the streets, Cyclops-style, with only one contact lens. Diesel-smoke particles congealed in a sticky layer of sweat and sunscreen, occluding my pores. I'd been wearing my money belt for so long that a rash of pinkish welts had appeared across my belly. (I knew better than to ask for sympathy, though. Even if I was bent double with bacillary dysentery, the response to any complaint would inevitably be: "You're a travel writer? I'd *love* to have your problems!")

The road was taking its toll. As yet another charter plane rattled the windows of my unventilated hotel room, I decided there was only one way to overcome my burgeoning spleen: I needed a vacation from my travels. It was time to go to Club Med.

§

The marriage of jet airplane and tropical beach, though a great leap forward in the development of the tourist bubble, wasn't foolproof. In spite of the perfection of airport transfers and beachfront security guards, it was still possible to encounter something foreign when one went abroad. It happened all too often: most notoriously, when the revellers at the Havana Hilton had their New Year's party crashed as Fidel Castro and his rebels swept into town from the Sierra Maestra in January 1959.

The antidote to such embarrassments was synthesized in a little tent village on the Mediterranean. Founded on the eve of France's generalized paid vacations by a White Russian living in exile in Paris, L'Ours Blanc vacation camp was a modest pre-war success, bringing 250 French vacationers by train and boat to the island of Corsica. After the war, it was reopened as the Club Olympique, attracting another Russian émigré, the London-based Reuters journalist Vladimir Raitz. Inspired by the enthusiastic staff and unpretentious atmosphere – reminiscent of the English seaside holiday camps of Billy Butlin, also launched in the Depression – Raitz chartered a plane to allow the British to enjoy the Mediterranean sun. Fighting Draconian post-war regulations and the British European Airways monopoly on short-haul routes, he flew 32 vacationers in a DC-3 to his own holiday tent village, the Club Franco-Britannique, in 1950, for a mere £32 10s a head. Offering two meat meals a day in an era of rationing, his excursion was an immediate success, and Raitz set up resorts in Benidorm and Majorca and named his company Horizon Holidays – which earned his clients the nickname the "horizontals" for their quick grasp of the sea, sex, and sun formula. Horizon succumbed during the 1974 energy crisis, but by creating the all-inclusive charter-flight beach-resort holiday, Raitz was responsible for a new travel paradigm. With meat-and-two veg, human pyramids, and copious pints of Watney's Red

Barrell, it was just like being in England, only with a better climate, whiter sand, and an ocean one could actually bathe in.

The original Club Olympique attracted another visitor: Gérard Blitz, Belgian water polo champion and a decorated Second World War resistance fighter. A communist from a Jewish diamond-cutting family, he was inspired by the conviviality he saw in Corsica to set up his own village. A simple poster in the Paris metro showed the sea, the sun, and his phone number. Hundreds called, and in 1950 his clients made the two-day train-and-boat trip from Paris to the first Club Méditerranée in Majorca. The Alcúdia camp was woefully underequipped: for 700 clients, there was a four-hole outhouse, three showers, and one stove. Against all odds, however, it was a success. The guests responded to setbacks with such cheerful alacrity that Blitz took to calling them *gentils membres* – his gracious members, eventually abbreviated, in Club parlance, to GMs. Associating with another Jewish communist, Gilbert Trigano (who had supplied him with U.S. army surplus tents), Blitz opened other villages in Tuscany and Montenegro. Soon, people were flying to Club Med camps on specially chartered planes. Baron Edmond de Rothschild visited the Arziv club in Israel, and after a diverting night of piggy-backing women around the camp, came to the founders' aid during a 1961 financial crisis by buying a third of the company. A half century after its founding, Club Med was a travel conglomerate, with its own cruise ships and 120 vacation villages in 36 countries.

From the start, Club Med was synonymous with hedonism. Conviviality was enforced with nightly singalong games like "Crazy Sign," "Agadoo," and "Hands Up," and the staff encouraged deadbeats by pushing them into the ocean. Corfu's Club Med village at Ipsos, set up in 1953, had been the first village with permanent, Polynesian-style huts, and the 60-hectare resort was initially capable of accommodating a thousand GMs. A security guard in a booth next to a roadside Club Méditerranée logo let me pass, and I walked down a winding road past red clay tennis courts. Soon I was among tree-shaded thatched huts, arranged by divisions like the aboveground tombs in Parisian cemeteries. After paying for a day-visit – the harried Greek woman at the desk put down my occupation as "Rider" – I made straight for the breakfast buffet, piling my tray with sectioned oranges and melon, muesli, thermoses of coffee, and watered-down orange juice, steering clear of a bowl of custard pudding crawling with wasps. Late risers were seated at picnic tables beneath the thatched roof, and I joined three Italian men finishing their coffees. They'd flown from Italy to Corfu via Athens and were staying for two weeks. Sebastiano, from Milan, was complaining about the gender ratio.

"It is something like 70 men for only 30 women. There is too much competition."

Francesco, a soft-spoken Fiat engineer with black hair swept back in the beginnings of a pompadour, objected. "Oh, is not so bad, Sebastiano. More like 60–40. There aren't so many people now, but maybe more women will come when the planes arrive this afternoon."

The setting certainly looked beautiful, I said. We could see people waterskiing from pontoons that stretched towards the hills of Albania.

"Eh," shrugged Francesco. "The beach, she not so good – not very large, and in the afternoon, very crowded."

After breakfast, Francesco showed me his hut. Individually named after extinct Greek gods, city-states, and currency – his was called Drachme – they looked like octagonal yurts with peaked roofs. Inside were two camp beds and an open armoire, where Francesco had carefully hung his pressed white shirts. Communal toilets, showers, and a roofless area with rows of sinks and mirrors could be found next to the cantina. Francesco, who had a swimming lesson scheduled, wandered off to the pontoons, and I headed to the bar, in a grove full of ancient olive trees whose gnarled trunks looked like pulled taffy. Most of the huts were on an evergreen-covered promontory, from which a narrow beach stretched back towards Corfu Town. Salsa music blared, and male GMs wandered around in Speedos and flip-flops, giving the rare women the once-over.

Club Med had been conceived as a utopian experiment in modern leisure. Money was banned – wallets were put into safes upon arrival, and drinks were paid for with coloured tickets – and *tutoiement*, the dropping of the formal "vous," was encouraged. "We are not pleased with the world as it is," Gérard Blitz had declared. "We are going to create another one." Club Med's brave new world, where the semi-nudity of beach life encouraged a superficial conception of free love, was timed perfectly with the appearance of oral contraceptives and women's liberation. At the infamous clubs in Martinique, Cancún, and Tahiti, *gentils organisateurs* (GOs), tanned and buff, scissored off the ties of arriving businessmen and suavely seduced new arrivals (while secretly cataloguing their conquests by carving notches into their bedposts). Micro-communities of free spirits, determined to cast off the strictures of urban life, dotted through balmy sites of the greatest natural beauty – a blueprint for paradise. If only the Club Med philosophy would spread, clients sighed, and all the citizens of the world one day lived as *gentils membres!*

The world had other ideas. Bubbles of privileged Europeans and North Americans indulging a noble-savage fantasy were bound to provoke reaction from the excluded citizens of the undeveloped nations in which they'd embedded themselves. In Corsica, where the Club Olympique was born, militant separatists who'd seen their island colonized by tourist operators from mainland France blew up eight bungalows at the Club Med village in Cargèse. In Paris, the Situationists, a group of far-left French artists and radicals, defaced billboards that read "Club Med – An Antidote to Civilization." (The Sex Pistols' Johnny Rotten would howl out a translation of the May '68 graffito a decade later: "A cheap holiday in other people's misery!") The "no-cash" illusion was undermined when armed robbers raided the tills of Club Meds in Mexico and Calabria, and a daring 1977 heist saw three masked gunmen bursting into the Corfu village, shooting a GO who tried to resist, and making off with half a million in cash and 600 passports. At villages like Les Boucaniers in Martinique, security guards started to patrol the beaches with submachine guns.

§

At the fringe of the public beach, a security guard checked my day pass – the other GMs wore hospital-style wrist bands. I sat down on a narrow strip of sand beneath a palm tree and gazed across the water, past the Italians floating on giant inflatable cellphones, towards the undeveloped coastline of Albania. The proximity to Europe's poorest nation had caused an enclave like Corfu problems in the past. In the 1970s, the Albanian coast guard strafed a dinghy of Club Med employees who were scuba diving too close to shore; a GO's decomposing body was found floating in the sea a few days later. When Albania plunged into anarchy after a series of pyramid schemes collapsed in the mid-1990s, several British vacationers were gunned down on their yachts, and the Greek navy had to be called in to patrol the straits.

All these geopolitical distractions seemed a world away on this sunny August day. The bathers on the Club Med beach were lithe and well formed, and as I paddled in the placid water I watched a man trot alongside some bikinied women, inquiring *"Italiana? Italiana?"* I have to confess I enjoy the voyeuristic spectacle of the beach, the sensation of deliquescing in the sun, the erotic charge of glimpsing breasts flattened against sand, the mild exhibitionism of standing to rub suntan lotion over my limbs.

I enjoy it for all of about two hours. Then I surpass my dose of solar radiation and start to wonder what the fuck I'm going to do for the rest of the day. Wandering back to the cantina just as it opened for lunch, I selected from the white fish, broccoli, boiled carrots, and french fries, and roamed with my tray until I spotted a vacant seat beside two French women.

"Est-ce que c'est libre?" I asked, hoping to sideswipe them with my New World French accent. Céline, her brown hair pulled back in a ponytail, gestured for me to sit down, as Marie, wearing a black bikini top, made room for me. I told them I was visiting for the day and asked how long they were staying. Céline, who had just left her job at Disney, said they'd flown down on a charter from Paris a week ago.

"We paid about 900 euros each," said Marie, who worked for Colgate-Palmolive. "That might sound like a lot. But it's the high season. If you take advantage of all the activities, the water skiing, the salsa lessons, I find that it's worth it."

I mentioned the complaints of gender imbalance from the Italian men I'd met that morning.

"Oh là là," said Céline, "they would say that! I think there are 600 Italians here now, maybe 400 French, 200 others. The problem is, there are far too many men. We both have boyfriends back home, and frankly, we just want to be left alone."

"It started in the plane," said Marie, rolling her eyes. "People were already checking one another out. Céline was trying to hide her head."

They described a fight at the bar started by a French man who objected to an Italian man's flirting – "Because there are also French people who are stupid, you know." (*Impossible!*) All in all, though, they'd had a good week.

"It's really a very special atmosphere here," said Marie, looking around at all the firm, tanned flesh. "There are only young people. There aren't many places left in the world like this."

What did they think of Corfu itself?

"We haven't left the Club Med at all," admitted Céline. "The island is supposed to be nice, *non?*"

They'd never find out; they were flying back to Paris that afternoon. I left them addressing a stack of identical postcards of a generic tropical island emblazoned with the Club Med trident.

My visit had been badly planned. Tuesday was the day the last week's *membres* left and the new ones arrived. Sitting on a low concrete stool, I watched bus after bus appear in the olive grove, to be surrounded by GOs in baby blue T-shirts who clapped along as a pumped-up remix of the old rhythm 'n' blues standard "Last Night" blared from speakers. As pale, blinking neophytes emerged from the shuttle, I was amused to note there were two men for every woman. Perhaps this imbalance was a localized phenomenon, but I suspected that Club Med's reputation as a pleasure dome appealed less to female fantasies than to some atavistic male vision of *Playboy*-era free love. All around me, disconsolate men were flipping through the pink pages of the *Gazzetta dello Sport*, playing chess, reading sandy-spined paperbacks. Paradise without the dames – it reminded me of the marines' camp in *South Pacific* before the nurses arrived. Beyond the gates, of course, there were plenty of women. Many of the Corfiot women I'd seen were gorgeous, thin-hipped, and pale-skinned, with blue slanted eyes suggesting the Norman genes in the local pool. The men at Club Med would never know, though – the only Greeks who penetrated their bubble were the middle-aged wait staff in drab blue-and-white gingham dresses.

I gave up on Club Med after a dinner conversation with more complaining French girls, preferring to finish the evening sipping an iced espresso at a seaside terrace in Corfu Town. The Arts Café was hidden from view by a wing of the Royal Palace, and Corfiots seemed to use it as a refuge from the summer hordes.

Apologists for the travel industry say that mass tourism can revive the flagging economies of poor and developing nations, but I'd never seen much redeeming value in all-inclusive resorts. They bring nothing to the locals, except perhaps a sense of alienation. Resort tourists don't eat at local restaurants, patronize local shops, or buy local crafts, and they leave their wallets at home or in safes, so there is virtually no trickle-down effect. The examples of their complete indifference to local conditions were legion: when a tropical storm left Martinique without safe drinking water, the local Club Med simply flew in a planeload of bottled Evian for its members. Rather than buy food from suppliers on the Spanish coast, a British tour operator set up a poultry farm outside Benidorm to provide rubbery omelettes for clients. There was never any morality involved in the touristic colonization of beach nations, only economics. It was fine, for example, for generations of Americans to sun themselves on the shores of a fascist dictatorship – Franco's Spain – but even now it was strictly forbidden to vacation in Castro's socialist dictatorship.

I headed over to a high stone wall that overlooked the water and the ramparts of the Old Venetian Fortress. A high-speed tourist catamaran had just zipped into port from Italy, and its wake buffeted a group of teenage swimmers, threatening to tangle them in a net strung across the inlet.

"That's bloody dangerous," said a woman with an antipodean accent. She was in her 40s, stocky, with a tan as deep as the worry lines around her eyes. "I happen to know my daughter was swimming there last week, quite drunk, and almost drowned." Originally from New Zealand, she'd met a Greek man and had been living on Corfu for 20 years.

I commented on the beauty of the scene.

"Ha!" she snorted. "There's things they don't tell you in the brochures. We've got the worst prison in the world here. All of the worst murderers. The walls are 20 feet thick, like those ones –" she pointed to the wave-slapped ramparts. I'd already noticed the panopticon-style building next to the British cemetery and the mental hospital. "There's no way to escape from that place. And don't forget, Greece is the poorest country in the EU. After my rent, I've barely got enough left over for food. And electricity is hideously expensive here. I take candles from the church and burn them

on the balcony at night to save on the bills. Sure, it's pleasant and all . . ."
She flicked a dismissive hand at the blue Ionian.

These were the backstage features most tourists preferred not to
glimpse. Better to imagine the Corfiots, with their donkeys and caiques and
evil-eye medallions, as superstitious peasants grateful for tourist dollars.
Judging by all the young Greeks walking around the old town with "English
First Certificate" workbooks under their arms, and the keen business
acumen displayed on the high streets, Corfu had a particularly cosmopolitan tourist-based economy, responding to the mixed blessing of great physical beauty with the usual blend of grace and greed. I'm always torn
between cheering and condemning locals who have acquiesced to letting
out their homes and re-enacting their own traditions for the benefit of
tourists. It's considered inappropriate for the privileged traveller to implore
people to remain picturesque fishers and farmers when the material
benefits of modernity – the opportunity to travel not least among them –
beckon so alluringly. But by surrendering their coast to foreign tourists and
their money, the Corfiots had acquiesced to their own colonization.

The woman from New Zealand had reminded me of a sacred source
near the royal estate of Mon Repos. According to a local tradition
described by Lawrence Durrell, a draught from this well means one will
never leave Corfu. The next afternoon, I found a shaded path between
some condos, descended a staircase littered with crumpled cans of Mythos
beer, and found a spigot next to a marble plaque set in a stone wall. A thin
trickle of the holy water of abandonment and forgetfulness dribbled to the
ground. I stared at it for a minute, imagined how good the cool water
would taste going down my throat. Then, thirst unslaked, I turned and
walked back up the steps.

§

There was one more place I had to see before I could abandon the sty to
the porkers. I took a bus down to a beach called Kavos, on the extreme
southern tip of the island. An out-of-print British guidebook had
described the place in obscurely rapturous terms: "Standing among a real
Old Guard of olive trees with tremendous trunks and shakos of silver-grey

foliage, even two-storey houses in Kavos allow the trees the ascendancy the eye delights in." The writer regretted that "a B class hotel was being built which will be only slightly out of scale." That was in 1980.

Twenty years later, the olive trees had given way to a grove of B-class hotels. A long strip of restaurants offered Toad in the Hole and Mushy Peas and Beans, bills payable in pounds. Though Kavos could now accommodate 8,000 tourists, I spent an hour plodding between hotels, their balconies hung with Union Jack towels, before I found a free room in a house in a back street. The Greek landlady explained that independent travellers almost never came to Kavos; it was fully booked by English outfits like Club 18-30, JMC, or Libra Holidays, which specialized in week-long getaways, mostly targeted at people under 30. After a late full-English breakfast – Libby's baked beans, stewed tomatoes, runny eggs, and cocktail sausages – I made for the beach. Foul trickles of brown water, slick with algae, meandered from between the hotels. I spent an hour on a beach chair, listening to the pale blonds next to me cackling. A Greek beach vendor came along, plaintively crying: "*wa*-ter-melon, *yel*-low melon, *cit*-rus fruits." The occupant of the next beach chair, a glabrous Londoner, looked up from his copy of the *Daily Mail*.

"Fuck off, you cunt," he said, and returned to the football scores.

That afternoon, Liverpool was playing Manchester United. Sports bars with satellite dishes and stools ranged before wall-size screens filled up with tipplers. The men went shirtless, and I counted the boils on backs, looked at the yellowish sheen of lager sweat purling over purpling skin. The women were thick-ankled and plain, wearing bikini tops with single-shoulder straps, fresh henna tattoos encircling their rolls of pink fat. Over dinner at the British Restaurant, the Greek waiter lingered over my table.

"You're not British?" he said. I shook my head. "I *hate* the British," he whispered with vehemence. He looked as if just saying it did him good. "I live in the next village, Lefkimi. I used to live here, but I couldn't sleep. Here, it is too crazy. Anything can happen."

I asked him about the sulphurous smell that was cutting my appetite for the fish and chips on my plate.

"When they build this place, they build it for too many people, they don't think. Now the sewerage system can't take it." Around 11 every morning, as thousands of alcohol-poisoned louts and laddettes discharged their bowels, an intolerable stench arose from the beach at Kavos.

〴

That night, I joined the carnival. Partiers were sitting on the patio below my room, starting the evening with vodka shots and Red Bull chasers. The music was already pounding on the main drag. "We *Will*, We *Will* – Rock You!," "ABC" by the Jackson Five, "Electric Avenue," lame techno – the night throbbed. The girls on the strip had traded their bathing suits for synthetic tops that made them look like inflatable dolls. The plainer they were, it seemed, the more glittery their outfits. The men had short hair, short-sleeved shirts, short tempers. A group of barechested yobs, wearing Chippendales' bow ties, were being led up the street by a horsey-looking tour leader, dressed in a corset and knee-high black boots, who yelled, domineeringly, "Keep to the right!" Walking past a bar called Crash Bandicoot, I was almost knocked to the ground as a knot of red-faced men poured into the street. A skinhead ripped the shirt off his narrow chest and tried to head butt a man with a pint in his hand before being thrown to the ground by four bouncers.

A tiny Albanian girl with a long flowered dress and a rose in her black chignon was trying to sell a glowing plastic rave stick to a passing lout. He wheeled and yelled, with inexplicable rage, "*Shakamak hakalak!*" His version of pidgin Greek, apparently. I was reminded of what a resident of the Canary Islands on the Santiago pilgrimage had told me about the German and English tourists who overran his home. "*Beben, rompen, salen,*" he'd said contemptuously. They drink, they break, they leave.

I strolled up and down the strip all night, goggle-eyed. People queued to leap head-first from a crane called the "New World Bungee Jump," and took shots on an invincible Greek goalie for the chance to win a bottle of champagne. By midnight, there were pools of vomit and broken glass outside every bar. People were borne on stretchers out of clubs. Every few hundred metres there was an infirmary ready to receive the victims of scooter accidents induced by *bomba*, the local surgical-spirit-and-mineral-water moonshine passed off as vodka or gin. A Greek family in a

small car were trying to drive through Kavos. Their eyes widened as a
drunk leapt on their hood and started licking their windscreen.

Back in my room, sated, slow-flying mosquitoes awaited my return. I
killed as many as I could, leaving red streaks of lager-lout blood on the wall,
consoling myself that any mosquito I'd missed would perish from cirrho-
sis anyway. Part of the nasty undertone of violence might have been the
bomba. But in Kavos, the old Marxist analysis seemed apt: vacation travel
was a kind of steam valve for the urban proletariat, providing an outlet for
the frustrated aspirations of alienated workers. The apologists for mass
tourism said this was too simplistic an explanation. Leisure time, now
available to all classes, was where people situated their independence and
creativity; it was time outside work, and hence the source of much hope,
discovery, and anxiety. In this ludic period, they might escape – perhaps
permanently – from sexual and social constraint, conceiving a new vision
of themselves.

Not bloody likely, I thought. More often, they opt for the convenience
of the tourist bubble, and when they get to the longed-for beach it's a
sewage-filled strip of grey sand where the locals cynically sell them a simulacrum of their long-vanished culture. Finding themselves among the
kinds of people they jostle with for standing room on the subway back
home, they resume a familiar pattern of competitiveness and sniping.
Hence the fantastic rages people fly into on vacation, as they discover the
bungalows, staterooms, and restaurants they've paid good money for
aren't up to standard. Not only have they sold their own time to their
bosses; the consolation they've worked for all year, their holiday, is the
same commercialized shuck they've left behind. The beach vacation – the
ritualized sexual licence of Club Med, or the Mardi Gras-like debauchery
of beach strips like Kavos – is a modern manifestation of Carnival, a
clearly demarcated time when the slaves can act like freedmen, ultimately
reinforcing the status quo. One that is doubly effective since the advent of
cheap charter jets because it inflicts the social and ecological conse-
quences of consumption and debauchery on distant cultures.

The Nazis would have been at home in Kavos; this was how they'd vacationed. Under the slogan *Kraft durch Freude* – "Strength through joy" – the
leader of the National Socialist Labour Front, Dr. Robert Ley, introduced

cheap collective holidays for workers in 1933. After abolishing unions and instituting six-month mandatory labour for young men, he set up ski and seaside resorts, and commissioned ten cruise ships to sail the Mediterranean and the Baltic. Like modern charter vacations, the Nazi *KdF* outings lasted one or two weeks and, by grouping fellow citizens from similar age groups, reinforced national values. One of the most ambitious projects was Prora, on an island off Germany's northern coast.

"When the visitor arrives at the resort, he must forget the past immediately," wrote Dr. Ley. "I want to construct it in such a way that he enters into a bustle of music, dance, and theatre that takes the breath away so that he forgets himself."

This had also been the Dionysian philosophy of the rave movement. I wasn't surprised to learn that the virtually indestructible Prora – at four kilometres, the world's longest building, big enough to house and amuse 20,000 vacationing Germans – had been claimed by the techno scene and turned into a cut-rate rave camp complete with Jet Skis and turntables. Strength through Ecstasy, with platform shoes instead of jackboots.

᛫

I checked out the next day. The landlady didn't seem surprised I was leaving so soon.

"We can't sleep either. The only time it is quiet is October and May. The English, there is something wrong with them. They drink so much," she said, flicking wrist to mouth.

The British do seem to have a special relationship with drink, a masochistic immaturity that borders on self-loathing. But the worst national traits start to dominate any group when you get them together in large enough numbers and offer them vast amounts of liquor.

When I got back to Corfu Town, I took a final stroll. Lured down a side street by manically tolling bells, I came upon a huge crowd of Greeks in a square in front of a simple whitewashed church. Triangular pennants had been strung across the road, and long-bearded Orthodox priests surrounded a gold-and-silver reliquary. It was the feast of St. Spiridion, patron saint of Corfu, whose skeleton was being borne through the streets in a glass bier, with marching bands and local dignitaries. He had saved Corfu in 1537, it was said, by conjuring forth a storm to drive off a Turkish fleet.

I stopped next to a woman who was lighting thin, gnarled tapers and handing them to her neighbours. A priest began to chant a monotonous verse in a sing-song voice. Led by a man with a baton, the crowd echoed him. It was haunting, beautiful.

Then a terrible thundering rent the heavens. I looked up and saw the pale underbelly of an inbound jumbo jet flash over our heads, winging in low towards the airport a kilometre away. The massed voices were drowned beneath the roar, and as people stared upwards in confusion, the voices lost their harmony. Spiridion's magic, which had driven away Sicilians, Catalans, and Turks, was ineffective against the new hordes of Anglo-Saxons, Romans, and Teutons. The Corfiots, it seemed, could no longer expect the saint's help.

But why should they? By leasing out their numinous shore, and thus renting their souls to the tourist trade, they'd consented to this final invasion.

Chapter 9

CRUISING IN
GREY WATER

*Marco Polo and Me – Youngest Man on the Cruise – In Which I Stuff My
Face – Why Writers Love a Good Cruise – Stuck with Marv at First Sitting
– Eggs Florentine and Dubrovnik – The Importance of Fitness at Sea – The
Earliest Cruises – "The K-Mart of the Caribbean" – A Tour of the Bridge –
"I Hope Here Is Nobody from Greenpeace!" – A Bout of Seasickness – The
Filipino Folkloric Show – $100 a Month and All-You-Can-Eat Dramamine
– Mistaken for a Terrorist – Wisecracks in Ephesus – No More Free Lunch*

The *Marco Polo* looked the way a ship was supposed to look – fit for
stuffing in a glass bottle. She was moored on the far side of the Stazione
Marittima in Venice. Longer and sleeker than I'd expected, she rode low in
the water, with a single striped funnel and a slight upcurve to her pointed
prow, calling to mind a Dutch clog or a Turkish scimitar. The radar
bubbles added a fantastic touch, as though a pair of Montgolfiers was permanently hovering over her bridge. I was particularly pleased with her
navy blue hull, a reminder that, though she currently bathed in the lukewarm Mediterranean, the *Marco Polo* sometimes ventured into the frigid
waters of the Antarctic and the Norwegian fjords. Not like those blanched
cruisers of the Caribbean, lollygagging between resorts in their all-white
tropical livery. Perpetually dressed in pre–Labour Day whites, such
immaculate ships would never have the fully rounded souls of craft that
had tested their mettle in the wintry waters of the North Atlantic.

I waited in line in a cavernous, high-ceilinged hall, passport in hand, with a hundred other passengers. With the possible exception of the Italian customs official, I was the youngest person in the room – though neither of us was especially young. After the college-age debauchery of Corfu, I was looking forward to a week in the company of my elders. People with regular habits, whose values included sobriety, restraint, good conversation – and, it appeared, a pathological obsession with matchmaking. Next to me, a tall, patrician-looking Pennsylvanian in his 60s was talking to a short fellow from Toronto with a squint and an unlit pipe.

"Did you notice," said the American, "all those fields of grain we flew over on the way in? What do you suppose the chief crop is here in Venice?"

"Tourists," the Canadian replied. Hearing me chuckle, he looked me up and down – though mostly up – and smiled vaguely.

"Young fellow, eh? Don't worry, we'll find a girl for you. I already saw one about your age. She'll be on the cruise."

The American's wife leaned over. "We've got three daughters. The middle one's still free, if you're looking. She lives in Manhattan."

My instant typecasting as an eligible prospect wasn't entirely unexpected. Unattached males in these settings are seen as volatile particles, rogue protons to be nullified by any passing neutron, restoring the prevailing equilibrium of double occupancy.

I didn't particularly want to hear it. Truth was, I deeply missed my girlfriend. I'd met Karen just nine months before I'd left on this trip. She was a dancer, working in Ottawa, a city two hours of bleak highway from my home in Montreal. It seemed typical of my travelling ways that I'd gotten into a semi-long-distance relationship, composed of dramatic Sunday afternoon partings, weekday longing, and euphoric Friday-night reunions in bus and train stations. I was tired of the pattern. Though Karen understood this trip would involve months of research, she'd encouraged me to go. Now, more than four months down the road, we were having trouble handling the separation. Karen was channelling her frustration into her choreography and a journal she promised to show me when I got back. I was fighting loneliness by trying to remain outgoing and curious, but lately I noticed my gaze lingering too long on beautiful backpackers. Not wanting this relationship to die of attrition, I'd exhausted dozens of phone cards and spent a fortune in Internet cafés keeping in touch. I told Karen I longed to end the longing, and I suggested we live together when I got back. She liked the idea, but at a pay phone on the sun-splattered Ionian I could hear the chill of the approaching Canadian winter in her voice.

"Hurry back," she'd said. I'd wanted to, then and there.

❧

Judging by the white-headed crowd milling outside the *Marco Polo*, temptation wasn't going to be an issue on this leg of my journey. By coming aboard, I'd be lowering the average age on the ship by about six months.

Up close, the hull, which seemed to rise at right angles from the water, was covered with indentations, suggesting dire nights shouldering past Newfoundland clumpers. Queuing outside, I scanned the railings for croaking crows or magpies – the illest of omens in Roman times – and watched with concern lest somebody sneeze on the gangway, another augur of catastrophe for ancient mariners. A beefy English mate with a shaved head and tattooed forearms directed us to the postern, and after passing through a metal detector, I was issued a "Cruise Card," to be swiped on entering and leaving the ship. A steward accompanied me to my cabin on the Main Deck, the fourth of the eight passenger decks. Dropping my day-bag on the bed, I turned and walked back out the door. I'd have a week to get to know my cabin. Venice, on the other hand, would be gone by the following afternoon.

I'd discovered the *Marco Polo* in an Internet café in Rome. Browsing for seaborne passage from Greece to points east, I'd come across the Web site of Orient Lines, a two-ship cruise company. The *Marco Polo* was going my way – following her namesake's route down the Dalmatian coast and around the rump of the Greek mainland, she would cruise through the Aegean islands and along the Turkish coast before heading up the Dardanelles to Istanbul, at the edge of Asia. I'd booked the "Venetian Odyssey" cruise with my credit card, and resigned myself to disrupting my journey's classical unity by doing a little backtracking to Italy. From Corfu, I'd endured another deck passage on the *Ouranos*, giving myself a sponge bath at a sink in Brindisi's train station, and dozed through a long

overnight train ride to Venice. Most of the *Marco Polo*'s passengers had
flown in from England or the United States and looked similarly bedraggled. But Venice's allures couldn't be denied, and the boat that left from
beneath the ship's stern was packed to the gunwales with jet-lagged passengers, exhilarated to be on the lagoon. When the day comes that I'm too
jaded to plunge into the Venetian labyrinth, I'll know it's time to swallow
my passport.

I spent the day prowling the canals, and came back to the *Marco Polo*
on the last tender, sleeping the sleep of the weary traveller who knows he'll
find chocolates on his pillow – the same pillow – for the next six nights.
Next morning I returned to town and got lost in the M. C. Escher maze of
bridges and stairs. With a population of only 70,000, Venice today has a
third as many residents as in its Renaissance heyday. Unless, of course, you
count the 12 million tourists – 170 visitors for each Venetian – who flood
the *piazze* and canals every year.

I was inclined to count every one of them, particularly those standing
between me and St. Mark's Square. Begging the time from a passerby, I'd
realized I had only 15 minutes to get back to the last launch before the
Marco Polo's one o'clock sailing. I made good time until I crossed the
humpbacked Accademia bridge, where I ran into hundreds of tourists –
the logo of another cruise ship stuck to their coats – clumped before a tiny
alley between long buildings. Their guides, holding aloft yellow umbrellas,
were funnelling them single-file down a lane no wider than a goat path.
Bobbing above a sluggish river of grey heads that meandered out of sight
several bridges away, I despaired of making the tender. Just then, three
Italian businessmen in Chicago-shouldered suits came power-walking up
behind me. With practised gruffness, they elbowed through the crowd
with perfunctory "*Permesso*"s. Following in their wake, I played ambulance chaser down interlinked alleys and was finally belched into the
relative freedom of St. Mark's Square. Scattering pigeons, I leapt onto my
launch with a minute to spare.

On the *Marco Polo*, there was an announcement from the bridge:
"We are missing one cabin, Mr. and Mrs. Bankers, from Cabin 456. And as
soon as Mr. and Mrs. *Bankers*" – the announcer spat out the name with
Scandinavian rectitude – "are on board, we can sail." I walked aft to the

open Belvedere Deck. The sun was burning through the late-morning fog, and the city was wreathed in a jaundiced, luminescent mist. The six-piece Amar Orchestra, dressed in white, struck up a ragtime version of "Anchors Aweigh," the ship's horn sounded, and the *Marco Polo* was pulled away from the dock by a tug.

I felt a poke in my kidneys. "Your money or your life!" a voice behind me said.

I turned around to find the Canadian matchmaker, his pipe stem at my back. Jerry was a freelance illustrator, responsible for the covers of more than 200 Harlequin romances. I asked whether he was taking any of the shore excursions.

"We signed up for that Turkish place," he said. "I can never remember the name."

Ephesus? I suggested.

"*Gesundheit!*" he replied. "No, just kidding, that's the place. I've never heard anybody saying anything derogatory about it."

We stared over the rail as we passed the beaches of the Lido, fronted by their dowager hotels, and the *Marco Polo* sailed into the Adriatic under its own power. I was happy to be underway: Venice, though agreeable, was a distraction. On a modern cruise, the ship was the thing, not its ports of call. Our destination, though nominally Istanbul, was in fact the *Marco Polo* itself, and I wanted to get around to abusing its facilities.

"Now we can get down to business," said Jerry, giving me a friendly nudge in my skinny ribs, as he headed off to the buffet. "It's time to *eat.*"

Jerry understood. He was a freelancer, too.

§

A cruise ship is the ideal home for a peripatetic writer. The tedious problems of nourishment – the headache of finding a calorific breakfast, the mid-day migraine of locating lunch, the crepuscular quandary of scanning crowded restaurants for a solo table – were resolved by the *Marco Polo's* two dining rooms and room-service snacks menu. There was a library full of guidebooks and travel literature, and a permanent link to the Internet in a bank of computers on the Sky Deck. For moments of lapsing inspiration, there were hundreds of metres of polished railings, perfect for scanning the horizon for the *mot juste*. If I was tempted, I could gather material for a tortured plunge into a personal abyss by patronizing the cocktail bar, or pursue my flirtation with Dostoevskian themes at the casino, where rigid-backed Filipinas in vests and bow ties awaited my downfall. If I ran out of ideas, there were the human dramas of the 545 other passengers and 325 crew members to explore. If I was feeling anti-social, I could cultivate my Superior Inside Life by withdrawing to my cabin and catching up on my journal. The *Marco Polo* was like a writers' retreat without the professional rivalry, one where the scenery changed as often as the towels.

Authors have long been charmed by the literary possibilities of the ocean voyage. The first true steamship cruise – as opposed to purposeful Atlantic crossing – probably took place in 1844, when the newly formed Peninsular and Oriental Steam Navigation Company, the same P & O that now owns Princess Cruises, sent the steamer *Lady Mary Wood* from Southampton to Egypt. The novelist William Makepeace Thackeray had agreed to write an account of his voyage in return for free passage, and he published *Notes on a Journey from Cornhill to Grand Cairo* under the pseudonym Michael Angelo Titmarsh. In Thackeray's travelogue, Victorian chauvinism and wry arrogance prevailed; the foreign was surveyed and found wanting. As an indifferent student of the Classics, Thackeray seemed to have it in for the Greeks: "I swear solemnly that I would rather have two hundred a year in Fleet Street, than be King of the Greeks . . . the shabbiness of this place actually beats Ireland, and that is a strong word." He denigrated the complexions of Mediterranean women: "They may talk about beauty, but would you wear a flower that had been dipped in a grease-pot? No; give me a fresh, dewy, healthy rose out of Somersetshire; not one of those superb, tawdry, unwholesome exotics, which are only good to make poems about." Dutifully singing for his supper, Thackeray endorsed the cruising experience: "It was one so easy, so charming, and I think profitable – it leaves such a store of pleasant recollections for after days . . . that I can't but recommend all persons who have time and means to make a similar journey."

For the next half century, such one-off pleasure cruises were the exception to the rule of the businesslike transatlantic crossing. Mark Twain's

1867 voyage from New York to the Holy Land, the first such American outing – and another all-expenses-paid junket – provoked a similar endorsement. He was duly impressed by the cancan in Paris, the beauty of the girls in Smyrna, and the mystery of the pyramids (where he watched another American tourist scale the Sphinx with a hammer to knock some souvenir granite off its face). "If the *Quaker City* were weighing her anchor to sail away on the very same cruise again," puffed Twain in *The Innocents Abroad*, "nothing could gratify me more than to be a passenger."

As early as 1883, the Pacific Coast Steamship Company was taking curiosity-seekers to Alaska's Glacier Bay, and six years later, the *Chimborazo* and the *Garonne*, Orient liners that plied regular routes in Australia, began seasonal cruises to the fjords of Norway. The first ship built specifically for cruising appeared with the new century, when Hamburg-Amerika launched the *Prinzessin Victoria Luise*, a small luxury vessel that included a private cabin for the kaiser. An experiment decades ahead of its time, with cabins that included sitting rooms and full bathrooms, she was lost on a sand reef off Jamaica in 1906. Purpose-built cruise ships wouldn't reappear in number until the invasion of outsized Caribbean vessels in the 1970s.

The *Marco Polo* was an example of the kind of ship people sailed on for most of the 20th century. Christened by the Soviets in East Germany in 1965 as the *Alexandr Pushkin*, she was built to navigate through broken ice, and crossed the waters between Montreal and Leningrad in a regular transatlantic service (provoking not entirely far-fetched rumours that the Russians were using her as a St. Lawrence spy ship). Bought from the Baltic Shipping Company by a British entrepreneur named Gerry Herrod, she was gutted and lengthened in a Greek shipyard and relaunched as the *Marco Polo* in 1993. Recently purchased (along with her sister ship, the *Crown Odyssey*) by Norwegian Cruise Lines, she was captained by a veteran of the Swedish merchant marine who had commanded the private yacht of the Aga Khan.

After clearing two plates of grilled red snapper, smoked salmon, vegetable ratatouille, and apple pie, I wandered inside, down the long, low-ceilinged Belvedere Deck. The shop that sold overpriced Murano glass and souvenir videos was called "La Boutique"; the gambling den, where three chain-smoking women were already planted in front of the slot machines, was called "Le Casino"; and the tiny cocktail lounge was dubbed "Le Bar." (The meretricious French articles – inexplicable francophilia on a Scandinavian ship named after an Italian explorer – stopped dead at the ship's *bibliothèque*, which was called, simply, "The Library.")

By the purser's desk, a young crewman in an Orient Lines suit and striped sneakers was keeping score as a group of middle-aged women putted golf balls across the gently rolling hallway. Unlike the current crop of mega-ships, the *Marco Polo* was no Mall of the Americas on the waves. Aimed at the nostalgia market, with a vague design nod towards Art Deco, she had teak decks, varnished railings, and an aquiline profile that conjured up classic Atlantic liners. Some of the first excursions, organized by shipping companies looking for off-season uses for their liners, were made on Hamburg-Amerika's *Cleveland* and *Cincinnati*. Before the First World War, they set a precedent by dispensing with the stratification of first class and steerage current on transatlantic trips, opening public spaces to all passengers on their costly round-the-world cruises.

After a mid-afternoon lifeboat drill (at which I was upbraided before the assembled passengers for the lax knot on my lifejacket), I got around to unpacking. My berth was at the end of a passageway that stretched out of eyeshot, with a noticeable midships sag, and the Orson Welles-does-Kafka atmosphere was aggravated by my porthole-free cabin. The decor was fine – submarine three-star, with a rust-coloured, low-pile rug, a pink upholstered chair between two single beds, and a mirrored closet with a safe inside – but deprived of the cues of sunlight and sunset, I have a tendency to feel like a twitchy Anthony Perkins in a circadian rhythms study. This wasn't helped by the room's loudspeaker, a Skinnerian device that suggested what daily life might be like in a dictatorship run by hedonists. The announcement of dinner's first sitting, preceded by a halting xylophone rendition of "Roll Out the Barrel," sounded as sinister as chimes heralding medication time in an Edwardian asylum.

With some trepidation, I walked downstairs to the Seven Seas restaurant. On a cruise, one dines with the same companions every night, and I'd heard stories of people gnawing off their own legs to escape the leghold trap of first sitting. I shared a small round table with two couples from

Oregon – a state, I was repeatedly informed, whose last syllable is pronounced "*gun*," not "*gone*." Sherry, with a round face, owlish spectacles, and a vast mane of curly blond hair, was travelling with her mother, Janet, and they were looking forward to a little jewellery shopping in Greece. The dominant personality at the table was Marvin ("Call me Marv!"), a real estate attorney in his 60s with a crooked nose, an impatient manner, and a braying laugh. He'd met his companion, Suzy, a plump-and-permed Hilton employee 15 years his junior, in an Internet chat room. Marv was full of pep, and his passions were legion: he was an ardent chef, and lovingly described multi-course Szechuan feasts and recipes for baked Alaska. He'd sailed the world, and he was an enthusiastic dancer, given to such ebullient declarations as "Polka is fun! It's a *fun* dance!" I also suspected that, given some tiny pretext, Marv could be a demanding boor.

I preferred Nestor, our imperturbable Filipino waiter, whose flat face and high forehead gave him a passing resemblance to the Dalai Lama.

"I don't want to see a single bell pepper in my food!" Marv warned Nestor. "I'm allergic to them. Red, yellow, green, whatever – I go into shock. And you don't want to see me in shock!"

After Nestor left, I asked Marv whether Suzy carried a syringe in case he went into anaphylactic shock.

"I'm not really allergic. I just don't like them!" He emitted his braying laugh. "And I want to make *damn* sure they don't put them in my food!"

We had risotto, salmon en croute, and a fondant-like chocolate *budino* covered in caramel sauce. I happily stuffed my face and, knowing that leaner days lay ahead, asked for seconds.

That night, I retired to my cabin early. A text bar on the cruise-cam TV channel showed that our latitude was 39° 50.27' N, our longitude 19° 08.90' E, and we were bearing south-southeast at 18 knots. I found this minutiae ludicrously soothing. There is something satisfyingly amniotic about a swaying private berth in a ship, combining as it does virtuous movement forward into the unknown with the abandonment of all responsibility. After sucking on my pillowcase chocolate, I fell into blissful sleep in my seismically challenged hotel room.

Having spent months trying to make croissants and coffee last till lunch, I took lavish advantage of the *Marco Polo*'s morning menu. "I love breakfast," I told the English couple with whom I was seated the next morning. I ordered eggs florentine, pancakes, fresh-squeezed orange juice, a side of hash browns, and a bowl of muesli.

"You must be American . . ." the woman said, as I plucked *pain au chocolat* and croissants from the pastry bowl. If I'd been wearing a trench coat, I would have stuffed my pockets with danishes.

"Canadian," I mumbled, between gulps. "You know, lumberjacks, fishermen, *coureurs du bois*. We need our calories."

They warmed up when they learned I was from the colonies. "We've sailed from Barcelona," said the man, who wore an Andy Capp-goes-to-Butlin's cardigan. "We were seated with some Americans last night – they were paralytic. Could barely stand up by the end of dinner."

"Oh, they were fine," said his wife. "It's some of *our* people that I don't like."

"True. There are too many what we call 'bar colonels' on board. They were probably only privates in the army. But they lord it over everybody, going on about world politics like they were experts. And they want to be waited on hand and foot by the Filipinos. I saw one fellow who dropped his napkin from a deck chair. Didn't make a move. Waited for a cabin boy to come by, had him pick it up and hand it to him."

I ate with a different couple every morning, all of them small-town British, elderly, and full of minor complaints, so that by the end of the cruise they had blended into a dimly perceived slow leak, a vague distraction from my efforts to consume every item on the menu.

After breakfast, glancing up from my newspaper, I noticed we were docking in Dubrovnik. Yet another benediction. The sun was out, and I went on deck to find us pulling up beside a suspension bridge, completed except for a tiny gap in the middle, which connected two plunging hillsides.

Expecting to find Croatia populated by gnarled peasant women wearing babushkas, I was surprised to be sharing the streets with well-tailored businessmen racing around in sleek Saabs and BMWs. The grey stone walls were studded with shrapnel holes, clumps of cacti, and satellite dishes. I circumambulated the parapets of the thick city walls, looking

down on the orange pantiled roofs that huddled up to the hemicycle of a
fort partially bracketing the old port. The walled city was tiny, a gridwork
of a few dozen streets, and inundated with cruise passengers. From a barbican on the city walls, I watched as the invaders scurried through side
streets, their antennae more sensitive to fellow tourists than Croatians, like
ants from neighbouring formicaries overrunning the same picnic blanket.

For a few hours, the streets of Dubrovnik were primarily populated
by cruise passengers. And then we all left. It was hard to imagine what
benefit our hit-and-run visit could have for the Croatians. Since most of
the passengers had opted for the walking tour and folklore show, there
had been no time to buy local souvenirs, let alone patronize a restaurant.
All we seemed to contribute to the local economy was congestion. (That
wasn't entirely true. At dinner the next day, Sherry told me that a *Marco
Polo* passenger had transferred a wallet containing $250 from his back
pocket to a shoulder bag, which, after a jostle in a narrow street, he found
sliced and emptied.)

Back at the dock, a row of souvenir stalls offering such traditional
Dalmatian coast crafts as "Hand-Painted Cheramics" and "Fridgemagnets"
was ignored by the returning passengers. I headed for the on-board
buffet and created a towering sculpture of spanakopita, breaded sole,
salade Niçoise, grilled mahi-mahi, french fries, and sushi on the biggest
plate I could find. Wandering out onto the open aft deck, I watched a
strange man with the features of an intelligent, hairless simian, devoid of
body fat, standing at the rail, making a complete video record of the
passing coastline.

I asked a pleasant-looking fellow if there was room at his table. He
smiled, showing buckteeth, and invited me to sit down. He was Bob, a residential designer from Virginia. Our introductions were muffled as the
band, whose matching sunglasses and polyester Hawaiian shirts demonstrated why Central Europeans shouldn't attempt tropical dress, kicked
out the jams on "Bye Bye Love." Bob's wife, Midge, appeared, a thin, pale
woman who managed a university bookstore. She grimaced as Teddy's
Group started a new song.

"It wouldn't be so bad if they knew how to speak English. But 'The
Girl from *Country* Down'? Come on!"

As we slid past an idyllic coastline of secluded coves, vacation homes, and rocky, cross-topped hillsides fringed with pines, Bob didn't seem inclined to find fault. "If somebody had told me last year I'd be eating lunch on the Croatian coastline, listening to a Polish chanteuse on a ship flying a Bahamian flag, I would have told them they were crazy. But this is lovely!"

Midge was staring distractedly at the swimming pool, which even Lilliput's Olympic team might have found too exiguous to do full laps.

"Who would want to swim in it?" she wondered aloud. "It's right in the middle of the lunch deck. And we're not exactly a bunch of Adonises and Venuses on board."

Taking the remark personally, I excused myself and went in search of the *Marco Polo*'s gym. Wandering past the deck chairs and Jacuzzis on the Sky Deck, where the sunbathers were already well into their Colin Dexter and Joanna Trollope paperbacks, I passed men with vast, pale bellies and vein-ridden, hairless calves. Women with cottage cheese thighs insisted on baking skin already puckered by decades of tanning. Elbows looked like parched earth, and hair sprouted where it shouldn't. Cruise ships provide countless object lessons in what happens to bodies left unattended over the years; once I found the gym, I hopped onto a treadmill and ran with real motivation for half an hour. The Scottish fitness instructor tried to talk me into taking the Total Body Conditioning class, but I demurred in favour of some weightlifting. (I wasn't surprised to see that the monkey-like videographer, who had donned skin-tight bicycle pants, was capering with the all-female aerobics class.) The selection of free weights was feeble but, rooting around, I discovered more serious poundages hidden in a wooden crate.

"Er," said the instructor, "we don't normally allow the passengers to use those weights. They're for the crew – they use the gym after 8 p.m." I assured her I would assume the risk and filed this away as further evidence of the growing evolutionary rift between the pampered Eloi and the buff Morlocks who serve them.

A photocopied program slipped under my door had reminded me we'd be spending the next 36 hours rounding the Greek mainland. Securing a deck chair, I contemplated the idea of a day and half at sea with real pleasure. I hadn't expected to enjoy the cruise so much. For a travel writer, the combination of self-indulgent leisure and directed movement was the perfect formulation of work-ethic sybaritism, like having sex in the afternoon while your clothes tumble-dry in the basement. Surprising, in fact, that it took the tourist industry so long to figure it out.

The early transatlantic liners had made most of their money from immigrants, stuck six or eight to a cabin in steerage (so-called because it was the section nearest the ships' steering mechanisms) and the under-populated first-class ballrooms and lounges consumed an enormous amount of deck space. When Prohibition was proclaimed in the United States in 1920, Americans started going on overnight "cruises to nowhere," where liners would make a quick jaunt into international waters so that passengers could drink with impunity. Soon, longer "booze cruises" took passengers as far as Nassau, Bermuda, and Havana on week-long expeditions. In the 1920s, the Italian Line introduced outdoor swimming pools on the *Rex* and the *Conte di Savoia*, which sailed from New York to Italy. Air conditioning replaced swaying punkahs – in 1935, the Orient Line's *Orion* was the first ship to boast a climate-controlled dining room and air-cooled luxury "flats" – making cruising the tropics a year-round possibility. During one-off pleasure cruises – round-the-world trips, or "positioning" voyages to introduce new liners – the class system was often abolished and public spaces were thrown open to all passengers.

Even so, most cruises were *de facto* first class, since the price excluded the working class. Evelyn Waugh took such a cruise aboard the *Stella Polaris* in 1929, continuing the by-then venerable tradition of churning out a book for a free ticket. (Waugh, I noticed, also enjoyed a good feed. In *Labels: A Mediterranean Journal*, he lingered lovingly over the one o'clock buffet, "laden with every kind of Scandinavian delicatessen, smoked salmon, smoked eels, venison, liver pies, cold game and meat and fish, sausage, various sorts of salad, eggs in sauces, cold asparagus, in almost disconcerting profusion.") The Norwegian vessel that Waugh took was a small ship, modelled after luxury private yachts. The first large vessel built specifically for cruising was the Cunard Line's *Caronia* (1948), so luxurious that its round-the-world cruises were patronized almost exclusively by millionaires and their kin.

Paradoxically, it was the jet revolution that led to the boom in cruising. By the mid-1960s, it was cheaper to cross the Atlantic by air than in a tourist class cabin, and dozens of palatial liners were made redundant. Those that weren't scrapped were converted into full-time cruise ships for tropical seas. In 1966, Knut Kloster, an entrepreneur from Norway, teamed up with an Israeli-born businessman named Ted Arison to launch the *Sunward*, the first of a new generation of warm-water cruise ships. Wedge-shaped, its stacks and decks layered like a wedding cake, the all-white *Sunward* was the harbinger of the geographically fruitless ocean voyage.

In 1971, Arison founded Carnival Cruise Lines, emphasizing week-long Caribbean getaways and advertising the ship, rather than the islands themselves, as the destination. He introduced on-board casinos, and turned the tedium-killing egg-and-spoon races of past voyages into round-the-clock, Las Vegas–style family fun. Derided as the K-Mart of the Caribbean, Carnival nonetheless sparked a revolution, shifting the industry's centre of gravity from New York to Miami. Thanks to the "fly-cruise" concept (on my cruise, many passengers had been offered free airfare to Venice) the airlines were enlisted into the service of their quondam competitors. With this Carnivalesque sea change – an inversion of the old class system – working North Americans could afford to be pampered like the nabobs their immigrant ancestors had glimpsed from steerage.

"We took a cruise on one of those mega-ships to Bermuda," said Midge at lunch one day. "It was terrible."

"They try to force you to have fun," Bob explained. "They had this big thing about how one of the horse racing pieces had been kidnapped, and they were constantly making announcements about this stupid horse. It went on for days. They came around to your table all the time and led you in singalongs – whether you wanted to or not.

"It was a rather long cruise," Bob continued, "from New York to Bermuda. So basically, there was nothing to do, no ports of call. People just ate and drank. I remember drawing into New York City on the last day. The sun was going down, it was a gorgeous evening, with the Statue of Liberty alongside. And people just had their noses down in their plates, shovelling up their free food."

Terrible, I agreed, just terrible, excusing myself to head for the dessert buffet. I'd noticed they'd wheeled out the gelato cart.

Considering the alternatives, I was happy to be on the staid *Marco Polo*, where the optional entertainment ran to cha-cha classes and Scrabble evenings. I tagged along with Bob and Midge for a tour of the bridge. The Second Officer, a soft-spoken Croatian named Davor, explained the runnings of the ship to the predominantly British crowd.

"Who's running the ship?" an elderly fellow with a hearing aid felt obliged to ask. "Not that fellow, surely?" He pointed to a tiny Filipino in a T-shirt, standing before what looked like the steering wheel of a Honda Civic.

"Yes, it is him who is driving. He is just practising," said Davor. "There are always two able seamans on deck." Craning his neck, he failed to locate the second, and shrugged.

Davor explained that the *Marco Polo* had a full keel, two propellers run by two separate engines, and an ice-certified double hull. As I almost leaned against an outsized red "Abandon Ship" button, I noticed that everything on the bridge looked like Pong-vintage high tech, with circular radar screens showing nearby ships as green dots. The only concession to the 21st century was a state-of-the-art Swedish satellite navigating system, which Davor said gave our real-time position in relation to nearby landmasses. For some reason it showed a close-up of the banks of the Mersey River in Liverpool. A little disconcerted, I asked Davor if the *Marco Polo* had ever been in an accident.

"Not that I know. But then, I have only been sailing on her for three months."

Somebody asked about the vast plumes of black soot we sent up whenever we were manoeuvring into port; the ashes tended to settle like blotches of smallpox on sun-creamed chests.

"I hope here is nobody from Greenpeace!" said Davor. "No – only a joke. This is from our bow thrusters, which produce much smoke."

In fact, pollution is one of the dirty secrets of the cruise industry. The *Marco Polo*, closely monitored because of her trips to environmentally sensitive Antarctica, had been equipped with new solid-waste sorters, compactors, and incinerators during her overhaul, and was relatively clean. But other cruise ships get away with murder. In a week-long cruise, a typical ship generates 800,000 litres of sewage, 3.8 million litres of "grey water" – soapy, shampoo- and detergent-laden water that's flushed untreated into the oceans – and eight tonnes of garbage. Of particular concern is the 95,000 litres of oil-contaminated water, which is supposed to be treated with costly separators and disposed of in port. Though the head offices of most cruise companies are now based in Florida, the ships fly flags of convenience, and the enforcement of environmental legislation in Panama, Liberia, and the Bahamas is effectively nil.

Royal Caribbean, one of the few cruise lines to be successfully prosecuted for environmental abuses, was fined $18 million for dumping oil in San Juan harbour and Alaska's Inside Passage in 1994. Investigators discovered a system of secret pipes that allowed untreated oil to be dumped directly into the water, amounting to a fleet-wide conspiracy to bypass anti-pollution laws. Other cruise companies had saved millions of dollars a year by jettisoning their waste in international waters, often at night. Cruise ship bilgewater, groundings, and anchor drops were also having a devastating effect on fragile coral reefs and atolls, the source of much of the ocean's biodiversity.

§

Sometime after clearing the Peloponnese peninsula, the *Marco Polo* began to pitch. I had felt a gentle roll on the treadmill which, since it was laid athwartships, meant that I was running alternately downhill and uphill, a sensation more amusing than nauseating. Pitching meant we were plunging along our longitude, bobbing like a triton's seahorse with its nose in the spray. On the open Belvedere Deck, a group of Englishwomen, well in their cups, laughed uproariously as the froth from the sloshing swimming pool settled on their Margaritas.

Midge had wondered who would be exhibitionistic enough to bathe in such a central wading pool. The monkey-man with the video camera had decided to relax after his aerobics class by descending into the pool at the moment of its greatest turbulence. (He was wearing, naturally, a tight-fitting, neon-toned Speedo.) As the ship pitched forward, the pool water churned, slapped the front wall, and sent up a spume of froth that soaked the upper decks. As the monkey-man was tossed around like a voodoo doll

in a boiling cauldron, the cackles of the women took on the sinister over-
tones of the weird sisters in *Macbeth*. For a moment, I thought the poor
guy was going to drown in less than two metres of water. Finally, he lunged
for the ladder and pulled himself onto the deck.

Given our predicament, the chimes for first sitting – "Edelweiss" this
time – sounded even more sinister than usual. Marv, who seemed to have
a strong stomach, was in his element. Making a solemn ceremony of
tasting a glass of wine, he replied to the busboy's request for his Cruise
Card with his standard comeback: "You just might get it, too!" followed by
the bray. The waiters were hard pressed to serve, and plates and glasses
could be heard crashing all around us. The pitching had only just started,
though, so our appetites were still good.

"Now," Marv expounded, "the Mediterranean is a relatively *deep*
ocean compared to the Caribbean, and it isn't known to have particularly
choppy seas. It's a good thing we're not rolling. That's what makes people
really sick."

I nodded, wolfing down pepper-seared tuna loin.

"And if you combine that with yawing, which is pivoting on a vertical
axis, like the ship was a bug with a pin through its back, then you start
seeing some *serious* vomiting."

I nodded, polishing off my smoked salmon farfalle.

As I walked the corridors after dinner, I regretted my confidence in my
gut's imperviousness. What had been amusing pre-prandial hallway
lurching became mad, green-gilled dashes for cabin sinks. In the halls, the
North Americans favoured the right and the British the left, leading to
last-second corrections at a time when nobody was feeling especially cour-
teous. Seasickness bags had been tucked beneath the railings, presumably
for instant access in case of a gastric emergency. I paid a visit to the
Ambassador Lounge, where a handful of hardy passengers were awaiting
the night's show.

"Tonight's performance is brought to you by the makers of Dramamine," a dry-mouthed Mexican-American comic cracked, hurrying off
stage after only a couple of cannibal jokes.

The Marco Polo Dancers were cancelled, the cruise director announced,
due to the risk of injury. I crawled onto my bunk, which was about as

comfortable as lying on the back of a bucking bronco. Next door, I heard a woman ask the steward: "Do you have any more bags – in case I don't reach the wash basin in time?" Feeling queasy but not nauseated, I turned on the television.

The night's feature was called *Speed 2*. The movie centres on a wrongly dismissed ship's engineer who listens to opera while attaching leeches to his back. After smuggling bombs on board in a golf bag, he hijacks a giant cruise ship and sends it careering through the Caribbean. A strange programming choice, I thought, like putting *Con Air* on the inflight screen just as the aircraft enters a zone of turbulence. That night, I dreamt I was doing laps with cackling chimpanzees in a pool full of vomit.

❦

On deck the next morning I found we were anchored in the perfectly calm waters of an extinct volcano's caldera. Santorini, an island in the Aegean, is a striking place to wake up. The sea-filled crescent where we were floating was once a mountain which, when it blew its top in 1645 B.C., utterly destroyed the Minoan civilization. The strange thing is that modern Greeks, in spite of earthquakes that caused massive damage in the area as recently as 1956, continue to build on the rim of the crater. The aerodynamically chamfered, white-walled hotels and homes of Santorini cling to the top of the 300-metre-high cliff like the nests of Cubist swallows. It looks about as sensible as building a subdivision on a Ste. Honoré cake.

I shared the cable car from the dock to the village with a flatlander from St. Louis who covered her eyes throughout the trip. Pointing at a small plaque, I told her not to worry – the gondola was built by the Swiss.

"Yeah," she moaned. "But it's maintained by Greeks!"

After a day spent walking the caldera's rim, I took the last tender back to the ship. Returning too late for first sitting, I contented myself with a solitary, multi-coursed dinner at Raffles, the ship's buffet restaurant. The after-dinner entertainment that night was a "Filipino Folkloric Show" and I watched, mortified, as the cabin crew staged re-enactments of traditional ceremonies. Filipinos have a reputation for being enthusiastic performers with huge repertoires, but they seemed stiff and resentful during the Santa

Cruz wedding ceremony, as busboys led barmaids in flat-topped hats beneath flowered bowers. Next, four Filipinos with halved coconuts strapped to their chests appeared on stage to re-enact the battle of the Muslims and the Christians over coconut residue, tapping out syncopated rhythms with shells held in their palms. Finally, my waiter Nestor appeared on stage, dressed in a long white shirt buttoned to the neck. As smoke billowed behind him, he played a creditable guitar and sang a pop ditty called "Do-Be-Do." I cheered enthusiastically.

Much as I liked to see Nestor cutting loose, it seemed a bit much that the Filipinos should be asked to parody their own cultural traditions for the same passengers who treated them like 19th-century domestic help. I'd been intrigued by the clickety-clack rhythms of Tagalog in the hallways, and in the corridor the next morning I struck up a conversation with one of the cabin stewards. A handsome young man from a town near Manila, he told me there were advantages to being on the ship.

"I love going to Antarctica. I have been three times. You can see humpback whales, blue whales – they rub themselves up against the ship to get barnacles off. There are emperor penguins, very tall. And hundred-year-old icebergs, transparent, as big as a city."

The work was hard – typically, he put in between ten and 13 hours a day, seven days a week. I asked how long he stayed at sea.

"Ten months. And then I have 45 days off, to see my family. I have two daughters. Every time I see them, they're much bigger." The company paid him $100 a month. "This is to send back to my family. The rest I get from tips from the passengers."

The farther east I headed, the more the Third World loomed. The average per capita income in the Philippines is $1,000 a year, so work on a cruise ship, with free room and board and the potential for tips, must look pretty good. Typically, prospective cruise ship employees go into debt by paying at least a month's wages to local agents, who are also responsible for sending money back to their families. Though most cruise companies are headquartered in the United States, flags of convenience mean they don't have to obey American minimum wage or labour laws. Few pay more than two dollars an hour. The only significant labour action in the United States was stymied, in 1981, when Central American workers went on strike aboard a Carnival ship in Miami, only to find themselves arrested as illegal immigrants and flown home, unpaid and unemployed.

Essentially, cruise ship "hotel staff," who are mostly from such countries as Jamaica, Haiti, and Indonesia, buckle under and do what they're told – whether it's by exploitative senior colleagues who steal their tips, the all-powerful agent, or the cruise company that can terminate their contract at a moment's notice. *Marco Polo* passengers went on about how happy-go-lucky the Filipinos were, how they relished the opportunity to work on the high seas – and then added that they were going to stiff their waiter because he hadn't brought their wine fast enough. Sleeping several to a cabin, slaving below decks in hot galleys or laundries for months at a time, being away from children who grew up without knowing them – cruise ship life seemed pretty far from the departed idyll of the Coconut Residue Dance. The closer you look, the more a cruise ship becomes a textbook example of the Fourth World – a First World setting with built-in pockets of Third World exploitation.

Ah, but there are no innocent pleasures. The next evening, after a long day spent in Mykonos – our landing in Delos was cancelled due to choppy waters – my fellow diners started to get on my nerves.

"We missed you at dinner yesterday," said Marv. "But then we got over it and ate anyway!" Atomized moussaka filled the air as he brayed at his own joke.

Suzy and Sherry were comparing the jewellery they'd bought in Santorini and Mykonos – almost all the women in the dining room were sporting pendulous gold earrings and necklaces. When Nestor brought a plate of veal, I congratulated him on the previous night's performance. A faint smile curved his lips, and I thought I saw the beginning of a blush.

"That was our waiter singing last night?" said Marv. "I didn't even know! Hey! Scoobee-Doo!" he yelled as Nestor bent over a cutlery tray.

"Marv," I muttered, "the song was 'Do-Be-Do.' And his name is Nestor."

Marv was unfazed. "Scoobee-Doo – get over here!" Nestor dutifully appeared. "You better make sure there are no bell peppers in my pasta!" he said.

I couldn't resist: "Or else there'll be a medical emergency?"

"That's right – I'll punch him right in the nose!"

I was thankful that I would only have to spend one more night with Marv's laugh.

It was getting harder to be sanguine about my pleasure cruise. Once, a busboy who upset a glass essayed a mild joke about getting his "sea legs," flashing a big Filipino smile. As soon as he thought he was out of eyeshot – backstage, as it were – his smile contracted to a surly frown, as though he loathed himself for pandering. After a run on the treadmill the next day, I leaned against a railing and watched a security guard approach. Uh-oh, I thought. He's got me pegged as a terrorist. Remembering the movie about the saboteur on the cruise ship, I realized I fit the profile perfectly: young man, travelling light, keeps to himself, avoids shore excursions. To make matters worse, the rent-a-cop had seen me alone on the top deck late one night, underlit in a burbling Jacuzzi, reading Machiavelli's *The Prince* – suspicious behaviour indeed.

But he only wanted to talk. Nodding to the sun-dried hills to port, and then at the barren hills to starboard, he said: "Greece and Turkey look not so different. Look same kind of country. All brown – no trees."

He was Nepalese, small and solid, with cheeks the colour of burnished hazelnuts beneath a white baseball cap. This was his first trip on the *Marco Polo*. I told him I hoped to visit his country soon.

"Ah! Good time to go. Many festivals. You will like. More trees in Nepal."

He exuded an air of peaceful watchfulness that seemed at odds with the perpetual air of low-grade, class-obsessed anxiety that infected the leisure of the passengers. Suddenly, I was happy to be heading east.

§

It seemed fitting to approach the frontier of Asia on a cruise ship. In a sense, it was the culmination of the millennia-long process of building the perfect tourist bubble. Since the 19th century, developed nations no longer had to rely on a rigid class system to separate the leisured few from the working masses. The two had merged – North American and European workers had long been able to afford cars, televisions, and their own vacations. These days, the great divide was not national – between classes within a country – but international, with the well-fed citizens of the First World relying on the resources and labour of the Third.

Inconveniently, it was the same Third World that seemed to possess a large share of the Exotic, the Authentic, the Traditional, and the Naturally Beautiful. What better way, after all, to see the Caribbean, Thailand, or Turkey than from a giant viewing platform that can turn tail and head for international waters at the slightest sign of trouble. As a means of separating the traveller from the world's economic realities, cruise ships were more refined even than beach resorts. Holiday spots in Jamaica, the Dominican Republic, and Indonesia were plagued by muggings, local uprisings, and a palpable undercurrent of native resentment. The workers on cruise ships, separated from their native soil, couldn't even draw strength from the moral outrage of the invaded. In this sense, cruise ships really were democratic. They allowed anybody with disposable income to purchase a week or two of feudalism.

Gated communities with stabilizers, the biggest cruise ships were in the mainstream of the future of travel. The workers' revolutions of the 20th century had struck at the urban palaces of the czars. It looked like the next wave of revolutionaries would have to use Zodiacs and helicopters to catch their exploiters.

As a metaphor for the direction the world was heading, the latest crop of cruise ships was pretty flagrant. The *Marco Polo* was a benign example – the emphasis was still evenly divided between shore excursions and shipboard entertainments. The future lay in behemoths like Royal Caribbean's *Explorer of the Seas*. With berths for 3,844 passengers, ten dining rooms, the biggest casino on the waves, a hockey rink, and a mall's worth of shops, it was the largest cruise ship ever built. Tellingly, many of the suites' portholes faced inwards, towards the promenade deck – it was the cruising experience that was the focus, not the sea voyage. Recently, an organization called ResidenSea had launched *The World*, the "first ocean-going luxury resort." Its 110 apartments, leased for 50 years at up to $10 million, were permanent homes for senior executives, guarded by Nepalese Gurkhas. Built in Norway, registered in the Bahamas, *The World* roamed unhampered by national laws, its residents freed from paying the income tax that might provide social programs for the unlucky plebs who lived onshore. Calling at the Monaco Grand Prix or the Cannes Film Festival, the industrialists of *The World* would never be affected by the pollution, poverty, and rising sea levels that their self-enriching entrepreneurship had inflicted on the rest of the world. With ten million clients a year, the cruise sector, which offered a sense of security in a world where unexamined privilege was so clearly provoking hatred, was the fastest-growing segment of the tourist industry.

I entered an elevator before dinner one night on the *Marco Polo*. A large couple with pronounced southern accents boarded with me, making the small elevator lurch noticeably under their weight. As we descended, the woman unleashed a lungful of hacking, phlegmy coughs.

"Oh, *excuse* me!" she apologized. "Please don't breathe! I just took an expectorant."

Essaying a mild joke, I said: "No fair – biological warfare."

Their faces froze instantly.

"That's not funny," she snapped. They left the elevator in offended silence, marching self-righteously in the direction of the all-you-can-eat buffet.

Right. Humourless, paranoid, and overprivileged. Model future citizens of *The World*.

◈

With just the slightest shift of perspective, I could allow myself to be fooled by the professional smiles of the Filipinos. After all, it was more comforting to leave the illusion unexamined: that we had earned our leisure, through hard work rather than the geopolitical happenstance of a lucky birth, and that the stewards and barmaids were enjoying opportunities – unlimited travel, hard currency tips – they would never have at home. Because this cruise was, undeniably, a pleasure. On our last day at sea, I was saddened by the knowledge that there would be no more "Pleasant Dreams" cards laid on my bedspread, no more nightly selection of movies, no more free lunches. I had stuffed my face for almost a week, and I knew the road ahead would strip what little weight I'd gained from my frame in no time.

When we docked at Kusadasi, I took my one and only shore excursion, to Ephesus. The guide, a handsome Turk with an easygoing manner and a good spiel, picked up the microphone.

"Welcome to Turkey! You will see many people trying to sell you things today. For the Ephesus booklets, you should pay no more than two dollars." An American groaned: "I paid three!" The guide shot back: "Thank you for helping the Turkish economy! Don't worry – the same thing happened to me in New York."

When Mark Twain had visited Ephesus with passengers from the *Quaker City*, they'd reached the site by donkey, and visitors were so rare that a government official had been dispatched from Constantinople to make sure they didn't steal any relics. ("They cannot afford to run the risk," explained Twain, "of having their hospitality abused by travelers, especially since travelers are such notorious scorners of honest behavior.") When we arrived, ours was one of scores of groups from at least four different cruise ships. Turkish guides with numbered paddles in their hands jostled for space in front of the columns of the ruined library.

"Two thousand years ago, the main income of this place was tourism," said our guide, giving us a reassuring vision of the continuity of things. "They came from all over to see the Temple of Diana. It was one of the Wonders of the World. In shops they sold idols. The apostle Paul lived here for three years."

Once a port town, Ephesus was now several kilometres inland; the Goths had pillaged the city in the third century, and the proximity of malarial swamps had depopulated it in the twelfth. We had to queue in order to get through the gate of the 25,000-seat theatre. On the way back, our bus deposited us outside a store that sold kilims, and we were ushered inside to shop for Turkish rugs.

I said goodbye to Bob and Midge that night, had my last dinner with Marv and the gang, tried to assuage my conscience by pressing envelopes full of greenbacks into the palms of my cabin steward, Nestor, and the maitre d'. The next morning, I awoke to a long-imagined sight. We were pulling into Istanbul's harbour; the domes of the Blue Mosque, piled like the teats of an upturned sow, were alongside the ship. Asia lay to starboard, Europe to port – I was entering a new phase of the voyage. I shuddered as a crow settled on the railing. It was grey-winged, with a murderous, gimlet-like bill, ideal for poking into carrion. The last time I'd seen one like it was in India.

On the final day of the trip, we were transferred to a high-rise businessman's hotel on Taksim Square. The cruise portion of my odyssey was over. Without really noticing it, I'd been pushed through a soapy, sun-squared surface and thrust into the invigorating and intimidating reality of modern-day Istanbul. On my way to the Fish Market, I ran into Jerry, chewing on his unlit pipe, waiting for the bus to take him to the airport.

"You never found me a wife, Jerry," I scolded him.

"Ah, I could tell you weren't really looking." The bus pulled up, and he loaded his bags into the luggage compartment. "Aren't you coming along?"

"Nah," I said. "I'm going to India."

He looked genuinely puzzled.

"Now why would you want to do *that*?"

But it was too late to explain; he was already on the other side of the bubble. The bus's door closed with a pneumatic whoosh.

Chapter 10

SHANTI TOWN

*Route Planning through Afghanistan – Asia on the Cheap – Seinfeld on
Emirates Airlines – A Shakedown at Mumbai International Airport –
Picking Up the* Lonely Planet *Trail – Traveller's Fare in Panjim – Chilling
with the Trustafarians on Palolem Beach – The Original India Trip –
Hindu Tourists Practise Karate Chops on My Head – Special Lassis in the
Hampi Bazaar – A Flash Bastard – 36 Hours to Varanasi – A Dead Man
on the Road to Nepal – Over the Hills with Over-the-Hill Trekkers –
Brownies on Freak Street – The End of the Road to Kathmandu*

In the Orient Express Bar of Istanbul's Pera Palas Hotel, I ordered a cappuccino and laid a map beneath the brass, cupid-shaped lamp on my table. My next stop was India, but the entire breadths of Turkey and Iran lay before me, a distance greater than all I'd traversed so far in western Europe. If this had been the heyday of the first great wave of post-colonial Orientalism, I certainly would have gone overland, booking a seat for £65 – the cost of passage in the late 1960s, on a budget bus with reclining seats, from London to India. In 1972, a British couple, Tony and Maureen Wheeler, bought a used Austin minivan and drove it across western Europe, the Balkans, and Iran. They sold it in Afghanistan and continued by bus, boat, and thumb before finally, nine months later, arriving penniless in Australia. The account of their voyage, the hand-collated and stapled *Across Asia on the Cheap*, was the incunabulum of *Lonely Planet's India*, the best-selling title in the catalogue of what is now the world's largest independent travel guide publisher.

I took a long look at the map. Things weren't as groovy in Afghanistan, Pakistan, and Kashmir as they'd been in the Wheelers' day. Much as I hated snapping the unbroken thread of my voyage, which so far I'd done entirely by land and sea, shopping for Afghan waistcoats in the bazaars of Kabul was no longer really an option. These days, the overland route meant contending with nuclear proliferation, militant fundamentalists, and Afghanistan's most recent plunge into chaos. After paying for my coffee with million-lire notes emblazoned with the Bela Lugosi scowl of Kemal Atatürk, I decided to make the sensible decision. The original road to Kathmandu wasn't paved with Air Miles, but these were clearly different times.

A few days later, I was in the Istanbul International Airport duty free, blowing the last of my lire on a key chain of blue eyeballs, the Turkish nazar symbol that wards off bad luck. Emirates Airline had been voted the best in the world that year, and it satisfied all the prerequisites of pre-packaged exoticism. The stewardesses, who spoke Arabic, Thai, Swedish, Bulgarian, and Swahili, wore beige scarves that hung from flat-topped red berets, and served meals of chicken biryani, Halal roasted lamb, and Turkish mezze with graceful bows. I sat next to a pair of buzz-cut sofa manufacturers from Ankara who spent the flight networking with a furniture shop owner from Delhi. On my personal television screen, which folded into my seat's armrest, I could choose from the latest American and British sitcoms.

Pleasant as the pampering was, for all the sensation of travel the plane afforded I might as well have been chloroformed – a flight simulator would have provided the same illusion of motion. Accelerating on the Istanbul runway, I felt as I always feel when travelling by plane: that I'd consented to be flipped from a catapult in a pressurized canister, to drop from the heavens, dazed and dehydrated, onto some absurdly remote patch of the globe a few hours later.

From Istanbul I was tossed over the Persian Gulf to the tip of the Arabian peninsula. After a few hours among the sheikhs and women in burkas at the Starbucks in the Dubai airport, I was lobbed skywards again, this time across the Arabian Sea towards the west coast of India.

All sense of insulation from reality broke when the canister touched ground in Mumbai. India, happily, will never allow itself to be homogenized by modernity. Here, the spectacle of western consumerism is subsumed by maya, the notion that the phenomenal world is merely an illusion, that all our Birkenstocks and cloned sheep are destined to fall to pieces like mangoes in the tropical sun. This was my second visit, and I was reminded of the vigour, the resistance, and the antiquity of a civilization whose spiritual capitals were thriving when Mecca and Jerusalem were just stretches of sand in the desert. Boarding a decrepit, stifling shuttle bus, I noticed the Coca-Cola logos near the airport painted on the collapsing wood and corrugated metal of the shanties that made up the largest slum in Asia. As I disembarked, I was mobbed by porters.

"Where from?" one asked.

Canada, I replied.

"Rich country!" he barked. "Dollar country! You give us one dollar each!"

I was carrying my own bag, I objected, and this was a free shuttle bus. Five pairs of unblinking eyes surrounded me.

"We make special trip to Terminal 2. Not free!"

I handed the ringleader a single greenback and pushed past them. I didn't blame them for shaking me down; I admired the fact that they were so clear. Exactly because it is so confident of its own unassailable quiddity, India will never let travellers forget just how foreign they are.

After having my luggage hand-checked, article by article, by soldiers on the runway (one table for men, another for women), I boarded my final flight. As a tabla-and-sitar version of "Strawberry Fields Forever" played on the intercom, I dozed, stirring to semi-consciousness only when the last in my relay of catapult shots had put me on a runway in Goa.

If this had been the 1960s, getting to Goa from Istanbul would have involved months of overland travel – on its own, the boat trip from Bombay (the city's name was changed to Mumbai in 1981) would have taken 24 hours. Goa, a region of 1.3 million inhabitants with a 100-kilometre coastline on the central western shore of India, would have been my first chance to bathe naked on the beach and recover from dysentery. Things had changed forever in 1987, when the first charter, a Condor flight from Frankfurt, touched down. Goa became a sun destination – a Corfu on the Indian Ocean. Discovered by DJs from London, it was briefly the centre of a thriving trance-and-jungle scene, until in 2000 the Indian government introduced a nationwide anti-noise law banning events of over 45 decibels after ten o'clock at night.

Crossing the runway in withering humidity, I was surrounded not by ravers but by vacationing Indians and a few European couples travelling with young children. In the taxi, I took in the lush riverine landscape, where white egrets and cranes waded beneath palm trees. A hand-painted billboard advertised a gigantic television monitor. "Videocom Bazoomba," it read. "Not just *thunderous*/but *wondrous!*" It was good to be back in a land where state-of-the-art technology was still advertised in 1940s-vintage English.

The driver dropped me on a side street off a creek that flowed into the Mandovi River in Panaji, Goa's biggest town. I'd asked him to take me to the Panjim Inn, the first place listed in the *Lonely Planet*'s "Mid-Range" accommodations section. A young man carried my bag up to a second-floor wooden *balcao*. In a common room, a couple wearing singlets and sarongs had retreated from the afternoon heat with Kingfisher beers and a video.

"It's *Romy and Michele's High School Reunion*," said the man, with a South African accent. "Utter bollocks, but kind of funny."

I noticed a copy of the guidebook, the same edition as mine, open on the table. It had taken a little effort – three planes, several hundred dollars, and 24 hours without real sleep – but I'd relocated the tourist bubble I'd left when I disembarked from the *Marco Polo*. In these parts, it was called the *Lonely Planet* trail.

❧

The *Lonely Planet* guide to India is thick as a brick. Its cover shows an out-of-focus crowd of women wearing colourful headscarves, beneath which a caption read "Saris, swamis & maharinis" – an assonant recipe for an exotic Oriental cocktail. (The name of the series came from Tony Wheeler's understanding of the song "Space Captain" by Joe Cocker, which includes a reference to "this lovely planet." Appropriate that one of the biggest corporate legacies of the hippie era was based on a misheard lyric.) The added weight is worth it: the *Lonely Planet* is an indispensable guide. Not for discovering India – anybody can do a better job by simply striking up conversations with English-speaking Indians – but for hunting down other western travellers.

In the last couple of decades, a kind of post-hippie banana-pancake route has been laid down through Asia. It has its own landmarks, stretching from Pokhara in Nepal, via the island of Ko Pha-Ngan in Thailand, up to Nha Trang in Vietnam and Yangshuo in southern China. After a stop at Angkor in Cambodia for the adventurous, it bifurcates north to the beaches of Boracay in the Philippines, or south to Kuta Beach on Bali. Often it ends, once the traveller's cheques have run out, with a spot of work in Sydney or Melbourne. It has its own vocabulary: gap-year wanderers – Britons taking their post-secondary break before university – meet with dreadlocked Britpackers to share bhang lassis at German bakeries and chai shops. It has its own literature: moisture-warped copies of Emily Barr's *Backpack*, Alex Garland's *The Beach*, and William Sutcliffe's *Are You Experienced?* are exchanged in guesthouses from Manali to Bali. In Sutcliffe's novel, Dave, fresh out of high school, follows Liz to India and heaps opprobrium on his fellow travellers without quite escaping the circuit himself. At one point, Liz asks a pompous Asia veteran how he located a certain restaurant.

" 'Just dug it out, I suppose. It's not in the book or anything.'

'Which book?' she said.

'The book. The Book. There's only one worth having.'

'We've got the Lonely Planet – is that the right one?' Her face was overcome with anxiety.

'It's not the right one.' He paused for effect. 'It's the only one.' "

Though it is slathered with contempt for backpackers, Sutcliffe's book, like the *Lonely Planet* itself, could be used as a route-finder to India's most happening travellers' scenes. Reading between the lines, McLeod Ganj was the place to smoke spliffs in the Himalayas, Pushkar was cool for its sacred lake and camel fair, Kochi was the must-see in Kerala before chilling on Kovalam Beach, and Varanasi was an Amsterdam on the Ganges. In all these places, you were guaranteed to find guesthouses exclusively patronized by other westerners. Now dominated by British, Australian, Canadian, Israeli, and South African travellers – Americans were severely underrepresented, particularly in India – the post-hippie

Asian circuit is developing into its own self-contained tourist rut, as resistant to the intrusions of anything foreign as the railpass-and-hostel party scene in Europe.

That evening, after a long nap, I flipped open the book – er, *The* Book – and looked for a restaurant. "The Hotel Venite," I was advised, "is one of the most character-laden restaurants in Goa. With four tiny balconies hanging over the street and rustic Portuguese decor it's a fine place to enjoy a meal or just a cold beer during siesta." I walked down a side street, surprised to find the architecture so reminiscent of colonial Latin America, and girls wearing old-fashioned print dresses instead of saris. Goa was settled by the Portuguese in 1510 and used as a kind of semi-official piracy base for terrorizing vessels on the Arabian Sea for centuries. Though Salazar's last minions had been driven away after an ignominious standoff with the Indian navy in 1961, the Portuguese had left a legacy of Catholic cathedrals, starched shirts, long siestas on shaded porches, and a kind of polite reserve at odds with the more rambunctious public life in the rest of India. I asked a chemist who was locking his door for the night for directions to the Venite.

"Just down the lane," he said, pointing.

"Is it good?"

"It is one of those restaurants recommended in a foreign guidebook. It is very popular with foreigners."

"And the food?"

"Allow me to suggest the Avanti," he said, diplomatically. "It is a favourite of Indian families. I am going to meet some friends there myself."

I promised I'd try the Avanti, but stuck to my plan. The Venite was located in a little travellers' complex, with a travel agency and an Internet outlet on the first floor. Upstairs, in a dimly lit single room, the "rustic Portuguese" tables were entirely occupied by travellers. Enya played on the stereo, her Prozac perennial "Sail Away" providing an easy-ambient apology for escapism. I saw the couple from my guest house sitting in one of the tiny balconies, and they invited me over. She was Lee, from South Africa; he was Nicki, from Namibia. They'd been travelling for six months, surfing in Bali and Lombok, then working their way through Thailand, most recently spending two weeks diving and going to health retreat on the island of Ko Tao. They were finding India a little hard to take.

"After Thailand, it's a bit of a shock," said Lee. "There you could find isolated beaches with only four or five people on them. We went up to Colva beach today on a scooter, and it was kind of mucky, and there were 40 or 50 people trying to sell you things."

My food arrived; a plate of rubbery calamaries in tomato sauce with fries and frozen vegetables, which I chased with a lemon pop called Limca. It was straight from the Pan-Asian travellers' menu of macaroni and tomato sauce, falafels, and cheese pizza – a strange, flavourless approximation of what westerners are thought to like. We ate looking down on a street scene of stray dogs and crows picking through garbage. Such elevated restaurants are favourites of travellers: they allow a voyeuristic perspective on the street while preventing actual contact with local poverty. (McDonald's had made a severe tactical error in Mumbai by keeping its picture windows; the clients had to eat their lamb-patty Maharaja Macs while starving children pressed their noses to the windows.)

I asked them which of Goa's beaches were the coolest.

"We've just come through Arambol, up north, which was OK," he said. "But we met loads of people who were heading down to Palolem and Gokarna, way down south. That's where we're going next."

The following evening, I took the chemist's advice and went to the Avanti Hotel, which hadn't made it into The Book. The restaurant, empty when I arrived, slowly filled with Goan families. Here, the calamaries were fresh, served in a mild, deeply flavoured chili paste, followed by pomfret, a delicious local fish, sliced into small steaks and bathed in a spiced gravy of Portuguese origin. It was also 30 rupees cheaper than the mediocre travellers' fare I'd had at the Venite. Afterwards, I chatted with Bernard, the cashier, a handsome young Goan with a high forehead, swept-back hair, and flashing eyes. His grandparents were Portuguese, and he had grown up with the language. He spoke with fierce chauvinism of his homeland.

"Goa is clean; other places in India are dirty. In the rest of the nation, they chew on *paan*" – a kind of betel nut–based digestive chaw – "and spit it all over the place. They closed all the *paan* sellers here – so there is no mess on the walls."

He offered me a shot of the local specialty, *feni*, which is distilled from cashews. I belted back the clear liquor. Not unlike lighter fluid, I thought, searching my palate in vain for some subtle hint of the nut. Observing my grimace, Bernard grinned.

"It tastes better with Limca," he said.

Right. With 100 parts lemon pop to 1 part *feni*.

Nicki and Lee had mentioned Palolem Beach. "This is Goa's 'paradise lost' according to some," advised The Book. "Accommodation is still mostly in beach shacks and village homes. It's still the most idyllic beach in the state, but fast filling up with travellers and the businesses set up to service them." Convenient: they were lamenting the very phenomenon they had created.

On the *balcao* of the Panjim Inn, I chatted with Jean-Marc, a Frenchman sporting dyed blond hair, a waist wallet, and a single earring, who had just flown in from Mumbai. He'd been travelling with his girlfriend until recently, but she'd had a bit of a *crise*, a breakdown.

"We decided to stop smoking shit" – it came out *sheet* – "when we came to India, because it can be dangerous to buy it here," he explained. "After a couple of weeks, she started to freak out. We were on a train to Udaipur and she started to tremble; she couldn't stand all the beggar children staring at her. I put her in an expensive air-conditioned hotel. As soon as I bought her some *sheet*, she was OK. But she wanted to fly back to Montpellier. So I am continuing on my own."

Shouldering my bag, I said perhaps we'd run into each other later.

"Do you really think so?" he snorted. "We are in a country of hundreds of millions of people, *tu sais!*"

I shot a meaningful glance at the French edition of The Book on the table.

"*Au revoir*," I insisted.

❧

Wedged into the back bench of a small bus between clean-cut Goans in short-sleeved shirts and slacks, I rode to Palolem Beach. The Book's first recommendation was Cozy Nook. "An excellent place in a great location at the far north end of the beach. Solid bamboo huts and treehouses are 350 [rupees]." Where the sand ended and the palms began, a morose-looking woman showed me ten thatched huts on stilts in the shadow of a palm grove. Mine was a simple affair, with no lock or sink – there were communal showers and toilets outside, and lockers for stowing moneybelts in the restaurant area – and a mosquito net that hung like a rectangular pup tent over the exhausted-looking mattress. I booked the hut for three nights.

I went to check out the scene in the open-walled beach restaurant. "No Woman, No Cry" seeped from the speakers – it jockeyed for number one on the banana-pancake circuit with the songs of Jimmy Cliff, Tracy Chapman, and the omnipresent Manu Chao – while I inspected yet another travellers' menu. Though the "Spinach Bugger with Chips" and the "Sweat and Sour Soup" sounded enticing, I settled for potato-and-spinach curry. Four neo-hippies plodded up the beach and sat down at the table next to me. They were caparisoned in the standard mix of appropriated tribal styles: biceps ringed by Celtic tattoos, eyebrows pierced, torsos wrapped in Malaysian sarongs. (Travellers' garb rarely has much to do with the place it is purchased. You can buy T-shirts with the all-seeing-eye symbol of Nepali stupas in Bangkok, and Nigerian dashikis, dyed by the Javanese batik method, in Goa's Anjuna flea market.) One of them, shirtless and with waist-length, wavy red hair, fished a sandy paperback copy of the anti-corporate manifesto *No Logo* from his Guatemalan knit bag.

"Did you ever notice that all bar codes have the number 666 in them?" he said, tossing his locks behind an ear.

"Oh, I love this song," said the woman next to him, a big-bosomed Mama Cass type with a booming voice. She started singing along to "Walking on Sunshine" in an affected contralto. "It's K.C. and the Sunshine Band, isn't it?"

He ignored her. "They say that in the future we're all going to have a bar code tattooed on our necks." Grabbing a pack of Marlboros from one of the other girls, he showed her how the Ms on three sides of the package could be made to look like Ks. "You see: K . . . K . . . K. It's like a code. They're made by Philip Morris. You know – the Deep South." He sucked on his *bidi* with satisfaction.

"You know that big sheet hanging in the hut?" said Mama Cass, obviously intent on pricking his bubble. "Don't use it; I accidentally hawked up a big lump of phlegm on it."

I almost choked on my *naan* bread.

"Bloody trustafarians," the guy next to me said, after the neo-hippies had shuffled off to play hacky sack on the sand. John was handsome, barechested, short-haired. A member of the Royal Shakespeare Company on a six-week break between seasons at Stratford, he was travelling with his new girlfriend, Victoria. They'd met during rehearsals of *King John*; as his Dauphin had repeatedly kissed her Blanch of Spain, they'd fallen in love.

"This is my second trip to India, but Victoria has never been to Asia. I didn't know whether she was going to be able to handle it. But we had a 16-hour trip down from Mumbai in a filthy sleeper bus – I mean, the mattress *reeked* – and she passed with flying colours."

Victoria sauntered up from the beach, put her arm around his shoulder. "Hey, babe," he said, putting his arm around her waist. Freckle-faced and carroty toned, she had loose red curls cascading over her shoulders. We chatted for a while, got along, and made a date for dinner a couple of nights later.

I spent the rest of the afternoon exploring the beach. At the south end, where the exhortation "No Topless" had been scrawled across a boulder, an establishment called Cocohuts attracted a crowd that favoured beach volleyball and soccer. It was also where the trustafarians were staying, and I saw the conspiracy-theory dude labouring over the chords to "Buffalo Soldier" on a guitar. All along the tideline, rotting arrangements of inflated blowfish encircled by glassy-eyed eels formed macabre Flemish still lifes on the sand. Thin-limbed Indian boys ran back and forth between listing wickets in all-day games of beach cricket. A Goan man in a loincloth plunged a metal pike into the surf and pulled forth a Picasso-faced flat fish, deftly skewered above its close-set eyes. I walked up and asked him what it was called.

"Want to buy some smoke?" he non-sequitured.

Palolem was that kind of place. I was on The Tropical Beach, after all, a durable travel cliché. Somewhere in the world, the story went, there was a stretch of powdery sand, coconuts, and hammocks that attained the

Platonic ideal of Beachness, where people lived like Fletcher Christian in an idyll of free love, body surfing, and guiltless sex. Maybe – but it sure wasn't Palolem. Giant sows, trailed by squealing piglets, snuffled through piles of garbage and seaweed. Every few hundred metres there was another complex of beach huts hidden beneath the palms (only Indira Gandhi's 1981 law banning major construction within 500 metres of the high-tide line had spared Goa giant shorefront hotels). If you sunbathed too far from your hut, you'd look up from a siesta to find a souvenir vendor had spread a small boutique's worth of snuffboxes, hashpipes, and nautilus shells encrusted with rhinestones on a blanket at your feet. In the collective unconscious, the shore of dreams – *The Beach* of Alex Garland's backpacker utopia – was uncommercialized, undiscovered by guidebook writers. And preferably, one suspects, uncontaminated by natives.

My immediate neighbour at Cozy Nook was a tall Frenchman with a perfect tan and a tight black Speedo who spent his days collecting shells and his nights trying to remember the lyrics to Manu Chao songs. I was sitting in the surf with a Spanish-born short-order cook from San Francisco, his head shaved except for a red topknot, when the Frenchman came up.

"*Tu fumes, toi?*" he asked me.

When I shook my head, he turned away and asked to borrow the Spaniard's rolling papers. Back on shore, I chatted with a green-eyed Israeli girl who was nervously flipping through a Hebrew translation of the *Lonely Planet*. As we talked of her military service, she stared at me expectantly, sliding a ring on and off her finger in a rhythmic gesture I had no trouble giving a Freudian interpretation. Later, I watched the Frenchman approach the Israeli girl. By sunset, they were sharing a hammock, beaming dopily at passersby with enormous grins. That night, the Frenchman's hut danced with candlelight, and, between coughs and puffs of smoke, I heard the whispered verses of Manu Chao's "Clandestino" being greeted with breathy coos of delight.

For all the Cozy Nook's air of jungle authenticity, it had been confected to appeal to backpackers. Amid the waterlogged paperbacks in the restaurant, I found a book called *Primitive Architecture*, full of Haida longhouses, Malian mud huts, and thatched stilt dwellings exactly like ours – the guesthouse's architect, I learned, had used it for inspiration. The owner was a shaven-headed Goan hipster named Aggi, always dressed in white, who'd got his start in hospitality working in the oil fields of Saudi Arabia. As he sat by the cash desk one night, I asked him whether he'd met the *Lonely Planet* writers.

"Sure. They came for three weeks. They didn't tell me who they were. They checked out all the places on the beach, made a map. And the day before they left, they told me they really liked the place and wanted to put me in the guide. I said: 'Of course!' I mean, I didn't pay them or anything." The mention had definitely helped business. "People used to come to Palolem and stay in somebody's house. After a night, they'd walk along the beach and find my place. The *Lonely Planet* thing just means they come straight here. It's better this way. I don't want to rent out my huts for charter flight tourists – these Indian 'folklore' nights. The tourists go, watch dances, that kind of shit, one night in a hut, back to their hotel."

If Palolem was a *faux* primitive construct for westerners, at least it was one that could also be enjoyed by Indian tourists. Merchant marine sailors, in impeccable white uniforms, strolled up and down the beach, flipping shells with the tips of their polished shoes. One afternoon, a group of portly Indian men stripped off their shirts and ran into the waves with stubby bottles of King's beer in hand.

"I sing to the horizon," a pot-bellied fellow declaimed, as he capered in a parody of modern dance, "the place where the sea comes to kiss the sky!"

"We are from Kerala!" another yelled, dog-paddling towards me. He was quite drunk. "That is a place in India! Coming from please?"

I confessed my nationality.

"My uncle lives in Toronto! Wait! I will give you his address!"

I lamented that I wasn't carrying a pen.

"OK! Later!" he yelled happily, and paddled away.

For the backpacking community, such middle-class Indian tourists had always been way too uncool; even the first hippies had dismissed them as "buffalos" and "full pants wallahs." In contrast, the Konkani-speaking locals – called "Junglies" by Christian Goans – who lived and worked on Palolem were sufficiently picturesque, if a little too real. Barefoot men shinnied up coconut palms like they were climbing ladders; a female construction team worked a patch of beach around the clock, removing sand on buckets balanced on their heads. One night, Cozy Nook was treated to an extended bout of domestic violence as a Goan chased his shrieking wife around the lot next door, a scene that ended with resounding slaps and prolonged wailing. A mutual exoticizing process was evident in Goa: the westerners took photos of fishermen pulling their mango-tree canoes onto the sand; well-groomed Indian men snapped shots of dreadlocked traveller girls tanning with their bikini tops unstrapped. Either way, there was a failure to connect, the two sides remaining in adjacent bubbles.

On my last night in Palolem, John and Victoria and I walked down the main drag – a strip of Internet outlets, travel agencies, and stalls selling toilet paper, Nivea suncream, and baggy tie-dyed pants. We ate pizzas made with buffalo milk mozzarella pulled from a brick oven by an Italian from Brescia. I commented that, except for the piglets rooting out back, we could have been on the terrace of a trattoria.

"Yeah, a little too familiar, isn't it?" John chuckled. "Sometimes I wonder if I'm getting jaded. When I came to Delhi on my first trip to India, I'd never even been on a plane before. It was in full monsoon. I'll never forget the shock – the dirt, the noise, the smells. I remember standing in a doorway and watching the rain come down. It was like an ocean dropping on the pavement. I rode 16 hours on a bus to Rajasthan that same night – no shocks, jammed in on metal seats. I thought I was dreaming. I just didn't get that feeling arriving in Mumbai this time."

Maybe it was the travellers who had changed, I suggested, not India. In the last decade, the emergence of the Internet and the proliferation of guest houses had completely changed the circuit. Travellers didn't take risks anymore – they preferred to hang out together. We were prime examples, I pointed out: here we were in Goa, eating *pizza al tonno*, surrounded by Europeans.

"But look what happened in the sixties," John objected. "It was embarrassing, wasn't it? All those people going to find themselves in Asia. They just got more lost. They may have burned their passports, but they all came crawling back to the embassies. Most of them ended up chartered accountants."

Perhaps. But some had also discovered new ways of looking at the world. The spiritual component – the willingness to be transformed by a place – seemed to be lacking in the *Lonely Planet* crowd.

John shrugged. This time, India was a two-week beach vacation, and he was enjoying playing the old Asia hand for Victoria's benefit.

After paying the bill, we said our goodbyes the modern way. No bear hugs, hand slaps, or wishes of good karma: we traded e-mail addresses.

§

Starting around 1966, the year I was born, a small but significant trickle of westerners started arriving in India and Nepal. Rejecting their parents' conception of travel – the ever-expanding post-war tourist bubble of beach resorts and jet planes – they risked the overland journey on gravel roads. The first contingent were mostly Americans (some flew direct, though most started in Europe) driven from home by the Vietnam War. After the street riots of May 1968, disaffected French students joined the trail. Pop culture played a role, as the Beatles and Donovan went to Rishikesh in the Himalayas to meet the Maharishi, followed by Mike Love of the Beach Boys and Mia Farrow (who took refuge on Goa's Colva Beach after freaking out at the Beatles' ashram).

Until the French *Guide Routard* appeared in 1973, the only travel guides available were Herman Hesse's *Journey to the East, The Tibetan Book of the Dead*, and Baba Ram Dass's *Be Here Now*. Travellers relied on word of mouth to track down guest houses and restaurants. About 47,000 Americans came to India and Nepal in 1966; five years later, there were 301,000 travellers, most from western Europe. Author David Tomory places the end of the hippie trail in 1973, the year American forces were withdrawn from Vietnam, oil prices increased, and the King of Nepal banned the legal sale of hashish in the pie shops of Kathmandu.

The hippie circuit, it was true, had been just as much of a rut as the current *Lonely Planet* trail. One stayed at the Gulhane in Istanbul, the Amir Kabir Hotel in Tehran, and the houseboats in Varanasi. The Crown Hotel in Delhi was celebrated: the rooms got cheaper and hotter the higher you went, and the management was famous for giving credit until money was wired from home (at which point they'd return your pass-port). Once in Delhi, people dispersed, heading for the Modern Lodge in Calcutta or the Hotchpotch in Kathmandu.

In spite of all the clustering, there was a spiritual dimension to the India Trip. For those overwhelmed by angst and Delhi belly after sleepless nights in third-class trains and one too many shouts of "Hello, Baba!" there were retreats such as the Sri Aurobindo ashram in Pondicherry, Sai Baba's in Puttaparthi, and later, the Rajneeshi complex in Pune. Though Hinduism is a religion that doesn't recruit converts, many travellers ignored caste and heredity and became wandering sadhus, donning saffron robes and meditating on the banks of the Ganges.

Eventually, even in India, the hippies were pursued by their reputa-tions as bubble-headed freaks. In 1971, the Indian director Dev Anand made a film called *Hare Rama Hare Krishna*, which parodied the hippie lifestyle. Suddenly, wherever they went, travellers were subjected to verses of the film's hit song, "*Dum Maro Dum*." Children raced after them, taunt-ing them with Hindi lyrics that meant: "Take a drag. Take a drag. I'm wiped out!"

When people complain that the good old days of Asian travel have vanished forever, they're only partly right. There are more international travellers – 2.6 million in 2000 – in India than ever before. In a nation of more than a billion, this still means the ratio of Indians to travellers is 385:1 (versus nine tourists for every citizen in the Bahamas). In spite of social changes – the swelling of the middle class, the boom in film production, the nation's emergence as a software giant, the spread of Hindu funda-mentalism – the good old India hasn't gone anywhere. By straying a few streets from the travel ghettos, you can still find yourself in communities where they till fields with neolithic hoes, struggle with leprosy and plague, and celebrate 3,000-year-old festivals. It's not so much India that has changed, but the way people travel.

At least some of the hippie travellers managed to break out of the travel rut. Embarrassing as the results could be, they sought experience, authenticity, and transformation, as Byron and Rimbaud had before them. With the appearance of the first *Lonely Planet* guide to India in 1981, everything changed. Travellers were given point-to-point instructions on how to find other travellers, and the circuit, with its full-moon parties, chai shops, and opportunities for casual sex became an end in itself. These days, backpackers aren't carrying The Book – The Book is carrying them.

As I walked down the main drag of Palolem to find an auto-rickshaw to the train station, I ran into blond-haired Jean-Marc, whom I'd last seen back at the Panjim Inn. Too cool to show any surprise at our chance reunion in a sea of humanity, he composedly shook my hand.

"I'm about to leave Palolem too," he said. "I can't stand the sound of techno in the bar next to my hut. I have just had four months of this beach life at home in Montpellier. This noise, boom-boom, first thing in the morning? *Non, merci.* And the people who come here, they don't really respect the Indians."

I humoured his Gallic tut-tutting – interesting to see that the French, even when backpacking, take pride in their finesse. When it came time to say goodbye, I again insisted on avoiding "*Adieu.*"

This time, Jean-Marc grudgingly returned my "*Au revoir.*"

§

From the platform of the tiny Canacona railway station, I watched the sun coming up. A lone bicycle rider traversed oddly European-looking fields, towards a church at the foot of a hill. A distant bell tolling the angelus wouldn't have sounded out of place. The sensation of being in a train station in Provence during tourist season was exacerbated by my company on the platform. An Irish couple was heading up to Mumbai. An athletic-looking, curly-haired young man with a surfboard-shaped pendant around his neck sat next to a huge black sports equipment bag. Two dishevelled English women complained about the sweet tea dispensed by chai vendors from stainless steel thermoses.

On the train, I started chatting with the man with the sports bag. I'd pegged him for an Australian – he had blond-flecked hair, an athletic carriage, and an easygoing demeanour – but Paul was actually an English triathlete. I asked him where he was headed.

"A place called Hampi," he said. "Do you know it?"

That's where I was going, I replied. The English women sitting across the aisle overheard me.

"That's fantastic!" one of them said. "That's where we're going too!"

Half an hour later, we got off at Margao and ran to the wickets to get our tickets. Once again, we all ended up in the same car. A conductor came along and said we could pay a small supplement to have reserved second-class seats a few cars up.

"You will be more comfortable there," he advised, with a slightly condescending wobble of his head.

I helped Paul get his bag down from an upper berth – it must have weighed 20 kilos – and followed him down the aisle past protruding, sockless feet. We arrived in a car inhabited entirely by Caucasians. *That's* what the conductor had meant – we'd be more comfortable surrounded by our own kind. My ticket assigned me a seat across from a pale German girl, engrossed in *Der Kleine Hobbit*. Her boyfriend, whose curly locks and chubby face made him look a bit like Bilbo Baggins, asked if I would mind sitting elsewhere. I joined Paul, who had already opened a copy of *The Celestine Prophecy*, and asked what was weighing down his bag. He pulled out a Sony mini-disc player.

"They're brilliant – you can carry three or four CDs on each one," he said. He showed me his top-of-the-line videocam. And his digital camera, which he took to Internet cafés to send travel snaps to the 150 friends on his e-mail list. He had a bulky, state-of-the-art iodine water purifier bottle, and wore a Nike digital watch.

"Maybe I have *too* much stuff," he said. "Sometimes it gets hard to carry."

Wasn't he worried about theft?

"Nah. I paid £400 in insurance. I got the deluxe policy – it includes kidnapping."

A beggar, his leg encased in an improbably narrow plastic tube, dragged his shrivelled limbs down the aisle, pausing before us to lift his eyes in mute supplication. Paul shrugged good-naturedly.

"Sorry, mate, I don't have any change. *No – rupees.*" He looked at me, puzzled. "What do you do? I never seem to have any coins to give."

Our Caucasian car hadn't yet filled up, so I excused myself and moved to another window seat to stretch my legs. At a town called Londa three young Indian men, dressed in shorts and tie-dyed T-shirts, boarded the train and sat in the vacant seats across the aisle from me. They too were tourists, students from Andhra Pradesh on the east coast, on their way to Jog Falls.

As we stopped in Hubli, open hands on thin wrists reached through the window bars, children begging for coins with plaintive whispers of "*Anna, anna.*"

"What do you think of all this poverty?" one of the Indian tourists asked.

"For a westerner, it's a shock," I admitted. "Sometimes I wonder if India's political class isn't more concerned with filling its own pockets than helping its citizens."

He nodded agreement. "We have food enough to feed everybody," he said. "The problem is the politicians. The British, they only put Gandhi in jail, they respected him. If Gandhi were alive today, the current government would not put him in jail. They would *shoot* him. They allow no protest. There was a demonstration recently in our state, against an electricity rate increase, and they shot and killed four people."

It was striking what a difference moving away from the *Lonely Planet* trail – even a few metres – could make. On my first trip to India, I'd carried a guidebook published by Cadogan, a British publisher. Highly literate, excellent on art, history, and architecture, it took me from Mumbai to Varanasi via Rajasthan, with stops in little-touristed forts in Orchha and Gwalior. I stayed at inexpensive hotels for Indian tourists – rather than travellers' guest houses – shared breakfast rooms with travelling Indians, and was usually the only non-Asian in the buses or trains. I shared pappadums with a family from Delhi on the second-class sleeper to Mumbai, got a lift from a student from Benares Hindu University on the back of his scooter, and watched a Hindi-language epic with two young Jains in a movie palace in Jaipur, meeting significant numbers of other western travellers only when I stopped at tourist spots like the Taj Mahal and the Elephanta Caves. This time, with the *Lonely Planet* guiding my steps, there was no getting away from them.

The girls, noses buried in Brit-chick fiction, seemed alarmed by the conversation, particularly when the Indian tourists started demonstrating karate moves with high-pitched Bruce Lee–style howls. Paul, however, was intrigued enough to come over. Struck by his good looks, one of the Indian tourists asked if he could touch his hair.

"It is so soft! And your eyes, so blue. Beautiful," he said.

Paul patted his hair self-consciously. "Yeah, right, but it's really dry. I lighten it with a spray, and it's made a mess of it."

In Hospet, Paul and I said goodbye to the tourists, and shared an auto-rickshaw from the train station to Hampi, bumping through an improbable terrain of immense, smooth-sided boulders that looked like they'd been sprinkled over a giant diorama by some prehistoric hobbyist.

"It's right out of *The Flintstones*," marvelled Paul.

The British girls, following in their own auto-rickshaw, pulled up before a row of guesthouses in Hampi. After poring over The Book, they rushed off to a recommended establishment. Shrugging, I followed them, and got the last room in the Padma Guest House, number six on the list.

§

In the 16th century, Hampi was a centre of the spice trade, a metropolis of half a million. Ransacked by a confederacy of Deccan sultanates at the height of its power, it had gone into swift decline. Now it had a permanent population of little more than a thousand, centred on the Hampi Bazaar, a dusty strip of guest houses, restaurants, and travel agencies that had grown up to service the *Lonely Planet* crowd. I rented a bike and rode among the 33 square kilometres of ruins, poking into overgrown temples and scaring the green parrots roosting on facades vaguely evocative of Mayan temples. It was a haunting place to lose oneself – a ghost empire – its furthest precincts patrolled by yawning security guards hired to foil gangs from Mumbai who were known to pillage the cameras and passports of errant tourists.

It was also a full-blown travellers' scene, with a heavy emphasis on drugs. At a rooftop restaurant, the waiter whispered an offer of opium. In addition to the standard mango and salted yogurt drinks, every menu included the coyly named "special" lassi – spiked with *bhang*, pollen from marijuana plants mixed with clarified butter. Groups of long-haired Israelis sat in bars, barking commands at the servers through clouds of hash. Though Hampi was a holy place and alcohol was technically banned, the waiters at most restaurants discreetly poured beer into metal cups beneath the tables.

In the Bazaar, I ordered a milk coffee in a restaurant whose sign boasted: "Geeta Restaurant – Recomended in Lonely Planet." A handsome Englishman in a collarless cotton shirt and baggy blue pants, yellow-lensed sunglasses balanced on his shaved crown, asked to borrow my map. With his sly leer, James was the living incarnation of the flash bastard, though I suspected his smooth verbosity was a side effect of benzodiazepines. Recently graduated from university in Bristol, he'd flown into Goa a month earlier and rented a brand new Enfield – the motorcycles are still cranked out in India to Second World War–vintage specifications – to buzz around the beaches.

"I stayed in Calangute. It was like package tourist central, but it was right in the middle of things. I found this great bar where they sold bottles of vodka for like, 120 roops. They had these three *wicked* dogs that would only bark when the cops were walking up the beach – which gave you largely enough time to dispose of the drugs.

"I'm really chuffed about all this Valium being about. I mean, the stuff is like gold in England, but they'll sell it to you here, no questions asked, for a few roops. I was with my mate on our motorcycles in Calangute and he had a really bad accident – you could see the sinews in his knee where he'd hit the pavement. So we went to a chemist's, completely paralytic, and said: 'Right! We'll have a box of Valium. That's right, 250 pills. And some amphetamine sulfate, please.' It was kind of pathetic, actually – we only had enough money left for the smallest bandage.

"Goa was *fan*-tastic. I met this girl from Paris, and we had a whirlwind fling. Here I was with a brand new Enfield – I mean, the chrome was still shining – riding around with this gorgeous *fox* from France. She was the best I'd ever had, on all levels: laughs, conversation, sex. When she left, I said to myself, I just can't face this night alone. So I downed a bottle of coconut *feni* on the beach. Last thing I remember, somebody said: 'Want

booking a ticket at Radiant Services, the only private bus service recommended in The Book, I remembered James and his tales of tranquillizers and decided to pop into a pharmacy. The druggist, his head on a wooden table, lurched into instant wakefulness when I cleared my throat. I asked for Valium.

"Certainly," he said, and dropped a blister pack of ten into a paper bag. Apparently he was used to servicing western travellers. "You want amphetamines? Ketamine? Liquid speed?" I politely refused.

The next morning I went to a travel agency near the train station to find a teetering mound of fluorescent backpacks and a knot of 50 or so travellers. The bus ride, essentially a shuttle for the *Lonely Planet* crowd, was a brutal affair. My knees were crammed against the seat back, and my thinly upholstered seat felt like it was welded directly to an unsuspended axle. The driver seemed to navigate by sound rather than sight, using his horn as a primitive form of echolocation. We broke down after two hours and limped to a gas station, where the bus was hoisted on a spindly jack until a replacement tire was found.

Once we got back on the road, I chatted with a laid-back Israeli girl who showed me out-of-focus pictures of snake charmers in Manali, sang along to a Hindi music cassette on her Walkman, and punctuated her conversation with the mantra "Shanti, shanti." After popping a Valium, I started to understand her perspective. When we swerved near the Nepalese border to avoid a dead man face down in the middle of the road, his dhoti rucked up around his thighs, I barely blinked.

By the time we got to Pokhara, a centre for trekking in the Himalayas, I was exhausted. Nonetheless, I hooked up with a young couple, he from San Francisco, she from Lille, and we hiked three days through mountain villages and along narrow forest paths. They'd hired a porter, whom they paid about 400 Nepali rupees (about $5.50) a day to carry their bags. Krishna, stoop-shouldered and pigeon-toed in his decrepit Vans, plodded along slow and steady. As we approached Poon Hill, we caught him singing a twist on a Nepali folk song.

"*Resum phri phri phri,*" he intoned in his sweet soprano. "Israeli monkey, Nepali donkey, *Resum phri phri phri.*"

We laughed, asked him to explain the lyrics.

"Monkeys crazy people, right? Israelis crazy too, like monkey, and they make Nepalis like donkey." I asked if he'd go trekking with them again. He put out a flat hand and yelled: "No!" It was the only time Krishna had raised his voice. "I try, two, three times. No good people. No worth the money. No tips. I like *no*."

Our guest house that night was filled with Dutch tourists. I chatted with the group leader, a care-worn physiotherapist reading a book called *Total Fitness*. He'd been coming to Nepal since 1993. A lot of the trekkers these days were in their 40s and 50s, he complained, and none too fit.

"In the beginning it was only backpackers, with their own bags. It was OK to guide these people. But now, they are older, and we have to guide the kind that go to Ibiza. They have all seen Brad Pitt in *Seven Years in Tibet*. They don't know what to expect, they have never hiked on a mountain. This time, one of them actually said to me: 'Harry – all of these steps. Now, when will we stop walking on all these steps and hills?' One of the men in our group has mental problems, from overwork. He started crying when he saw all the dirt and poor children in Kathmandu, he wanted to turn back. Finally, I had to force him – just get in the bus. Take one step at a time. Ah! It is not like the old days."

In fact, the median age on the Annapurna circuit seemed to be approaching the cruise-ship average. Deciding I'd strayed too far from the backpacker trail, I bid adieu to my trekking companions in Ghorepani. We toasted Krishna with shots of raiksi, a nasty millet wine served from a kettle. It tasted not unlike sake – if sake were made with mouldy brown rice and adulterated with mountain meltwater.

By the time I got back to the Lakeside travellers' ghetto in Pokhara, a cold bug had lodged itself deep in my sinuses. I spent the hair-raising bus trip to Kathmandu, past gossamer foot bridges that spanned milky-green mountain rivers, lightly stoned on over-the-counter cold medication. Glancing over a cliff, I'd seen a bus that had just passed us, now 30 metres below in the river, black smoke pouring from its doors. When we stopped in a roadside rest stop, I asked a thin-lipped Israeli with a ponytail whom I'd met on the bus from Varanasi how he was handling the ride.

"I have a Nepali next to me, he's being obnoxious," he said, spreading his legs to demonstrate. "And that loud Hindi music they are playing. Horrible."

No earplugs? I asked.

"Foreigners should not be forced to listen to this disgusting music. I took my nail scissors and cut the wires next to the window. But I think this wire, it was not for the speakers. Maybe the brakes?"

Christ, I thought, I'm riding with a sociopath. I fumbled in my bag and took another Valium.

§

Finally, after a month of crimping my backbone on bad transportation, my road to Kathmandu came to an end. And, to paraphrase the Grateful Dead, what a long, strangely familiar trip it had been. Following the *Lonely Planet* trail, I'd passed through the world's largest democracy, a nation that boasted 18 official languages, 1,600 dialects, and 330 million deities, without having had any but the most glancing and superficial encounters with actual Indians. Which isn't to fault the *Lonely Planet* – it's accurate, detailed, and well-researched, as thorough, in its way, as a 19th-century Baedeker. It's the self-perpetuating trail it has spawned that's the problem.

What makes it particularly offensive in the Asian context is the pretensions of the current crop of western travellers. Sure, it's essential for young people to have a look at the world, to see how the great majority of humanity still struggles with hunger, religious strife, and disease in pre-industrial conditions. A contemporary Grand Tour of Asia, South America, or Africa also provides insight into modernity's great hidden truism: that Europe and North America owe their wealth and power to their continuing exploitation, through the intermediary of western-oriented local elites, of the Third World's resources. But to use the freedom of a fortuitous birth to hide behind mini-disc players and clouds of hash in all-traveller buses, on groovy beaches, and in guest-house ghettos is a squandering of privilege.

There were exceptions – like the guy in Varanasi who'd stopped travelling to help the lepers. There were those who, eyes opened by what they'd seen, would return to help with micro-electricity projects in the Nepalese Terai, community banks in Gujarat, and the victims of "kitchen accidents" (unwanted wives who are locked into kitchens and burnt with kerosene after their dowry is spent) in Kolkata. But the great mass of travellers treat the Third World like a resort – one that will give them a spurious aura of experience back home – all the time complaining about the shoddiness and filth that inconvenience their vacation. By the time I got to Kathmandu, I was inwardly applauding when the locals stole expensive Sony digital cameras and videocams. It seemed fitting that the devices used to exoticize and objectify the poor – any one of which could buy an entire village family out of debt and indentured labour – were being filched from overstuffed backpacks.

My imaginary Kathmandu had been a medieval Zermatt in the Himalayas, an overgrown hamlet surrounded by high mountain peaks, where everything was made of wood, snow drooped from overhanging eaves, and hard-core voyagers draped in wool blankets drank yak tea as they planned mountain expeditions. I was surprised to find a stifling, sprawling metropolis, plagued by vicious Enfields and Nissans, the distant snow-peaks barely visible through a Southern Californian pall of exhaust. As I checked into the Kathmandu Guest House, a Gurkha-guarded enclave among the fast food joints and trekkers' outfitting shops in the Thamel tourist ghetto, my head cold reached its zenith and the dust and pollution prompted me to best my personal record for sneezing: 25 times in a row, a bout that left me reeling and exhausted.

Kathmandu was the one place where remnants of the old hippie contingent remained. I made the pilgrimage to the legendary Freak Street, off Durbar Square. In the Snowman Restaurant, a pair of neo-freaks with dreadlocks, goatees, and red tikka marks on their foreheads peppered a laconic German conversation with "peace and love" and "cool." (While the groovy travellers all dressed like bastard sons of Grace Slick and Sai Baba, the Nepali drug dealers in Kathmandu favoured Guns 'n' Roses T-shirts and Ramones-style leather jackets.) A Captain Beefheart tape was playing on the stereo, and the waiter brought us apple crumbles and milk coffees. I sat down with a scraggly haired character in his late 40s who went by the Sanskrit name Tarachandra. Wearing a droopy knit sweater, he told me he lived in San Francisco but had been coming to Nepal to study Sanskrit and the Tantra since the 1970s.

"When I first came here, Thamel didn't exist. It was all Freak Street. And there were drugs all around. This place was full of pie shops, with Nepalis and hippies sitting around smoking chillums. Man, you didn't need to smoke – you just had to inhale. Now, it's still happening, but it's more low-key – people keep it hidden."

I asked if today's travellers were different.

"Well, you never used to see the trekker types. I guess our generation was different because with everything going on – the Vietnam War, all that – we felt like we had nothing to go back home to. I mean, what was there for us in the States? It was better to be in India, rather than go home and be drafted."

I met another old hippie, this one from Australia, in the New Orleans Café in Thamel. We talked over ice cream and brownies while a choir of Nepali children in Newari costumes sang, "If you're happy and you know it, clap your hands" (over and over and over again). His name was Terry, and he'd been coming to Nepal for 12 years, buying crafts to sell at fairs near his home in Adelaide.

"I don't make money at it, but I love it. And it helps the Nepalis. In the villages, people are lucky to get one meal every two days. In the remote areas, a single hailstorm can wipe out a crop and kill a whole village. I know the farmland looks rich, but that's only what you see in the trekking areas. Most of these people farm for 12 months, but they can only provide for six months. I mean, I've had friends in the villages; I've come back a year later and they've starved to death. I used to spend a lot of time crying about it. But there's not much you can do." He shot me an earnest glance. "I hope I'm not bumming you out."

I told him he was, and pushed aside my brownie.

"Look, enjoy your dessert. The Nepalis would enjoy it if they were in your place. And who's to say – maybe in a hundred years we'll be the ones hoping for a single bowl of *dal bhaat* a day."

That just made it worse. Terry looked at me with paternalistic concern. He was in his 50s and had two grown sons. "You know, you look tired," he said. "Sometimes the best thing to do is *just go home*. You can't take the entire world on your shoulders. Start with your family back home. Take care of your neighbours, take care of the ones you love. That's where you have to start."

He was right. I *was* tired. Exhausted. Longing for home, sick of packing my bags every few days, aching to hold Karen. What I needed was a place to call my own – not a sublet apartment, nor a storage spot and the promise of a couch. It was time to think of finding an apartment that felt like home – maybe even buying one. I could pick out some house plants and work on sticking around long enough to keep them alive.

Meanwhile, though, I had more pressing problems. The incessant travelling had gotten to me, and my long-observed resolution to avoid drugs had shaken free, dropped somewhere along the road like a bulky, too-often-read paperback.

Coconut *feni*, millet *raiksi* – perhaps these qualified as local specialties. But Mother's Little Helper? Things were getting out of hand.

Chapter 11

I SHOT THE TOURIST

"Amazing Thailand" – I Find Myself a French Wife – Ten-baht Túk-túk
Rides on Khao San Road – A Night at Patpong's Vaginal Olympics – The
True Cost of a Rented Girlfriend – A Short History of Intoxication &
Intercourse – Gauguin, Loti, and Other Lubricious Travellers – "Mysteries
of the Long-Necked People" – A Hill-Tribe Trek – In Which I Discover that
Some of My Fellow Trekkers Are Idiots – The Fire Dance – A Massage and
Some "Oplium" – The Problem with Authenticity – Gastrointestinal
Meltdown During an Elephant Ride – "I Shot the Tourist!" – The Hit Man
at Silver Sands – Never a Dull Moment in Pattaya

I needed to chill. Thailand, I hoped, would be just what I needed.

Aboard the Thai Airways flight to Bangkok, a sloe-eyed stewardess in a purple gown presented me with dinner, and I thought I tasted Indochina in the curry and coconut milk, sensed the approaching Far East in the bacteria-free exoticism of the longan and papaya dessert. After all the flyspecked sugar bowls in India and Nepal, the prospect of sweetening my coffee with individually sealed saccharine packages in the air-conditioned 7-11s of Southeast Asia had a certain antiseptic appeal. On the backpacker's circuit, Thailand was known as the place to go for reclining-seat luxury buses, cheap massages on white sand beaches, and guilt-free fast food binges, a kind of westernized resort from the rigours of travel. Who needed drugs when you had perfectly powdered sand, pristine tropical forests, and all-you-can-eat *pad thai*?

The glossy "Amazing Thailand" tourist brochure I'd picked up in a Kathmandu travel agency showed photos of jungle orchids, cloud-draped mountainscapes, bungalows set among verdant cliffs, and kaleidoscopes of tropical fish scattering before scuba divers. The target market, it seemed, was the big-spending ecotourist. "Most popular with visitors is the hill country of the North, a region of teak forests and jungle-covered peaks where the folds of the mountains hide secret little valleys, any one of them a contender for Shangri-La." The highlight was Chiang Mai, where trekking companies offered "low-impact" hikes through pristine forests to non-touristic hill-tribe villages.

Since the 1990s, ecotourism has been touted as a unique innovation: a way of minimizing the impact of mass tourism on fragile environments and far-flung cultures by emphasizing small groups and responsible touring practices. Focusing on such developing-world destinations as Costa Rica, Kenya, the Galapagos Islands, and Southeast Asia, it promises to bring economic benefits to Third World nations that desperately need to preserve fading indigenous cultures and threatened ecosystems. After seeing how Grand Tourists overran the *piazze* of Italy and lager louts had ruined Corfu, I longed to believe there was a way of travelling without laying waste to a culture.

Looking out the port window, I could see we were flying level with the sunlit peaks of the Himalayas – a striking image, as we had just reached 9,000 metres. One of the travel industry's dirtiest secrets is that planes are incommensurate belchers of greenhouse gases; the picturesque trail our jet left in the Asian sky was injecting nitrogen oxide directly into the upper atmosphere, increasing ozone concentrations and hastening climate change. Any British ecotraveller who flew to Brazil to trek in the rain forests was responsible for burning 2.2 tonnes of carbon – an individual passenger's share of the plane's total emissions – twice what the average African produced in a year. Though I was proud of the fact I'd never owned a car, I knew that by flying across the Atlantic and then taking these short hops across Asia I was spewing as much carbon as if I'd commuted to work in an SUV every day for a year. Ecotravel, in that it encourages the privileged to take polluting jets across the globe to rusticate in the thatched huts of the Third World, will always be more successful as an oxymoron than as a buzzword.

Besides, how many of the ten million or so visitors to Thailand every year – 70 percent of them single men – actually came for the hill tribes and coral? The tourist bumpf highlighted untouched wilderness; the sex tourists knew how to read between the lines. For them, Thailand was the place to enjoy fun-loving bar girls and prescription-free Viagra while paid-off cops looked the other way.

§

After cashing a traveller's cheque – an American dollar bought 45 baht – I waited outside the Bangkok airport in the subtropical heat for a bus. Air-conditioned Corolla taxis were filled by a succession of quick-moving young Thai women, their slender arms dripping with Duty Free bags, accompanied by large, sluggish white men in shorts and loud shirts. I asked a tall backpacker in his late 20s about getting to Khao San Road. Dirk was German, and explained that he was stopping for the night in Bangkok before heading to a guest house he ran with his Thai girlfriend in the north. We found a common language in French, and Dirk suggested we cut costs by sharing a hotel room.

It was well after sunset, and through the windows of the A2 bus Bangkok looked like a metropolis of skyscrapers caressed by sinuous overpasses. After the low-wattage night of Indian cities, the nightscape – a roadside slide show of Marlboro and cellphone billboards – seemed brash and brilliant, a Los Angeles built entirely in the last decade. Dirk led me down a *soi* – an urban lane – full of massage parlours and laundries, to a quiet back street lined by guest houses. After checking into a grim but cheap room, we ambled down Soi Rambutri in search of drink. Our desultory conversation over Cokes attracted the interest of a French girl at the next table.

"*Vous permettez?*" she asked, pulling a lacquered wicker chair to our table.

Cécile had flown in from Australia a week before, and confessed she'd been having trouble penetrating Bangkok's nightlife. "It's all right if you're a man," she complained. "You just plunge right in, and nobody objects. But I want to see these famous go-go bars too!"

Dirk sympathized. "Yes, they don't really like the *farang* women in Patpong."

Farang was the Thai term for white foreigners, and Patpong was the district – three parallel *sois*, cross-hatched by even narrower alleys – where the strip bars were clustered. I told Cécile I wanted to see the Patpong girls myself – but only to look, not to touch. Perhaps we could foil the touts by posing as husband and wife. We made a dinner date for the following night, and she wrote down her room number in a nearby guest house.

"*Salut, chéri!*" she said, leaving me with a pair of sticky-cheeked kisses.

Dirk arched an eyebrow. "You sure you need a French wife?"

I already had one, I said, and could probably handle a temp.

In the morning, Dirk strode off to catch the train north. Cutting across a complex of temples and schools, I arrived at Khao San Road, the celebrated backpacker's ghetto. Superimposed signs protruding from multi-storeyed guest houses competed for eye space: Welcome Travel, Hello Internet Café, Rainbow Silver, and, at the end of the street, my favourite: Aporia Books – a haven, surely, for the doubt-ridden traveller. A driver trolled for custom, gesturing rakishly towards the stuffed vinyl seats of his three-wheeled motorcycle rickshaw:

"*Túk-túk* drive?" he asked. "Only ten baht!"

Travel agencies offered minibus rides to Phuket, visas to Cambodia, and trips to "Heaw Suat Waterfall, as seen on film THE BEACH." A pharmacy window discouraged dubious customers with a firmly lettered "No Diet Pills" sign, and a squat woman with a porkpie hat and a face covered with moles sold folded paper envelopes of deep-fried grasshoppers and grubs. (I bought a spoonful of the latter. Bursting against the gums with an unpleasantly evocative "pop," they tasted not unlike greasy teabags stuffed with dirt.)

Over a banana pancake breakfast at an establishment called Lucky Beer, I took in the scene. Rows of Triumphs and BMW motorcycles, many with sidecars, were parked outside bars where backpackers watched DVDs of the latest Hollywood films. Knots of fresh-off-the-plane English darted between taxis. With their brand-name athletic sandals and singlets emblazoned with the two head-butting bulls of a Thai vitamin drink, they looked like they'd all been outfitted by the same tropical welcome wagon. Khao San Road was Asia reduced to a one-stop backpacker's mall; it would be on a strip like this one, an obvious concentration of loudly partying young westerners, that 180 backpackers and vacationers would later be killed by a car bomb in Bali's Kuta Beach.

Cécile and I met for dinner in a restaurant in a tree-filled courtyard. Over a plate of red prawn curry, I complimented her: she'd put on a dress, made up her face, and gathered her hair in a bun.

"What do you expect? You start to get a complex, with all these men walking around with these Thai women, skinny like this . . ." She flourished her little finger with disgust.

She'd been laid off from her job as a high school teacher and, thanks to a new wrinkle in the French social security system, was entitled to 912 days of unemployment benefits. Deciding to make her money last, she'd come to Thailand by way of Sydney.

"I don't think I am going to stay in Bangkok, though. It is too depressing for a foreign woman. With all these little go-go girls around, we don't stand a chance!"

I asked what she thought of the Thai men.

"Ah! *Ça, par contre!* Some are very cute, with their skinny hips. *Oui,* maybe *une petite aventure* would be amusing. Provided he had his own scooter. But if he asked me to pay for his dinner and his drinks . . . *Ça, non!*"

We took a taxi to Thanon Surawong, a modern thoroughfare lined with banks and skyscrapers in the centre of Bangkok's business district, and pulled up to a section of the sidewalk where crowds overflowed into the gutter. Before my foot hit the curb, a middle-aged man with a thin moustache had grabbed my arm.

"Where you going?" he asked, pushing a laminated card in my face. "Come see show!"

"*Pussy Ping Pong Pussy Egg Pussy Dart Pussy Razor Pussy Smoke Cigarettes,*" the faded typescript promised.

I'd heard about Thailand's "Vaginal Olympics," a kind of gynecological Barnum & Bailey approach to stripping. Cécile followed me down Soi Patpong 1, a narrow street crowded with stalls of a night market selling counterfeit Calvin Klein wallets, Versace sunglasses, and T-shirts with the Coca-Cola logo in Thai script. The buildings were dumpy, two-storey affairs; every few metres the neon-lit facade of one beer bar succeeded another. American tourists in white chinos, wide-bodies all, shuffled past serried sidewalk tables, shadowed by nimble Thai men. It was the kind of setting that made my wallet tingle as if it were spliced into my nervous system. I circumspectly transferred it to my front pocket.

We followed the tout down a sidestreet called Soi Crazy Horse, and stopped outside a bar called King's Lounge. Up a narrow flight of stairs, a half-dozen leggy girls were lazily gyrating on a stage in an empty room.

"This doesn't look very interesting," said Cécile, and I agreed. When we reappeared in the street a minute later, the tout furrowed his brow in annoyance and followed us, waving his pussy-tricks card at us menacingly.

"Why you no stay? You come back!"

Shrugging him off, we crossed to the other side. "Pussy Galore," read the old-fashioned sign in neon script, and the facade had a sign that promised "Go Go Girls – Hot Stuff for Lovers." A chubby woman in bulging blue jeans greeted us at the door and pointed to the drinks sign.

"Singha cost 90 baht. Heineken 100. You come?"

I nodded, and she planted a hand in the small of my back, pushing me up the stairs. I heard the door being unlocked, and a middle-aged hostess in a tight-fitting dress ushered us to seats on the edge of the stage.

Something above my head exploded. As my eyes adjusted to the light, I saw a woman lying on her back, blowing darts through a tube wedged between her labia at sausage-shaped balloons pinned to a pillar next to the stage. Pussy Galore was a small, rectangular room, with a raised, boxing-ring-like stage surrounded by tables, and, nearer the walls, rows of couches. The hostess treated us with the edgy, eyes-wide attention a Pomeranian focuses on a new house guest. To our right were three dapper Arab men in dress shirts, flanked by topless women. They applauded as the girl leapt up from the dirty stage, plucking the tube from her crotch. As "Start Me Up" came over the PA, a half-dozen thin-bellied girls began to shuffle listlessly around the stage, swinging their elbows in an approximation of a rock 'n' roll dance.

I felt hands inexpertly kneading my shoulders. Two topless girls had appeared behind us. "You tense! You want massage?" the one behind me asked.

"I think they're trying to drop something in my beer," whispered Cécile. She moved the bottle away from her masseuse and covered it with her palm.

Since the girls on stage were already naked, there wasn't any stripping to be done. They couldn't dance, so there wasn't much technique to be admired. In the absence of talent, they concentrated on self-debasement. A woman removed a fluorescent plastic chain from her innards as "Itsy Bitsy Teeny Weeny Yellow Polka Dot Bikini" played. Another girl flourished an egg, forcefully inserted it, and then dropped to the floor, slamming her concave belly three times against the stage. She then leapt up, laid the egg – a scene from Georges Bataille's *Story of the Eye* flashed into my mind – and held it aloft to show it was still unbroken. The girl who had blown the darts stuck another tube into herself, and, as the barman presented her with a soiled cake with petrified icing, she contracted her belly and blew out its four listing candles. She then inserted a trumpet between her legs and tooted it three times.

Cécile's mouth was agape. "Can you imagine if I did something like that during sex? '*Attends, chéri*, I want to show you something . . .' And I pull out my little trumpet!"

Girls milled on stage, their knees level with our eyes. "How can they be so thin and still have stretch marks?" Cécile wondered aloud.

Shortly after we arrived, a tall man with a prominent Adam's apple and thick glasses sat down across from us. He was instantly the centre of all gazes, and the Pomeranian hostess rushed to bring him a Heineken. Though he looked like some unloved programmer from Sausalito, he was received like a conquering rock star, and was soon surrounded by eight topless girls. Overwhelmed by the attention, he bought drinks for his groupies. After the last event of the Olympics – we were spared the infamous Pussy Razor Show, in which a string of blades is pulled from a sack concealed in the vagina – he singled out an angelic girl, who couldn't have been more than 18. She leant her head against his shoulder as if they were old sweethearts. Negotiations with the hostess ensued, the girl returned from a backstage room wearing a glittering tank top, and they preceded us down the stairs into the Bangkok night.

The hostess followed us to the door. "OK, OK," she said, giving me a gentle push. "You have good time? Good. Bye!" The door slammed behind us. Patpong had little patience, apparently, for sociologists, couples, and voyeurs.

Cécile and I wandered down a dead-end lane, past bars like Screw Boy Go-Go and Pinocchio's that catered to the gay crowd. A barker lured us into a ground-floor establishment, where rows of buff, slender Thai men in glossy green g-strings and top hats were finishing a revue. To discourage Cécile, the doorman demanded we pay an entrance fee of 500 baht – over $10. I refused.

"It's not fair," she moaned. "You got to see the women!"

To make up for it, I bought her a tequila sunrise from a Volkswagen van with a pop-top roof that served as a kind of mobile disco, complete with turntables and mirror ball. Exchanging chaste *bises* on Khao San Road, I thanked her for being a marvellous – and highly tolerant – wife.

"*C'était un plaisir, mon cher!*" she said with a formal curtsy, a jab at my failure to flirt.

I was too far gone – and too close to the end of the road – to be turned on by a strip-bar date with a Frenchwoman. The Patpong girls, with their perfect breasts and long legs, were gorgeous, but the setting was about as sexy as a factory farm full of battery hens. My imagination needs to be stimulated before I get aroused; and lately, all my imaginative effort had been pouring into thoughts of Karen and home.

I found a quiet table at a guest house bar and considered what I'd seen. The nerdly punter I'd watched at Pussy Galore had been a model client. He'd taken his pick of the bar girls – they were there for that purpose – and paid the hostess the "bar fine," about 500 baht, that would free her for the night. They'd probably go back to his hotel room. She might ask 1,500 baht for a night's work, and if they got along she'd ask for a gift and arrange to meet him again. Thailand was famous for the institution of girlfriend rental, and it produced improbable couples: balding Europeans with black socks riding up hairless calves, trailing a nimbus of lager-and-sausage sweat, being pulled by seraphic girls in high heels into the gold shops of Chinatown.

If you accepted the sex tourists' version, Thailand was a respite from the hypocrisy of the Western world. Thai girls were tender, they argued, certainly more so than mechanistic, all-business American and European prostitutes; their culture taught them to respect and love older men; and they could cite many flings that had developed into love and even marriage. Adept at blending sentiment and commerce, the prostitutes at Patpong favoured the long con. Once they found a boyfriend, they would milk him for money for their parents, their sister's weddings, or their malaria-stricken baby brother back in their villages in the north of Thailand. Men who were schmucks back home – who had let overwork, drink, or bad communication doom their relationships – were heroes in Thailand, the centre of grateful gazes as their "gifts" saved entire families from vice and poverty. In fact, the family usually only got a fraction of the cash – the rest was spent on clothes, gambling, sometimes drugs – as the bar girl strung along several boyfriends at a time.

At least 200,000 adult females worked as prostitutes in Thailand. (Some non-governmental organizations put the number of sex workers, including men and children, at two million.) Long before mass tourism, it was true, prostitution had been an institution in Thai society. Men were seen as naturally mischievous and irresponsible, and the Thai version of Buddhism accorded women low status. Only by acquiring merit in this life could a Thai woman hope to be reborn in a male body. Thai men were expected to frequent brothels, which, now as at the beginning of the last century, were hidden behind shops in working-class districts.

It was the Vietnam War that brought prostitution out into the open. Though nominally an independent kingdom – ruled by His jazz-loving Majesty Bhumibol Adulyadej, whose bespectacled image could be seen in backlit posters at every major intersection in Bangkok – Thailand became a *de facto* American military outpost in the 1960s, a base from which B-52s carpet bombed North Vietnam. U.S. Secretary of Defense Robert McNamara signed contracts with the Thai government in 1967 allowing American soldiers to use the nation for R & R – or I & I (Intoxication and Intercourse), as the GIs more accurately called it. If Patpong go-go bars like Suzie Wong and Goldfingers still favoured Creedence Clearwater Revival and Jimi Hendrix, it was because both they and their clients had come of age in the 1960s. Thousands of aging American veterans still live in Thailand, unable to pull themselves away from a sexual Never-Never Land where their comparative affluence buys them the status and respect they could never find at home.

The sex tourists who followed – Japanese and Arabs on package tours, Englishmen who hummed "One Night in Bangkok" as they poured out of charters – took advantage not only of cultural traditions that sanctified men and devalued women, but also of the social space created by grunts who had frequented the go-go bars and kept (and then abandoned) *miachao*, rented wives. While the war was still on, McNamara became president of the World Bank, encouraging "Thailand to supplement its export activities with an all-out effort to attract rich foreigners to the country's various tourist facilities." The plan worked: by 1980, 2.2 million tourists a year were coming to Thailand, providing the country with money to pay off its World Bank and IMF loans. Along with illegal logging and drugs, receipts from the industry sparked a speculative building boom (whose collapse trashed the Thai economy and led to the 1997 devaluation of the baht). Though technically illegal, prostitution and its associated industries are Thailand's leading source of foreign exchange.

Some feminist scholars argue that prostitution is an empowering option. For a woman from the impoverished Isan region of northeast Thailand, where most Patpong girls come from, working in go-go bar might look better than being a *saphay* (a female in-law, treated like a slave) or a *chee* (a religious disciple who begs for a living, lower in status than a monk). Working behind a sewing machine in the rag trade might earn her 825 baht ($18) a week; she could make as much in a few hours on Patpong. Such women aren't necessarily ostracized; they return to their villages with money and sometimes buy their parents new homes.

But only the lucky few work for long in Patpong. If a woman in a bar like Pussy Galore fails her HIV test, she is bumped down to a "low charge" brothel, to work alongside ethnic-minority women sold into indentured servitude, forced to pay off ever-mounting debts to traffickers. Such brothels are frequented by migrant workers, who take disease back to their wives in rural villages. For much of the 1990s, Thailand downplayed the prevalence of AIDS. Lately, the government has admitted that 100,000 Bangkokians are infected with HIV, and one in 60 Thais carries the virus. Even these figures are probably face-saving underestimates. One thing is certain: AIDS is now the nation's leading cause of death.

Because sex tourism in Thailand is, more than anything, a matter of face. From the exterior, it can look like a happy arrangement for both the deluded client and the insouciant sex worker who uses a talent for tenderness, real or simulated, to profit herself and her family. But the real sexual slavery – catering to Japanese businessmen, Chinese who pay extra to deflower virgins, and local working-class Thais who patronize hill-tribe girls – takes place behind closed doors. It's an enormous pan-Asian industry, and its clients pay a premium for the young and the undiseased. The fact that wealthy western tourists so blatantly promenade with prostitutes on the streets of Bangkok puts a tacit stamp of approval on the institution. Only when you tally up its cumulative social tolls does sex tourism assumes its true face: as a slow-motion disaster that is hastening the breakdown of family, traditional ways of life, and plunging the poor into ever-larger urban slums.

An improbable couple teetered past my table on Soi Rambutri. She was delicate and thin-boned, wearing high heels and a diaphanous dress printed with orchids that hinted at the black panties below. He, lurching and belching, was twice her age, a waddling warning against deep-fried Mars bars and chip butty.

"C'mon, honey," she said, steering him down a sidestreet. "We almost there."

If I ran into him on the Chao Phraya River Express the next day, he'd boast about his new girlfriend – not a whore, mind – and how he'd bought her a counterfeit Cartier watch at the Weekend Market. For most sex tourists, saving face meant denying that they were paying outright for sex and companionship.

Of course, sex tourism is a venerable travel tradition. For generations, western men have been casting off the strictures of corrupt civilization to find liberation in the supposedly looser mores of the East. Julien Viaud voyaged to Tahiti in 1872, fell in love with a woman named Rarahu, and assumed a new identity: from then on, he was Loti, the name the Polynesian girls had bestowed on him. It was Viaud's account of the affair, *Le mariage de Loti*, that lured Paul Gauguin to the South Seas paradise. (Gauguin was eventually so disfigured by the syphilis he'd brought from Europe that even the 13-year-old girls he preferred as sex partners stopped accepting his "gifts.")

By romanticizing Thai prostitutes and inscribing them in the noble savage tradition (which portrays them as naturally tender, unselfconsciously sexual beings), modern punters attempt to dignify pedophilia and paid sex. This ignores the whole sexual revolution and the fact that for the last 40 years consenting adults have been meeting in the bars of the western world to have one-night stands without money changing hands. (One catch, of course: since the 1960s, women have had the social and economic power to demand that the men they select be in some way attractive.) The sex tourists crawling over Southeast Asia claim to be fleeing society's hypocrisy. To me, it looked more like they were exporting their own corruption.

Ecotourism, from this perspective, was minor cosmetic surgery, an optimistic nip-and-tuck to make an aging drab look decent for the brochures. Bangkok itself certainly didn't have much ecology to offer. It is one of the most polluted cities in Asia, and 17 percent of its population lives in slums, choking in fetid lanes where dust-particle levels reach 106,000 milligrams per cubic metre, more than ten times the safe limit. I spent a day riding the new elevated Skytrain, visiting the tourist enclaves of the gilded royal *wats*, getting peripheral-vision glimpses of shanties on sluggish canals. By early evening, my throat was rasping from the smog. The *sois* and underpasses were haunted by peasants picking through garbage and tiny girls selling squirming puppies. Addiction to *ya ba* – "crazy medicine," a Burmese amphetamine pill – is widespread; a third of all traffic accidents are thought to be caused by the drug. Between the lethargic shuffling of starvation and the manic lunging of speed-induced psychosis, navigating the sidewalks of Bangkok was about as relaxing as rollerblading through a Moroccan souk.

§

It was a relief to hop a northbound train from Hualamphong station the next afternoon. I was served vegetables with prawns and rice on pink Melamine plates by an attendant dressed like an Avon lady, and given a body-length towel to make my upper berth cozy. I awoke the next morning in Chiang Mai, the capital of the north, and took a *túk-túk* to the Kavil

Inn, catching glimpses of plump tourist calves on sidewalks as my head stretched the plastic of the low-slung roof.

The pace was slower up north – marginally. Thailand's second city had fewer highrises, and the 121 temples in its old town were surrounded by a square moat that recalled Chiang Mai's status as capital of a medieval kingdom. But an international airport brought in charter flights from Europe, a six-lane ring road surrounded the city, and even at mid-day bar girls beckoned me into their gloomy abodes. Streetfront signs advertised Thai Cookery schools, with photos of satisfied-looking California blonds chopping up chilis, and endless institutes offered courses in massage, meditation, and rock climbing. As I walked past the Hill Tribe Hemp Café ("Wheatgrass juice fresh from our juicer"), the German Hofbräuhaus (a Thai girl dressed in an Alpine dirndl held up a menu of wiener schnitzel), and the Chiangmai Saloon ("Best damn food in town"), packs of aging bikers wearing "Chrome Devil" vests roared along the avenues, loosening bricks from the city's crumbling fortifications.

Chiang Mai is the centre for excursions into the traditional territories of the minority peoples, who make up less than 1 percent of Thailand's population. "Attractive figures in this breathtaking landscape are the colourful hilltribes, semi-nomadic people who follow independent life-styles" – the Tourism Authority brochure reduced them to picturesque effigies. Every few hundred metres, another agency was plastered with descriptions of treks. One showed a faded photo of a tribal woman, her perfectly oval face dotting the "i" formed by a long shouldertop column of golden neck rings. "Mysteries of the Long-Necked People," the sign read. "Let's Visit & Touch Them Together."

Or I could opt for thrill-seeking in the Jungle Bungy Jump, or prurient anthropology in Pasang, "Town of Beautiful Women." Confused by this embarrassment of riches – there were 300 tour operators in Chiang Mai alone – I walked into the Night Bazaar, a permanent market for hilltribe crafts, and approached a rustic-looking wooden stand. "GREAT TRAVEL CENTRE CO. LTD.," the sign read. "I am not like the rest, I have been here [since] A.D. 1983." (Good. I had a strict policy against pre-Christian travel agencies.)

The Thai man in a faded jeans vest at the counter pulled out a photo album of sweating tourists trudging through rice fields. "This is our most popular," he said, "Number 11. Leave tomorrow morning."

At 40 bucks for a three-day trek, I couldn't carp about the price. He wrote out a receipt in looping, baroque script: "2 night 3 days Heighest point of Thailand Elephant Riding Bamboo Rafting visit hill Tribe villages water fall. 1,800 baht."

Next morning, I climbed into a *sawngthaew* – a pick-up truck with two rows of wooden benches in back – and we drove through Chiang Mai's grid of one-way streets, adding trekking companions at every guest house. At first they came in couples: a pair of physiotherapists from Tasmania; blond students from Denmark; married computer programmers from Roscommon. A Korean school teacher, Hyung, squeezed on. The last additions were Mark and Alan, shaven-headed men in their 20s from Lincolnshire. We sat facing each other, like prisoners in a paddy wagon, gripping the bar that ran the length of the *sawngthaew* to reduce the jolting. The English lads were sipping from little bottles of Red Bull, the Thai-made caffeine-and-taurine spiked drink popular on the club circuit.

"We've been living off the stuff," said Mark, the less excitable of the two. "We're trying to pack as much as we can into our three weeks here, only getting three or four hours of sleep a night. We've been doing it *all*. We went to Ko Phi-Phi, saw the place where they made *The Beach*. Then we went to Phuket, visited a snake farm and a shooting range. They gave me a .45. The power of those things! I understand why people go on rampages."

As we left Chiang Mai, Alan pulled at his Camel brand trousers. "They're brilliant. When it gets too hot, you can zip off the legs, make 'em into shorts." He was wearing a new Adidas jersey and carrying a Diesel backpack. "They're counterfeits, but like, really *good* counterfeits. Got 'em at the Weekend Market in Bangkok. I'm going to pay for my whole trip by auctioning these things back home on the Internet."

They worked at an industrial bakery, squirting garlic butter into baguettes on a production line. "Then our company sells them to supermarkets in France," said Mark. "Crazy, isn't it?"

The *sawngthaew* lurched and juddered; the only scenery was the strip of receding highway visible out the back of the truck. After a half-hour stop in a covered market, Alan and Mark returned with two bottles of rice whisky and a pair of peaked straw hats.

We finally pulled off the paved road and descended from the truck in a village called Khun Wang. Our guide, who'd been sitting in front with the driver and his female cousin, introduced himself as Tim. ("My Thai name is too difficult for tourists," he explained.) Baby-faced at 20, he epitomized the East for me: he had the tongue stud of an East Village hipster, spoke with an East London accent, and dressed like an East L.A. gangsta. He was tiny, barely five feet, and carried a pack stuffed with trekkers' food that was twice as heavy as the bag of the broad-shouldered Irishman, who towered over him.

He gave us a perfunctory briefing. "Today, we're going to walk for about an hour and a half to the next village, where we'll sleep for the night." We set off in a line, 11 western tourists in shorts and T-shirts, stumbling into the Stone Age.

Or so we thought. Khun Wang was, in fact, a village of the Hmong tribe, one of the 13 recognized minorities that live in northern Thailand. The hill tribes were animistic swiddeners – non-Buddhist slash-and-burn farmers – who came from Vietnam, Laos, Burma, and the south of China. Some tribes migrated in the last century, but others, like the Karen, have lived in the Thai hills for generations. Our group tramped across a soccer pitch and paused to watch a semi-circle of children tossing balls at a marker in the dirt. The Korean, Hyung, who would prove an utterly shameless ethnologist, strode over and snatched up the marker.

"It is made of wood!" he said, holding it close to his glasses. "So interesting!"

The infant players, their scoring ruined, leapt up and down in consternation.

I noticed rows of vegetables growing beneath plastic sheets, and a Thai flag flying over the schoolhouse. The village didn't look too traditional to me.

"The king came here a few years ago," explained Tim, "and got the Hmong to grow vegetables instead of opium. There are tomatoes, papayas, and" – pointing to shoots sprouting underneath platforms – "these are chilis."

We walked through forest where wild orchids grew out of tree trunks, crossed a river over a felled log, and trod Indian-file along the raised ridges between plots in rice paddies, dry and shorn after harvest. Before we'd come to our stop for the night – a low hilltop that looked out over forested valleys – the English lads were already taking swigs of whisky. I quickly explored the village; it was only a couple of shacks surrounded by scrawny roosters with iridescent ruffs, an outhouse, and the table where Tim's cousin brought us a meal of curry chicken, vegetables, and rice. I asked Tim if anybody lived there.

"A couple of old people. But we built this village for tourists."

I liked Tim. He was soft-spoken, disabused, and sweetly sardonic. (At one point we heard echoing reports in the hills. I asked what they were shooting. Cocking his head, Tim replied, "Canadians," and kept walking.) He watched Alan and Mark with some concern; they had started working on the camp's supply of Chang beer and were already slurring their words.

Mark didn't finish his dinner. "I can't take spicy foods any more," he told me. "My doctor says eating too much HP Sauce gave me an ulcer. As soon as I get back to Chiang Mai, it's straight to the Kentucky Fried Chicken – for the potatoes. I can't stand all this fucking rice."

When the sun went down, the chill set in. The Chiang Mai region was experiencing a never-before-seen cold snap, and our trek coincided with the worst of it. Tim built a campfire with the help of a wizened old man wearing a pom-pom-topped wool cap, and we gathered on benches close to the flames. The English lads were getting abusive.

"All right!" yelled Alan. "Who's got the Mekong whisky? Bring it out!" He looked at Hyung. "Hey – dog man. Yeah, you, dog-eater! Are you hiding my bloody whisky?"

Hyung, irate, yelled, "Why you call me dog-eater?"

"Look, it's a fact. You already fucking admitted that people eat dogs in your country. I wouldn't mind if you called me a beef-eater, would I?"

The fellow with the pom-pom walked by, and Alan made a grab for him. "Hey, old man! Where's the opium? You *know* what I'm talking about!"

Tim said quietly: "I don't think there's any opium in this village."

Alan was incensed. "Bring out the bloody pipe! C'mon! We want the pipe!"

To placate him, I passed the bottle of Johnny Walker Red. Alan upended it over his mouth and looked comically perplexed until realization dawned. "Who put the fucking cap on the bottle?" he bellowed. Untwisting it, he drained the remaining two inches of whisky in a single slug.

A rickety wooden frame had been built around the fire, and Alan threatened to clamber atop it. "I'm going to do the fire dance! Mark, get a picture of me doing the fire dance!" Pulling himself up on the platform, he balanced precariously for a second, threatened to tumble face down into the flames, then crashed backwards over the bench on his ass, recovering with that Gumby-like flexibility that blesses the intoxicated. I hadn't had a drop to drink, and I was mortified to share the same skin colour as these halfwits. I excused myself and found a distant corner of the longhouse, put in my earplugs, and shivered myself to sleep in my thin sleeping bag.

Awake at cock crow, I sat down next to a thick iron pot, where an old Hmong woman was boiling eggs for breakfast. To my surprise, Alan, proud possessor of a 26-year-old-liver, sat down next to me, wincing but coherent after four hours' sleep. He tugged at a milky stain on the sleeve of his track suit.

"See this?" he said. "It's all over my sleeping bag. It's that bloody Korean. He spat on me last night when I was asleep, just 'cos I called him dog-man. Good job for him we're going back or he'd find himself swimming in piss tonight."

It was more likely, I thought, that Alan had drooled all over himself. I asked whether he'd spent any time with Thai girls on his trip.

"Yeah, after Bangkok, we loaded up on Vallies" – Valium was as easy to buy in Thailand as it had been in India – "and flew down to Phuket. The girls down there were all over us. We hung around with these prostitutes for three days, paid their bar fines, 400 baht, another 1,000 baht for the night, drove them down to the beach on our motorcycles. And by the end, they were saying: 'When you meet me? When you come back to bar? You come back at seven o'crock?'"

His voice took on a clipped, angry tone. "I said: 'Listen, we're going down to the boozer, then to the beach, and we'll meet you at seven o'clock like we said!' I tell you – it was like having a fucking girlfriend again!"

He'd bought a house with a woman back in England, he said, but ended up dumping her. "I don't know – I have problems being with women. They just make me mad. They're always saying: 'When are we doing this? When are you going to buy me that?' Not that I'm a wife beater or anything. I've just decided I like being single. I'm a bit worried, though. I was having sex with one of those bar girls in Phuket and the johnny broke. First thing I get home I'm having the AIDS test."

It was hard to absorb this sad tale of early-onset misogyny at seven in the morning. Fortunately, Alan and Mark had signed up for the abridged two-day version of the trek, and Tim's cousin took them back towards Chiang Mai after breakfast. I watched them go, skinheads sporting counterfeit jerseys and hangovers, disappearing into a Southeast Asian forest.

❦

Things were quieter once the lads had gone. We spent the day hiking, pausing atop Doi Inthanon, Thailand's highest peak, for a lunch of rice and vegetables wrapped in banana leaves. The view was a panorama of forested valleys; the agency had done well to choose a national park for its featured trek. In 1960, more than 60 percent of Thailand was covered with trees; but rampant logging, much of it illegal, has reduced the forest cover to just 20 percent, and trekkers who insist on visiting untouched, non-touristic hill-tribe villages often find themselves hiking through vast clear-cuts.

That day we endured a five-hour march that had everybody looking forward to a rest. Chickens scattered as we emerged from the forest into a backyard. A Karen village in a river valley spread out before us – a few dozen houses on stilts, separated by dirt lanes and towering stands of green bamboo. Tim talked to the head of the household, then said we could leave our bags in his house. Between the gaps in the floor made of bamboo slats, I could see a big black sow chained to one of the stilts that raised the house off the ground. The pigs and chickens below made convenient garbage disposal units: fallen rice and peelings were simply swept between the slats and into their gullets.

Outside, a squint-eyed old lady clenched a corncob pipe between her teeth, Popeye style. Women carried their babies slung around their shoulders on their sides, and wore white-and-pink scarves around their heads. Hyung sat at a long table, dandling a runny-nosed infant on his thigh, watching a woman operating a foot lever that raised and lowered a pestle into a stone well filled with dried rice.

"Taras!" he said. "What is this machine?"

Looks like a rice crusher, I replied.

Putting down the child, he simply pushed the woman's leg aside with his sandalled foot and gave the husks a couple of good smacks.

"So interesting! This is not how we make rice in Korea."

Uh-huh. But that was obviously how he treated women in Korea.

At a long table, we ate a communal meal of chicken, spicy papaya soup, and rice, followed by instant coffee served in mugs made of cross-cut bamboo. As I chatted about Northern Ireland with the computer programmer, the owner of the house asked if I wanted a massage. The man didn't look robust enough to knead a piglet, and everybody else had turned him down. But my shoulders were aching, so I followed him back to the longhouse. I lay down on my sleeping bag and let his gnarled hands rub my limbs. The massage was a cursory affair. As he put his bare foot on my back and pulled my arms behind me, bending my torso like a bow, he whispered:

"Oplium? You want?"

Smoking a few bowls of opium was one of the unadvertised highlights of hill-tribe treks in Thailand, as Mark and Alan had been well aware. When I admitted that I did want, the old man gestured for me to follow him into the kitchen. It was a tiny cell at one end of the longhouse where the family slept when trekkers had taken over the main quarters. Tim followed me in, closing the door behind him.

"I told the old man I thought you might be interested," he said. "But I didn't want to do this when those English guys were around. They were too drunk and noisy." We knelt on the bamboo slats beneath a dim electric bulb; the old man fashioned a tiny boat out of aluminum foil with his thumbs. He then produced a fingernail-sized, bladder-like plastic packet of white powder.

"It will be 100 baht to smoke, OK?" said Tim.

Just over two dollars. I nodded.

"You know . . ." he started, then paused.

"What, Tim?" I asked.

He looked away. "I'll tell you later."

The man slit open the packet with a long fingernail, tapped it over the foil. He lit a match and handed me a rolled-up 20-baht note, which I placed between my dry lips. The powder evanesced instantly when I held a match beneath the foil, and an evocative arabesque of smoke leapt into the air. I snatched at it with a suck on my paper tube. The medicinal smoke felt cool in my lungs, and I exhaled and sensed a bitter aftertaste on my lips. Tim sat down facing me, and we alternated puffs. All the pain in my back and thighs deliquesced, and a familiar feeling, as of being in tepid amniotic fluid, washed over me. Not unlike being stoned on heroin, I thought – a sensation I hadn't felt for eight years. We continued to puff; the old man slit open another packet, tapped it with his finger. All my uneasiness at being an interloper was swept into some back room of my mind. I felt completely reconciled to this hut of bamboo and thatch, as if I'd rediscovered an ancestral home, a good warm place I'd left long ago. I smiled benignly at an infant in an oversized Liverpool football club shirt in the corner, watching us with deep black eyes.

"What were you going to tell me, Tim?"

He leaned back, exhaled. "This isn't opium we're smoking. It's heroin."

I accepted this information passively. I knew that opium came from the resin that oozed from the slit pods of poppies, and was smoked in sticky black balls. I'd told myself that opium was a local specialty – like aguardiente in Galicia, or Koum Quat liqueur in Corfu – and, as a traveller, I should leave myself open to the experience of smoking it in an authentic setting. Heroin, on the other hand, was a street drug I'd spent my early 20s dabbling with, a serious flirtation I'd extricated myself from with difficulty. I knew exactly what it looked like, and knew that tangling with it again would be a severe blow to my psychological integrity. But I'd looked at the white powder, willfully blurred my vision, and inhaled.

Opiates, fortunately, provide the perfect solace for even the gravest existential doubts. When I came back to the fire, all eyes were upon me – but my pupils were pinpricks, and I couldn't meet the gaze of my fellow trekkers. They were playing a round-robin game that involved naming cities and countries; as my eyelids drooped, my replies came so slowly they eventually skipped my turn. I spent the night in blissful half-sleep, gazing at the thatched ceiling like it was a planetarium light show. The next morning, the other trekkers complained that I'd snored like a fat old man.

§

Like Baudelaire's Oriental lair, transformed into a ragged room on the Seine with the coming of dawn, the village was a different place by daylight. I'd convinced myself I was in an inaccessible hill-tribe settlement, but the trappings of modernity soon became evident. There was a torn Thai election poster pasted to the inside of our house, and beneath it a battered tape player with a stack of cassettes. A helicopter flew overhead – Tim told me it was the police on patrol. The women in our house were wearing traditional shawls, but their neighbours wore track suits and running shoes. I noticed the Thai flag flying over a government school where some barechested European trekkers were playing soccer with local boys on a red-dirt pitch. As I tried to make out their nationality – Dutch, I thought – a young man who had followed me down the lane came up to me and tried to sell me some more heroin. With his dirty sweatshirt and clouded left eye, he could have been a *ya ba* dealer in some sodden Bangkok *soi*.

Next to an outhouse beside the school, I waited for the Irish computer programmer to finish washing himself. A half-dozen pre-school boys approached me shyly, and I gave them a tentative smile. Suddenly, the biggest of them – I was seated on a concrete stoop, so we were eye to eye – snapped his bare foot towards my face and ran away. One by one, the others followed, simulating kick-boxing blows to the head, their tiny toes stopping a couple of inches shy of my nose. I took it passively; it seemed an honest reaction to trekkers. That morning, I felt I deserved a good kick in the face.

The hill-tribe family seemed relieved to see us go. As we walked towards the rice fields, one of the women stuck in a cassette of Thai pop music and cranked the volume, as if suddenly free to drop the facade of primitiveness. For the rest of the day, I trailed behind the group, feeling sweaty and corrupt, troubled by how effortlessly I'd gone from shots of local liqueur to heroin. But there was something else nagging me. By acquiescing to my own deception, convincing myself that I was participating in something authentic by smoking "opium," I'd crossed a line. Until then, I'd been following the world's travel ruts with a kind of aloofness, attentive to the ropes and sandbags in the wings of a stage obviously set for my deception. This time, I'd allowed the desire for the authentic to cloud my judgment; I'd swallowed the facade of what the sociologists call a "staged back region": a hill-tribe village that simulated Stone Age primitiveness but showed all the characteristics of being a government-built reserve shot through with drug addiction and other contemporary social problems. In the highlands of Thailand, I'd let myself become just another of history's great hordes of self-deluded tourists.

The realization depressed me. This long trip, with its solitary nights away from the woman I loved, had given me too many excuses to dabble with untried intoxicants. If I didn't watch out, when I got home I'd need to start my own 12-step group – Local Specialties Anonymous, a church basement filled with travel writers addicted to Czech absinthe and Oaxacan mushrooms.

§

As our trek ended, we emerged by a road in a Shan village. Three girls in oversized T-shirts detached themselves from the group of trekkers ahead and ran up to us, dangling bead necklaces from their palms.

"Hello! Ten-baht!" they cried, in sing-song voices.

Tim chuckled, a little sadly. "That's the only English they know – ten-baht, ten-baht."

We bought Cokes from the Thai woman who ran a roadside store. (Few of the shops we saw were run by villagers, who derived little benefit from trekkers, and only a few dozen baht of the fee I paid went to the hill-tribe families who accommodated us. The Thai middlemen and the agency in the Night Bazaar got most of it.) A team of Thai workers was finishing a road across the paddies where Shan women were tossing rice into the air from circular screens.

By the early 1990s, the trickle of trekkers in Northern Thailand that started in the 1970s had swollen to 60,000 a year, bringing remote villages into the orbit of Chiang Mai. It's a process called spearheading, in which travellers in search of remote beauty and authentic cultural experiences pave the way for later tourist development. In hill-tribe regions, the process is particularly nasty. Guides promise to lead trekkers to "nontouristic" villages. When too many tourists come, leaving in their wake football club T-shirts, roads for easier access, and piles of Coca-Cola cans, trekkers start complaining that the village isn't authentic enough. The guides abandon the village they've ruined – many of whose families have given up agriculture because of the promise of sustainable ecotourism – and seek out an even more remote setting. Village by village, the hill tribes are brought into the sway of modern urban Thailand. Locally harvested opium had once been used for ritual and medical purposes; many villagers, their traditional agriculture disrupted by the Thai government's war on drugs, were resorting to heroin, produced by labs in Burma. This can be directly attributed to the trekker and the tourist, who were one and the same. And I was part of the problem.

It got worse. The "Long-Necked Women" whose photos I'd seen on signs in Chiang Mai are actually Burmese refugees, members of the Kayan tribe, who had been settled in three northwestern villages by the Thai government. Tourists paid armed police guards 250 baht to view the women who, from the age of five, were fitted with brass neck rings that pushed down their shoulders and collar bones, earning them their "giraffe women" epithet. If the rings are removed, the women, whose neck muscles have never developed, can suffocate. The practice was dying out before mass ecotourism hit Thailand; but, encouraged by monthly stipends from the Thai government, at least 100 women have taken to wearing the rings. The Kayan women, driven from their homes by ethnic warfare, can never go back to their traditional way of life; nor, with their stretched necks, are they likely to integrate into mainstream Thai society. Every visitor who paid the admission fee was subsidizing the maintenance of a human zoo.

I looked at the floppy-haired Shan girls trying to sell us necklaces. In a few years they would be old enough to attract the interest of traffickers –

who would come to the highlands via the road built for the trekkers. The hill tribes were one of the leading suppliers of Thailand's low-charge brothels. The Karen girls in particular were prized for their light skin, and families were known to sell daughters to traffickers for as little as 5,000 baht. Until recently, the Thai government had refused to give tribal people national identity cards. Without them, they were stateless people, and hilltribe girls found outside their districts could be arrested. Brothel owners kept them prisoners of the sex trade by threatening to report them to police. The cops wouldn't help – they were among the brothels' most faithful customers.

I felt sick in body and soul, disgusted by the all-too-visible effects of the trekkers – of people like me – in these hills. It occurred to me that it was less harmful to join the hordes who clog the squares of Italy and the ruins of Greece. At least developed-world sites can handle the crowds – they've been dealing with tourists for a couple of millennia. Like the kid with the mud-caked boots who won't fess up to filling the hall with footprints, trekkers are tourists in denial of their impact. Ecotravel, in the final analysis, is just tourism trying to feel good about itself.

§

We were driven to the Mae Wang River. As I sat on a bamboo raft – nine hollow green poles lashed together – my innards began to feel like they were liquefying, the usual morning-after side-effect of opiates on my digestive system. Every shift in the turbulent green water provoked a new gastro-intestinal crisis. A dead dog floated next to the raft, and the bare tree branches along the river were tangled with plastic bags, tampons, plastic dish racks, and old magazines, as though we were downstream from the cloaca of a major city. Teetering onto shore an hour and a half later, I realized my ordeal wasn't over: the elephant ride was next. Hyung and I shared a perch on the back of the lumbering beast, and the nausea-inducing ride was aggravated by the Korean teacher's incessant questions.

"Taras!" he exclaimed, as we simultaneously rolled, yawed, and pitched. "What is the average cost of tuition fee in Canada?"

I didn't have those figures at hand, I muttered through gritted teeth. A spasm ripped through my bowels.

"Taras! Why are you freelance writer?"

I groaned as I gripped the wooden seat to avoid being thrown over the elephant's trunk.

"No security!" he pursued, as our plodding mount picked its way across the river. "In Korea, most important thing is security! Teacher is a much better job!"

I promised Hyung I'd consider it. Dismounting at a wooden platform, I ran for an outhouse, a roll of toilet paper unspooling behind me.

A couple of hours later, the *sawngthaew* dropped me back at my guesthouse. I lay on my bed, hating myself. My dabbling with local specialties would have to come to an end. Ultimately, the desire for escape – from routine, from home, from myself – was an addiction that expressed itself in many different ways. The euphoria of travel wasn't so different from the intoxication of drugs, and here, near the end of my road, I'd allowed the two to become conflated. I rooted through my toiletry bag, found the blister pack of Valium I'd bought in India, and used a bucket of water to flush it down the toilet bowl.

Tim had invited us to join him at a bar for farewell drinks. Now that he'd collected his tips, all pretense of being the deferential eco-guide was gone. He had a bottle of Saeng Som rum in front of him, and I watched him knock back shot after shot, as if he was trying to drown something he'd swallowed but could never fully digest. He had to take another group of tourists on a three-day hike the next morning. One of his friends, a handsome Swiss-Vietnamese, played electric guitar and sang "Sultans of Swing" on a stool a few metres from us. While the Danish and the Irish couples shot pool, Tim invited me back to his place to smoke some more "opium." I said that I was tired, and that he was too drunk to double me on his scooter.

"You don't trust me, do you?" he said. "You don't trust me!"

As the guitarist started playing an old reggae standard, Tim leapt up and grabbed the microphone, clutching his rum bottle like a pint-sized Keith Richards.

"*I shot the TOURIST!*" he ad-libbed, in his East London accent, "*but I swear – I swear it was in self-defence!*"

I joined him in a chorus. After a week in Thailand, shooting tourists seemed like a wholly defensible domestic policy.

§

Back in Bangkok, I booked a ticket to Hong Kong. Though I'd had enough of Thailand, Thailand wasn't finished with me. My flight wouldn't leave for a week, so I decided to celebrate my birthday on Ko Samet, an island in the Gulf of Thailand. In the air-conditioned mini-van, two urine-hued Germans gripped their Chang beer like baby bottles and demonstrated the national talent for drinking all day without getting drunk. A half-hour ride in a decrepit ferry had me on white sand beaches, and I found a guest house in a cove called Ao Phutsa.

Officially Ko Samet was a national marine park, as I learned when I was forced to pay a 200-baht entrance fee to uniformed guards, but I'd never seen a national park that looked more like Acapulco. Most of the island's east coast was encrusted with bungalows and dotted with travellers in open-air bars drinking crushed-ice cocktails and watching bootlegged DVDs on big-screen televisions. Older gay tourists frolicked in the surf with their slender Thai boyfriends. Stray dogs roamed the beaches (signs in every cove assured us Ko Samet was a "RABIES FREE ZONE"), and the Thai barkeeps drove away the emaciated curs with homemade slingshots. The northern beaches, dominated by Bangkokians, were the most polluted. The urban Thais tossed water bottles and styrofoam containers onto the sand, and buzzed the shore in Jet Skis and speedboats. The Jet Skis were illegal – their vibrations degraded the coral reefs – as were the bungalows, but somebody was obviously getting paid off. Snorkelling near the southern tip of the island, I saw as many jettisoned San Miguel beer cans as I did sea urchins. Thailand boasts that 15 percent of its land area is set aside for environmental protection and national parks, one of the highest percentages in the world. If Ko Samet was any indication, the figure was meaningless.

As a beach resort, though, Ko Samet was pleasant. I spent my birthday at a bar called Silver Sands with a pair of hard-drinking Irishmen. Sprawled on bamboo mats, we watched shirtless beach boys juggling flaming batons.

A tattooed Thai man who had been necking with a British girl leaned over and boasted that he was a professional hit man.

"I used to be kick-boxer. I win 20 match, never lose. But then I kill man, and to get out jail, police make me kill people for them. Drug dealers, bad people – who they say, I kill."

Now he was in exile, waiting on tables at one of the beach bars because he was unable to return to his hometown.

"Ko Samet very nice," he said. "Many *farang* girls. But what I hate – always have to smile at tourists." His face twitched into a rictus. "I don't want to smile at fucking tourists. I hate tourists! When I smile I think: maybe I kill you instead!"

❦

Amazing Thailand, "Land of Smiles." As a tourist who wasn't in search of young girls or booze or Viagra or parasailing, I saw the famous Thai smile fade again and again. Thailand, in this sense, was the culmination of a long historical process. For millennia, people had travelled abroad in search not just of relaxation and escape, but also of some elusive experience that would prove they'd had a real interaction with the place they were visiting. Tourism, an institutionalized intersection of cultures, is a kind of kernel of modernity embedded in the past. Early on, it taught people they could benefit from representing themselves – their dances, rituals, beliefs, their entire culture – to visitors from another, usually more powerful, civilization. Inauthenticity evolves when the notion of representing oneself, rather than simply being, enters a civilization. Travellers, from the discreet anthropologist to the gawking hordes, are the forbidden apple: they bring to a culture the original sin of self-consciousness. With the camera-bearing outsider comes the possibility of self-representation for profit – and, eventually, an industry of simulated authenticity.

A romantic, even mystical, current in western society situates the notion of authenticity in sex, in the physical union of bodies. Most tourists are content to go abroad and merely witness some simulacrum of authenticity. The sex tourists in Thailand believed they were crossing an important boundary: they were claiming the foreign on their own terms, by paying for the company of Thai girls and boys. Part of them believed it was love, since the bar girl seemed so tender and playful; part of them knew they had paid for it, bought it like any commodity, and they could be replaced by another *farang* the minute they boarded their flight home. The high-charge prostitutes of Patpong, who situate their cores with their families and their Buddhist identity, have learned to exploit this developed-world confusion. Which is why there are so many sad, lost sex tourists stranded in the streets of Bangkok, caught in a hall of mirrors, wondering whether their rented girlfriend really feels the affection she simulates so well. For allowing love – one of the few relationships in life that can be unmediated by capitalist notions of exchange – to enter the realm of the commodity, these men deserved their confusion.

Of course, I'd also fooled myself into thinking I could purchase an authentic experience. By letting desire authorize disbelief – by briefly convincing myself that Burmese powder on foil was as authentic as a pipe full of opium – I'd willfully blinded myself to the realities of hill-tribe life. What had the little boy in the Liverpool shirt seen? A westerner, one of the globe's privileged elite, smoking drugs in his hut. For all the example I'd set, I might as well have been promenading through the streets of Bangkok with an underaged prostitute.

The tourist who aspires to be more than a tourist longs to touch the untouched. Hence the emphasis on virginity, both cultural and physical, among travellers. The greater the immaculateness of the desideratum, the greater the prestige associated with its defilement. The demanding sex tourist soothes his corruption by deflowering the barely post-pubescent virgin; the discriminating ecotraveller longs to be the only visitor in the hill-tribe village or the perfect secluded beach.

Strolling through the Karen village, feeling voyeuristic as I glimpsed scenes of family intimacy, part of me hoped to experience something I didn't possess. My mobility was a form of decadence, and in travelling the world, something in me was seeking its antithesis. I'd come halfway around the globe to sit in a bamboo hut, searching for groundedness, tradition, and community – all the things I'd abandoned for the endless novelty of travel. And by fooling myself into thinking I'd bought something real, I'd become a chump, a despoiler. In a word, a tourist: somebody who travels abroad to purchase a simulated antidote to an existential lack, and then denies that the transaction has taken place.

Identifying the problem didn't comfort me. It made me feel more lost.

§

I had one more place to visit in Thailand. On the way to the Bangkok airport, I stopped for a couple of nights in Pattaya: "A colourful and vibrant place where a complete spectrum of watersport amenities is combined with a wealth of on-land entertainment to ensure there is never a dull moment, night or day," according to the brochure.

During the Vietnam War, Pattaya had been the biggest headquarters of American I & I, and it still lived up to its reputation. I was dropped outside the Porn Hotel, near a bar called Angels of Sleaze ("All Employees Registered with Authorities," said a sign on the blacked-out window). I wandered past open-air bars on the shorefront, where literally hundreds of girls in corral-style bars swivelled their necks as I passed, mewling, "Welcome! Welcome!" like chicks opening their beaks to the worm. On the narrow beach, every wavelet brought watermelon rinds, vegetable oil bottles, styrofoam containers, plastic bags, dead fish. A Caucasian man-mountain – a phenomenon, perhaps 200 kilograms – sat in a street-front restaurant, inhaling some kind of green leaf from a soup bowl, his petite Thai girlfriend at his side. She couldn't have weighed more than one of his thighs.

Through the grate in my hotel room's bathroom, I could hear everything that went on next door.

"Shower? Pussy!" said an old Germanic voice.

A young woman laughed. The man became angry.

"You shower – pussy! Pussy! Wash! Wash!"

There was a commotion in the hall, and I poked my head out. Four maids in pink uniforms were shouting. A blond-wigged Thai prostitute backed out the door, bulging out of a gold lamé top, rocking back and forth on her high heels. A man in a blue shirt, tie thrown over his shoulder, came out of the room, carrying a shirtless, shoeless European, in polka-dot boxer shorts, who convulsed as his head lolled back. I called the elevator for them. A few minutes later, in the lobby, I saw the man sitting on a vinyl sofa, vomiting into a garbage can. Indeed: never a dull moment in Pattaya. It was 4:15 in the afternoon.

The next day, when I went down to settle my bill, a tall Danish man was at the desk. There were two Thai children, a boy and a girl, no more than seven or eight, standing beside him. They were crying.

When I came back from breakfast, the Danish man was on the sofa, holding some ice to his eye and moaning. The children were gone. I asked a red-faced young man standing by the elevator what had happened.

"*Ja*, that man over there is an *asshole!*" he yelled, pointing. The man on the sofa turned away, sobbed. We both stepped into the elevator, and the fellow seemed to calm down a little as the doors closed.

"I too am Danish, I was on the same plane with this man. He seemed like a good man, a nice man. He got a Thai man, a guide, to find these children for him. Today, they were crying. And he tells me: 'You will not believe what I have been doing with these children in my room.' So of course I hit him. Women, teenagers are one thing – but little children?"

Yes, of course. One has to draw the line somewhere in this world.

Chapter 12

THE END OF
ELSEWHERE

*Christmas in Hong Kong – My Triskaidekaphobia Gets the Better of Me –
A Non-Psychotic Canadian Free of Eggplants – The Eiffel Tower on the
Pearl River – Tibetans Pose for the Han – The Lowdown on Chinese
Tourism – "China's Hawaii" – A Mysterious Lotion – My Taxi Driver
Tries to Take Me to Borneo – Giant Boulders Make Great Photo Op –
The Beach at the End of the Earth – The Last Sunrise*

There's a pregnant orange moon maundering above the hills of China.
From my front seat on the top floor of the double-decker airport bus, it
looks gravid and sluggish, listless with evening sickness. It's making me
recall all the other moons I've seen over the last seven months: the robust
Galician globe hanging over the lighthouse of Fisterra; the blinding crys-
talline circle in the pure air of the Alps; the slightly louche scoop of
Neapolitan ice dolloped over the cone of Vesuvius. It was on the party
beaches of Corfu that the moon's disc started yellowing, and it was in
Varanasi, over the human bonfires on the Ganges, that its tinge fully succumbed to jaundice. Now, in the subtropical Far East, it looks inflamed
and fulvous, threatening to spill its load over the New Territories. I sense
it will be a breach birth, a C-section, and whatever is born will kill its
mother. I don't want to be around for the delivery.

It's been a long time now since I felt the euphoria of motion. Lately all
I experience is leaden dread, a mounting thrum of anxiety over the missed
connection, the lost notebook, the passport left on the taxi seat. With

every takeoff, at the moment the front tires leave the ground and the cabin starts to tilt skyward, I fight the irrational fear that the back of the fuselage will clip the runway, sending us crumpling into a fireball.

When this voyage started, at the other end of the Eurasian landmass, I was wide-eyed and ready to seek out the best in everyone I met. Now, after being taken for one too many rides by auto-rickshaw drivers, I've become splenetic and skeptical, suspecting the worst of people and grimly satisfied to have my suspicions confirmed. Every curious local who asks about my nationality is trying to get at my wallet; my fellow travellers are self-deluded tourists running from unexamined lives; the very landscape I'm moving through is a mock-up built to appeal to some shoddy taste for exoticism.

On this night of the full moon, the universe is also toying with my triskaidekaphobia. On the way to the Bangkok airport from Pattaya, my cab driver had chosen toll gate 13. On my route map, the bus stop for the hotel I've chosen in Kowloon is 13. It's December 1 – 1/12 – I add date and month and come up with 13. My trip is so close to its end that I've become morbidly attentive to portents, and today they all seem to be pointing to disaster. As I step off the bus, a splay-footed woman wearing a semi-official vest spots my backpack.

"Mirador Mansion?"

I nod, and she leads me up the crowded sidewalks of Nathan Road to a grim concrete building, straight to a guesthouse on the 13th floor. "Here is your room!" she says, throwing open the door on a windowless meat-locker with a mattress. I make my excuses, tell her the number 13 is not an auspicious one for me.

"Oww!" she says, seeming to understand perfectly.

I walk to the guest house one floor up, where the owner is eating drooping greens at the reception. She shows me a room with a window; when I crane my neck, I can see the green neon of the Rolex signs spanning the street far below. The linen stinks of night terror, and the only possible way to occupy the closet-like space is prone on the mattress. But I take it, grateful that the number on the door is 7.

Next morning, I walk down to the promenade at the southern tip of Kowloon and look across the channel at the Hong Kong skyline, the world's

largest billboard for electronic equipment. "Season's Greetings," the buildings say, but also, reading from left to right: Sanyo; Sharp; Bosch; Hitachi;
Siemens; Canon; and Toshiba – broadcasting the propaganda of consumption towards a China that no longer needs to be convinced. Today is
Filipina day, Sunday, when all of the underpaid domestic workers are free,
and Hong Kong has become a metropolis of single women. The maids are
wrapping huge parcels in brown paper outside the General Post Office, or
picnicking beneath the postmodern columns in front of the Cultural
Centre. I glance at a Scrabble game on an upturned bucket: HOWL – AJAR
– JEST – BEAM – DUMB – GLAR, the board reads, as one of the players
triumphantly lays an "E" on a triple word score. Outside the Chungking
Mansions, an Indian man sweeps his arm over a cardboard box full of pens.

"Mont Blancs?" he asks.

Another fellow pulls up his sleeve: "Watch? Copy watch?"

A security guard dispassionately whacks the hawker on the head with
a rolled-up newspaper. Farther up Nathan Road, the banyan trees near the
mosque, veined and twisted like skinless anatomical dummies, are strung
with Christmas lights. At the Starbucks by the Peninsula Hotel, "Jingle
Bells" is playing, and the employees wear elves' caps. Christmas in Hong
Kong; it feels like a Tom Waits song.

A cold droplet from an air conditioner splatters on my crown, and I
look up to see a neon sign on the building's facade: "Shoestring Travel 4/F."
A tiny female tout has seen me coming.

"Visa?" she asks. When I nod, she gives me a proprietary shove
towards an elevator. "Fourth floor, OK?"

Down a hall where Hindu worshippers are chanting before marigold-
draped idols, a disgruntled-looking young woman in an Adidas track suit
fields calls in Cantonese and English. I fill out my Chinese visa application
and buy airplane tickets. I can tell she doesn't want to be working on
Sunday, doesn't want to be working at all; she looks like she's on the verge
of a breakdown. Come back with another passport-sized photo, she tells
me impatiently. I catch a glimpse of her screen-saver, scrolling across a
baby-blue monitor. It reads: "Don't put off your HATE till tomorrow!!!"

The day my visa is ready, I board the Kowloon-Canton Railway. A ride
through the burgeoning bedroom communities of the New Territories

brings me to the Lo Wu border crossing. An official on the Hong Kong side with a black glove on his right hand inspects and then returns my passport. I go upstairs, join a second lineup (for Foreigners and Taiwan Passport Holders), and wait in the long queue with families carrying plush bears and bags of Harry Potter memorabilia. A sign on the wall informs me I'm prohibited from importing eggplants. I fill out the entry card as I shuffle forward. Are you suffering from: Psychosis, Jaundice, Cough, H.I.V. (including AIDS)? As a non-psychotic Canadian free of eggplants, all I get is a glance verifying that my photo matches my face. After crossing a concrete-lined moat, with razor-wire-topped fences on either side of the water, I'm in Shenzhen. The first face I see, on a panoramic backlit poster, is Tiger Woods's.

§

Twenty-five years ago Shenzhen was a fishing area inhabited by 30,000 members of the Hakka tribe. In 1980, Deng Xiaoping declared it a Special Economic Zone, a vivarium for a new generation of capitalists, and since then its population has grown to 4.3 million. The vital statistics read like the P.R. of some San Fernando tech town in the boom days: the average age is 30; Shenzhen's construction workers can add a floor to a skyscraper in less than three days; 150 new cars hit the road every day. At last count, there were 17 McDonald's, 600 hotels, eight golf courses, and a thousand karaoke bars.

I hop a red Volkswagen Jetta cab on a Stalinian square surrounded by gargantuan shopping centres, and we merge onto a dual-carriage motorway, passing ranks of cheaply built apartment buildings with burglar-bar cages encasing the balconies. In Hong Kong, they drive on the left, take cream tea at the Peninsula Hotel, and speak English with a British accent. In Shenzhen, they drive on the right, treat themselves to American hamburgers, and don't speak much English at all. In days to come, I will move through a landscape of ill-translated signs, misconstrued hand gestures, and mounting loneliness and irritation – a tourist bubble for masochists.

The alphabet has changed one too many times on this trip – from Spanish to Greek to Hindi to Thai – for me to be enthralled by the novelty of the ubiquitous ideograms. I'm finding I've attained the meretricious cosmopolitanism of the senior travel editor, able to construct elaborate pronouncements like, "Of course, a Neapolitan espresso is almost as short as a Roman *ristretto*" or "The snake soup in Hong Kong is slightly less pimenté than in Bangkok." Though I'm still taking in impressions, diligently noting what I see, I'm numb, as if deep down aware of the impossibility of entering into a meaningful relationship with this place. I fear that my soul is now so far behind me that I'm becoming a *gweilo*, a foreign ghost, and I dread the moment the automatic doors stop sliding apart for me. In Shenzhen, a non-place full of non-residents, all of my relationships are now mediated by money – in this case, the almighty *yuan*.

The lobby of the Crowne Plaza Hotel is decorated Venetian style, the giant winged lion of St. Mark's on its roof. Female gondoliers in tasselled straw hats welcome clients; I inquire about the price of a room, hoping for an exchange rate miracle, but it's as expensive as a five-star hotel anywhere. By Happy Valley, a vast amusement park complete with roller coasters and a Kentucky Fried Chicken outlet, I spot a youth hostel and buy a room for the night. Down a long hallway, shirtless men stare at me blankly through open doors, smoking, hawking up phlegm, clipping their nails. I leave my bag in a huge room I have to myself and buy a ticket for the monorail, the "Happy Line," that trundles along the snaking track at less than walking speed.

"Hello passengers!" a recorded voice in the car announces. "We are now heading south towards the Seaside Mangroves!" A Muzak vibe solo plays on the loudspeaker, and this could be Niagara Falls in 1971 – if it weren't for the cranes, both feathered and metallic, wheeling on the Pearl River Estuary.

China underwent a theme park boom in the 1990s. Most of the parks, hastily confected from styrofoam and chicken wire, have been failures. But the four well-conceived examples in Shenzhen, grouped in the Overseas Chinese Town, are exceptions: since 1989 they've attracted 60 million visitors, and Window of the World – consisting of 118 reduced-scale tourist attractions – is one of the most successful.

A replica of the Pyramid of the Louvre, its glass lozenges emblazoned with the Window of the World logo, stands before a ticket booth in a loggia modelled on St. Peter's colonnades. Crossing the World Square, I pass India's Ashoka pillar, and walk beneath the bearded lions of the Pergamum gate towards the centrepiece of the park, the Eiffel Tower. At 108 metres, it's about a third the size of the original. A group of voluble Chinese tourists follow me into a tiny elevator, and we rise to the glans of the gossamer phallus. The view is striking: skylights shoot up from skyscrapers, and a hovercraft skims across Shenzhen Bay towards a thicket of buildings on Hong Kong Island. Beneath me is the park: I can make out the Tower Bridge, the Arc de Triomphe, and the Pyramids.

I've arrived at Window of the World just two hours before closing. Though there are crowds in the central square, buying noodles and fresh coconut slices from the Café de Eiffel, much of the park is deserted, an Epcot Center after the N-bomb. I wander through a poorly lit Grand Canyon and a switched-off Niagara Falls. It's eerie and unsettling, as if I'm moving through addled memories of a travelling life, an impression exacerbated by the soporific version of "Sounds of Silence" on the loudspeakers. I come across replicas of painted totem poles in Vancouver, the city where I grew up. There's a miniature Manhattan Island in a lake, Twin Towers still standing, with a recording of honking cars and a male chorus singing: "New York – it's a helluva town!" I finally get to see the Manneken Pis – the pissing icon of Brussels is much, *much* smaller than I expected. I can't miss the shark's fin of the Matterhorn, its flanks covered with out-of-proportion skiers. Rome's Spanish Steps are set among shrubbery rather than palazzos, and have mysteriously become "The Great Steps of Spain." St. Mark's Square, pigeon-free, shares a lagoon with the Sydney Opera House. On the other side of the World Square is Thailand's Grand Palace, the royal *wat* I wandered through two weeks ago in Bangkok. The place is like an executive summary of the last eight months of my life.

Thanks to parks like Window of the World, one no longer needs a passport to see the world. Disney proved this long ago, of course. Before the Epcot Center, tourist bubbles had been flawed: beach resorts or pedestrianized Old Town cores implanted in foreign locales were constantly invaded by local reality. By gathering the world's great monuments in one convenient location, Disney actually supplanted the authentic, obviating the need for travel. (For insularity, the theme park's only competition was the cruise ship. Disney now owns two.) Artfully duplicated, cleaned up, its salient features gathered on a single site with convenient parking, "elsewhere" became irrelevant.

In the 1970s an eloquently supercilious Umberto Eco toured fake gold-rush towns, Disney's reconstruction of New Orleans, and the seven "authentic replicas" of the Last Supper between San Francisco and Los Angeles. He decided that this penchant for hyperreality was a particularly American phenomenon. The States gave its people faithful renditions of world masterpieces and monuments (or even improvements: Eco came across a Venus de Milo with her arms intact) so that they would feel no need to see the original. Been there, done that, was the checklist philosophy of the Epcot Center. If Eco made his tour today, he would find a continent enamoured of gated communities, where the voyage into hyperreality has only accelerated. In the new Las Vegas, steam spews out of fake manhole covers at the New York–New York hotel complex, where guests stay in a smaller version of the Chrysler Building and a Coney Island–style roller coaster loops through the skyscrapers.

But the penchant for genuine fakes is no longer particularly American: the world has enthusiastically taken to hyperreality. The first televised reality show, *Big Brother*, was Dutch; France has had its own Disneyland since the early 1990s; and amusement parks, from Japan's indoor beach bubble of the Phoenix Seagaia Resort to Thailand's FantaSea, abound throughout Asia. What's unique, and poignant, about Window of the World is that it is the be-all and end-all of foreign travel for the Chinese. Though a growing minority of China's burgeoning middle class can now afford to be tourists, they can't leave the country. An American who visits the 165-metre-tall Eiffel Tower in the Paris Las Vegas complex can, if he so chooses, also go see the original on the Champ de Mars. For the Chinese, this replica Eiffel Tower, emblazoned with flickering digital ideograms, is the only one they will ever see. Shenzhen is at once a Special Economic Zone and a vast gated community encircled by razor wire and check points, designed to keep out unregistered citizens. Like Cubans, the Chinese need special permission – the coveted urban residence permit – just to move to another city. Near the Korean pagoda, I buy a souvenir passport, to be stamped at stalls throughout the site. It feels like a cynical mockery of a freedom most Chinese will never have.

Most visitors to Shenzhen's amusement parks are mainland Chinese. Surprisingly, there are few children, and the only white foreigner I see in two days of exploring is a blond man in his 20s outside a theatre called Kaiser's Palace. He asks me something in an unfamiliar language; I make out the word "*spasiba*." Noticing my puzzlement, he says, "You are not Roosian?"

I shake my head.

"*Nichevo, nichevo*," he mutters, and walks on.

Entering the hall, beneath a blue neon sign that promises a "Fervorous Paris Night," I realize he's mistaken me for a countryman. Thousands of Chinese are sitting on benches, watching blond Cossack dancers in black pants and red satin shirts re-enacting European folk dances. Then a Chinese girl in a diamond tiara introduces the next number, a crab-walking procession of frozen-faced women in Russian peasant costumes. The crowd is demonstratively bored. Some are talking loudly on cellphones; others are clipping their nails; the girl behind me has her head down on the table, asleep. After the dancers execute a costume change and embark on yet another geometric display, many people simply walk out.

The next day, I visit an amusement park called the China Folk Culture Villages, where the scale is life-sized and the implications are more disturbing. China is home to more than 400 ethnicities, of which 56 are officially recognized *minzu*, or minority groups. The Han majority accounts for 95 percent of the population, and modernization has fostered a condescending fascination with the culture of the others in their midst. The park focuses on 21 separate ethnic groups, from the nomadic Kazaks in their yurts to the hunter-gatherer Li in their boat-shaped huts. I pass the McDonald's outside the gates and buy another ticket – at 150 yuan, or $18, admission to each park is steep – pausing to watch a businessman who has paid to be carried in a wooden chair, like a mandarin of old, by workers dressed as coolies. Each of the minorities is grouped in a separate village of full-sized native dwellings. A brochure summarizes the park's philosophy in opaque English.

"Be from life and yet go up onto a higher plain than life itself" – Eco would approve of the transcendent leap into hyperreality – "Absorb what is good and reject what is bad."

Rejecting what is bad seems to involve a cultural cleansing of all that clashes with state ideology. I watch a performance by the Uigurs, comely pale-skinned girls in long pink and yellow dresses twirling before the filigreed arches of a traditional home.

"Uigur people live in Xinjiang in the northwest and have a population of 7,210,000," explains a sign. "Uigur people live flat-roofed houses. On the roof is a skylight or a 'garden on the roof.'"

Uigur people are also a Muslim minority whose persecution the government justifies by claiming their leaders are Afghan-trained terrorists. The only allusion to Islam in the Folk Culture Villages is the "Muslem Building" outside a full-sized replica of a mosque, which is used as a boutique to peddle Uigur blankets, carpets, and neon plastic "Funny Sphere" gewgaws.

Wandering the site, I realize I'm in a giant, totalitarian version of my Thailand hill-tribe trek, a theme park that exploits, even more cynically, the same touristic longing for authenticity. The Chinese have gathered representatives of their remaining indigenous peoples in one place, eliminating the need for tiresome hiking. Amid the grass-skiing hillside and the pulley ride over the Green Lake, I watch tourists clapping along with the barechested, grass-skirted Dong villagers. Hani men, famed for their addiction to nicotine, sit in their huts smoking one hand-rolled cigarette after another.

The worst is the Tibetan area. In a large Lamasery, the 1951 invasion – which the government refers to as the "Peaceful Liberation of Tibet" – is justified with a replica of a fresco depicting the marriage of a Tibetan king and the daughter of a Tang dynasty emperor. Among the prayer flags is a two-storeyed home full of Tibetan extras in traditional garb. In a kitchen hung with copper pots, a woman in a silk shirt, hair pulled back by a rolled head band, sits in a picturesque pose, playing a tortoise-bellied stringed instrument. A strikingly handsome man, with a spreading mane of black hair, a sleeveless black jerkin with golden piping, and leather riding boots, sits wide-kneed on a wooden sofa covered with rugs as tourists jostle to snap his photo. At least in Thailand there was some pretense of respecting the integrity of the hill-tribe setting. The scene in Shenzhen, where the ancestral traditions of China's *minzu* groups are re-enacted in a staging ground for capitalism, stinks of coercion.

First-century Romans travelled to the Greek city of Neapolis to watch concerts and don the Hellenic *chlamys* of the sophisticated culture they'd supplanted; the English tossed baksheesh to the colonized Egyptians to shinny up the pyramids; post-war Americans of the Marshall Plan era shipped home Rhine castles, brick by numbered brick. Today, the democratization of tourism means that both the working class of the developed world and the middle class of the developing world – lager louts in Corfu and Indian families on European bus tours alike – can jet off to other continents. In Lucerne, I watched the Swiss play their alpenhorns for Japanese salarymen. In its industrialized form, where the bubble has long solidified, tourism is the trite but harmless spectacle of one culture representing itself to the others. Here, on the frontiers, the inequalities are haunting.

§

That evening I wait for a China Northern flight at Shenzhen International Airport. There are aquariums filled with dragon fish in the waiting lounges and foot-powered delivery bikes on the landing strips. Ushering us onto the narrow MD-82, a stewardess tells us we can choose whatever seat we like.

"Waaaaa!" goes a chorus of voices as we lift off.

My seatmate speaks fluent English. A young executive at the China Construction Bank, he was born in Fujian province but now lives in Shenzhen and is a member of the new generation of business-school capitalists. He wears glasses and a natty business suit, and tells me to call him Michael. I ask him whether he's ever been outside China.

"No," he replies. "Even going to Hong Kong is difficult for us. We have to have good reason, apply for visa."

I ask what he would have to do to vacation in Thailand.

"I would have to pay a deposit of 10,000 yuan" – about $1,200 – "to government, to make sure I come back. And the travel agency would have to guarantee that I come back as well. And I would need people, from my company, perhaps, to recommend me."

Savouring my inflight coconut milk, I ask Michael whether he could travel as I do, independently.

"No, that would not be possible. I would have to go with group, with agency."

It's easy to forget that travel is a privilege enjoyed by the citizens of the world's richest nations. Per capita, the Swiss make the most international trips, followed by the Dutch, the English, the Canadians, and the Germans. (Americans place tenth.) Large swaths of humanity – Israelis and Palestinians; Thai women and Caribbean men; North Koreans and Arabs – have enormous difficulty obtaining visas and crossing borders. Small wonder that the travelogue is a genre dominated by white Europeans and North Americans. For an Iranian woman, travel writing just isn't a viable career path.

There have also been great historical periods when tourism simply disappeared, to be replaced, at best, by R & R. During the Thirty Years War, Napoleon's battles, and the two global conflicts of the last century, European travel came almost to a standstill. War, that ineluctable onslaught of authenticity, is the antithesis of tourism. Waves of ethnic and religious hatred tend to make short work of the benign representation of cultural differences in tourist spectacles: the jolly men in lederhosen at the Oktoberfest put down their beer steins, pick up Lugers, and start slaughtering their neighbours. The picturesque Burmese villagers prove to be chain-smoking Christian guerrillas led by messianic child generals. War's impact on travel tends to be temporary (though, in the right conditions, war itself can be spectacle: Thomas Cook conducted English tourists to Boer battlefields while the war still raged). And war can sometimes, paradoxically, enable tourism: after the corpses are buried, the conquerors can go romp in the land of the conquered.

Just before I left Corfu, two jets slammed into the World Trade Center. For a while I considered going home. The chief instrument of mass tourism had been turned into a weapon of mass destruction, and I feared that, for a few months at least, world tourism would simply stop. To my surprise, apart from a spate of cancellations on the *Marco Polo* (which allowed canny English couples to snatch up drastically reduced cabins) and the disappearance of all but the most obdurate Americans from the guest houses of India, the world's travel trails remained well populated. According to the World Tourism Organization, tourism remains the world's biggest legal industry, accounting for 11 percent of the global gross domestic product. In 1999, there were 652 million international trips. In 2001 – in spite of the terrorist attacks – the figure had risen to 692 million. Though travellers were favouring destinations closer to home, a year after the attacks in America, international trips were on their way to reaching levels higher than pre-9/11 totals. The hijackings of the 1970s, the fuel price hikes of the Energy Crisis, the Gulf War, and, most recently, the al-Qaeda attacks – tourism may suffer temporary setbacks, but, decade by decade, the grand total of international travellers continues to rise. With the infrastructure of world travel so firmly in place – allowing people with disposable income to jet off to whatever geopolitical bubble happens to be considered secure for the time being – only a global conflict could completely put an end to our millenia-old wanderlust.

China, as it happens, is probably the safest place on earth to be travelling right now. We touch down in Sanya, the southernmost city, on the island of Hainan, and as we cross the humid runway Michael offers to give me a lift to my hotel. His colleagues, jovial young bankers primed for a tropical junket, are waiting for him in a minivan, and when the hotel recommended in my guidebook proves not to exist, Michael does the talking at the front desks along a beachfront strip until he finds me an inexpensive room. We shake hands; I give him my e-mail address, and – forgetting myself – invite him to come visit me one day in Canada.

"I don't think that is too likely," he says with an embarrassed smile, leaving me kicking myself for my slip. Meeting Michael has allowed me to step out of my tourist role for a couple of hours; the credit, for having studied the tongue of a foreign visitor, is all his.

It's a temporary reprieve. In the hotel, a foil pouch of liquid sits on the bedside table. "Yirenbao Man Lotion," says a plasticized sheet. "The Necessity for a Successful Person. No one can feel free about something embarrassing in his busy social life and Yirenbao will help relieve at ease.

As the green product, Yirenbao, made by high-tech AZONE process, is the super-concentrated Chinese medicinal preparation in dew form, which contains no saponin and chemical agents. Usage: Knead repeatedly inside and outside of your private parts for two to three minutes." Alone? Before sex? After? How do I get the product *inside* my private parts? I'm tempted to call reception for a demonstration, but instead I drift off watching a musical variety show in which a chubby-cheeked woman in military uniform belts out an aria before a grand piano.

I wake up to a Southeast Asian Hawaii – coconut-palm-lined roads filled with motorized tricycles called *bop-bops*, a white sand beach at the end of a broad concrete promenade, the sea an inviting green. This, my last stop, is Hainan, an island the size of Taiwan in the South China Sea, about 50 kilometres south of the mainland. During the Tang Dynasty, it was considered the remotest place on earth, the edge of the known universe. For disgraced courtiers and political outcasts, it was the farthest point from Beijing, and the tenth-century exiles who were sent here were quickly felled by untreatable tropical diseases. Later, Madam Mao and the Gang of Four vacationed at a villa in Sanya, near where I'm staying. An American spy plane was shot down here recently, its crew detained while the Chinese took a leisurely look at its espionage equipment. Since the 1980s, Hainan has been a Special Economic Zone, a Shenzhen in the tropics. Eighty percent of its income derives from tourism, and the beaches are lined with five-star hotels catering to honeymooners and newly affluent businessmen. Most of its eight million inhabitants are Han Chinese, but there are also 1.2 million Li tribespeople, who until the 1930s still lived a hunter-gatherer existence, and the Hmong, members of the same wide-ranging tribe whose villages I'd tramped through in Thailand.

Today, the tribespeople roam the roadside along the broad highways of Sanya, trying to sell ropes of misshapen pearls to tourists. The government appropriated the Li's shorefront farmland a few years ago, offering meagre restitution, in order to build hotels like the one I'm staying in. At the desk, I get the clerk to write down my final destination in Chinese characters.

"*Tianya Haijiao!*" I say as I hop into a cab, and the driver executes a prompt U-turn, cutting off a *bop-bop*.

The name is sometimes translated as "The End of the Sky, the Corner of the Sea," but it's more succinctly known as the End of the Earth – the southernmost point in China. We buzz along a straight, four-lane highway, past a minibus that has crashed into a concrete divider planted with purple flowers. On a quiet stretch of road, my driver pulls over, turns off the engine. He looks back at me, floods me with Mandarin. He's an older man, with a sweating, furrowed brow. I point at the card the clerk has given me.

"*Tianya Haijiao!*" I repeat, precisely imitating the Chinese tones that Michael taught me on the flight down from Shenzhen. The driver takes my card, scratches his head.

"*Tianya Haijiao! Tianya Haijiao!*" I insist, irate. I know this is a scam; but my inability to communicate makes me impotent. He pulls off the road at a shorefront concession stand. Grabbing my arm, he takes me to a ticket booth.

"*Tianya Haijiao?*" I ask the girl at the wicket. She furrows her brow in annoyance and points at a sign: 90 yuan. I pay the admission. My cab driver hurries me down to a pier, where I'm handed an orange lifejacket and told to get into a speedboat. The boat takes off, its prow slapping the waves. I'm praying we'll round a headland, make for some inaccessible beach, but we're heading due south, in the direction of Borneo. I look behind me – my cab driver is sitting there, life jacket askew, grinning.

Ten minutes later, I step ashore. A sign announces that I'm on West Island, a scuba diving centre. My taxi driver points delightedly at the open-air restaurant, the sea urchins visible in the shallow water. I am tempted to slap him.

I look him in the eye, and enunciate as clearly as I can: "*Tian-ya Hai-jiao.*" A man walks past and overhears me.

"This is West Island," he says, with a precise American accent. "*Tianya Haijiao* is a beach, you can see it over there."

He points to a stretch of sand back on Hainan. Feeling myself redden, I ask him to explain this to my cab driver, who nods attentively and feigns dawning comprehension. I stomp back to the boat, and we ride back across the waves. A five-minute drive later, I see a blue road sign hanging from a gallows-like pole that says, in clear English letters below the Chinese equivalents: "The End of the Earth."

"*Tianya Haijiao!*" I shout, triumphantly.

"Owww!" my cab driver says. "*Tianya Haijiao ...*" He doesn't look surprised when I stiff him for the tip.

It comes as no shock that there's a hefty admission fee to get to the End
of the Earth. Pretty much every step I've taken so far in China has cost me
a bundle of yuan. This is an "official scenic spot," which means, in this
communist nation, that citizens have to pay a fee to stroll on their own
beach. Out of sorts, I pay up and walk towards the shore, past a spotted
deer tied to a tree. I'm trailed by a tiny woman in a straw hat holding forth
a conch shell, but I lose her in a copse of cacti next to an elephant being
tended by two men in red track suits. Plodding along white sand, I head
for the main attraction: huge sandy-coloured boulders lapped by the
waves, stained black from their crests down, rimed with barnacles near the
high water line. The biggest are six metres tall; some are pointed, others
bulbous and squat. Many are inset with red ideograms, lines of Chinese
poetry. The few English translations are shaky.

"Ancient Ya State stands being explored / Fertile land nurtures / the
distinguished and admirable, / Where is the earthly paradise? / Ever green
is Tianya-Haijiao!"

Tourists are taking snapshots of one another. I was virtually alone at
Cabo Fisterra, but I share this end of the earth with thousands of Chinese.
They've come in groups, wearing beach ensembles, matching tops and
knee-length shorts plastered with palm trees and vacation slogans in
cursive script: "No Problem," "Master Cowfish," and "Welcome to
Seychelles." Their guides wear plasticized name tags and herd them into
position for group shots. I can see how this place might have inspired an
exiled Tang official to poetry a millennium ago: the green hills descending
towards a vast sea, whose edge lay somewhere in eternity; the mysterious,
smooth-sided boulders, gathered at the shore like the protruding vertebrae
of sand-swaddled sea dragons. As a diagonal beam of light pierces the sky,
staining the sea with a strip of mercury, I try to conjure up a fitting sense of
awe and nostalgia. But the pot-bellied guy in turquoise flower-print bathing
trunks, posing for a photo with a Marlboro in hand, foils my efforts.

N

From the hotel in Finisterre to the tour buses of Tianya Haijiao, from one end of the earth to the other, I've crossed the Eurasian landmass – 10,700 kilometres in all – encountering, essentially, this: tourists with cameras. It is now possible to travel the entire world without leaving the tourist bubble. In one of its most venerable stretches, the bubble extends through the backroads of the hills of northern Spain. It follows Michelin signposts along the highways of France and the itineraries devised by Thomas Cook between the capitals of Europe. It shrinks into exclusivity in the various Germanic Baden, bursts with the British fluid in Zermatt, weeds out some of the less fit at the top of the Matterhorn, and crosses the Alpine passes with a railpass into the promised land of Italian hostels and pub crawls. It shields the kids at Corfu's Pink Palace and the Club Med from Albanian pirates and Greek culture; it provides satellite links to CNN and Hotmail on Mediterranean cruise ships. In South Asia, it crops up in the guesthouse ghettos of Pushkar, Goa, and Hampi, linked by tourist buses and trains, before swelling to cover much of Thailand with its seductive air, a faint odour of orchids and counterfeit Chanel.

By now, most of the world has become inured to the crowds. Larger civilizations in particular are robust enough to adapt to the schizophrenic demands of tourism. The Indian subcontinent and the Middle Kingdom had sufficient sophistication and artifice to confound and bedazzle all comers. It is the more fragile and remote peoples, Asian hill tribes and Amazonian Indians, that suffer most from modernity's *nostalgie de la boue*, our complex urge to touch simplicity. When travellers find that yesterday's unknown village is today's tourist hell, that the locals have turned cynical from peddling Kodak film and diving for coins, the tourist bubble continues to elongate. Like a capillary system extending into new flesh, the bubble moves in tiny self-contained bursts – guides carrying boxes of powdered banana pancakes into the inner reaches of the rain forest, to the last untouched villages in New Guinea. What happens when 700 million people on this fully mapped globe of six billion are in motion every year? When there's a *Lonely Planet* guide to Antarctica, package tours to Burma, snowboarders on Everest? When even the Ends of the Earth are part of the spectacle? Simple – it's the end of elsewhere.

We aren't quite there yet, of course. For all the incursions of modernity, I know that the authentic is all around me. But getting to it requires work: learning languages, listening carefully, offering friendship. Had I undertaken this voyage with a different attitude, travelled by camel and sampan rather than rented car and cruise ship, and engaged with locals rather than fellow travellers, I would have discovered that the world remains a wonderful place, populated by people with beliefs and views as varied as their dialects. Travelling well means not travelling farther, but finer; it means establishing connections and maintaining them. Ultimately, of course, everything I've seen is authentic, from the German skateboarders outside Baden-Baden's *Kurhaus* to the Thai teenagers smoking speed while they flip patties at a Bangkok Burger King. Real travel is a matter of keeping one's eyes open and working to understand real lives, rather than being satisfied with the ongoing reality show of staged authenticity. Even here, in this ridiculous Chinese scenic spot, the authentic persists; it suffices to direct one's gaze at the pulleys, props, and technicians in the wings.

"Supervise the market by law," an Orwellian sign entreats below the palms. Another demands: "Serve as economic guard." The pearl saleswomen trying to interest the Chinese tourists in their wares, wearing Snoopy and X-Files T-shirts beneath their straw hats, are tribespeople or illegal Han migrants from the mainland. Some are members of the Li minority whose farmland was appropriated to make room for tourist hotels. The lucky ones, the attractive ones, have been given jobs. They're posing at the entrance to the site, fair-skinned women in red dresses, inviting tourists to photograph them and their chained peacocks. At 4:40 there will be a performance of the nose-blown vertical flute, the bamboo skipping dance, and other Li and Hmong rituals in an octagonal theatre on the beach – for Tianya Haijiao is also a diminutive version of the China Folk Culture Villages.

But the authentic drama is happening out on the beach. Chinese government soldiers in fatigues squat on the rocks; others patrol the sand, making the pearl and shell saleswomen flee beneath the cover of the palm trees. One squeals as a soldier traps her by her skinny bicep and leads her off the site. This is what the tourist bubble, at its most naked, both encourages and tries to shield us from: the dispossessed being ushered from their land for failing to serve up a pleasing simulacrum of their supplanted culture.

§

Many months ago, I watched the sun go down over the Atlantic. Before this trip can end, I need to see it rise over the Pacific. Pulling myself out of bed before dawn, I shuffle down the concrete promenade to the beach, and unfold a dew-covered beach chair.

The scene brightens imperceptibly, like a stage light on a rheostat. It starts with the pinkening of a single cloud. As the horizon begins to glow, I realize I'm not alone. Down the sand, there's an old man doing Tai Chi, thrusting his arms out loosely from his sides. Dime-sized translucent crabs scuttle along the tide line. The first of the pearl hawkers is out, making a diagonal beeline for the first tourists emerging from their hotel. A man with glasses, pant legs rolled up, walks shoeless along the surf, talking into a cellphone. A taxi pulls up to the edge of the sand. While an older man pays off the driver, his escort, a young woman in a tight dress, runs down to the water and leaps in, fully clothed, emitting a little yip as she throws her hands into the air. The disc of the sun, orange, pokes through a bank of grey clouds. As its rays spread, I feel a thin optimism occupy my weariness. It's 7:10 a.m., and there's no more road left. I've reached the End of the Earth. It's time to go home.

That is, if I have a home to go back to. I wonder if my possessions are still safely in storage; if, after all these months of Hotmail exchanges and echo-plagued Internet telephone conversations, Karen will welcome me back.

This trip has taught me a few lessons. First, the slower you go, the richer you travel. For this purpose, trains are good, and so are boats; but going by foot is even better. (Staying put – for weeks, months, whatever you can manage – is best.) Second, I am not temperamentally a nomad; few people are. Before I can travel again, I'll need to drop anchor, good and deep. (Montreal, I figure, will make a decent harbour.) Finally: the fundamental problem with tourism is also my problem. By locating my hope for a fulfilling existence in the chimeric Arcadia of elsewhere, I've allowed the camaraderie of the road and the allure of the foreign to keep me from establishing deep connections where they matter most – at home. Obsessed as I've been with seeing how green the grass is elsewhere, I haven't noticed how badly my own lawn has gone to seed.

Pulling myself out of my beach chair, I head back to the hotel to pack up my road-frayed possessions one last time. Something inside me snapped on this trip. Though I will certainly travel again, at some deep level I really don't need to. I'm not chasing after elsewhere anymore. I've been there – for longer than I ever planned – and frankly, I'd rather be somewhere else.

From now on, all my journeys will take me home.

Fiction
Crime
Noir

Culture
Music
Erotica

dare to read at serpentstail.com

Visit serpentstail.com today to browse and buy
our books, and to sign up for exclusive news and
previews of our books, interviews with our
authors and forthcoming events.

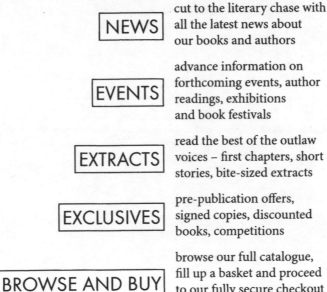

NEWS — cut to the literary chase with
all the latest news about
our books and authors

EVENTS — advance information on
forthcoming events, author
readings, exhibitions
and book festivals

EXTRACTS — read the best of the outlaw
voices – first chapters, short
stories, bite-sized extracts

EXCLUSIVES — pre-publication offers,
signed copies, discounted
books, competitions

BROWSE AND BUY — browse our full catalogue,
fill up a basket and proceed
to our fully secure checkout
– our website is your oyster

FREE POSTAGE & PACKING ON ALL ORDERS…
ANYWHERE!

sign up today – join our club